The Explorer Sven Hedin and Kyoto University

The Explorer Sven Hedin and Kyoto University
Central Asia Fosters East-West Cultural Exchange

Kyoto University Press

First published in Japanese in 2018 by Kyoto University Press.

This English edition published in 2019 jointly by:

Kyoto University Press
69 Yoshida Konoe-cho
Sakyo-ku, Kyoto 606-8315
Japan
Telephone: +81-75-761-6182
Fax: +81-75-761-6190
Email: sales@kyoto-up.or.jp
Web: http://www.kyoto-up.or.jp

Trans Pacific Press
PO Box 164, Balwyn North, Melbourne
Victoria 3104, Australia
Telephone: +61-3-9859-1112
Fax: +61-3-8611-7989
Email: tpp.mail@gmail.com
Web: http://www.transpacificpress.com

© Kazuko Tanaka et al. 2019

Copyedited by Karl Smith.

Designed and set by Sarah Tuke, Melbourne, Australia.

Book cover designed by Hana Mori, Kyoto, Japan.

Printed by Asia Printing Office Corporation, Nagano, Japan.

Distributors

Australia and New Zealand
James Bennett Pty Ltd
Locked Bag 537
Frenchs Forest NSW 2086
Australia
Telephone: +61-(0)2-8988-5000
Fax: +61-(0)2-8988-5031
Email: info@bennett.com.au
Web: www.bennett.com.au

USA and Canada
Independent Publishers Group (IPG)
814 N. Franklin Street
Chicago, IL 60610
USA
Telephone inquiries: +1-312-337-0747
Order placement: 800-888-4741
   (domestic only)
Fax: +1-312-337-5985
Email: frontdesk@ipgbook.com
Web: http://www.ipgbook.com

Asia and the Pacific (except Japan)
Kinokuniya Company Ltd.
Head office:
3-7-10 Shimomeguro
Meguro-ku
Tokyo 153-8504
Japan
Telephone: +81-(0)3-6910-0531
Fax: +81-(0)3-6420-1362
Email: bkimp@kinokuniya.co.jp
Web: www.kinokuniya.co.jp
Asia-Pacific office:
Kinokuniya Book Stores of Singapore Pte., Ltd.
391B Orchard Road #13-06/07/08
Ngee Ann City Tower B
Singapore 238874
Telephone: +65-6276-5558
Fax: +65-6276-5570
Email: SSO@kinokuniya.co.jp

The research project for this book was supported by the Grant-in-Aid for Scientific Research (B) of Japan Society for the Promotion of Science (Grant No. 15H03275) and the 2017 Kyoto University Expenses. The publication for this book was supported by the 2018 Kyoto University Expenses, and the 2017/2018 Special Expenses for National University designated by the Ministry of Education, Culture, Sports, Science and Technology.

All rights reserved. No reproduction of any part of this book may take place without the written permission of Kyoto University Press or Trans Pacific Press.

ISBN   978–1–925608–89–2

Contents

Figures and Photos — vii
Tables — ix

Foreword — xi
Contributors — xiii
Map: Sven Hedin's route and camp   *Tanaka Kazuko* — xiv

Section I: Album: Sven Hedin's Original Drawings, Reproductions
  Discovered in the Department of Geography, and Images of Tibet
  a Century Thereafter   *Ikeda Takumi & Satō Ken'ei (photographer)*

Preface — 2

1 Tashi Lhunpo Monastery — 10
2 People of Shigatse — 48
3 Trans-Himalaya — 62
4 Tibetans — 70
5 Tibetan Temple Monasteries — 114

Epilogue — 137
Supplementary Table: List of Reproductions, Original Artworks,
  and Illustrations in Hedin's Books, etc.
  Ikeda Takumi & Tanaka Kazuko — 138

Section II: Reports: Hedin's Tibetan Expedition and Modern Japan

1 The Headwaters of the "Exploration University"   *Yamagiwa Juichi* — 147
2 Hedin's Reception in Kyoto, 1908   *Tanaka Kazuko* — 152
3 The Legacy of Sven Hedin's Stay in Kyoto: Reproductions of
   Original Art by Hedin Left at Kyoto University   *Tanaka Kazuko* — 171
4 Exploration, Science, and Understanding Others: Thinking Through
   Hedin's Trajectory   *Matsuda Motoji* — 183
5 Sven Hedin as Artist and Photographer: Extending the Techniques
   of Cartography and Illustration at the Turn of the Last Century
   Håkan Wahlquist — 199
6 Hedin and Classic Chinese Texts   *Kizu Yuko & Tanaka Kazuko* — 217

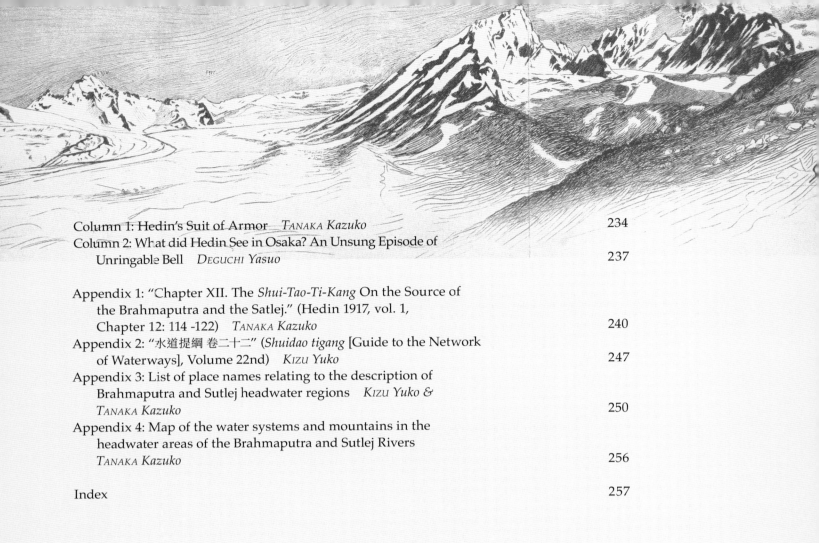

Column 1: Hedin's Suit of Armor *Tanaka Kazuko*	234
Column 2: What did Hedin See in Osaka? An Unsung Episode of Unringable Bell *Deguchi Yasuo*	237
Appendix 1: "Chapter XII. The *Shui-Tao-Ti-Kang* On the Source of the Brahmaputra and the Satlej." (Hedin 1917, vol. 1, Chapter 12: 114 -122) *Tanaka Kazuko*	240
Appendix 2: "水道提綱 卷二十二" (*Shuidao tigang* [Guide to the Network of Waterways], Volume 22nd) *Kizu Yuko*	247
Appendix 3: List of place names relating to the description of Brahmaputra and Sutlej headwater regions *Kizu Yuko & Tanaka Kazuko*	250
Appendix 4: Map of the water systems and mountains in the headwater areas of the Brahmaputra and Sutlej Rivers *Tanaka Kazuko*	256
Index	257

Figures and Photos

Section II

1.1	Chimpanzee (sketch by Itani)	149
1.2	Turkana tribesman (sketch by Itani)	149
1.3	How to hold a smoking implement (sketch by Umesao Tadao)	149
1.4	Structure of a horse-riding saddle (sketch by Umesao Tadao)	150
1.5	Lamasery (sketch by Wazaki Yōichi)	150
2.1	Professional fields of the people involved in the welcome reception given to Hedin by the Tokyo Geographical Society.	154
2.2	Activities of Hedin and President Kikuchi in Kyoto during Hedin's stay (November 28–December 12, 1908)	157
2.3	Faculty members from the College of Letters who took part in the welcome reception for Hedin on November 29	159
2.4	Faculty members from the College of Science and Engineering who took part in the reception for Hedin on November 29	159
2.5	Three books autographed by Hedin	165
2.6	Members of the Society of Historical Research (1908–1911)	168
3.1	The paper envelope and card stock enclosing the sixty reproductions	171
3.2	An example of a reproduction	172
3.3	Original painting by Hedin	172
3.4	An exhibition of Hedin's paintings	172
3.5	Links between people closely involved in Hedin's reception	176
3.6	Portrait of Ishibashi Gorō.	177
3.7	Sample handwritten annotations	178
3.8	Sample handwritten annotations	178
4.1	The white explorer grapples with the beast as Africans flee in terror	195
4.2	A native African kneels	195
4.3	Young Woman (Sketch by Hedin)	196
4.4	Young Man (Sketch by Hedin)	196
5.1	Sounding the depth of Little Kara Kul, Pamir, September 1894 (photo)	200
5.2	Sounding the depth of Little Kara Kul, Pamir, September 1894 (sketch)	200
5.3	The Potala Palace in Lhasa and its surroundings as depicted in Athanasii Kircheri "China Monumentiis," 1667.	200
5.4	The Salt Lake Tso Mitbál, in Pangkóng, Tibet.	201
5.5	Ludvig Hedin at work with his wife Anna, Stockholm 1890s	203

5.6 Ludvig Hedin 1859; architectural drawing for the front of "Eldkvarn" in Stockholm. (From the Stockholm City Archives) 203
5.7 The Hedin family in their summer home 1898 204
5.8 Sven Hedin surrounded by his remaining siblings 1948 204
5.9 "Special", route map depicting the Kubi Gangri area, where Sven Hedin argued that the source of Yarlung Tsangpo/Brahmaputra can be found 1907 205
5.10 Hypsometrical map of the Kailash-Manasarowar area 205
5.11 The photographic and hand-drawn panoramas of the sources of the Brahmaputra at Kubi Gangri compared. Sven Hedin 1907 206
5.12 Sven Hedin surveying the Lop Desert between the dried-up basin in the north and the basin in the south 206
5.13 Bruno Hassenstein's second-generation map 1898, of an area in north-east Tibet, based on Sven Hedin's route maps of 1897, with inserted panoramas 207
5.14 Campsite in Tibet, Sven Hedin 1901 208
5.15 Panorama across Shemen Tso, Tibet, Sven Hedin watercolors. From Camp 320, 06 February 1908 209
5.16 Photographic panorama of the mountain ridge south of "Lake Lighten" in the Aksai Chin Area of northwest Tibet, Sven Hedin from Camp 15 at an altitude of 5095 meters. 18 September 1906 209
5.17 Drawings of Bactrian camels. Sven Hedin 1896 210
5.18 Sven Hedin sketching the portrait of a Mongolian woman 1927 210
5.19 Mohamed Togda Bek, 66 years old, resident of Kapa, Xinjiang. Sven Hedin 1896 211
5.20 Men constructing a ger, sketched by Sven Hedin in Inner Mongolia 1927, later redrawn with ink. 211
5.21 Sven Hedin delivering a lecture on his Tibetan expedition, in front of a quickly constructed map, Simla, 1908 212
5.22 Map of the area around the Northern Mazar Tagh, Tarim Basin. Compiled by Otto Kjellström and Herman Byström, based on Sven Hedin's route maps from his first two expeditions 213
6.1 A list of five Chinese texts (with English translations) 230
6.2 A letter to Hedin from Kikuchi Dairoku (September 17, 1911) 230
C.1 A record of the purchase and gift of the suit of armor noted in the Equipment Inventory 234
C.2 Catalogue of commemorative gifts presented to Hedin. 234
C.3 Suit of Japanese armor given to Hedin at the Museum of Ethnography, Stockholm. 235
C.4 A mannequin of Hedin wearing long leather boots. 235
C.5 Photo of Hedin in ethnic garb published in *Trans-Himalaya*. 236
Reproduction of a page from volume 22nd of the *Shuidao tigang* [Guide to the Network of Waterways] by the Qing period scholar Qi Zhaonan 齊召南 248

Tables

2.1	Hedin's reception in Tokyo (November 13–27, 1908)	153
2.2	Hedin's reception in Kyoto (November 28 to December 12, 1908)	156
2.3	Summary of participation in the reception for Hedin on November 29	158
2.4	Hedin's books and expedition materials exhibited for the university lecture	161
2.5	Reports on Tibet and Central Asia exhibited for Hedin's lecture	161
2.6	Chinese geographical materials exhibited for Hedin's lecture	162
2.7	Tibetan and Western Buddhist scriptures exhibited for the university lecture	163
2.8	Inscriptions and old maps exhibited for Hedin's lecture	163
2.9	Hedin's university lecture and other events in the first two years of the Society of Historical Research	166
3.1	Faculty members from Kyoto Imperial University listed in Kanokogi Takeshirō's Chijin meibo (Name book of friends and acquaintances), (1915 to 1933)	180
6.1	(4) Chinese Geographical Treatises on Central Asia	222
6.2	(5) Chinese Writings on Tibetan Geography	222
6.3	(6) Western Chinese Buddhist Scriptures, including Tibetan Buddhist Scriptures	223
6.4	Principal works cited by Hedin	227

Sven Hedin

Foreword

This volume reports on the findings of the "Cross-Disciplinary Study of Sciences and Sven Hedin in Modern Japan Using Newly Found Pictorial Materials," which was undertaken as a three-year project from 2015 to 2017 with support from a Grant-in-Aid for Scientific Research from the Japan Society for the Promotion of Science (JSPS).

The original impetus for this project was the discovery of a collection of surprisingly fine pictures in a stained and dirty envelope labeled "Central Asia; Terrain; Customs; Reproductions" in calligraphic brushwork that was found by Tanaka Kazuko in early 2014 while organizing materials in the Department of Geography. Together with other pieces found sandwiched between thick card stock, the trove amounted to sixty works, including watercolors, pen drawings, and pencil sketches vividly depicting diverse subjects including mountain landscapes, temples, and people. Goaded by my own curiosity about these pictures – their intrinsic allure demanded that questions be answered – I undertook a preliminary study that soon developed into a joint research project. Readers interested in the details of these background circumstances are invited to read "Preface: In the Footsteps of Hedin: Depictions of Tibet in Century-Old Reproductions" (Ikeda Takumi) in Section I and the column in Section II titled "Hedin's Suit of Armor" (Tanaka Kazuko).

Participants in this joint research project included Matsuda Motoji (Social Anthropology), Kizu Yuko (Chinese Language and Literature), Mizuno Kazuharu (Physical Geography), and Tanaka Kazuko (Human Geography) from Kyoto University's Graduate School of Letters, as well as Ikeda Takumi (Studies on Sino-Tibetan Languages) of the University's Institute for Research in Humanities, Hirano Shigemitsu (Modern Western-style Painting) of the Kyoto Municipal Museum of Art, and Håkan Wahlquist (Anthropology and History of Exploration) of Sweden's Hedin Foundation. Although they may have taken part because something about the project piqued their interests, each represents a different field of study, and with the diversity of their respective interests – a spectrum that included Sven Hedin, Tibet, cross-cultural encounters, art, and Ogawa Takuji – they constituted a truly cross-disciplinary lineup.

Following workshops in Kyoto, a survey in Stockholm, and fieldwork in Tibet, a symposium was held in December 2016 (hosted by the Graduate School of Letters), followed by an exhibition in December 2017 (hosted by the Graduate School of Letters with support from the Swedish Embassy). This volume, in a sense, presents a summary of this series of research activities. Other participants invited to participate in our workshops included Kaneko Tamio (an expert on Hedin), Shirasu Jōshin (History of modern explorations of Inner Asia), Kōmoto Yasuko (Comparative Cultural Theory and Modern Japanese History), and the photographer Satō Ken'ei. When we began planning this volume for publication, we invited contributions from two additional scholars: Yamagiwa Juichi (President of Kyoto University, Primatology), on account of his particular interest in exploration, and Deguchi Yasuo (Graduate School of Letters, Philosophy), a scholar closely associated with Shitennō-ji Temple, one of the sites visited by Hedin. We must take this opportunity, also, to acknowledge that Hirano and Wahlquist put in great efforts on our exhibition, from preparations to the opening.

This volume consists of two sections: Section I "Album: Sven Hedin's Original Drawings, Reproductions Discovered in the Geography Department, and Images of Tibet a Century Thereafter" and Section II "Reports: Hedin's Tibetan Expedition and Modern Japan." The focus of Section I is on photographs and paintings. By juxtaposing original works by Hedin and their reproductions by art students from the Kansai Art Academy with recent photographs from Tibet, the authors contrast Tibet as portrayed by Hedin a century ago with the region as it is today, illuminating their comparison with additional commentary (Ikeda and Satō). Section II is a collection of essays. Beginning from the "headwaters of the exploration university" (Yamagiwa), this section includes discussions of Hedin's 1908 visit to Japan and the creation of the artistic reproductions (Tanaka), explorations and cross-cultural representation (Matsuda), Hedin's proficiency and qualities as they relate to art, cartography, and photography (Wahlquist), and Hedin's relationship with Chinese texts (Kizu and Tanaka), as well as columns on Hedin's suit of armor (Tanaka) and the great bronze bell (*tsurigane*) of Shitennō-ji Temple (Deguchi).

Hedin arrived in Japan and visited Kyoto in the winter of 1908. We can perhaps imagine the excitement and exhilaration of the people who welcomed this world-renowned explorer, with the latest information about Tibet. Hedin's lectures on his exploration in Tibet had a great visual impact on his audience as he showed his original sketches and maps to them. Hedin's welcoming events in Kyoto involved people in a variety of academic and artistic fields. Every day, newspapers carried enthusiastic articles of welcome. Likewise, as Hedin wrote in his books, he was greatly stimulated by his first stay in Kyoto. In 1908, many of the encounters and exchanges engendered by Hedin's visit may have held the power to stir up powerful curiosity about the unknown and an energy that would lead to new activities. The chance encounters and exchanges engendered in Kyoto at the turn of the 20th century have a significance and appeal that remains current even in the 21st century.

The reproductions of Hedin's original art that were discovered in 2014 are fascinating materials possessed of a strange, and curious quality that has no parallel outside Kyoto. These reproductions are a product of Hedin's visit. From a different perspective, that the discovery of the reproductions would provide an opportunity for a joint research project, and that the publication of the present volume has come about as a result, can be seen as the present-day fruit of a legacy Hedin left in Kyoto a century ago.

In the realization of our joint research project and the publication of this volume, we have benefitted from the tremendous support of a great many individuals. In the editing and publication of this volume, we are grateful for the enormous assistance provided by the editors of Trans Pacific Press and Kyoto University Press. I would like to convey my heartfelt thanks to everyone involved.

January 2019
Kyoto University Graduate School of Letters
Tanaka Kazuko

Contributors

Deguchi Yasuo
Graduate School of Letters, Kyoto University
Philosophy

Håkan Wahlquist
The Sven Hedin Foundation at the Royal Swedish Academy of Sciences
Anthropology and History of Exploration

Ikeda Takumi
Institute for Research in Humanities, Kyoto University
Studies on Sino-Tibetan Languages

Kizu Yuko
Graduate School of Letters, Kyoto University
Chinese Language and Literature

Matsuda Motoji
Graduate School of Letters, Kyoto University
Social Anthropology

Tanaka Kazuko
Graduate School of Letters, Kyoto University
Human Geography

Yamagiwa Juichi
President of Kyoto University
Primatology

Photography

Satō Ken'ei
Photographer

Images attributed to Hedin were provided by The Sven Hedin Foundation

Map: Sven Hedin's routes and camps

Sven Hedin's routes and camps (1906–1908 expedition in central Asia): The identified places are presented through referring to the memos described in 60 reproductions of Hedin's original paintings and drawings.

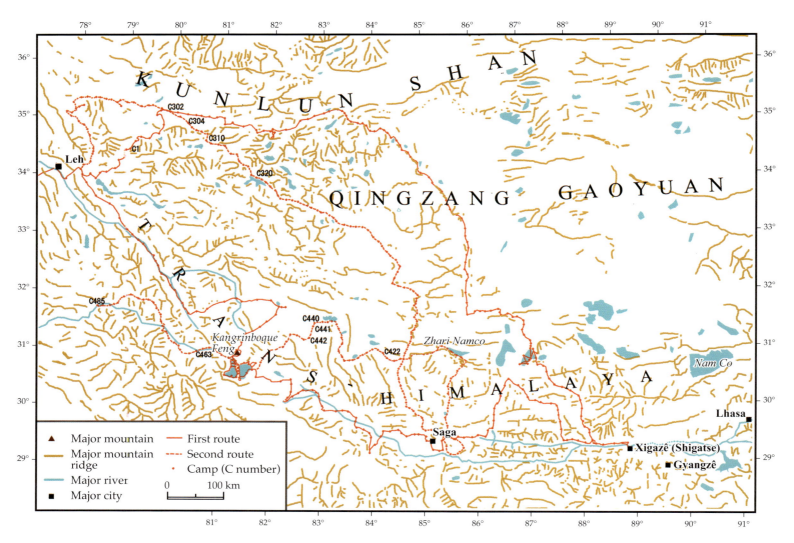

Map: Tanaka Kazuko
References: (1) "Map of Tibet showing Sven Hedin's Routes 1906–1908" in Hedin, S., 1910, *Trans-Himalaya*, Vol. II. (2) "Overview map of Sven Hedin's Expedition in Central Asia" (Aoki, Hideo translated. 1965. Trans-Himalaya (Jō). (*Hedin chūō Ajia tanken kikō zenshū* 4 [Complete Collection of Hedin's Journeys in Central Asia, 4], Hakusui sha, Inner cover) (3) *Sekai dai chizu chō*, Seventh revised edition [The Atlas of the World]. 2015. Heibon sha. (4) *Taimuzu sekai chizuchō*, 13 han [The Times Atlas of the World, 13th edition], 2011, Times Books Groups Ltd., (Japanese version: Yūshō dō).

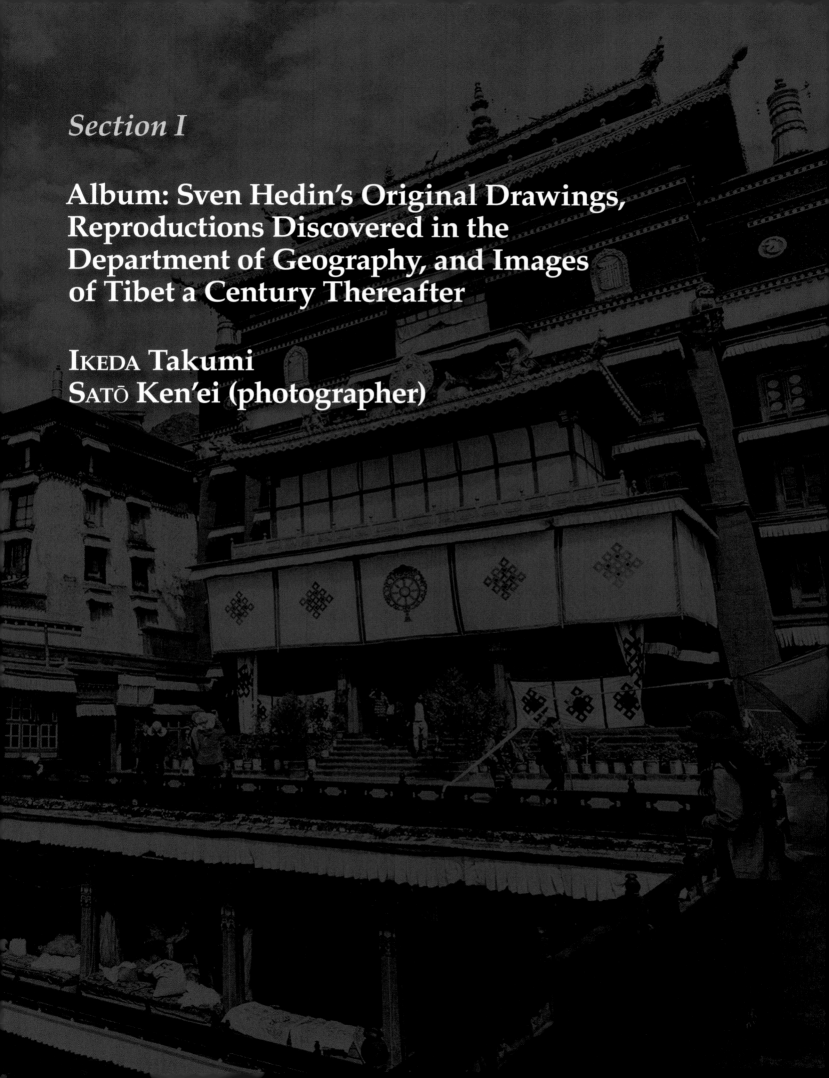

Section I

Album: Sven Hedin's Original Drawings, Reproductions Discovered in the Department of Geography, and Images of Tibet a Century Thereafter

Ikeda Takumi
Satō Ken'ei (photographer)

Preface
In the Footsteps of Hedin: Depictions of Tibet in Century-Old Reproductions

IKEDA *Takumi*

Stonework carved with mantras from prayers (Lhasa: Near rock carvings on the hill of Chakpo ri) ©IKD

It was in the early summer of 2014, I think, that I received a telephone call from Professor Kizu Yuko 木津祐子 at Graduate School of Letters, who hoped that I might come take a look at some sketches of Tibet of unknown provenance in the Department of Geography at Kyoto University. Over the phone, Kizu mentioned that the sketches were quite old – likely produced sometime around Japan's Meiji 明治 period (1868–1912) – and included a few watercolor paintings. In the Meiji period, vectors for obtaining information about Tibet were extremely limited, and all Japanese travelers who visited Tibet at the time can be identified. When Tada Tōkan 多田等観 (1890–1967), the monk and Buddhist scholar who laid the foundations of Tibetan Studies in Japan, first arrived in Tibet in 1912, it had been just over 11 years since the first journey into Tibet by Kawaguchi Ekai 河口慧海 (1866–1945), the monk of the Ōbaku 黄檗 school of Zen who, as a Buddhist scholar and explorer, became the first Japanese to visit Tibet in 1900. But I had never heard tell that either of these men had left behind collections of sketches they had assembled themselves, or of having brought back sketches made on their travels. And while the illustrations that accompanied the newspaper serialization of Kawaguchi Ekai's チベット旅行記 [Journey to Tibet; published in English as *Three Years in Tibet*] contributed greatly to the shaping of the popular imagination of Tibet in Japan, these can hardly be said to have been very realistic. We should also remember that at the time Kawaguchi was making his reputation on the back of his adventures, he was also being accused of peddling tall tales.[1] So, if he had in fact been in possession of such lifelike drawings, he surely would have wasted no time in making these public. And I thought that while this leaves the possibility that they might be drawings copied from photographs taken by someone in Tibet, there were no color photographs in the Meiji period. But perhaps they were colorized interpretations of black and white photographs…

1. The reproductions left in the Department of Geography

Arranging to visit Tanaka Kazuko 田中和子, a professor of geography, I was shown to the geography storeroom in the Kyoto University Museum building, where I saw the 60 drawings. A variety of sketches of all sizes had been stored in two sheaves, the first sandwiched between card stock labeled in calligraphic brushstrokes with the words "Ishida Kinzō 石田金三, Nishimura Junji 西村純二, Adachi Itarō 安達伊太郎; Reproductions; Central Asia (?) Terrain and Customs I," the other in a paper sleeve labeled on the front, again in calligraphic brushstrokes "Central Asia; Terrain; Customs; Reproductions II." Looking down from the wall of the storeroom where I had been brought was a portrait of Ogawa Takuji 小川琢治, who had taught geography in the Faculty of Letters at Kyoto Imperial University following his appointment as Professor of Geography in 1908. Ogawa was the father of the widely admired "scholar siblings" Kaizuka Shigeki 貝塚茂樹 (oriental history), Yukawa Hideki 湯川秀樹 (physics), and Ogawa Tamaki 小川環樹 (Chinese literature), all graduates of Kyoto University.[2] Tanaka told me that several of the drawings were signed by the artists who had made the reproductions – the individuals whose names were written on the card stock – and in some cases, also featured annotations thought to be written in the transcription of Tibetan language. These artists had apparently been students at Kansai Bijutsuin 関西美術院 around the end of the Meiji period. All the drawings had been made using the orthodox and realistic techniques of Western-style portraiture, and both the drawings and the watercolors appeared to demonstrate a considerable degree of accomplishment. Judging from the available evidence as well as what is generally known about their history, there is no reason to believe that either Kawaguchi or Tada, as Japan's earliest known visitors to Tibet, could have produced such works of Western-style art.

2. Line drawing of a soldier riding a yak

While the reproductions certainly featured scattered instances of the penciled addition of what appeared to be the names of Tibetan places and people, these were written in halting cursive script. And although some of the words seemed to be transcriptions of Tibetan pronunciations, the unfamiliar spelling conventions made them largely illegible. According to Tanaka, the annotations were also lacking in any calendrical information that would allow them to be dated with any accuracy. And while many of the images had been drawn with pencil or pen, there were also vivid watercolors depicting women's costumes and the interior of temples and monasteries. Scrutinizing the images one by one, my eyes were drawn to a sketch that showed a panoramic view of a large monastery as seen from a rooftop perspective. Although the drawing had been done in fine pencil, I recognized the layout of the building and its characteristic roof. I had a memory of standing in almost that same spot, looking down on similar scenery. In the memories that were awoken, the building's red walls and their golden-hued roof came to life in vivid contrast. "This has to be the Tashi Lhunpo Monastery in Shigatse in central Tibet," I explained to Tanaka. The accurate tones of the watercolor depicting the altars and temple interior could not possibly have been accomplished without reference to direct observation at the site. I ventured to Tanaka that the colors never could have been added to paintings based on photographs from mere imagination. The second bundle of reproductions, in the paper sleeve, included several portraits, many depicting soldiers bearing firearms. One of these caught my eye – a line drawing of a militiaman riding a yak. I had seen this picture somewhere before. Searching my memory, it dawned on me that it was almost certainly one of the illustrations from a book by Sven Hedin about his exploration of Tibet. Come to that, the other pictures would not have been out of place as illustrations for Hedin's books, either. In fact, perhaps these reproductions *might actually be copies* of the illustrations in Hedin's books…

3. Illustrations from Hedin's works?

At this point, Tanaka and I decided that the first thing to do was to split up and begin a search of Hedin's published works. Hedin made three expeditions to central Asia; his book *Trans-Himalaya: Discoveries and Adventures in Tibet* (published in three volumes in 1909, 1910, and 1913) is a celebrated and detailed record of his third expedition to Tibet, also widely known in Japan thanks to the translation by Aoki Hideo 青木秀夫 (two volumes, Hakusuisha 白水社, 1979). When I consulted copies of the first two volumes of the English edition (London: Macmillan) held in the library of the Institute for Research in Humanities, Kyoto University, I found that the published illustrations corresponded to many of the pictures from the trove of reproductions. Also, learning that an album of drawings by Hedin had been published (1964; trans. By Kaneko Tamio 金子民雄 1980), I obtained and checked a copy from a secondhand bookstore, whereupon I again found several pictures corresponding to the reproductions. Tanaka had made a similar check at the library of the Graduate School of Letters, and once we reconvened to compare notes, the facts we had been able to glean, and our ideas based on these, were as follows.

1. Most of the reproductions were based on pictures drawn at the time of Hedin's third expedition to Tibet.
2. A considerable quantity of the pictures had been used as illustrations in Hedin's work.
3. However, the illustrations in the publications had been shrunk to a very small size.

The reproductions corresponding to the illustrations were much larger in size, and in some places, had very intricately drawn details that were hard to distinguish in the illustrations. Also, whereas the trove of reproductions included vivid watercolors, the illustrations were in black and white, and there were some reproductions for which a corresponding illustration could not be found. From these facts, we arrived at the conclusion that these reproductions could not have been made with reference to the books after the publication of Hedin's work.

The reproductions had to have been produced based on Hedin's original drawings. This then raised the question of when these art students could have possibly seen Hedin's drawings.

4. Hedin's visit to Kyoto

Having completed his third central Asia expedition, before returning to Europe, Hedin received an invitation to come to Japan, where he received a welcome reception in Tokyo. He then spent an extended visit in Kyoto, where he delivered academic lectures at Kyoto Imperial University. It must have been during this sojourn in Kyoto that the art students were able to see the original drawings and that the reproductions were produced. But even so, who had arranged to have them reproduce the sketches from Hedin's Tibet expedition and for what reason? And why, having done so, had they ended up being left in the Department of Geography?

We launched a two-pronged investigation into these questions, with Tanaka following up on the circumstances that had led to the creation of the reproductions while I investigated the Tibetan society depicted in the sketches.

What sort of academic impact would Hedin's visit have had on Kyoto Imperial University, and what would have been its lasting influence? Perhaps the reproductions we were confronting could be described as symbolic of this legacy. Tanaka pursued her study from the perspective of academic and artistic encounters in the context of a modernizing Japan, which led to the clarification of the various circumstances and historical background concerning Hedin's arrival in Japan and the creation of the reproductions, as well as the spread of their influence. Readers interested in these details are encouraged to refer to the discussions collected in Section II of this volume.[3]

In the meantime, having experience of the region through my own research into the Tibetan language, I decided to look carefully into the landscapes, people, and objects that Hedin had drawn. I suspected that the question of why these images were chosen for reproduction might be clarified by examining Hedin's experience in the field in Tibet. The results of this are presented in Section I of this volume as "A Vicarious Expedition to Hedin," so to speak.

5. Hedin's original drawings in Stockholm

At the outset of our study, our hopes of first checking Hedin's original drawings were happily realized in the autumn of 2015 thanks to the cooperation of Håkan Wahlquist of the Sven Hedin Foundation in Stockholm. Wahlquist is an anthropologist specializing in the Tibetan and Himalayan regions and was appointed as director of the Sven Hedin Foundation after a long career at the Museum of Ethnography in Sweden. As I was acquainted with Wahlquist through research exchanges at Japan's National Museum of Ethnology (国立民族学博物館), I arranged for his introduction to Tanaka and, along with Professors of Graduate School of Letters Kizu, Matsuda Motoji 松田素二, and Mizuno Kazuharu 水野一晴, we visited the Museum of Ethnography (Etnografiska Museet) in Stockholm in November 2015 to ascertain the whereabouts of the originals and compare them with the reproductions. As a result, we found that among the 60 reproductions, the originals for 11 had been lost. We also found that the art students who had made the reproductions had been highly skilled, as the originals had been copied faithfully and with careful precision. A significant takeaway from this research visit was that we were able to confirm Hedin's own annotations on the original drawings. The original sketches were signed by Hedin and dated with the year in which he made them – details not included in the reproductions. After Tanaka photographed these annotations and organized a series of enlargements, juxtaposing these with the annotations on the reproductions enabled us to increase the legible portions with details such as camp numbers, as well as place names and the names and ages of the people depicted in the images. The information in these annotations constituted important basic data for identifying places to be visited during fieldwork.

In addition, the Museum of Ethnography had also received the bequest of a scrapbook of newspaper clippings from the time of Hedin's stay in Kyoto. Glancing through these articles, we were able to get a sense of the contemporary hospitality Hedin was shown. The museum's display also featured a set of samurai armor that had been presented to Hedin by Kyoto Imperial University in commemoration of his visit.[4]

6. Fieldwork in central Tibet

In August 2016, I set out for a stint of fieldwork in Tibet accompanied by the photographer Satō Ken'ei 佐藤兼永. The number of sites along the route of Hedin's Tibet expedition that were generally accessible to foreign tourists remains extremely limited, extending only to the areas around the central Tibetan settlements of Lhasa, Shigatse, and Gyantse, which are now open to tourists, and the pilgrimage routes of Lake Manasarovar and Mount Kailash in Western Tibet. Of course, we had not even broached the subject of our intention to conduct fieldwork in connection with a survey of Hedin's entire expedition route. Accomplishing a follow-up survey in the mountainous areas of Western Tibet – the region that Hedin dubbed Trans-Himalaya – would be extremely difficult without organizing an appropriately-sized academic research team. We limited our objective to revisiting the parts of Tibet that Hedin had sketched. Accordingly, we narrowed the focus of our fieldwork down to the Tashi Lhunpo Monastery in Shigatse, where Hedin had spent approximately a month, and which featured in many of the sketches he left behind. Carrying with us a thick file of color photographs of the reproductions, we visited the monastery on several occasions, where, with the aid of local guides and temple monks, we searched for the places depicted in the sketches and the exact spots where Hedin would have stood to draw them.

Ultimately, we were able to identify the precise vantage points from which Hedin must have worked for only a few of the sketches. However, I could not help but be surprised at how Tashi Lhunpo Monastery, thoroughly ravaged during the Cultural Revolution, had been so faithfully restored and had maintained traditions since the time of Hedin's visit. Elsewhere, I had been powerfully struck at how places like the Drepung Monastery in Lhasa, which we visited during our fieldwork, had changed so drastically in appearance since I had visited in 1991,[5] to the point that I struggled to recall what they had looked like only 25 years earlier. This was not only due to the progress that had been made in restorations and the construction of many new buildings, but also to new features such as the concrete-encased visitor's route provided for tourists. Indeed, while a major reason that I had not visited Lhasa over the last quarter of a century had been the fact that my principal area of research has been the Garzê Tibetan Autonomous Prefecture in Sichuan Province, which had not afforded me any opportunities to visit central Tibet, my Tibetan friends had also been unanimous in conveying to me that if I knew what Lhasa was like in the 1980s, it would be better for me to just cherish those memories and avoid visiting there today.

7. Inheritance and resilience

Nevertheless, in Tashi Lhunpo Monastery as well as in contemporary Tibetan society, we discovered what has most recently been spoken of in anthropology and psychology as *resilience* – the ability "to rebuild, to recover, to bounce back" or "to flexibly adapt and survive even in the face of difficult conditions." That proved to be one of the major fruits of our fieldwork. The people depicted in Hedin's sketches lived in these Tibetan lands a century ago, but they are here no longer. Yet, while the culture of their day could not have escaped the vast changes resulting from historical upheavals brought on by destruction, repression, and the tide of modernization, more than a little of Tibet's legacy has survived or been recovered and passed down to subsequent generations.

To contextualize and understand the historical significance of those sketches whose subjects have been lost, we decided to take photographs that would demonstrate the forms in which the Tibetan society and culture that Hedin had depicted has been inherited today, even when this meant differences of time and place. Satō Ken'ei, the photographer who accompanied me on this fieldwork, has provided a wealth of vivid shots taken with this idea in mind. But, while Satō is responsible for most of the photographs of Tibet found in Section I of this volume, some of my own photographs seeking the perspective in the reproductions are also included.

Commemorative mural painted above the entrance to an apartment where Hedin once lived (Stockholm) ©IKD

8. The publication of *Sven Hedin as Artist*

The sketches and watercolors from the trove of reproductions were all made during the Tibetan survey expedition from 1906–1908. Of all the sketches recording this expedition, what were the criteria by which these 60 pictures were selected to be copied and preserved as reproductions?

The most convincing clue to an answer to this question was found in Hedin's commentary about these pictures.

To mark the centenary of his birth (1865–1952), an album was published in 1964 that collected many of the sketches he had produced to record his explorations. The book was edited by Dr. Gösta Montell, a pupil of Hedin's, and the album was published simultaneously in both Swedish and English under the title *Sven Hedin as Artist* (*Sven Hedin som tecknare*). A Japanese translation by Kaneko Tamio 金子民雄 was published in 1980 as *Hedin sobyō gashū* 『ヘディン素描画集』 (Hakusuisha 白水社). According to this volume's "Translator's Afterword," the commentary by Hedin that Kaneko had translated from Swedish seemed to have been revised by Montell, probably from an original draft manuscript. Also, some of Hedin's drawings had been published in a book prior to *Sven Hedin as Artist*; according to Montell's foreword, in 1920, Hedin had staged an exhibition in Stockholm of his own sketches and watercolors to benefit the School for War Children, for which occasion a pamphlet of drawings was produced under the title *En Levnads Teckning* (Sketches of a Life-time) (Albert Bonnier, Stockholm, 1920). Montell writes that in this book "for the first and only time the artist tells how with pencil and sketch-book in hand he rambled through his Asia." Kaneko writes that "this commentary [from the 1920 book] provided the basis for the present text [i.e.,

Brightly colored thangka (Tibetan Buddhist paintings on silk) illuminated in a dimly lit temple
(Tashi Lhunpo Monastery: Shakyamuni Hall) ©IKD

the 1964 book]. However, this pamphlet [*En Levnads Teckning*] contained a mere twelve sketches." It should also be mentioned that *En Levnads Teckning* is an extremely rare book, one that I have not yet been able to see for myself, as no copies are available from any public institutions in Japan.

9. Hedin's commentary on the sketches

Sven Hedin as Artist was published at a time when producing color art books entailed many difficulties, both technically and economically. It seems that this is why it was primarily an album of *drawings*, rather than watercolors. This can be inferred from Montell's comments in the foreword about the marvels of reproducing the sketches by lithographic printing. However, Hedin's commentary in *Sven Hedin as Artist* contains descriptions of many sketches not included in the album and frequently refers to details such as the color tones of the (absent) watercolors. As Kaneko points out, it seems clear that this text was based on a commentary written for the exhibition of sketches and watercolors originally held in Stockholm in 1920.

While re-reading the Japanese translation of *Sven Hedin as Artist*, I noticed that a considerable proportion of the 60 drawings that had been preserved as reproductions fit very well with the content mentioned in the four chapters of commentary dealing with "The Tashi Lhunpo Monastery," "People of Shigatse," "The Transhimalayas," and "Tibetans." When I tried arranging the reproductions in conjunction with the text, they seemed to fit very well. Almost, I thought, as if the commentary had been written for the reproductions that were left in the Department of Geography at Kyoto University. Such structural coherence could not possibly be a coincidence. What could this mean?

10. For reporting findings from the field

Presumably, when we report on our fieldwork today, we arrange photographs chosen according to the broad outlines of our story to think about the composition of our slideshows. It seems likely that Hedin, too, when presenting his lectures in various places, must have given explanations while presenting drawings he had selected in line with his stories on each theme in order to efficiently and accurately deliver his commentary in a limited time. Hedin's text, written as the commentary for an exhibition, would have been a manuscript for introducing drawings based on the arrangement of just such a presentation.

Therefore, in Section I of this volume, I have classified the reproductions in line with Hedin's commentary as included in *Sven Hedin as Artist* and rearranged them divided into the four chapters noted above on "The Tashi Lhunpo Monastery," "People of Shigatse," "The Transhimalayas," and "Tibetans." I have placed Hedin's own commentary at the beginning of each chapter, arranging spreads of reproductions, originals, field photographs, and additional commentary as necessary, to illustrate the story as it unfolds.

These pictures, exhibited at the time of Hedin's visit to Japan in 1908, considering the world situation at that time, represented the latest dispatches from the unexplored reaches of central Asia. The early twentieth century had nothing like today's video techniques, and although the Autochrome dry plates for color photography had by this time been invented, their use was still far from widespread. Even for black and white photography, the necessary dry plates and equipment were heavy and took a considerable amount of time to expose, to say nothing of the expense they entailed. The dim interiors of Tibetan temples, illuminated only by the faint light cast by butter lamps, would have been extremely difficult to shoot with the photographic technology of the time. The most reliable means of vividly conveying details of the field site under such conditions were therefore high-precision sketches and vibrant watercolors.[6]

11. Re-evaluation as historical materials

At the time of Hedin's visit to Japan, the records of his local investigations – including his numerous sketches – were undoubtedly the very latest information of academic or journalistic interest. Information relating to the topography of central Asia was of great interest to a variety of fields in the context of the contemporary world situation and the trends of the age. However, the impact of Hedin's expedition on the field of Tibetan studies was relatively minor in comparison to its achievements in geographical circles.[7] Chief among the reasons for this are that Hedin's accounts of the field and his observations, predating ethnographic description achieved by the methods of modern research, amounted to little more than an "account from the Age of Exploration," as well as the fact that Hedin himself did not seem to have any interest in Buddhism or textual sources, and thus did not actively contribute to those fields which constitute the core of Tibetan studies. On this point, there was a large divide in the evaluations accorded to the contributions of those scholars who collected primary materials with a focus on textual sources like Kawaguchi Ekai and Tada Tōkan from Japan, Aurel Stein from the United Kingdom and Paul Pelliot in France, all of whom were active in the same period, and those of the "explorers" who also contributed a large amount of research information to the academic community despite their different aims and orientations. In contrast to the precision of Hedin's sketches of geographical landscapes and architecture and the realism of his portraits, the Buddhist images and art depicted in temple interiors convey a surprisingly naïve or rough impression. This is inevitably pointed out by Tibetans on seeing the reproductions. Herein I wonder if we might be seeing a symbolic expression of Hedin's lack of interest in the forms of traditional Tibetan Buddhist art, which do not conform to the techniques of Western portraiture.

More than a century after Hedin's visit, his preserved sketches and their reproductions have assumed increased gravity as historical materials, imbued with a new value that is quite unlike the purpose for which they were initially created.[8] There is no question that Hedin's surviving sketches provide records of the earliest scientific field study of Tibet. To give an example, Hedin's sketch of the mausoleum and memorial tower at Tashi Lhunpo Monastery as they once were, before they were destroyed, having fallen mercy to modern history, show them as they stood in their heyday, and thus have great value as graphic records of their former glory. In fact, Hedin's sketches and photographs of Gyantse Dzong have reportedly been used as reference for restoring the dzong in recent years.[9]

Hedin's sketches of Tibet, are valuable records of a lost time and place, but also important evidence of the resilience of the Tibetan people and of Tibetan society.

Notes

1 The formation of the popular imagination of Tibet in Meiji Japan is detailed by Kōmoto Yasuko 高本康子 (2010), who argues that Hedin's arrival in Japan had an enormous impact in that it led to the regeneration and expansion of the popular imagination of the Asian mainland in the pre-war period.

2 What I did not know then, and what Tanaka Kazuko's study has revealed, is that at the time of Hedin's visit to Japan, Ogawa Takuji played a central role in arranging Hedin's invited lectures and academic interactions at Kyoto Imperial University. See Tanaka's chapter in Section II of this volume (chapter 2), on "Hedin's Reception in Kyoto, 1908." On

November 29, 1908, Ogawa, together with Naitō Torajirō 内藤虎次郎 (aka Naitō Konan 内藤湖南), staged an exhibition of Chinese texts – mainly geographical documents – in conjunction with an exhibition of Hedin's sketches, and they presented Hedin with an English translation of a passage about Tibet from the 22nd volume of the 18th-century *Shuidao tigang* 水道提綱 (Guide to the Network of Waterways). On the Chinese texts that Hedin used with Ogawa's help, see the chapter by Kizu Yuko and Tanaka Kazuko in Section II of this volume (chapter 6) on "Hedin and Classic Chinese Texts."

3 That the Western-style painter Kanokogi Takeshiro 鹿子木孟郎, who had helped organize Hedin's reception, was closely involved in the making of the reproductions is demonstrated by a careful study of contemporary records and the exchanges between academic and artistic circles in Kyoto. See Tanaka Kazuko's chapter in Section II on "The Legacy of Sven Hedin's Stay in Kyoto: Reproductions of Original Art by Hedin Left at Kyoto University" (chapter 3), which discusses how the reproductions came to be made and the art students who were responsible for their creation.

4 See the column by Tanaka Kazuko in Section II of this volume on "Hedin's Suit of Armor."

5 Cf. 雲上の秘境 チベット [*Tibet: Untrodden Region in the Clouds: Its Treasures, Traditions, and Lifestyles.*] 2 vols. (VHS) EMI Music Japan; (Laserdisc) Toshiba EMI, 1992.

6 The photographs taken by Sven Hedin and his photographic equipment, and the techniques he used in his sketches as a cartographer and artist, are discussed in detail by Håkan Wahlquist in the chapter entitled "Sven Hedin as Artist and Photographer: Extending the Techniques of Cartography and Illustration at the Turn of the Last Century" in Section II of this volume (chapter 6).

7 Also relevant was a historical context in which the geographical expeditions of the day were inextricably linked to the politics of powerful territorial ambitions and balances of power; even today, Hedin's Tibetan explorations have not received any evaluation in China. For a discussion of the fraught context of international politics at the time of Hedin's expedition, see Shirasu Jōshin 白須淨眞 (ed.) (2014).

8 Matsuda Motoji analyzes Hedin's ideological background through his praxis and representations of other cultures. In this reassessment, Matsuda argues that although Hedin made his debut as an explorer in the late nineteenth-century "Age of Exploration," in an era where the meaning of praxis was transitioning from exploration to academic study, he created a new perceptual framework that overcame the dichotomy between civilized and primitive societies that had been the dominant paradigm of cross-cultural recognition in his own time. See Matsuda's chapter in Section II of this volume on "Exploration, Science, and Understanding Others: Thinking Through Hedin's Trajectory" (chapter 4). Also, it was after the Age of Exploration that Kyoto Imperial University started to actively adopt the methods of modern scientific research, beginning to attempt more sophisticated "academic explorations" and "field surveys" before and after the Second World War. This historical trajectory is introduced in another chapter in Section II of this volume, by Yamagiwa Juichi 山際壽一, entitled "The Headwaters of the 'Exploration University'" (chapter 1).

9 An architectural treatise has been published on the restoration of Shigatse Dzong that includes discussion, if only briefly, of the historical materials surveyed in carrying out the restoration. See Chang Qing 常青 (2015).

Section I Bibliography

* A list of the principal publications referred to in the commentary in Section I.

Hedin's Publications and Japanese Translations

スウェン・ヘディン [著] 深田久弥・榎一雄・長沢和俊 [監修]
    (1964–1966)『ヘディン中央アジア探検紀行全集』全11巻. 白水社;
    (1978–1979)『ヘディン探検紀行全集』全15巻・別巻2. 白水社;
    (1988–1989)『スウェン・ヘディン探検記』全9巻. 白水社.
スウェン・ヘディン『トランス・ヒマラヤ』上/下, 青木秀男 [訳]
    (1965)『ヘディン中央アジア探検紀行全集』4–5;
    (1979)『ヘディン探検紀行全集』7–8;
    (1988)『スウェン・ヘディン探検記』4–5.
Sven Hedin. *Trans-Himalaya: discoveries and adventures in Tibet.* London: Macmillan. (1909) I; (1910) II; (1913) III.
スウェン・ヘディン (1992)『チベット遠征』金子民雄 [訳] 中公文庫.
Sven Hedin (1934) *A Conquest of Tibet.* New York: E.P. Dutton and Co.
スウェン・ヘディン (1980)『ヘディン素描画集』ヨースタ・モンテル [編] スウェン・ヘディン [文] 金子民雄 [訳] 白水社.
Sven Hedin (1964) *Sven Hedin as artist: For the centenary of Sven Hedin's birth.* Gösta Montell [revis.], Donald Burton [trans.]. Stockholm: Sven Hedins Stiftelse: Statens Etnografiska Museum.

Hedin's Life and Explorations

金子 民雄 (1972)『ヘディン伝 偉大な探検の生涯』新人物往来社;(1989)『ヘディン伝 偉大なシルクロードの探検者』中公文庫.
金子 民雄 (1982) 『ヘディン 人と旅』白水社;(2002) [増補改訂文庫版]『ヘディン交遊録』中公文庫.
白須 淨眞 [編] (2014) 『大谷光瑞とスヴェン・ヘディン 内陸アジア探検と国際政治社会』勉誠出版.

In the Footsteps of Hedin: Depictions of Tibet in Century-Old Reproductions

The Panchen Lama and Tashi Lhunpo Monastery

牙 含章［編著］ (1987)《班禅额尔德尼传》西藏人民出版社.
苏 发祥［主编］ (2009)《历辈班禅额尔德尼》青海人民出版社.
イザベル・ヒントン (2001)『高僧の生まれ変わり チベットの少年』三浦順子［訳］世界文化社；
　　　　　　　　(2006)［修訂文庫版］『ダライ・ラマとパンチェン・ラマ』ランダムハウス講談社.
Isabel Hilton (2001) *The Search for the Panchen Lama*. New York: W. W. Norton.
蒙 紫廖 频［編輯］ (1993)《班禅大师驻锡地 札什伦布寺》丹迴・冉纳班杂（第五世）［撰文］外文出版社/民族出版社.
彭措 朗杰［編著］ (1999)《扎什伦布寺》中国大百科全书出版社.
彭措 朗杰［編著］ (2010)《中国西藏文化之旅 扎什伦布寺》中国大百科全书出版社.
喻 淑珊［編著］ (2010)《中国文化知识读本 扎什伦布寺》吉林文史出版社.

Tibetan Culture and Personal/Geographical Naming Conventions

常 青 (2015)《西藏山巅宫堡的变迁 —桑珠孜宗宫的复生及宗山博物馆设计》同济大学出版社.
杨 清凡 (2003)《藏族服饰史》青海人民出版社.
曽布川 寛、基信 祐爾［監修］ (2009)『聖地チベット ポタラ宮と天空の至宝』（展覧会図録）大広.
王 贵 (1991)《藏族人名研究》民族出版社・
星球地图出版社［編］ (2009)《中国分省系列地图集 西藏自治区地图集》星球地图出版社.
中国地图出版社［編］ (2016)《中国分省系列地图册 西藏》中国地图出版社.

History of the Exploration of Tibet

河口 慧海 (1904)『西藏旅行記』上/下. 博文館；(1978) 日本山岳会［編］〈新選覆刻日本の山岳名著〉上/下. 大修館書店；
　　　　　(2015) 高山 龍三［校訂］上/下. 講談社学術文庫.
多田 等観 (1984)『チベット滞在記』牧野文子［編］白水社；(2009) 講談社学術文庫.
ピーター・ホップカーク (2004)『チベットの潜入者たち ラサ一番乗りをめざして』今枝由郎・鈴木佐知子・武田真理子［訳］. 白水社.
金子 民雄 (2013)『聖地チベットの旅』連合出版.
薬師 義美 (2006)『大ヒマラヤ探検史』白水社.
高本 康子 (2010)『近代日本におけるチベット像の形成と変遷』芙蓉書房出版.
江本 嘉伸 (1993)『西藏漂白 チベットに魅せられた十人の日本人』上，(1994) 下, 山と渓谷社；
　　　　　(2017)『新編 西藏漂白 チベットに潜入した十人の日本人』ヤマケイ文庫.

Explanatory Notes

* Translations of Tibetan names shown after Tibetan script are spelled in the Wylie system.
* Sources of quotations from the writings of Hedin are abbreviated as follows:
  As Artist　*Sven Hedin as Artist*. ed. Gösta Montell, tr. Donald Burton. Stockholm: Sven Hedins Stiftelse, 1964.
  Trans-Himalaya I, II, III　Sven Hedin, *Trans-Himalaya* Vols. I, II, and III. New York: The Macmillan Company, 1909 (I), 1910 (II); London: Macmillan and Co., Limited, 1913 (III).
* The Panchen Lamas are commonly identified by numbers that begin three generations (posthumously designated) before the first actual Panchen Lama, who Hedin identified as "first." For clarity in this text I have indicated Hedin's numbering as e.g., "[1st]-generation", followed by the standard numbering in Roman numerals: "[1st] Panchen Lama IV" (note also that Hedin uses the alternate title "Tashi Lama" for the Panchen Lama).
* Satō Ken'ei provided all photos in Section I, except those marked ©IKD, which were taken by Ikeda Takumi, who also wrote all the captions.
* Ikeda titled all of the reproductions in Section I after consulting reference materials. Sven Hedin had not titled his original artwork.

Acknowledgments

In preparing the account in Section I, I received kind instruction from Dawa Trashi ཟླ་བ་བཀྲ་ཤིས་, Hoshi Izumi 星泉, Ōba Emi 大羽恵美, and Iwao Kazushi 岩尾一史 on various aspects of the depiction of Tibetan culture. I express my appreciation here. Nevertheless, any errors or inappropriate expressions should be attributed entirely to a lack of understanding on the part of the author.

Chapter 1: Tashi Lhunpo Monastery

THE TASHILHUNPO MONASTERY
Now our caravan moves north to Tibet.

From every camp where fires burned between our tents, from every pass where our horses were caressed by the wind I sketched a panorama. On the long diagonal journey through the whole of Tibet I had no human beings or dwellings to draw. For three months we passed through uninhabited tracts and then through scintillating cold. Now the photographic equipment, too, was constantly in use. But Hladje Tsering, the Governor of Naktsang, I could not pass over [*as Artist* 106]. He looks like an old woman, smokes his pipe and is clad in the Chinese style. It was he who in the year 1901 compelled me to go back when I was trying to push on to Lhasa, but who now put no obstacles in my path on the way to the great monastery of Tashilhunpo, south of the upper Bramaputra or Tsangpo.

The year 1907 had passed before we reached this famous monastery, after Lhasa the finest in Tibet, and situated beside the country's other city, Shigatse. In Tashilhunpo resides Tashi Lama, the Pope of southern Tibet, in holiness higher than Dalai Lama, in temporal matters more powerful than he.

The monastery is situated at the amphitheatrically falling foot of a mountain arm and constitutes in itself an entire town of different houses. A picture in Indian ink, like all the others done on the spot, gives some notion of a part of this temple-town [**Reproduction 1**]. Three of the five mortuary chapels are visible. In each of these rests a Tashi Lama under a roof built in the Chinese style and coated with a thick layer of real gold.

Another picture, where the colours are only hinted at, shows the façade of the finest temple-building [**Reproduction 2**], called Labrang. On the stone terraces before this and the other buildings a number of sepulchral pyramids are erected. At the foot of a couple of these characteristic monuments a crowd of monks and women have collected to observe my incomprehensible occupation [*as Artist* 108].

From smaller courtyards wooden steps lead up to the veranda-like open vestibules from which one enters each of the five high-priestly mortuary chapels [**Reproduction 3**]. These entrances are lacquered in extremely motley fashion, the predominating colour being intensive blood or cherry red. On the two side walls and on the wall-surfaces confronting the visitor on either side of the entrance-gate fantastic pictures are painted alfresco, representing the four spirit-kings who are the masters of all the evil flying about in the air and who keep guard at the entrance to the innermost sanctuary and chase away all the cruel spirits of the air [**Reproduction 4**].

Tashi Lhunpo Monastery

The entrance is closed with two massive doors of old wood, which are painted with dark-red lacquer and have brass mountings and heavy rings in hemispherically curved shields.

When the lama, who had been charged by the high-priest himself to show me round and point out all the glories of the temple, had got the doors to swing slowly on their hinges and open inwards to the sanctuary [Reproduction 5], I found myself facing a high altar-with a different design in each of the five chapels [Reproduction 6]. In tall temple vessels of silver and gold, in form resembling goblets with stem, butter, rice and water are offered as sacrificial gifts to the images of the gods. And above them, as background to the altar, is a cjorten with mountings of thick silver plate studded with precious stones, in which a Tashi Lama sleeps the eternal sleep [Reproduction 7].

My cicerone led me back to a large temple hall with columns, sky-light in the ceiling and long benches and table at which novices sat bent over pages from the sacred texts [Reproduction 11]. It was not easy to sketch this scene, as I kept in the shade behind the columns in order not to disturb the lesson. It was strange that they let me alone and did not object to my presence. But I was already a familiar figure on the premises and Tashi Lama's guest. They therefore went on reading in a sing-song rhythm after the introductory chant by an instructing lama [Reproduction 10].

One of my pictures shows the kitchen in Tashilhunpo [*as Artist* 116]. Tea-kettles of copper, as large as round bath-tubs, are inbuilt in a stone foundation, and their bottoms are licked by the flames of the furnace. At the top are seen a couple of cooks who with ladles the size of oars are stirring the Tibetans' national drink.

SVEN HEDIN AS ARTIST pp. 41–42

Profile of Hlaje Tsering (*Sven Hedin as Artist* 106)

The kitchen at Tashi Lhunpo Monastery (*Sven Hedin as Artist* 116)

A large discarded kitchen cauldron (Lhasa: Sera Monastery precincts)

[Reproduction 1] Adachi Itarō, Pencil, 25.1 × 35.4 cm

1 View of Tashi Lhunpo

The Tashi Lhunpo Monastery is located in Shigatse, Tibet's second largest city. Headed by successive generations of Panchen Lama, it has played a significant role in Tibetan history as the most powerful rival to the authority of the Dalai Lama in Lhasa. Both figures belong to the Gelug school of Tibetan Buddhism and are objects of worship and veneration by the Tibetan people: the Dalai Lama as a reincarnation of the Bodhisattva Avalokitesvara, and the Panchen Lama as a reincarnation of the Buddha Amitabha. When we compare a sketch by Hedin with a photograph of Tashi Lhunpo taken recently at approximately the same angle, we see that while the basic configuration of the buildings has survived, including their layout and coloring, there are some differences in detail. The tall flat-roofed building visible at the rear left in the photograph is the Maitreya Hall constructed in 1918. This houses a gilt-bronze statue of the seated Bodhisattva Maitreya, which at 26.2 meters high, is the largest such figure in the world; it had not yet been built when Hedin visited in 1907. In front of that is the mausoleum of the [7th] Panchen Lama X, who died in 1989; built in 1993, this is the newest structure. Inside is a stupa housing the remains of the Panchen Lama. The gold-colored roof at front center in the picture belongs to the mausoleum of the [1st] Panchen Lama IV. All of the Panchen Lama tombs now on view are reconstructions, the originals having been destroyed during China's Cultural Revolution; hence, they are not exactly as Hedin saw them.

Tashi Lhunpo Monastery

[Original 1] Sven Hedin, 1907, Pencil and Pen, 25.1 × 35.4 cm

Mausoleum structures and façade of Tashi Lhunpo Monastery (Shigatse)

[Reproduction 2] Nishikawa Junji, Pencil, Pen, and Water Color, 25.0 × 35.2 cm

2 Tashi Lhunpo Monastery: Façade of the Labrang

The lower left of both the reproduction and the original carry the word "Labrang," while the original is further annotated with Hedin's signature and the figure "08", denoting the year. Regrettably, no additional information is available about this picture, which is not included in either *Trans-Himalaya* or *Sven Hedin as Artist*. The annotated term *labrang* refers to a dwelling in which a lama resides. In Tibetan, it is pronounced either *laprang* or *Latrang* (བླ་བྲང་ *bla brang*). This structure doubled as both the Panchen Lama's residence and his offices. The entryway was situated in a large entrance plaza, in front of which stood a building whose interior served as a corridor while its exterior doubled as another façade. Although the Labrang, as well as the mausolea, was built from the east, each time the mausoleum of another Panchen Lama was built to the west, the façade structure was also extended sideways, forming a single contiguous wall. The façade was dyed in the same red color as the walls of the mausolea. Hedin has depicted a terrace above the front entrance of the Labrang through the front garden from atop the roof of the building that constitutes the façade. Hedin, in the explanation given in this chapter, briefly mentions this picture as well.

Tashi Lhunpo Monastery

[Original 2] Sven Hedin, 1908, Pencil, Pen, and Water Color, 25.1 × 35.4 cm

Another picture, where the colours are only hinted at, shows the façade of the finest temple-building, [built as the residence of the High Lama], called Labrang. (*Sven Hedin as Artist*, p. 41)

At present, it is no longer possible to ascend to the top of this façade structure, but tourists are free to go on to the roof of a building further in front of the façade, and from there a path has been opened for visitors to visit the stupa. The photograph of the façade and mausoleum was taken from this visitor's path.

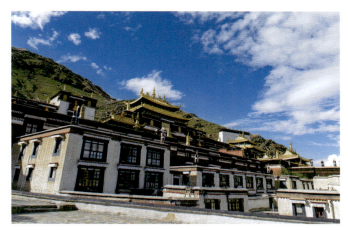

Mausoleum and its façade (Tashi Lhunpo Monastery)

Commentary
The Panchen Lama and the Dalai Lama

The Panchen Lama is the head abbot of the Tashi Lhunpo Monastery visited by Hedin. Hedin had an audience with Thupten Chö kyi Nyima (1883–1937) the [6th] Panchen Lama IX, at which the two men photographed each other. Today, the photograph taken by Hedin is widely known as a portrait of "Panchen Lama IX."

The Panchen Lama is known in Tibetan as པན་ཆེན་བླ་མ་ (spelled *pan chen bla ma* using Wylie transliteration). Although rendered as *Banchan lama* 班禪喇嘛 in Traditional Chinese, the title typically used in Tibet is Panchen Rinpoche (པན་ཆེན་རིན་པོ་ཆེ་ *pan chen rin po che*). The term "Panchen" is an abbreviation of the Sanskrit word *pandita* "scholar" and the Tibetan word *chenpo* "great", while "Rinpoche" connotes (someone or something worthy of respect as) a "precious jewel." The head abbot of Tashi Lhunpo Monastery has also been known as the "Tashi Lama" – and indeed was referred to as such by Hedin – but this appellation is no longer in common usage today.

As living reincarnations of Buddha, the Panchen Lamas are believed to be avatars of the *Tathāgata Amitābha*, repeatedly incarnating as high priests to bring salvation to all sentient beings. In Hedin's writings, Thuptän Chö kyi Nyima is described as the [6th] Panchen Lama in accordance with the contemporary system of reckoning incarnations (the Ganden Phodrang system). However, in the Chinese style of reckoning now used at Tashi Lhunpo, which recognizes three predecessors to the first Panchen Lama to adopt this name, he becomes Panchen Lama IX. For convenient reference, in this volume, the latter reckoning is noted in Roman numerals after the former.

In the dominant Gelug school of Tibetan Buddhism, the Panchen Lama enjoys religious standing comparable to that of the Dalai Lama. It is sometimes said that "as the sun and the moon are to the heavens, the Dalai Lama and the Panchen Lama are to the world of men." However, whereas the successive Dalai Lamas were both religious authorities and supreme temporal leaders as the kings of Tibet, the authority of the Panchen Lamas was basically religious.

From the perspective of their supporters, the Panchen Lamas, as incarnations of the Buddha of Infinite Light (the *Tathāgata Amitābha*), are figures whose importance in terms of Buddhist doctrine exceeds even that of the Dalai Lamas, who are seen as incarnations of the *Bodhisattva Avalokiteśvara* (the *Tathāgata* is one who has attained enlightenment, whereas a bodhisattva is seen as a practitioner who aspires to enlightenment). On the other hand, from the perspective of the supporters of the Dalai Lamas, since the 5th Dalai Lama's accession to supreme authority over the religious state, the Panchen Lamas are said to no longer have any involvement in politics. The Panchen Lama, as Tathāgata, already belongs to the world of clean thought and is no longer involved in the secular world. Since bodhisattvas are practitioners who are supposed to engage in altruistic practice for the relief of all sentient beings, it is seen as proper that the Dalai Lama, as the incarnation of a bodhisattva, should actively engage with the secular world.

However, even in the context of secular authority, a rivalry has existed between the Western Central Tibetan district of Tsang (གཙང་ *gtsang*), centered on the seat of the Tashi Lhunpo Monastery in the city of Shigatse (གཞིས་ཀ་རྩེ་ *gzhis ka rtse*), and the Eastern Central Tibetan district of Ü (དབུས་ *dbus*), centered on Lhasa (ལྷ་ས་ *lha sa*), with a history of attempts orchestrated by each to exert control over the other. After the establishment of political authority of the Dalai Lama in 1642 with the conquest of Tibet by the Mongol ruler Güshi Khan, the virtuous monk Lopsang Chö kyi Gyältsän (བློ་བཟང་ཆོས་ཀྱི་རྒྱལ་མཚན་ *blo bzang chos kyi rgyal mtshan*; 1570–1662), who had been mentor to the contemporary 5th Dalai Lama, died. In gratitude to the monk who had chosen him and served as his ceremonial teacher, the 5th Dalai Lama conferred him with the title of Panchen and designated that his subsequent reincarnations would inherit the position of head abbot of Tashi Lhunpo Monastery, whereupon he selected and recognized Lopsang

Yeshe (བློ་བཟང་ཡེ་ཤེས་ *blo bzang ye shes*; 1663–1737) as the [2nd] Panchen Lama.

However, it was not long before the Panchen Lama of Tashi Lhunpo Monastery became a focal point for forces opposing the Ü region; with the beginning of interference and control by the Qing Dynasty at the turn of the eighteenth century, the Panchen Lama and his circle began to show an attitude favorable to the Qing. For its part, as well, the Qing Dynasty was also seeking to utilize the authority of the Panchen Lama to undermine that of the Dalai Lama.

In Hedin's sketches as well, many of the figures portrayed appear to be Tibetans dressed in Chinese clothing. These drawings are therefore a valuable record pointing to the presence at the time of a significant number of individuals in the circles close to the Panchen Lama whose sympathies lay with the Qing Dynasty.

Commentary
The history of Tashi Lhunpo Monastery and changes to its mausoleum

The first mausoleum: The original Panchen Lama

Tashi Lhunpo Monastery is in Shigatse, Tibet's second largest city. Along with the "great three" monasteries of Ganden, Sera, and Drepung in Lhasa, it is one of the four great monasteries of the Gelug tradition. Formally, it is known as བཀྲ་ཤིས་ལྷུན་པོ་དཔལ་གྱི་སྡེ་ཆེན་ཕྱོགས་ཐམས་ཅད་ལས་རྣམ་པར་རྒྱལ་བའི་གླིང་ *bkra shis lhun po dpal gyi sde chen phyogs thams cad las rnam par rgyal ba'i gling*, a Tibetan name meaning "All fortune and happiness gathered here, at this glorious great community, a monastery victorious in all directions." The name "Tashi Lhunpo monastery" is an abbreviated name for the "Monastery of Mount Sumeru, the mountain of Bliss." The monastery was founded in 1447 by Gendün Druppa (དགེ་འདུན་གྲུབ་པ་ *dge 'dun grub pa*; 1391–1474), a former disciple of Je Tsongkhapa (the founding patriarch of the Gelug tradition of Tibetan Buddhism), who would later become the first Dalai Lama. In 1600, a large-scale expansion was carried out under the abbotship of Lopsang Chö kyi Gyältsän (བློ་བཟང་ཆོས་ཀྱི་རྒྱལ་མཚན་ *blo bzang chos kyi rgyal mtshan*; 1570–1662), another eminent monk of the Gelug tradition. In 1662, the 5th Dalai Lama, one of Gyältsän's students, conferred his former teacher with the posthumous honorific title of Panchen Lama and designated that his reincarnations would inherit the abbotship of Tashi Lhunpo Monastery. When Lopsang Chö kyi Gyältsän passed away at the remarkable age of ninety-two, his remains were interred in the Great Maitreya Hall and prayers were invoked to appeal for a swift reincarnation. After the corpse was mummified, a memorial stupa embossed with gold to preserve it and a mausoleum covered with a golden roof were erected to house them all. Thus, at Tashi Lhunpo Monastery, with the passing of each successive Panchen Lama, a mausoleum and a memorial stupa to store the remains were constructed, expanding the monastery. The abbot at the time of Hedin's visit to Tashi Lhunpo was the [6th] Panchen Lama IX. Given special dispensation by the Panchen Lama, Hedin visited all the mausolea of the successive abbots of Tashi Lhunpo, leaving a record of his detailed observations in the first volume of *Trans-Himalaya*. In both the commentary in this chapter as well as in the first volume of *Trans-Himalaya*, Hedin repeatedly mentions the existence of five mausolea from which we know that mausolea were built for the [1st] IV through [5th] VIII Panchen Lamas. And while visitors to Tashi Lhunpo today can see three mausolea buildings and the palace dedicated to *Maitreya Bodhisattva* (see the photo ©IKD below), these are the result of renovations and reconstructions that have taken place as a result of the destruction wrought over the past century by upheavals such as the Tibetan uprising and China's Cultural Revolution; the mausolea that Hedin saw have not all survived into the present in their original forms.

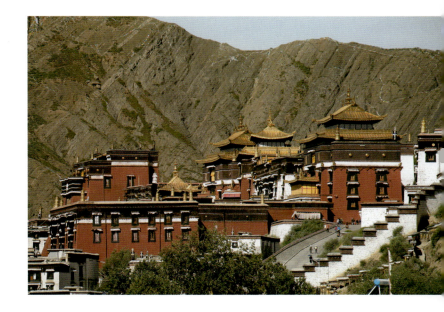

Tashi Lhunpo Monastery

Hanging map in thangka painting style: Abbotship of the [4th] Panchen Lama VII

Surviving materials which reveal aspects of the construction of the mausolea include mounted artwork like a kind of *thangka* (photo on the facing page). On a sacred map depicting a bird's-eye view of Tashi Lhunpo Monastery and its surroundings, the upper half shows the great temples and lamaseries of the monastery city set against the backdrop of Mount Nyima. Although slightly offset relative to its actual position, the Shigatse Dzong is drawn on the center right of the panel, with the old city of Shigatse spreading out below. The Panchen Lama's summer palace is at the bottom of the screen, where the figures of three elephants can be seen kept in an enclosure. At the upper right (east) side, an enormous painting of three Buddhas is suspended on the giant *thangka* wall (Terrace for the Ceremonial of Buddha's Portraits), while on the left side, the vivid red hues of three mausolea can be seen. All of this suggests that this picture was painted during the era of the [4th] Panchen Lama VII, known by the dharma name Pälden Tänpai Nyima (དཔལ་ལྡན་བསྟན་པའི་ཉི་མ་ *pal ldan bstan pa'i nyi ma*, 1782–1854). Formerly, the mausoleum on the eastern side was known as the Eastern Chapel (མཆོད་ཁང་ཤར་ *mchod khang shar*; lit. Eastern Offering Hall) (it is currently a mausoleum in which the V through IX Panchen Lamas are enshrined together). The appellation, still in use today, of the "Central Chapel" (མཆོད་ཁང་དཀྱིལ་ *mchod khang dkyil*; lit. Central Offering Hall), probably dates from this period (the current Central Chapel was rebuilt as a mausoleum for the [1st] Panchen Lama IV). The Western Chapel (མཆོད་ཁང་ནུབ་ *mchod khang nup*), in which the memorial stupa of the [3rd] Panchen Lama VI was once interred, was destroyed during China's Cultural Revolution, and no structure bearing that name currently exists. (See the commentary for Reproduction 8: *Framed sign over the entrance to the mausoleum of the [3rd] Panchen Lama VI*). This picture, from the collection of Tashi Lhunpo Monastery, is reproduced in the 《班禅大师驻锡地 札什伦布寺》 [The Hidden Tradition: Life Inside the Great Tibetan Monastery Tashilhunpo] (1993) published in China, and was featured at an exhibition staged in Japan in 2009 entitled 『聖地チベット―ポタラ宮と天空の至宝―』 [*Tibet – Treasures from the Roof of the World*] (according to the exhibition catalogue, it measured 61.0 cm in height by 41.5 cm in width). Notably, several prints of the picture also seem to have been issued, and have occasionally come to auction in foreign countries.

Fold-out illustration in Das (1902): Abbotship of the [5th] Panchen Lama VIII

A comparatively well-known map of the precincts of Tashi Lhunpo Monastery may be found among the colored fold-out illustrations featured in Das (1902) (bottom of this page). The mountain that provides the backdrop is tinted green and the mausoleum and façade are tinted red, but for the most part, the other temple quarters and halls of study are left without coloring, giving an overall effect approaching that of a line drawing. Sarat Chandra Das (1849–1917), a notable pundit, was a Tibetan

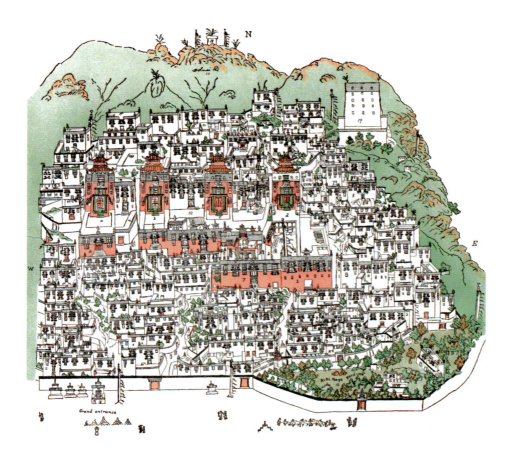

scholar from India. Travelling to Central Tibet in 1879 and 1881–1882, he visited the Tashi Lhunpo Monastery and Lhasa and explored the Yarlung Valley. In 1902, he published a memoir of his travels, edited by W.W. Rockhill, entitled *Journey to Lhasa & Central Tibet*, a book that would have undoubtedly caught the eye of Sven Hedin. Moreover, it is a matter of record that Kawaguchi Ekai, who also sought access to Tibet, studied the Tibetan language under Das and obtained information from him. Comparing this fold-out illustration with the *thangka* painting described earlier that showed three mausolea, the principal differences in Das's picture are that the giant *thangka* wall at the upper right (east) side does not feature a suspended Buddhist image, but instead, a white wall inset with many small windows, and that the number of mausolea inked in red has grown to four. Accordingly, it is speculated that this picture was painted during the era of the [5th] Panchen Lama VIII, known by the dharma name Tänpai Wangchuk (བསྟན་པའི་དབང་ཕྱུག་ *bstan pa'i dbang phyug*; 1855–1882). While the coloring methods used for the fold-out illustration and the *thangka* painting differ considerably, they share many points in common, not only in terms of composition, but also in terms of the way that the details of the line drawings of the mausolea and temple quarters were drawn. It seems likely that a new temple map was produced based on the *thangka* map after the period when there were only three mausolea, but the finished product has not survived. Das must have acquired a line drawing (possibly a rough sketch) of a picture of the four-mausolea period, accurately traced it to produce this picture, and then added commentary based on his own interviews (an English-language explanation is included in the lower right of the fold-out map, but has been omitted here). While we have no more information on this matter, since no detailed mention of this picture is to be found in the main text of Das (1902), it is a fairly accurate picture of substantial value as a historical document.

Artwork in 『チベット旅行記』 [A Journey to Tibet], by Kawaguchi Ekai

Kawaguchi Ekai, who studied Tibetan and collected information under Das, set out for Tibet from Nepal in 1900. After making a pilgrimage to Mount Kailash in December, he visited Tashi Lhunpo Monastery, where he stayed for several days on his way to Lhasa. Thuptän Chö kyi Nyima, the [6th] Panchen Lama IX, whom Hedin would later receive an audience with, was eighteen years old at the time. At the time of his own visit, Kawaguchi states that the Panchen Lama was away at his summer residence, and his hopes for an audience were unfortunately dashed. Illustration no. 54 in Kawaguchi's account of his travels, 『チベット旅行記』 [A Journey to Tibet] (1904), captioned チベット第二の府に到る [Arriving at Tibet's second seat of government], features a sketch of Tashi Lhunpo Monastery (bottom of this page). Compared with the hanging map in *thangka* style drawn using

Tashi Lhunpo Monastery

Tibetan painting techniques and the fold-out map in Das (1902), the shape of the mausolea and other details closely resemble a Chinese Buddhist temple; with the three-layered roofs atop the foundations, the image does not appear to be very lifelike. Nevertheless, we see that five mausolea are present with the background of the mountain, and given that the giant *thangka* wall is drawn on their right, it is conceivable that the image accurately depicts the mausolea around the time of Kawaguchi's visit. Although it is a rough sketch, it is noteworthy that it carefully includes the basic elements signifying Tashi Lhunpo Monastery: the number of mausolea, the religious monument visible on the mountain peak, and the shape of the giant *thangka* wall with the two trees on its roof (although there are too many small windows), as well as several objects near the center of the precinct that resemble Buddhist stupas (drawn as dark, thin forms). While it is possible that Kawaguchi drew this illustration based on a sketch made at the time of his visit, given the similarity of the picture's composition and the fact that Kawaguchi and Das enjoyed a close relationship, it seems likely that it was drawn based on information provided by Das. Since Kawaguchi returned to Japan and serialized his travel account in the newspaper in 1903 and the account of Das's travels was published in 1902, it is certainly possible that he saw the fold-out map, but whether he referred to it remains in the realm of speculation. The important thing is that whereas there are four mausolea on Das's fold-out map, five such structures are correctly drawn in Kawaguchi's illustration.

A picture scroll of the monastery precincts: Abbotship of the [6th] Panchen Lama IX

Another image that has survived at Tashi Lhunpo is a picture scroll depicting the monastery's precincts (the image above). A rather large object, horizontal and vertical creases are visible showing where it was folded for storage. While this picture is also to be found in 《班禅大师驻锡地 札什伦布寺》 [The Hidden Tradition: Life Inside the Great Tibetan Monastery Tashilhunpo] (1993), the publication does not include any information about the scroll's actual size. Although the photograph is somewhat unclear, judging from the way it is drawn, it appears to be quite precise and realistic, to the point of including details of individual buildings, suggesting an inheritance of the technique used in the *thangka* painting produced during the period when there were only three mausolea. What is notable about this picture is that we know it to have been drawn during the abbotship of the [6th] Panchen Lama IX because it shows five mausolea. The number of temple quarters has increased, and within the cramped and detailed drawing, we can see that a *chorten* (stupa) has been drawn slightly to the left (west) of center. Meanwhile, the appearance of the mountain in the background is vague and, notably, five tree-like objects can now be seen on the roof of the giant *thangka* wall. Although depicting the same five-mausoleum period, Kawaguchi's illustration differs from this picture sufficiently to establish that his drawing did not refer to this picture. With this picture scroll, too, it seems that several copies were produced; another map was shown to the journalist Isabel Hilton when she visited "Tashilhunpo in exile," a monastery rebuilt in Dharamsala under the auspices of the Dalai Lama's government in exile. She reports "a man [...] unrolled for me a huge painting of Tashilhunpo Monastery as it used to be" (Hilton 2001: p.248). This was most likely a copy of this same scroll. However, Hilton's account records another tradition relating to the production of the scroll.

Construction of a new memorial stupa: The [6th] IX and [7th] X Panchen Lamas

In 1914, the [6th] Panchen Lama IX, with whom Hedin had an official audience, oversaw the construction of a palace dedicated to Maitreya Bodhisattva to house what was to be the world's largest seated statue of Maitreya Bodhisattva, measuring 26.2 m high. Thereafter, caught up in the swirl of world affairs, the Panchen Lama was forced to leave Tibet after the deterioration of relations with the 13th Dalai Lama and the Ganden Phodrang. Although he died in 1937 at the age of fifty-four in the town of Jyekundo (སྐྱེ་དགུ་མདོ་ *skye dgu mdo*; Yushu in Qinghai Province), arranging for his remains to be returned to Tibet proved to be difficult; it was 1941 before his remains made it back to Tashi Lhunpo Monastery. After his arrival, in accordance with tradition, a memorial stupa was created to inter the monk's dharma body. Records show that a mausoleum was also constructed at this time. Soon, Lopsang Trhinläy Lhündrup Chö kyi Gyältsän (dharma name བློ་བཟང་འཕྲིན་ལས་ལྷུན་གྲུབ་ཆོས་ཀྱི་རྒྱལ་མཚན་ *blo bzang phrin las lhun grub chos kyi rgyal mtshan*; 1938–1989) was identified as the [7th] Panchen Lama X, as his predecessor's reincarnation.

After the exile of the 14th Dalai Lama following the Tibetan Uprising, [7th] Panchen Lama X became the leading representative of Tibet under the Chinese Communist Party regime. Since he, too, continued to issue political proclamations, he was imprisoned during the Cultural Revolution, where he remained for the next fourteen years. Although the Red Guards' storm of destruction swept across all of Tibet, and the [7th] Panchen Lama X was criticized, commentaries and other writings published in China suggest that the Panchen Lama had a political relationship with the Communist Party, which may have contributed to the fact that the damage inflicted on his seat at Tashi Lhunpo Monastery was light in comparison with that suffered by other temple institutions. And while other accounts seem to attribute the destruction experienced by Tashi Lhunpo Monastery to pillaging during the second campaign of the Tibet-Gorkha war in 1792 (also known as the Sino-Nepali war), the most significant damage clearly took place at the time of the Cultural Revolution. Even at Tashi Lhunpo Monastery, a full third of the buildings were destroyed, while the memorial stupas of the [2nd] V through [6th] IX Panchen Lamas were despoiled and their contents reportedly scattered and thrown into the river. While Chinese sources are silent on the specifics of these outrages, Hilton (2001) presents oral testimony from several living witnesses. With the end of the Cultural Revolution, the [7th] Panchen Lama X was also released and rehabilitated. In the 1980s, while serving in a political role as a standing committee chairman of the National People's Congress, he devoted himself to the restoration of Tibetan culture as a representative of Tibet under China's reform and opening-up policy. Securing government aid for the reconstruction of memorial stupas of the former Panchen Lamas destroyed in the Cultural Revolution, as well as for a formal dedication ceremony, in conjunction with his visit to Tibet for New Year's ceremonies in 1989, a grand ceremony was held to dedicate the new memorial stupas jointly enshrining the [2nd] V through [6th] IX (see the photo ©IKD below of the courtyard in front of the joint mausoleum, where the ceremonies were held). Sadly, the [7th] Panchen Lama X passed away shortly after the completion of the ceremony. The remains of the Panchen Lama were interred in the new memorial stupa in accordance with tradition, and the newest mausoleum was built at Tashi Lhunpo Monaster in 1993.

Tashi Lhunpo Monastery today

Tashi Lhunpo Monastery as we saw it during our fieldwork in the summer of 2016 was a beautiful temple city of study halls and monastic buildings laid out in intricate patterns nestled in the gentle foothills of a mountain ridge that provides a semi-circular backdrop for the city against a piercing blue sky. Situated about 4,000 m above sea level, the precincts of the compound run up a slight incline, which leaves one short of breath after only a short stroll. Worshippers walk slowly, climbing the road to the mausolea one step at a time. A single path leads from the monastery entrance to the building known as the "Central Chapel" (མཆོད་ཁང་དཀྱིལ་ *mchod khang dkyil*), the mausoleum in which the [1st] Panchen Lama IV was reinterred at the time of its reconstruction in 1989. After paying their respects at the joint mausoleum enshrining the [2nd] V through [6th] IX Panchen Lamas, visitors circumambulate the temple, following the pilgrimage route that stretches from beside the giant *thangka* wall or Buddha display wall (གོས་སྐུ་སྤེལ་ *gos sku spel*; literally "cloth-image spread") to the mountain beyond, making their way to the old town that looks out over Shigatse Dzong. Numerous prayer wheels are installed along the walking path that traverses the mountain. Atop the mountain behind the monastery, prayer flags known as *lung ta* (རླུང་རྟ་ *rlung rta*; meaning "wind horse") and five-colored flags printed with verses from sutras flap in the wind. It is said that when the flags flutter, the words of the sacred sutras written upon them are carried by the winds to distant places far away. The wind also gently ripples the white cloth decorations hung in the windows of the temple quarters.

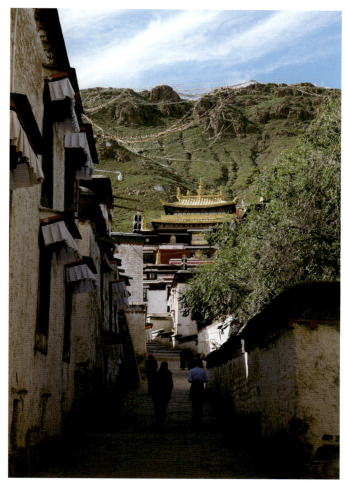

Looking toward the front of the Central Chapel (Tashi Lhunpo Monastery) ©IKD

The mountain pilgrimage route leading to the old city district (Tashi Lhunpo Monastery)

Sven Hedin as Artist 108

Stupas at Tashi Lhunpo Monastery

One impressive sketch depicts monks congregating around white Tibetan-style stupas known as *chorten*. Although not one of the drawings that was reproduced, this is one of the few sites drawn by Hedin that we were able to identify from local interviews. Since it is also described by Hedin, we would like to give it particular mention.

> On the stone terraces before this and the other buildings, a number of sepulchral pyramids are erected. At the foot of a couple of these characteristic monuments, a crowd of monks and women have collected to observe my incomprehensible occupation.
> (*Sven Hedin as Artist*, p. 41)

This picture is included as illustration no. 108 in *Sven Hedin as Artist*, with the caption "Chorten in Shigatse,

Tashi Lhunpo Monastery

Stupas have become a part of the pilgrimage route. (Tashi Lhunpo Monastery)

1907." It is also included as illustration no. 151 in the first volume of *Trans-Himalaya*, where it appears with the caption "Chorten in Tashi-lunpo." The term *chorten* (མཆོད་རྟེན་ mchod rten) refers to a Tibetan-style stupa in the shape that can be seen in this sketch. While the chorten that can be seen today at Tashi Lhunpo Monastery have reportedly undergone restoration in recent years, when we follow the thread offered by the drawings of Tashi Lhunpo Monastery in the past, we find that stupas already stood in this location at least since the era of the [4th] Panchen Lama VII (i.e., the latter half of the seventeenth century), and have been depicted in all of the pictures drawn over the subsequent eras. In contrast to the changes that have befallen the mausolea, stupas have stood consistently in this location, making them a symbol of the traditional inheritance of Tashi Lhunpo Monastery.

[Reproduction 3] Nishikawa Junji, Pencil, 25.5 × 35.3 cm

3 Staircase to the mausoleum of the [5th] Panchen Lama VIII

According to the writing on both the original and the reproduction, this is the mausoleum of the [5th] Panchen Lama VIII. The picture appears as Illustration 133 in *Trans-Himalaya* I with the caption "Staircase to the mausoleum of the fifth Tashi Lama in Tashi-lunpo." The handrails on the stairway, which leads up to the entrance hall, are distinctive. The door to the entrance is behind two decorated pillars, with murals painted on either side, and a row of lion-head reliefs arrayed above the door. Although this is not clearly discernible in the original or in the reproduction, a photograph of the reconstructed joint mausoleum of past Panchen Lamas shows a row of seven lion-head reliefs above the entrance door, suggesting that similar ornamentation appeared above the entrance to the mausoleum of [5th] Panchen Lama VIII when visited by Hedin. Both the mausoleum and stupa of this Panchen Lama were destroyed during the Cultural Revolution and are no longer standing.

Tashi Lhunpo Monastery

[Original 3] Sven Hedin, 1907, Pencil and Pen, 25.0 × 35.3 cm

A relief of Chinese guardian lions at the entrance to the joint mausoleum (Tashi Lhunpo Monastery)

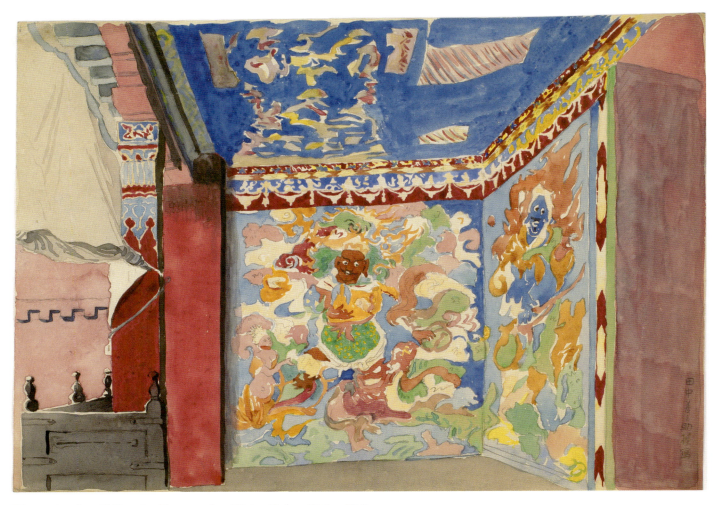

[Reproduction 4] Tanaka Zennosuke, Water Color, 25.4 × 35.2 cm

4 Four Deva Kings outside a mausoleum entrance

A monochrome photograph of this picture appears as the frontispiece of *Trans-Himalaya* III. The painting shows a mural to the left of a chapel entrance that portrays two of the four Deva Kings guarding the entrance. Which of the guardian deities appear here could not be identified from the monochrome photograph, but with the discovery of this reproduction and access to the original painting, the colors of the kings' faces were obvious. Facing the front of the picture plane, i.e., at the left end if one were facing the chapel entrance, is the red-faced Virupaksa, while the blue-faced Virudhaka appears to its right, i.e., to the immediate left of the door. Hedin's caption for the picture simply reads: "Temple vestibule in Tashi-lunpo. Two of the spirit kings which guard the entrance" without identifying the location. Although the four Deva Kings were also painted at the entrances to the mausoleums of past Panchen Lamas, the shape of the column in this picture does not match those depicted in Hedin's sketches of the mausoleum entrances of the [5th] Panchen VIII and [3rd] Panchen VI Lamas. However, *Trans-Himalaya* introduces the mausoleum of the 4th Tashi Lama (i.e., Panchen Lama VII) accompanied by a detailed description of the four Deva Kings, suggesting that the picture is of the entrance to the mausoleum of the [4th] Panchen Lama VII. Still, there is no hard evidence of this, in the form of sketches or otherwise. Entrance murals of the Deva Kings are faithfully reproduced the position and the style at the joint mausoleum at Tashi Lhunpo today. It is interesting to compare a recent photograph taken at the same angle as the reproduction: the entrance hall to the joint mausoleum extends some distance back, and there is no wall at the left end.

Tashi Lhunpo Monastery

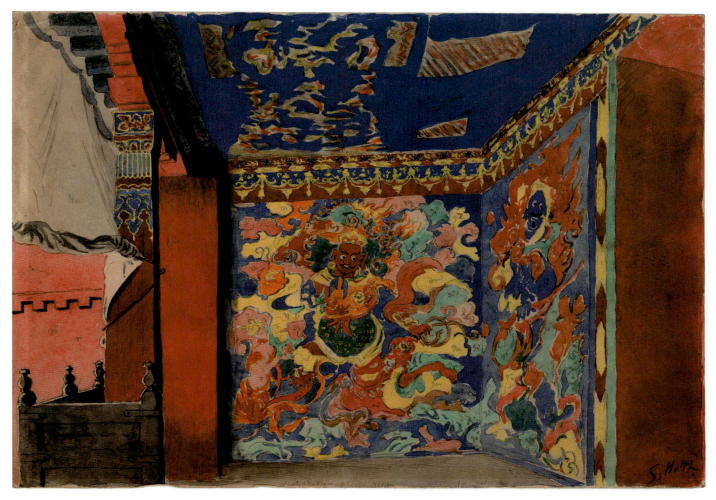

[Original 4] Sven Hedin, 1907, Water Color, 25.0 × 35.3 cm

Depiction of *Virūpākṣa* at the entrance to a study hall at Drepung Monastery (Lhasa)

Left side of the entrance hall at the joint mausoleum (Tashi Lhunpo Monastery) ©IKD

[Reproduction 5] Nishikawa Junji, Pen and Water Color, 24.9 × 35.1 cm

5 Monk opening the door to the mausoleum of the [5th] Panchen Lama VIII

Regarding his visit to this mausoleum, Hedin wrote:

> The entrance is closed with two massive doors of old wood, which are painted with dark-red lacquer and have brass mountings and heavy rings in hemispherically curved shields. When the lama, who had been charged by the high-priest himself to show me round and point out all the glories of the temple, had got the doors to swing slowly on their hinges and open inwards to the sanctuary, I found myself facing a high altar. (*As Artist*, pp. 41–42)

Hedin further writes that at the time, the mausolea of the Panchen Lamas through the 4th generation (VII) were closed to the public, who could only visit that of the [5th] Panchen Lama VIII, which was therefore thronged with pilgrims (*Trans-Himalaya* I, p. 338). When Hedin visited in 1908, the Panchen Lama was the 6th generation (IX), and the mausoleum of his predecessor, the 5th generation (VIII), was the newest. Hedin remarks, "As this mausoleum is only about twenty years old, it looks fresher and cleaner than the others" (ibid).

A picture of a child playing the flute can be seen on the wall to the right of the doorway. This child is an acolyte of *Dhṛtarāṣṭra*, one of the Four Great Kings in Tibetan Buddhism (see Commentary p. 120), and so we find that Dhṛtarāṣṭra has been painted holding a dram nyän (a kind of Himalayan lute) to the right of the doorway. And now, at the entrance of the reconstructed joint mausoleum consecrating the [2nd] V through [6th] IX Panchen Lamas, again, Dhṛtarāṣṭra and his acolyte, the child playing the flute, have been painted to the right of the doorway, showing that the reconstruction has been accomplished in keeping with tradition.

Tashi Lhunpo Monastery

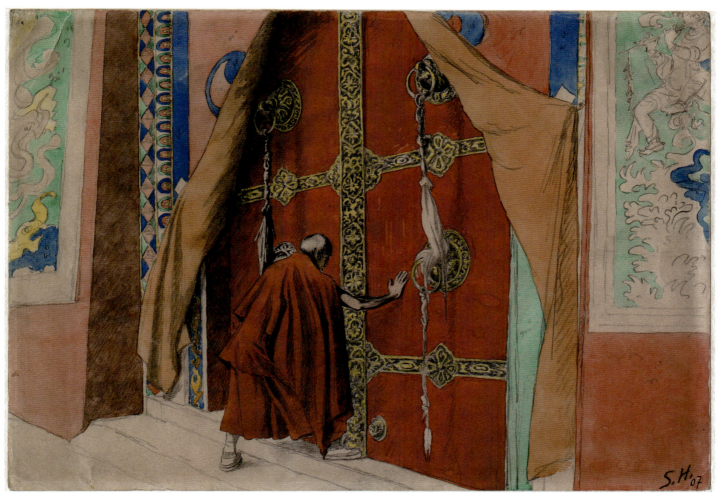

[Original 5] Sven Hedin, 1907, Pen and Water Color, 25.2 × 40.1 cm

Door to the joint mausoleum and altar in front of the memorial stupa (Tashi Lhunpo Monastery)

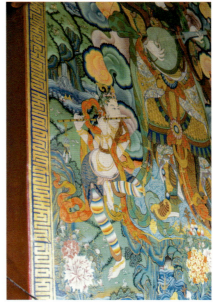

A child playing a flute: An acolyte of *Dhṛtarāṣṭra* (Tashi Lhunpo Monastery)

[Reproduction 6] Nishikawa Junji, Pen, 35.2 × 25.2 cm

Tashi Lhunpo Monastery

[Original 6] Sven Hedin, 1907, Pen, 35.3 × 25.1 cm

Altar in the joint mausoleum (Tashi Lhunpo Monastery)

6 Altar before the stupa of the [5th] Panchen Lama VIII

Both the original and the reproduction are line drawings in pencil, whereas the Illustration 126 in *Trans-Himalaya* I is a monochrome watercolor highly reminiscent of sumi-ink painting. Very possibly, shadowing was added with watercolor to a copy of the original sketch for inclusion in the book. Because it is monochrome, it effectively expresses the darkness of the mausoleum interior. The note written at the lower left corner of the picture, "Tembe Oantjuk," is a transliteration of the name of [5th] Panchen Lama VIII, Tänpai Wangchuk (བསྟན་པའི་དབང་ཕྱུག *bstan pa'i dbang phyug*) (1855–1882). The statue at the base of the stupa would seem to be a likeness of [5th] Panchen Lama VIII. About this mausoleum, Hedin wrote:

> [It] is particularly richly and gorgeously decorated without and within. The front of the *chhorten* glitters with gold, turquoise, and coral. A glass candelabrum from India looks out of place amid the pure Lamaist convent style, as also some common balls of blue glass and looking-glass – cheap wares, such as are seen in country gardens and in front of village inns. They hang from a ledge in front of the sarcophagus receptacle. On the altar stand the usual votive vessels, many of them strikingly elegant and tasteful. A large bowl on a tall foot is of gold, and contains a burning wick. On the right, on nails, hang simple gifts of poor pilgrims. (*Trans-Himalaya* I, p. 338)

The altar of today's mausoleum is also adorned with numerous ritual implements. If we compare the photograph shown here, the altar appears to be a relatively faithful reconstruction, differences in the shape or design of specific implements notwithstanding. Photographs of the Panchen Lamas IX, X and XI are arranged in front of the stupa.

[Reproduction 7] Nishikawa Junji, Pen and Black-and-white Color, 35.3 × 24.8 cm

Tashi Lhunpo Monastery

[Original 7] Sven Hedin, 1907, Pen and Black-and-white Color, 35.4 × 25.0 cm

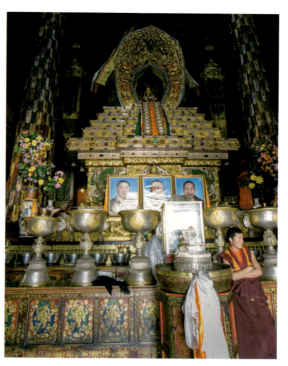

A joint memorial stupa enshrining the remains of the V through IX Panchen Lamas. The Buddhist divinity niche at the top of the stupa contains a portrait of the [6th] Panchen Lama IX. (Tashi Lhunpo Monastery)

7 Stupa of a Panchen Lama

This stupa houses the remains of a Panchen Lama. The picture does not contain any written explanation, so it is impossible to verify which Panchen Lama is interred here. In *Trans-Himalaya*, Hedin writes the following about a Panchen Lama stupa:

> The tomb itself, in the interior, is a *chhorten* in the form of a pyramid with steps, ledges, and cornices, and may be 20 to 23 feet [6 to 7 meters] high. All the front is decorated with gold and silver in arabesques and other designs, and is studded with precious stones. At the very top stands a *gao* [prayer-box], a yard [1 meter] high, somewhat like a sentry-box, with a front of lotus leaves, and in it sits a statue of the deceased wearing the usual [yellow] mitre, with which Tsong Kapa [founder of the Gelug school] is always represented, and of which we saw so many specimens during the [New Year] festival. A number of long silken *kadakhs* [ceremonial scarves] have been placed in the uplifted hands of the statue, and hang down over the monument in long festoons and streamers. This is also draped with a multitude of *tankas*, temple banners which are painted in Lhasa and Tashi-lunpo, and represent scenes from the life of the founder of the religion and of the Church fathers. Among and behind them also hang standards and pennants of coloured cloth narrowing to a point at the bottom, and all are old, dusty, and dingy. (*Trans-Himalaya* I, p. 332)

Hedin's description is of the stupa of the [1st] Panchen Lama IV, but this sketch does not depict the "standards and pennants of coloured cloth narrowing to a point at the bottom." In a contemporary photograph of the mausoleum, we can see pennants of this sort wrapped around the pillars on either side of the stupa. White khata (ཁ་བཏགས་ *kha btags*: "ceremonial scarves") like those in Hedin's sketch also hang next to the monk standing with arms folded.

[Reproduction 8] Adachi Itarō, Pencil, 35.1 × 25.1 cm

Tashi Lhunpo Monastery

[Original 8] Sven Hedin, 1907, Pencil and Pen, 35.3 × 25.2 cm

Framed statement mounted beside the lecture court: "Protecting the Nation to Benefit the People" (Tashi Lhunpo Monastery) ©IKD

8 Framed sign over the entrance to the mausoleum of the [3rd] Panchen Lama VI

The handwritten note "Tjuckan-nup" visible on the reproduction probably indicates a *chökang* or chapel (མཆོད་ཁང་ *mchod khang*). Since *nup* (ནུབ་ *nub*) means "west," we can surmise the following from the note. There is a building referred to as the *chökang* within the current reconstructed precincts of Tashi Lhunpo; it is the mausoleum of Panchen Lama IV. Its Tibetan name transliterates to the Chinese characters 曲康吉 (qǔkāngjí). 曲康 (qǔkāng) is the equivalent of the Tibetan *mchod khang*, while the final 吉 (jí) is a transliteration of kyii (དཀྱིལ་ *dkyil*), meaning "center." Thus, the mausoleum of the [3rd] Panchen Lama VI viewed by Hedin may have been located immediately to the west of today's 曲康吉 (Qukangji; known after his reinternment as the "mausoleum of the [1st] Panchen Lama IV"), which was considered the center. Hedin's sketch shows a framed sign with Chinese characters. Considering the historical context, we may surmise that this was a gift from the Qianlong Emperor, with whom the [3rd] Panchen Lama VI was in direct contact. Hedin himself suggests as much in *Trans-Himalaya* I (p. 333), though the circumstances are unknown. The characters on the sign in the sketch are also difficult to decipher; if one might hazard a guess, they appear to read (from right to left) 亨相益宗, meaning something like "Advance and benefit to the doctrine." This sign has been lost, and no reference to it could be found in the literature; the author welcomes any information about this. At Tashi Lhunpo today, a sign is posted that is said to have been presented by then-General Secretary Jiang Zemin during the completion ceremony for the mausoleum in 1989.

[Reproduction 9] Nishikawa Junji, Pencil, 25.0 × 35.2 cm

9 Double colonnade alongside the lecture court

This sketch of an atmospheric double-colonnade corridor appears as Illustration 142 in *Trans-Himalaya* I. That figure, however, is a monochrome watercolor, which Hedin may have personally copied from the original sketch, adding shadowing for inclusion in the book. The reproduction shown here was clearly made from the original. The reconstructed mausoleum for past Panchen Lamas (V through IX) at Tashi Lhunpo (which was the mausoleum of the [1ˢᵗ] Panchen Lama IV when Hedin visited) is fronted by a broad inner courtyard known as the lecture court. This was where the ceremony commemorating the completion of the joint mausoleum was held in 1989. Adjacent to the lecture court on the west side is the Library Hall, the entrance of which faces a section of the corridor enclosing the court; this is a fairly wide space supported by a double row of pillars. It is called the Thousand-Buddha Corridor because of the numerous Buddha images painted on the wall. The central section of this wall served as the assembly place for young monks participating in the scripture reading at 6 pm every evening. Called by the sounding of a conch shell, trainee monks gather in the corridor, and then enter the Library Hall. Standing at the library entrance where the religious service was held, Hedin had an oblique view of the long rows of pillars in the corridor, dimly backlit so that he depicted them in silhouette. We stood where we thought Hedin had made his sketch and photographed the scene. The note written on the drawing and the reproduction appears to be a Tibetan word, possibly ཀ་བྲང་ ka brang, or colonnade, though it is not clear. It could also be ཀ་དབྲག་ ka dbrag, or space (between pillars).

Tashi Lhunpo Monastery

[Original 9] Sven Hedin, 1907, Pencil, 25.0 × 35.4 cm

Double corridor in front of the Lecture Hall: "Hall of a Thousand Buddhas" (Tashi Lhunpo Monastery)

[Reproduction 10] Tanaka Zennosuke, Pencil, 25.1 × 35.2 cm

10 Trainee monks reading scriptures

This scene at Tashi Lhunpo shows an inner room where monks are reading scriptures. Though drawn in pencil, the heavy shadowing richly conveys the darkness of the temple interiors. The monks sit in orderly rows before long low tables, on which are placed lateral scrolls of Tibetan scripture from which the monks can be seen to be reciting. All the monks are wearing capes, and the angle of the light striking their garments and the pillars suggests that it is entering from skylights in the high, atrium-like ceiling. In the center rear of the picture, a supervising monk can be seen standing and making his rounds among the reciting monks. Hedin titled this picture "Novices in reading hall. Tashilhunpo 1907." (*As Artist* 114). From our own visit, we were able to determine that the dark shadow on the right is most likely a senior monk serving as an instructor. A photograph taken on-site shows, on the right, a high-ranking lama viewed from behind as he teaches while sitting on a high cushion against a pillar. The large silhouette on the right of Hedin's sketch appears to be a slightly abstract rendering of a similar figure of an instructing monk.

Tashi Lhunpo Monastery

[Original 10] Sven Hedin, 1907, Pencil, 25.0 × 35.3 cm

Monks at a religious service in the Chanting Hall: Instructor and practitioners (Tashi Lhunpo Monastery) ©IKD

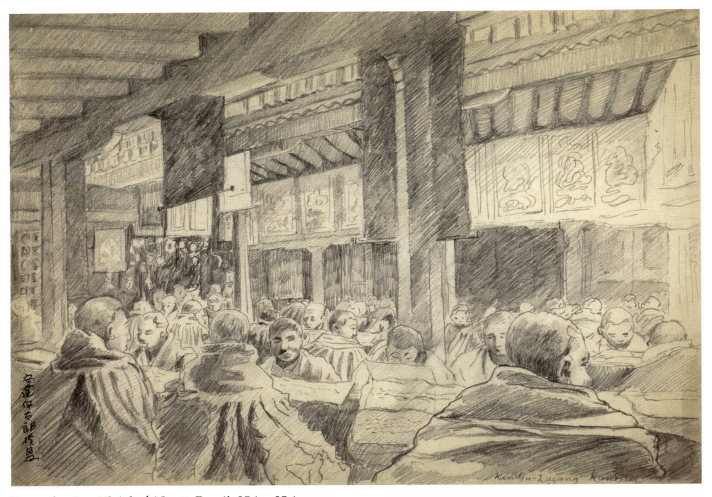

[Reproduction 11] Adachi Itarō, Pencil, 25.1 × 35.4 cm

11 Trainee monks reading scriptures

This picture also appears in *Sven Hedin as Artist* with almost the same title as 114, "Novices in reading hall. Kandjur-lagang 1907." (*As Artist* 115). However, the original sketch has been lost, and it could not be confirmed to be in the possession of the Museum of Ethnography in Sweden. The caption gives the place and year as "Kandjur-lagang 1907." *Kanjur-lhakang* (བཀའ་འགྱུར་ལྷ་ཁང་ *bka' 'gyur lha khang*) is the word for a scripture library. There is a courtyard, known as the lecture court, in front of what is now the joint mausoleum of past Panchen Lamas, and the evening scripture readings that took place in the library adjoining the double-colonnade corridor on the west side of that courtyard were open to the public. Donning the yellow capes and hats of the Gelug school over their dark red monastic robes, monks gather in the corridor next to the library. When the doors open, the monks form a line, file inside, and sit down in their respective seats. Once inside, they remove their hats and place them to one side, but keep their capes on. The fringed objects, made of the same yellow fabric as the capes, that sit next to the monks in the photograph are their folded caps. As in Hedin's sketch, the scroll-like Buddhist paintings known as *thangka* hang in profusion from the ceiling beams. The thick pillars are not repainted, and in places are blackened as if charred. Unlike in Hedin's sketch, however, the trainee monks did not read from texts, but rather recited scriptures from memory in response to the supervising monk. In a process that appeared to be for the benefit of young monks who had just begun training, supervisors also guided the monks whose attention flagged. It was a scene that truly matched the caption "Novices in reading hall," demonstrating that the tradition witnessed by Hedin 100 years ago had been preserved over all that time.

Tashi Lhunpo Monastery

Sven Hedin as Artist 115

Young novice monks wrapped in capes chanting sutras (Tashi Lhunpo Monastery)

[Reproduction 12] Adachi Itarō, Pencil and Water Color, 25.2 × 17.5 cm

Tashi Lhunpo Monastery

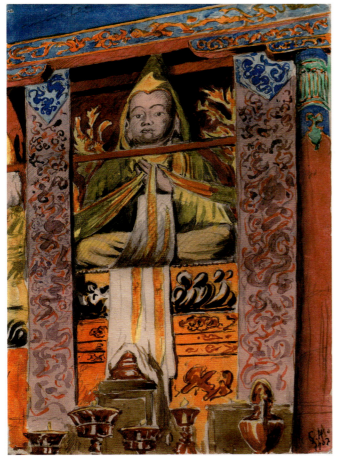

[Original 12] Sven Hedin, 1907, Pencil and Water Color, 25.1 × 17.5 cm

Statue of Je Tsongkhapa (at the Shakyamuni Hall) (Tashi Lhunpo Monastery) ©IKD

12 Statue of Tsongkhapa in the Namgyal-lhakang [watercolor]

This picture appears in color as Illustration 129 in *Trans-Himalaya* I with the caption "The Namgyal-lhakang with the figure of Tsong Kapa, in Tashi-lunpo." The copy contains no inscription at all, while the original has only Hedin's signature and the year 1907, indicating when it was drawn. The formal name of this building at Tashi Lhunpo today is Gandän Namgyäl Lhakang (དགའ་ལྡན་རྣམ་རྒྱལ་ལྷ་ཁང་ *dga' ldan rman rgyal lha khang*). It was built by the [6th] Panchen Lama IX, who Hedin met, and lies adjacent to the Maitreya Hall built by the same Panchen Lama in 1914, seven years after Hedin's sojourn. However, the Namgyal-lhakang must have been built earlier if that is where Hedin saw this statue of Tsongkhapa. The present-day Namgyal-lhakang houses a 3.78-meter-high sitting figure of Tsongkhapa, flanked by statues of his disciples Dharma Rinchen (དར་མ་རིན་ཆེན་ *dar ma rin chen*) and Gelek Pälzang (དགེ་ལེགས་དཔལ་བཟང་ *dge legs dpal bzang*). Now the building is in two tiers, the main hall on the first floor and the Tsongkhapa on the second floor. However, it may have undergone repairs at some point after Hedin visited. During my visit, the Namgyal-lhakang was not open for viewing, so I was unable to take a photograph of the statue of Tsongkhapa there. The photo here is of a different statue of Tsongkhapa that sits in the Kyikang Dratsang or Exoteric Buddhist Seminary (དཀྱིལ་ཁང་གྲྭ་ཚང་ *dkyilkhang grwa tshang* [lit. Central College]) at Tashi Lhunpo.

[Reproduction 13] Tanaka Zennosuke, Pencil, 25.1 × 35.6 cm

13 Statue of Tsongkhapa in the Namgyal-lhakang [drawing]

The reproduction contains no inscription and the original has only Hedin's signature and the year 1907, indicating when it was drawn. This picture does not appear in either *Trans-Himalaya* or *Sven Hedin as Artist*, so unfortunately, we have no further information about it. It depicts a statue of Tsongkhapa sitting on an altar behind columns, most likely the same statue shown in the previous watercolor (Reproduction 12). Of this statue of Tsongkhapa, Hedin writes: "Our next visit is to the so-called Namgyal-lhakang, the temple of Tsong Kapa, a large pillared hall with a huge statue of the reformer; [...] Tsong Kapa's name is as famous and as highly revered in the Lamaistic Church as that of Buddha himself: I cannot recall to mind that his statue is absent from one of the many temples I have visited in Tibet" (*Trans-Himalaya* I, p. 335). Tsongkhapa (1357–1419) is credited with the revival of Tibetan Buddhism and the founding of the Gelug (Yellow Hat) school. His ordained name is Losang Drakpa (བློ་བཟང་གྲགས་པ་ *blo bzang grags pa*), meaning "fame for conscience." "Tsongkhapa," an honorific name bestowed by later generations, means "man from Tsongkha," his birthplace in the Amdo region of Tibet (now Qinghai province), near where Kumbum Monastery is today. At age 16, he entered central Tibet, traveled to the great monasteries of the various schools, and studied with as many as 30 great teachers and scholars. At age 24, he was fully ordained as a monk. From 1393, he led a religious reform movement that emphasized Buddhist precepts. In his work, *The Great Treatise on the Stages of the Path to Enlightenment* (*Lamrim Chenmo*), he compiled the teachings of Tibetan Buddhism based on the concept of *lamrim* ("stages of the path" to enlightenment), which unifies various Buddhist doctrines under the framework of the path of practice taken by ascetics from

[Original 13] Sven Hedin, 1907, Pencil and Pen, 25.0 × 35.4 cm

ignorance to enlightenment. The year after holding the Great Prayer Festival at the Jokhang temple in Lhasa in 1409, he founded the Ganden Monastery outside Lhasa. He died at Ganden in 1419 at the age of 63. Historical accounts mention over 100 disciples of Tsongkhapa. The last of these, Gendün Druppa (དགེ་འདུན་གྲུབ་པ་, *dge 'dun grub pa*; 1391–1474), who later came to be considered the first Dalai Lama, founded Tashi Lhunpo in 1447 with assistance from the nobles of Ü-Tsang. Construction reportedly took 12 years.

Statue of Je Tsongkhapa stored on a Buddha shelf at the back of the Exoteric Buddhist Seminary (Tashi Lhunpo Monastery) ©IKD

Chapter 2: People of Shigatse

PEOPLE OF SHIGATSE

During my stay in Shigatse I had my tent set up in a garden on the outskirts of the city, and here were encamped the whole of my caravan and the few animals I had left. Our rest lasted for a month and a half, and a large part of my time was taken up with photography and sketching. I wandered freely around in the temple and took home with me a rich collection of illustrations therefrom. Besides the sketches of inanimate objects already referred to, I also drew lamas and lay-brothers performing various duties.

I will only draw attention to the young lama who is blowing a *tung* or conch, where the conch is silver-mounted in an unusually magnificent way.

Another picture shows two lay-brothers or serving lamas who in large brass-mounted copper pots are carrying tea to the monks, whether the latter are in their cells or sitting in a row in one of the courtyards.

From the remarkable dance of incantation I have also immortalized some amusing figures [*as Artist* 123, 125, 126]. They are wearing weird, frightening masks, intended to scare evil spirits.

To these pictures may be added a collection of portraits of townspeople, peasants, pilgrims and other wanderers who had come to the New Year's festival. The sixty-year-old Panjol was a droll type [*as Artist* 129]. He served as custodian in one of the temple-halls and always nodded in a friendly and comfortable way when I came prowling around with sketch-book or camera.

Here are also some countrymen and their womenfolk from Tengri-nor or Nam Tso, the great lake to the north of the eastern Transhimalayas, and an itinerant mendicant monk [*as Artist* 128] and a sort of wandering nun, Mimar [*as Artist* 132],(1) who in a melancholy, monotonous song explains the meaning of the religious pictures painted on a canvas. She hangs up her canvas at a street corner, collects a small group of listeners and occasionally gets a coin.

The whole of this droll carnival trooped to our camp. Here danced boys beating shrill little drums, here sang mendicant monks, who are all their lives afoot on an endless pilgrimage, hither came couriers, travellers and occasionally a Chinese official, indeed, even the women in Shigatse honoured us with repeated visits.

Some further portraits of women give some idea of the strange arches with which especially the ladies of Shigatse adorn their heads [Reproduction 16]. It cannot be denied that these often twelve-inch high contraptions with their rows of intensively blue turquoises are decorative. They are seen to excellent effect when during the festival days the women are assembled in thousands in the galleries and on the roofs of the temples.

SVEN HEDIN AS ARTIST p. 43

(1) This must be a typical Tibetan name: *Mig dmar*

People of Shigatse

A young monk blowing a Tibetan conch-trumpet (*dung dkar*) (Tashi Lhunpo Monastery). Reproduced from 《扎什倫布寺》(1993)

The comical Panjol (*Sven Hedin as Artist* 129)

A woman's hair ornaments, reproduced from Das (1902)

Masked Cham dance performers (*Sven Hedin as Artist* 123, 125, 126)

[Reproduction 14] Adachi Itarō, Pencil, 25.1 × 35.8 cm

14 Shigatse Dzong

A *dzong* (རྫོང་ *rdzong*) is a fortress-like structure that serves as the district government administrative headquarters in Tibet. Though the word originally meant "fortress," it has come to refer to the entire district under the jurisdiction of the resident administrator. In the past, the occupant of the *dzong* was called the *dzongpön*, a governor appointed for a fixed term by the central government. In Tibet today, under the governance of the People's Republic of China, the word *dzong* is used as the Tibetan equivalent of the Chinese 县 (county). There are several sketches by Hedin of the Shigatse Dzong; the original of this copy appears in *Sven Hedin as Artist* (107). In *Trans-Himalaya* I, Illustration 134 (p. 343) is a watercolor depicting the same fortress from a different angle. The title in the former book is "The castle in Shigatse, 1907"; in the latter, it is "Shigatze-dzong (the fortress)." Shigatse Dzong is located atop a hill on the outskirts of Shigatse at a bit of a remove from the mountains surrounding Tashi Lhunpo. A majestic structure looking down on the town, it was entirely demolished in 1968 during the Cultural Revolution, leaving only the foundations. The structure seen today was rebuilt on the same site beginning in 2007; completed in 2010, it now houses a museum and meeting hall. Photographs taken by Hedin were reportedly among the reference materials used for the restoration. Lhasa, by contrast, did not have a *dzong* because the Potala Palace, residence of the Dalai Lama, was the seat of government and served the same function as a *dzong*.

People of Shigatse

[Original 14] Sven Hedin, 1907, Pencil, 25.1 × 35.3 cm

Shigatse Dzong, rebuilt in 2010 (Shigatse)

A photograph taken by Hedin used as reference material for the reconstruction

[Reproduction 15] Nishikawa Junji, Pencil, 25.2 × 17.6 cm

People of Shigatse

[Original 15] Sven Hedin, 1907, Pencil, 25.0 × 17.5 cm

15 Mendicant monk with a prayer wheel

The caption of Illustration 84 in *Trans-Himalaya* III describes the person depicted here as a "Mendicant lama." According to *As Artist* 133, his name is Tsurup Tensin, and the portrait was drawn in Shigatse in 1907. He wears a monk's habit, a hat with ear flaps, and a long rosary hanging from his neck. In *Trans-Himalaya*, we find a description of this monk in a passage between mentions of the dates February 19 and March 4 during Hedin's stay in Shigatse, suggesting that the portrait was drawn during that period: "[A] mendicant lama comes with his praying mill in his hand and two hand-grooves hung by a strap round his neck. In these he pushes his hands as in a curry-comb, when he prostrates himself on the ground in making a circuit of the temple" (*Trans-Himalaya* I, p. 383). The "praying mill" or prayer wheel in the mendicant's hand is called a *mani khorlo* (མ་ཎི་འཁོར་ལོ་ *ma ni 'khor lo*) in Tibetan. This is a Buddhist prayer implement; a metal cylinder containing prayers is set on the end of a long sturdy handle, and the centrifugal force of a small weight attached to the cylinder causes it to revolve clockwise. Each turn of the cylinder is deemed equivalent to one recitation of the prayers inside. Tibetans of both sexes and all ages and walks of life habitually walk around holy sites with these prayer wheels in hand to accumulate merit. There are various types and sizes of wheel portable enough to be held in the hand.

Fixed prayer wheels installed on the Lhasa lingkhor, or sacred path

Commentary
Mani wheels

On pilgrimage routes around temples or holy sites, rows of large fixed prayer wheels are arrayed along building walls or streets so that people can rotate them in turn via the wooden handles at the base of the cylinders as they walk along chanting mantras. At the entrance to a temple there is often a small pavilion housing a gigantic prayer wheel several meters high. Some regions have wind-powered prayer wheels on the roof, or water-powered prayer wheels housed in their own building. Recently there are small, ornamental, hi-tech versions that run on a solar battery which are frequently seen on car dashboards.

Small clay Buddhas and stupas called tsa-tsa dedicated under fixed-position prayer wheels (at Pelkor Chode, Gyantse)

The rich variety of handheld prayer wheels include specimens that are multilayered, those attached to umbrellas, and large examples mounted on long poles. Special belts are also available

People of Shigatse

Commentary
Prostration in prayer

Just above the prayer wheel held by the mendicant monk in Hedin's picture, we can see him cradling something that resembles a shoe sole with nails in it. This is presumably a hand pad used for performing prostrations. In *Trans-Himalaya*, Hedin describes this as a pair of "hand-grooves" into which "he pushes his hands … when he prostrates himself on the ground in makinfg a circuit of the temple" (*Trans-Himalaya* I, p. 383). These "hand-grooves" (ཕྱག་ཤིང་ *phayg shing* in Tibetan) are usually made of wood with a cloth or leather strap attached for inserting the fingers. Though it is difficult to discern from the sketch, a sheet of leather is tacked to the back of the board to soften the impact when the hand strikes the ground. The bottom of one hand pad is visible in the sketch; the leather on it is torn and frayed, and what looks like a bent nail sticks out from one side. Several other small round objects may be tacks in the leather or possibly pebbles that have become stuck to it. Now hand-grooves with metal soles are also used on the stone pavement streets in Lhasa.

Around the Potala Palace, the figures of parents and children were also seen carrying out a prostration pilgrimage.

Chakshing (*phyag shing*) affixed with metal.

In front of Jokhang Temple Monastery in central Lhasa, crowds gather every day to prostrate themselves in prayer.

[Reproduction 16] Adachi Itarō, Pencil, 35.7 × 25.6 cm

16 Woman of Shigatse with a headdress

Hedin made several sketches of the unique hair ornaments worn by Shigatse women. These ornaments, called *patru* (ཕ་ཕྲུག *spa phrug*) in Tibetan (transcribed as 巴楚 in Chinese), consist of jewels arranged on a wooden frame; in the Tsang region, they serve as formal dress for women. Hedin's sojourn in Shigatse coincided with the *Losar* (ལོ་གསར་ *lo gsar*) New Year festival in 1907, so he had the fortunate opportunity to see Shigatse noblewomen dressed in their finery. In *Trans-Himalaya* I, Hedin recounts his personal observations: "On the gallery below [the officials] sit their wives and other ladies of rank, quite buried under the most varied and extraordinary adornments: their dresses are red, green, and yellow; they wear necklaces and silver pendants, silver cases inlaid with turquoise, and at the back of the neck tall white aureoles, thickly set with jewels and other ornaments. Their coiffures are of various forms: some have a parting in the middle, and hair, like polished ebony, puffed

People of Shigatse

Sven Hedin as Artist 134

Figure of a Tsang woman dressed in a traditional costume exhibited at the Tibet Museum (Lhasa)

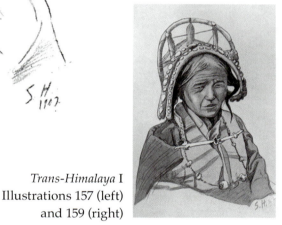

Trans-Himalaya I
Illustrations 157 (left) and 159 (right)

up at the sides; others have the hair plaited in a number of thin switches, which are fixed up and decorated with beads, etc." (*Trans-Himalaya* I, p. 305).

In outward appearance, the headdress resembles the frame of a wide braided-straw hat. The wooden frame is thickly painted with red lacquer and decorated with coral and turquoise, and sits on the head with the base extending to the sides. The tightly braided hair is parted to the left and right and entwined with this frame. The headdresses of noblewomen also boast pearls and other precious jewels; photographs remain that attest to the crafting of some truly luxurious and beautiful head ornaments in the past (see Das [1902] p. 120). There are various types of headdress, with their shapes varying from district to district. Those in Lhasa have a thick V-shaped frame that sits flat on the head with the divided part facing the front. Women in Tsang are said to wear two types of headdress: *palung* (སྤ་ལུང་ *spa lung* 巴隆) and *chiku* (སྤྱི་གུ་ *spyi gu* 基古), but how they differ could not be ascertained. Today such headdresses are preserved as family heirlooms and rarely worn. They can be seen at traditional festivals or as part of the costumes in Tibetan dance performances. At the Tibet Museum in Lhasa, we saw a display of a woman of Tsang wearing traditional clothing and a headdress.

[Reproduction 17] Nishikawa Junji, Pencil, 33.3 × 25.3 cm

People of Shigatse

[Original 17] Sven Hedin, 1907, Pencil, 35.4 × 25.1 cm

A central Tibetan woman dressed in a traditional costume, photo likely from a festival in the 1980s. Reproduced from *Tibet: A Complete Guide* (Passport Books, 1986)

17 Girl of Shigatse with a headdress

Both the original and the reproduction identify the subject as "Burtso, 17." Although this sketch appears in neither *Trans-Himalaya* nor *Sven Hedin as Artist*, one finds a detailed (and by today's standards, quite prejudiced) description of this young woman in *Trans-Himalaya* I (p. 381). Since it follows a passage that begins "Under February 19 the following entry stands in my diary," we can assume that the sketch was done around that date in 1907. "Burtso was a little Shigatse lady of seventeen summers, and bore the dirt of those seventeen summers on her face. Like most of the others her features had the sharply marked characteristics of the Mongolian race – oblique narrow eyes contracting to a point at the sides, and the lower part of the eyelid telescoped into the upper so that a slightly curved line is formed and the short lashes are almost covered; the iris is dark chestnut brown, and appears black within the frame of the eyelids; the eyebrows are usually only slightly marked, are thin and irregular, and never form the finely curved Persian and Caucasian arch like a crescent. The cheek-bones are rather prominent, but not so high as with the Mongolians; the lips are rather large and thick, but the nose is not so flat as among the Mongols." (*Trans-Himalaya* I, p. 381)

[Reproduction 18] Nishikawa Junji, Pencil, 25.2 × 17.6 cm

People of Shigatse

[Original 18] Sven Hedin, 1907, Pencil, 25.1 × 17.5 cm

The wife of the Panchen Lama's younger brother and five female attendants (*Trans-Himalaya* I, Illustration 168)

18 Four people in front of a temple entrance

This rough sketch appears in neither *Trans-Himalaya* nor *Sven Hedin as Artist*, and there is no text written on it to provide clues as to the location or subjects depicted. The picture shows four Tibetans walking in front of the door to a temple. The woman on the left wears a type of headdress worn by noblewomen in Shigatse. The brass ring attached to the door behind them indicates that it is a temple door. Since the original is signed by Hedin and dated 1907, the figures are probably local worshippers visiting Tashi Lhunpo at the time of the New Year festival.

Chapter 3: Trans-Himalaya

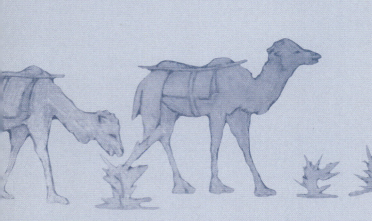

THE TRANSHIMALAYAS

During the years 1907 and 1908 I crossed on eight lines the immense mountain system situated just north of and parallel to the Himalayas, being separated from this mountain range by the continuous valley of the upper Bramaputra and the upper Indus, in which also the sacred Lake Manasarowar has its dark-green expanse of water between two of Tibet's most celebrated mountains, Kailas, the most sacred of all, to the north and the mighty snow-capped cupola of Gurla Mandhata to the south.

To give here even a fugitive description of the several hundreds of panoramas I brought home with me from this journey would mean writing a new account of my travels.

Among the coloured pictures from this period I will mention here only the views over Lunpokangri, Kantjungkangri, Shakang-sham and Kailas. These are followed by divers[e] panoramas of snow-capped chains situated between those mentioned above or lifting their ridges from the plateau country in central and northern Tibet or Chang-tang, the northern plain, as these parts of the country are called by the nomads. A pencilled panorama [*Trans-Himalaya* II 242] done in greater detail shows the series of pyramid or prism shaped peaks belonging to the Himalayan chain Kubikangri, from whose glaciers spring the sources of the Bramaputra.

Let me also refer to some coloured panoramas of the salt lakes filling flat depressions in the Transhimalayan orographic system. Among those that may be specially noted one might mention Lake Terinam Tso, beautiful in point of colour, but otherwise extremely desolate and surrounded by dead landscape.

This sheet of water is a dazzling turquoise blue, as if the whole sky were mirrored in it. The Mediterranean itself pales by comparison. The mountains in the vicinity are shot with shades of brown and red, chains and peaks on the other side of the north shore have light pink and violet tints, becoming airier with increasing distance, and showing here and there eternal snow-fields on their ridges.

Panorama of Kubi-gangri and the glaciers that constitute the source of the Brahmaputra River (*Trans-Himalaya* II Illustration 242)

When one is on one of the high passes, with a view extending 60–90 miles in every direction, one becomes a prey to the illusion that one is gazing out over sea, on whose gigantic petrified waves the highest crests break in snow-white wreaths of foam. Along the shores of Terinam Tso one sees distinctly in different coloured belts the marks from the slow drying up of the lake.[1]

Wild asses, wild sheep, antelopes and yaks roam on the shores of these salt lakes. Nomads, too, bend their steps in this direction if the pasturage there is tolerable. The more well-to-do mountain-dwellers transport their tents and belongings on yaks, the less well-to-do on sheep. It sometimes amused me to make rapid sketches of the animals while they walked or grazed – in order to try to catch their movements on the paper.

SVEN HEDIN AS ARTIST p. 44

1 While it is unfortunate that reproduction of "Teri-nam-tso" (བཀྲ་རི་གནམ་མཚོ་ *bkra ri gnam mtsho*; 扎日南木错 Zhari Namco; also known as Lake Trari Nam) so praised by Hedin were not made, several reproductions that allow us to envision the beautiful vistas of the lakes of the northern Trans-Himalaya do remain. All of these are watercolors depicting Camps no. 302, 304, 320, and 310 in the Kashmir region, far to the north of the Trans-Himalaya.

Mountain highlands and prayer flags on the outskirts of Lhasa

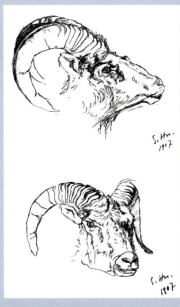

Sven Hedin as Artist 103 (top) and 104 (bottom)

Chapter 3

A stone cairn near Yamdrok Lake (in Nakartse, approximately 70 km southwest of Lhasa)

19 Landscape with people resting by a lake and a cairn

A mountain range rises in the distance across a lake and, on the left, two men tend to a bonfire in front of a cairn. To the left of the figure wearing a red hat, another person wearing a hat and Tibetan clothing is seen from behind in silhouette. The object to the right, however, is farther away and not clearly defined. Insofar as it is painted the same color as the mountains, lacks distinct outlines despite the sun shining on it, and appears to blend with the colors of the ground, one may surmise this to be a cairn – but it could also be a sitting human figure. Since this sketch appears in neither *Trans-Himalaya* nor *Sven Hedin as Artist* and the original was lost, unfortunately, we cannot be certain what it portrays. The notation L302 at bottom right is a camp number; from Hedin's expedition route map, we can determine that this is Aksai Chin Lake.* Tibet's lakes are all holy places, so the cairns of "mani stones" known as *dopung* (རྡོ་ spungs *rdo phung* or རྡོ་ spungs *rdo spung*) in Tibetan can often be seen along their shores. The photograph shows a cairn above Yamdrok Lake not far from Lhasa.

* Aksai Chin Lake is located in the Kashmir region, where the borders of China, India, and Pakistan converge. Aksai Chin region, where the lake is located, is a basin at the northwest corner of the Tibetan Plateau between the Karakoram Range and the Kunlun Mountains in southern Hotan. The basin is over 4,000 meters above sea level, while the surrounding mountains reach heights exceeding 6,000 meters. As a result of the Sino-Indian Border Conflict in 1962, it is under the effective control of China, though India continues to claim ownership, arguing that the region is part of Ladakh. According to China's administrative divisions, most of the area falls under the jurisdiction of Hotan Prefecture in the Xinjiang Uygur Autonomous Region, while a section in the south is part of Ngari Prefecture in the Tibet Autonomous Region. Since ancient times, it has been a strategic point on routes connecting East Turkestan (新疆 Xinjiang) with India, and the Tarim Basin with the Western Regions (西域 Xiyu).

[Reproduction 19] Ishida Kinzō, Pencil and Water Color, 8.0 × 25.2 cm

Trans-Himalaya

[Reproduction 20] Nishikawa Junji, Pencil and Water Color, 9.9 × 25.1 cm

[Original 20] Sven Hedin, 1908, Pencil and Water Color, 9.9 × 25.0 cm

20 View of mountains on the Changtang Plateau

Camp number L304 is written on this picture. According to Hedin's expedition route map, it is located around 35° north latitude, 80° east longitude, and was the second camp after Aksai Chin Lake. Judging by the lay of the land, it appears to be on a gently sloping plateau among low mountains. The picture is inscribed with the year 1908, suggesting that this is along the route of the latter half of Hedin's third central Asia expedition, after he returned from Shigatse to Leh in Ladakh and reorganized his caravan. The location would be shortly after entering the Changtang Plateau following departure from Leh. Hedin uses soft coloring to depict the complex shadows of the mountains in the sun while also faithfully reproducing the colors of the high-altitude vegetation of the plateau, demonstrating both his observational skills as a geographer and his sure eye as an artist. The many similar panoramic color landscapes he painted were invaluable references for the creation of topographic maps of the region.

A distant view over the pastures of the Tibetan Plateau (Outskirts of Nakartse) ©IKD

21 Lake and mountains in the moonlight

This evocative painting of a white full moon over mountains across a lake does not appear in either *Trans-Himalaya* or *Sven Hedin as Artist*, and the original has been lost. The only clue to its location is camp number L310 written at the upper left. According to Hedin's route map, camp L310 was near 31° east longitude, between 34° and 35° north latitude, placing it in what is now the Aksai Chin region. The name of a lake, Tsaggar-tso, appears just under the camp site, so that is probably the lake in the picture. However, this lake cannot be found on maps published by the People's Republic of China today. The Tibetan Plateau at night is pitch-dark when there is no moonlight, but at this high altitude, the stars that fill the sky seem so close you can touch them, and you are treated to the sight of one shooting star after another.

[Reproduction 21] Ishida Kinzō, Water Color, 9.6 × 25.1 cm

[Original 22] Sven Hedin, 1906, Pencil and Water Color, 7.8 × 25.1 cm

Trans-Himalaya

Tarcho (prayer flags) suspended from the bare mountain rock, tinted by the morning sun (Shigatse)

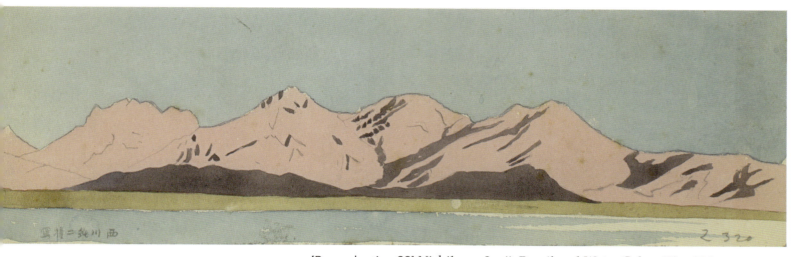

[Reproduction 22] Nishikawa Junji, Pencil and Water Color, 7.9 × 25.1 cm

22 Snowy mountains in the setting sun

Both the original and the reproduction of this picture are inscribed with the camp number L320 at the bottom right. The original additionally bears Hedin's signature and the number "06," but this picture must have been painted in 1908, so the incorrect date was probably added later. Checking camp L320 on the route map, we find that it is on the shore of Shemen-tso, a lake located at 34° north latitude. On current Chinese maps, the corresponding lake is named *Lumajangdong* 鲁玛江冬错 (ལུ་མ་བྱང་སྟྲོང་མཚོ་ *lu ma byang strong mtsho*) or *Cogzo* 措作错 (ཚོགས་གཙོ་མཚོ་ *tshogs gtso mtsho*), which differ from Hedin's map. However – perhaps because the area is near the national border – contemporary maps published in China do not provide detailed information on topography or place names. Based on Hedin's map, it appears that the camp was on the north shore of the lake, but because the lake's contours are so convoluted, we cannot be certain that the mountains are those to the south of the lake. The pink tinge of the entire snowy range suggests that the picture was painted while the mountains were bathed in the setting sun.

[Reproduction 23] Ishida Kinzō, Pen, 21.0 × 63.5 cm

23 Mountain landscape in the Bongba district

This powerful pen-drawn panoramic view of mountains has camp number 422 and the place name Tarok-tso written in pencil outside the picture frame. The picture appears as Illustration 299 in *Trans-Himalaya* II with the caption "Panorama from Camp 422, Bongba." On Hedin's route map, Bongba is a province crossed by numerous mountain ranges from north to south, including the Gangdise and Nyenchen Tanglha ranges. Camp 422 lies about 100 kilometers due west of Terinam Lake, located around 31° north latitude. Buptsang-tsangpo, the name of a river flowing into lake Tarok-tso, is written virtually atop the location of the camp. On contemporary Chinese maps, the lake is named *Taro* 塔若错 (ཐ་རོ་མཚོ་ *tha ro mtsho*) and the river *Buduo* 毕多藏布 (བུལ་ཏོག་གཙང་པོ་ *bul tog gtsang po*). The incorrect date on the original sketch might have been added later.

Trans-Himalaya

Paved roads extend even to the Tibetan Plateau (Nojin Kangtsang in Nakartse County) ©IKD

[Original 23] Sven Hedin, 1907, Pen, 21.4 × 64.6 cm (28.5 × 70.0 cm)

Chapter 4: Tibetans

TIBETANS

From the camp-sites and valleys of the Transhimalaya I have harvested the greater part of the collection of Tibetan folk-types in my cartons. The great majority are nomads in whose neighbourhood we had camped and who came to visit us from their own tents.

When I left Shigatse orders were issued from Lhasa that a special escort was to accompany me during the first weeks, to be relieved subsequently by new riders – all this so that the authorities might be assured that I really left their country.

In the different escorts, relieved at regular intervals, I found a rather amusing set of types in characteristic costumes and with a barbaric arsenal of swords and guns. I used as a rule to sketch these representatives for the rural militia in full-length portraits, in order to get down all the details, even to the comical, in actual life parti-coloured and decorative felt boots [Reproduction 26].

Most of them are bare-headed. Their thick, dense, teeming hair is a good substitute for headgear. Others have folded, cherry-red cloths wound like turbans round the crown of the head, while others again wear a ring-shaped cloth roll or pad threaded through some broad bone-rings like a crown on top of their heads [Reproduction 28]. Occasionally one finds them in winter wearing cowl-like caps of fox-skin, covered on the outside with red cloth. The militia from the tracts round Terinam Tso wore picturesque hats of conical shape and with broad straight brims [Reproduction 30].

The characteristic way in which the Tibetans wear their sheepskins is seen from the drawings [Reproduction 39]. They tie a belt round the waist and then pull up the sheepskin so that it hangs round the entire waist like a bulging bag. In this way they get a space that serves them instead of pockets, and is, moreover, stuffed with all sorts of small articles, amongst other things a supply of food and tobacco. The Tibetans also gain another advantage by drawing up their sheepskins in this fashion: the coats become so short that they scarcely reach to the knees, and thus do not hinder them when they walk.

A generally current usage in Tibet, especially in summer-time or at home in the tent, is to have the right arm and the right side of the trunk bare, exposing the beautifully bronze-brown and weather-bitten skin [Reproduction 43].

The chiefs are recognized at once by their more bedizened costume. They often wear red cloaks over their sheepskins or have the latter lined with red cloth. I have a chief here in the crowd, Tagla Tsering [Reproduction 37] from Terinam Tso, who is wearing an extra belt over his sheepskin which is studded with *gaos*[(1)] of silver and copper, all containing images of gods.

Tibetans

Finally, I will mention some female types from Kyangyang in the western part of the Transhimalayas. These I have coloured-not to produce anything that might deserve to be called a water-colour, but only to give some notion of the glaring colour characterizing their costumes. Red predominates, but also yellow and green and occasionally blue enter in the mosaic of patches and fields of which such a costume is composed. Not least gay is the headgear of inferior corals, silver coins and glass beads, forming as it were a net-like veil which leaves only the face free [Reproduction 44]. From the crown of the head a broad roll of red cloth falls down the back, increasing in width towards the bottom and becoming multiple. It is covered with silver coins and lids of *gao*s and shells [Reproduction 46] and reminds one of the head ornaments of the Ladak women.(2)

SVEN HEDIN AS ARTIST pp. 45–46

Tibetan hat with earflaps. Also commonly known as a "Lhasa hat"

(1) A "Buddhist prayer-box". See the comments on Reproduction 37.
(2) The head ornament of the Ladakhi woman mentioned here is likely the one seen in *Sven Hedin as Artist* (96).

Jankit, a twenty-year-old woman in Leh (*As Artist* 96)

Inhabitants of the region near the source of the Sutlej River (Photo by Hedin; reproduced from *Trans-Himalaya* II, Illustration 271)

Dance by Ladakhi women (reproduced from *Trans-Himalaya* II, Illustration 282)

[Reproduction 24] Adachi Itarō, Pencil, 32.0 × 21.3 cm

24　Portrait of the bodyguard Nima Tashi

Both the original and the reproduction bear the written note "Nima Tashi, age 35, Saka" (the subject's place of origin). The original also has the year 1908 with Hedin's signature. This picture appears as Figure 146 in *Sven Hedin as Artist*. The subject is a chief bodyguard named Nima Tashi (ཉི་མ་བཀྲ་ཤིས་ *nyi ma bkra shis*) of Saga (ས་དགའ་ *sa dga'*), who is also shown in the next watercolor (Reproduction 25). Since his pose is the same in both the sketch (a frontal half-length portrait) and the watercolor (a full-length portrait from the side), the two pictures were probably made on the same occasion. Several things can be discerned by comparing the two images. For example, the man grasps the hilt of a long sword in his left hand, the tip of which can be seen in the lower right corner of this picture. In the half-length sketch, two belts cross his chest diagonally; from the full-length portrait, we can see that the upper belt crossing from his right shoulder down to his lower left side is a rifle belt; the belt underneath crosses

[Original 24] Sven Hedin, 1908, Pencil, 32.2 × 20.1 cm

Rural militia from Bongba led by Tagla Tsering (*Trans-Himalaya* II, Illustration 365)

from his left shoulder and has a number of objects shaped like chili peppers dangling from it, which are also visible in the full-length portrait. These are powder flasks, or *dzä-khu* (རྫས་ཁུག་ *rdzas khug*) in Tibetan, made from yellow-brown bull horns. A metal fastener is attached to the base of the horn and hung from the belt. A small hole is cut open at the tip and plugged with a piece of wood after the horn is filled with gunpowder. A single *dzä-khu* contains enough powder for a single round from a muzzle-loading matchlock rifle, which can thus be loaded with the right amount of powder without spillage by unplugging the horn and inserting it directly into the muzzle. The object hanging between two *dzä-khu* is probably a metal "fire-striking sickle" *meja* (མེ་ལྕགས་ *me lcags*) used to produce sparks by striking a flint.

[Reproduction 25] Adachi Itarō, Pencil and Water Color, 25.4 × 20.2 cm

Tibetans

[Original 25] Sven Hedin, 1908, Pencil and Water Color, 25.4 × 20.1 cm

Costume of a man whose hair has been bound in red tassels called trapshu (exhibited at the Tibet Museum in Lhasa)

25 Standing figure of the bodyguard Nima Tashi

This picture appears in color as Illustration 353 in *Trans-Himalaya* II. The caption reads "Nima Tashi, commander of the government-escort on the way to the Teri-nam-tso." At his left side, on a belt slung from his right shoulder, he carries a traditional Tibetan rifle phönda (བོད་མདའ་ *bod mda*), a muzzle-loading matchlock. His left hand grasps the hilt of a long sword. In Hedin's watercolor, however, the deep shadowing (owing perhaps to the bright sunlight) makes it difficult to tell that this object is really a sword sheath. Possibly for that reason, the hilt grasped by the left hand and the sheath of the sword appear misaligned in the reproduction. In the full-length watercolor portrait, we see something that looks like a red cloth wrapped around the head and woven through the hair. This is a man's head ornament known as a *tapshu* (སྐྲ་གཞུག་ *skra gzhug*), literally "hair tassel," consisting of a bundle of braided silk threads. Though it is commonly described as an ornament worn by men of the Kham region (eastern Tibet), it is often seen in other regions as well. The white felt coat worn by Nima Tashi is of a type said to be favored by men of the Shigatse district (楊清凡 2003) [*History of Tibetan Dress*. p. 200].

[Reproduction 26] Adachi Itarō, Pen and Water Color, 25.4 × 20.3 cm

Tinderboxes with flint and steel known as *me ku* are still sold at Buddhist emporiums and antiques stores. They are said to be used as decorations rather than applied to practical use ©IKD

Tibetan boots. The simple type placed at the left of the front row and in the back are men's boots known as pho zom (men's boots), while the ones embroidered with a flower pattern are mo zom (women's boots). (Shigatse: Shopfront in the antiques district) ©IKD

26 Young militia boy with a rifle

This picture does not appear in either *Trans-Himalaya* or *Sven Hedin as Artist*, and the original is lost. The reproduction lacks any name or other inscription. Hedin drew many sketches of Tibetan militia men and wrote about them as follows: "I used as a rule to sketch these representatives for the rural militia in full-length portraits, in order to get down all the details, even to the comical, in actual life parti-coloured and decorative felt boots" (*As Artist* p. 45). The young militia boy carrying the rifle on his back is wearing a pair of Tibetan wool boots. In Tibetan, the traditional felt boots are called *son pa* (ཟོན་པ་ *zon pa*) or *som pa* (ཟོམ་པ་ *zom pa*). However, a distinction is made between men's boots with sturdy soles and simple designs, which are called *pho som* (ཕོ་ཟོམ་ *pho zom*, "men's shoes"), and those for women, with narrow soles and flowery embroidery, which are called *mo som* (མོ་ཟོམ་ *mo zom*, "women's shoes"). Though they are no longer worn as often in the course of daily life, Tibetan boots are still considered a must when people dress up for traditional Tibetan events. As for the item hanging from the boy's belt that resembles a wallet, this is a leather accessory case known as a *me ku* (མེ་ཁུག་ *me khug*). The top pocket contains a small flint, while a sickle-shaped metal plate for striking the flint is attached to the bottom. Metal or stone ornaments are often attached to the leather lid of the pocket for decorative effect.

[Reproduction 27] Nishikawa Junji, Pencil and Pen, 20.4 × 25.2 cm

27 Bodyguard riding a yak

The original bears Hedin's signature and the year 1908; other than that, there is no inscription on either the original or the reproduction. The picture appears as Illustration 348 in *Trans-Himalaya* II, with only the caption "Trooper of the escort." The bodyguard is riding a yak – one of the long-haired bovids that are native to the Himalayan region at elevations over 3,000 meters and are the representative livestock of Tibet. Herders in Tibet put yaks out to pasture, weave fabric and make tents from their hair, use them to till fields and carry loads, burn their dried dung as fuel, and depend for sustenance on the yogurt, cheese, and butter made from their milk. In Tibetan, the word *yak* (གཡག་ *g-yag*) refers only to the mature male; a different word, pronounced *mbi* or *ndri* (འབྲི་ *'bri*), is used to refer to the female. Which means that "yak's milk" is an oxymoron. As Hedin writes, "The more well-to-do mountain-dwellers transport their tents and belongings on yaks" (*As Artist* p. 44). They would not only use yaks as pack animals, but also saddle and ride them. In the 1980s, before Tibet had much in the way of roads, cars, or other infrastructure, yaks still served as a mode of transport in rural areas, and children could be seen riding them to school (see photo). Yak meat is aromatic and tasty. During my 2016 visit, I had the opportunity to eat a "yakburger" at the restaurant in our hotel in Lhasa. It was extremely delicious – far better than a typical American hamburger.

[Original 27] Sven Hedin, 1908, Pencil and Pen, 20.2 × 25.4 cm

Children traveling on yaks. 1980s. Reproduced from *Tibet: A Complete Guide* (Passport Books, 1986)

[Reproduction 28] Nishikawa Junji, Pencil and Pen, 25.3 × 20.2 cm

[Original 28] Sven Hedin, 1908, Pencil and Pen, 25.3 × 20.1 cm

28 Young shepherd of Bongba

The name and place of origin of the subject is written at the lower left on both the reproduction and the original. The inscription appears to have been added to the original later in block capital letters in pen and ink, overwriting a cursive note in pencil. The original also bears Hedin's signature and the year 1908. The name is given as Tamding Angal, probably spelled རྟ་མགྲིན་དབང་རྒྱལ (*rta mgrin dbang rgyal*) in Tibetan, from Kebjang in the province of Bongba. Though no age is given here, the next picture, which portrays the same person (Reproduction 29), indicates he is aged 19. The picture appears as Illustration 350 in *Trans-Himalaya* II with the caption "Young shepherd of Bongba." On Hedin's route map, the place name Kebyang (i.e. Kebjang) is near camp 420 in the province of Bongba. Among the copies of Hedin's drawings is a panoramic view in ink of the mountains of Bongba (Reproduction 23; see the description under "Mountain landscape in the Bongba district"). In *Sven Hedin as Artist*, Hedin appears to be describing the headgear of the subject of this picture when he writes of the men dispatched to serve as his escorts: "[O]thers again wear a ring-shaped cloth roll or pad threaded through some broad bone-rings like a crown on top of their heads" (*As Artist* p. 45). What Hedin calls a "bone-ring" is actually made of ivory and is called an "ivory ring" *paso tikor* (བ་སོ་ཐིག་བསྐོར *ba so thig bskor*) in Tibetan. It is interesting to note that the front of this man's head ornament features what appears to be a woman's *gao* (གའུ *ga'u*), an oblong amulet originating in the lid of a Buddhist prayer-box.

[Reproduction 29] Pen, 25.5 × 20.1 cm

[Original 29] Sven Hedin, 1908, Pencil and Pen, 25.3 × 20.0 cm

29 Two guides from Bongba

Two guides from Bongba are depicted. The name of the man on the left, hatless with one shoulder bare, is written as Tevi Dortje, probably spelled བསྟན་འཕེལ་རྡོ་རྗེ་ (bstan 'phel rdo rje) in Tibetan, and his place of origin as Kebjang. The man on the right wears a hat and what appear to be sunglasses. Labeled "Tamding Angal, 19," also from Kebjang, he is the man depicted in the half-length portrait above (Reproduction 28). In Tibetan, his name is རྟ་མགྲིན་དབང་རྒྱལ་ (rta mgrin dbang rgyal). In these two portraits, his name, hat, and head ornament are all identical. The picture of the two standing men appears as Illustration 323 in *Trans-Himalaya* II with the caption "Two guides (inhabitants of the province of Bongba)." After Nima Tashi's escort departed beyond the Mendong Gompa monastery near Terinam Lake, these local shepherds were probably Hedin's guides on his westward route. What looks like a pair of sunglasses on Tamding, on the right, is in fact an eye mask to protect against the glare from the snow. Called *mik ra* (མིག་ར་ *mig ra*) in Tibetan, these masks are woven from the thick hair that grows under a yak's belly.

[Reproduction 30] Nishikawa Junji, Pen, 25.6 × 20.0 cm

Tibetans

[Original 30] Sven Hedin, 1908, Pencil and Pen, 25.4 × 20.1 cm

A man who had come from the Kongpo region. He was wearing the characteristic hat of the region, called a kongsha (Lhasa: Drepung Monastery)

30 Young man wearing a broad-brimmed hat

The notes written on both the reproduction and the original in pencil appear to name the subject Kamdul, but the corresponding Tibetan name is unknown. His age is given as 25 and his place of origin as Mapisa, presumably located in the province of Bongba. The picture appears as Illustration 324 in *Trans-Himalaya* II with the caption "Boy with hat (inhabitants of the province of Bongba)." The broad-brimmed hat worn by the young man, called *arsha* (ཨར་ཞྭ་ *ar zhwa*) in Tibetan, is of a type worn by nomads living on the Changtang Plateau of central Tibet, where the sunlight is intense. Fancy felt hats of this sort with red chin straps are worn as formal attire at festivals and religious ceremonies. In Illustration 365 in *Trans-Himalaya* II, a group photo of militia men, the one in the center appears to be the same man shown here. The caption of the photo merely says, "Group of Tibetans at the Teri-nam-tso [i.e., Terinam Lake]." In the Japanese translation of *Trans-Himalaya*, however, the caption for the same photo reads "Attendants of Tagla Tsering," suggesting that the young man in question belongs to the guard of Tagla Tsering, a local chief of the Naktsang district (Reproduction 37).

31 Militia man with a spear and long sword

Both the reproduction and the original contain handwritten inscriptions with the word "Mendung" (The spelling is questionable; and it is unclear whether this is the subject's place of origin, or the place where the picture was drawn), the name Sonam Tundup, and his age, 26. The original bears Hedin's signature and the year 1908. In Tibetan, the name Sonam Tundup is probably spelled བསོད་ནམས་དོན་གྲུབ་ (*bsod nams don grub*). This picture appears in *Trans-Himalaya* II as Illustration 346, with the caption "Armed Tibetan from the country between the Teri-nam-tso and the Dangra-yum-tso." There is also a reproduction of a vivid watercolor of the Mendong monastery near Terinam Lake (see Reproduction 49, under the heading "White-walled brick monastery and monks").

Changing of the guard by local militia (*Trans-Himalaya* II, Illustration 246)

[Reproduction 31] Nishikawa Junji, Pen, 25.5 × 20.2 cm

[Original 31] Sven Hedin, 1908, Pencil and Pen, 25.4 × 20.1 cm

Tibetans

[Reproduction 32] Nishikawa Junji, Pencil and Pen, 25.3 × 20.2 cm

[Original 32] Sven Hedin, 1908, Pencil and Pen, 25.2 × 20.1 cm

32 Standing militia man with a rifle on his back

The note in cursive script on the reproduction is difficult to decipher. Instead of a person's name, it appears to be something like "Mardangni" or "Mendongni," followed by a question mark. One possibility is that it stands for the Tibetan སྨན་སྟོང་ནས་ (*sman stong nas*), meaning "from Mendong" – the handwritten "ni" may be the Tibetan postpositional particle ནས་ *nas* (pronounced *ne* or *ni*), meaning "from." The subject is 45 years old. The reproduction also contains the note "Duntsing Kuntsen," the meaning of which is also unclear, though it could stand for བདུན་ཚོགས་འགོ་འཛིན་ (*bdun tshogs 'go'dzin*), "chief of a seven-man unit." I welcome further analysis. This picture appears in *Trans-Himalaya* III as the middle figure of three soldiers standing in a row in Illustration 63 with the caption "Soldiers of Sonam Ngurbu." The somewhat more elegant attire, with its decorative pattern, worn by this individual suggests that he may be a leader of the soldiers. The name may be a misspelling of "Sonam Norbu" (i.e., བསོད་ནམས་ནོར་བུ་ *bsod nams nor bu*).

33 Standing militia man holding a rifle

Both the reproduction and the original have written in pencil the name Tundup Tsering, age 43, with "Saka" given as his place of origin. In Tibetan, the name would be དོན་གྲུབ་ཚེ་རིང་ (*don grub tshe ring*). The picture appears as Illustration 344 in *Trans-Himalaya* II with the caption "Soldiers of the garrison of Saka-dzong, belonging to our escort." This soldier and the others no doubt belong to the militia brought from Saga (pronounced as *saka*) by Nima Tashi (Reproductions 24 and 25). A dzong (རྫོང་ *rdzong*) is the fortress-like government office built in provincial cities in Tibet (see Reproduction 14, "Shigatse Dzong," for an explanation). However, "Saka-dzong" (ས་དགའ་རྫོང་ *sa dga' rdzong*) may refer to not only the government office in Saga, but also the area administered by that office, since *dzong* is often used in the sense of a district or a county.

[Reproduction 33] Nishikawa Junji, Pencil and Pen, 25.4 × 20.1 cm

[Original 33] Sven Hedin, 1908, Pencil and Pen, 25.3 × 20.1 cm

Tibetans

[Reproduction 34] Nishikawa Junji, Pen, 25.5 × 20.0 cm

[Original 34] Sven Hedin, 1908, Pencil and Pen, 25.4 × 20.3 cm

34 Militia man holding a rifle

This picture does not appear in either *Trans-Himalaya* or *Sven Hedin as Artist*. On both the reproduction and the original, the subject's name "Puntså," age 56, and place of origin "Saka" are written at the lower left. On the original, Hedin's signature and the year 1908 are also inscribed near the subject's foot. The Tibetan equivalent of "Puntså" is ཕུན་ཚོགས་ (*phun tshok*). He is presumably another of the soldiers brought from Saga by Nima Tashi (Reproductions 24 and 25).

An old Tibetan matchlock with an attached mobile bipod gun rest (Tibet Museum) ©IKD

[Reproduction 35] Ishida Kinzō, Pencil, 34.0 × 23.3 cm

35 Dorche Tsuen, governor of Saga in profile

Hedin temporarily returned to Leh in Ladakh after his sojourn in Shigatse during the first half of his third central Asia expedition. He then reorganized his caravan and once again crossed the Changtang Plateau, this time on a diagonal course with the aim of exploring Bongba, a province lying between the Gangdise and Nyenchen Tanglha ranges that appeared as a blank area on maps. However, his presence was detected somewhere near Saga Dzong, resulting in a confrontation with the governor of Saga in a place called "Semoku" (Tibetan spelling unknown; the current Chinese transliteration is 斯莫苦 Simoku), near the Yarlung-tsangpo River on April 27, 1908. The governor was the personage described here as "Dortje Tsuän (རྡོ་རྗེ་བརྩོན་

Tibetans

[Original 35] Sven Hedin, 1908, Pencil, 30.2 × 20.3 cm

rdo rje brtson), age 42," with whom Hedin negotiated the route he would be allowed to follow henceforth. This picture appears as Illustration 327 in *Trans-Himalaya* II. Hedin writes: "Pun Dorche Tsuen is an unusually tall Tibetan, forty-three years old, of sympathetic and refined appearance, dressed in a Chinese costume of silk, with a small silk cap on his head, a pigtail behind, and velvet boots. He is a man of wealth, owning large flocks in the province over which he rules and a stone house in Lhasa, his home, for he is an upa or domiciled inhabitant of the province U, the capital of which is Lhasa" (*Trans-Himalaya* II, p. 355). *Pun* (དཔོན་ *dpon*) means "chief" in Tibetan. In Tibet, under the authority of the Dalai Lama, *dzong* (རྫོང་ *rdzong*) referred to both the administrative office/fortress in each district and the administrative unit under the jurisdiction of a governor known as a *dzongpön* (རྫོང་དཔོན་ *rdzong dpon*), who was appointed for a fixed term and dispatched by the central government. *U pa* (དབུས་པ་ *dbus pa*) means a person from Ü province. Central Tibet was traditionally divided into the provinces of Ü (sometimes pronounced as *wu* or *yu*), where Lhasa is located, and Tsang, where Shigatse is located. They were respectively transliterated to Chinese as 衛 (wei) and 藏 (zang) and were also referred to as "Front Tibet" and "Back Tibet." The portrait shows a man in profile smoking a pipe, wearing Chinese clothing, and boasting a conspicuously large earring. Known as a *sok-jil* (སོག་བྱིལ་ *sog byil*), this earring served as a sign of his high status as a man of Ü and an official of the regional government.

[Reproduction 36] Tanaka Zennosuke, Pencil, 32.4 × 21.2 cm

Tibetans

[Original 36] Sven Hedin, 1907, Pencil, 32.1 × 21.2 cm

36 Official of Saga: Portrait of Ngavang

This portrait is of the governor of Saga Dzong. His name (དགའ་དབང་ *ngag dbang*) is written "Ngavang" on the reproduction, and nothing else. The original carries Hedin's signature and the year 1907, as well as a number of unknown meaning, 84. The picture appears as Illustration 78 in *Trans-Himalaya* III with the caption "The governor of Saka-dzong." It also appears as Figure 135 in *Sven Hedin as Artist* with the caption "Aristocratic Tibetan, Shigatse 1907," indicating some confusion in the records. In *Trans-Himalaya*, this personage makes an appearance together with Dorche Tsuen, the governor of Saga Dzong portrayed in Reproduction 35 above: "Ngavang, his coadjutor, is a little, fat, kindly man in Tibetan costume, but with a Chinese cap and pigtail" (*Trans-Himalaya* II, p. 355). The description perfectly matches this picture. There is no previous mention of him in *Trans-Himalaya*. Thus, the year 1907 written on the original and the caption in *Sven Hedin as Artist* would seem to be unrelated information that somehow slipped in. The man in the picture is wearing Chinese clothing (probably of quality silk), not Tibetan. However, the fact that he sports the status symbol of a large *sok-jil* (སོག་བྱིལ་ *sog byil*) earring as Dorche Tsuen does makes it clear that he is a high-ranking Tibetan official.

[Reproduction 37] Nishikawa Junji, Pen, 32.3 × 21.3 cm

[Original 37] Sven Hedin, 1908, Pencil and Pen, 32.3 × 21.4 cm

Buddhist amulet boxes (ga'u) sold at an antiques market. (Shigatse) ©IKD

37 Portrait of local chief Tagla Tsering

When Hedin negotiated with Saga governor Dorche Tsuen (Reproduction 35), he was refused permission to head for India via Shigatse. Instead, it was agreed that he would turn north to Terinam Lake, then west under escort (and surveillance) by the militia of Nima Tashi (Reproduction 24). However, Hedin saw an opportunity to visit the uncharted holy lake Dangra-yum-tso to the east of Terinam Lake and repeatedly expressed his desire to do so. Nima Tashi therefore contacted the local chief, Tagla Tsering, who appeared with several dozen armed men and stopped Hedin from proceeding to Dangra-yum-tso. As a result, Hedin and his group headed westward past the Mendong monastery near Terinam Lake. This picture is a portrait of the chief in question; both the reproduction and the original are inscribed in pencil with the name "Tagla Tsering" (probably སྟག་ལགས་ཚེ་རིང་ *stag lags tshe ring* in Tibetan). The original also bears Hedin's signature and the year "08." The reproduction is clearly copied from the original sketch. Figure 144 in *Sven Hedin as Artist* is also a pen-and-ink drawing, accompanied by the caption "Chief Togla [sic] Tsering. Terinam Tso 1908." However, Illustration 329 in *Trans-Himalaya* II appears to be a monochrome watercolor that was very likely copied from the line drawing, with watercolor shadowing added for inclusion in the book. The caption reads, "Tagla Tsering, the chief who refused to let me go to the Dangra-yum-tso." Of this individual, Hedin writes that he is "wearing an extra belt over his sheepskin which is studded with gaos of silver and copper, all containing images of gods" (*As Artist*, p. 45). The gao (གའུ་ *ga'u*) is a small box made of gold, silver, or copper that contains a small Buddhist image or prayer and is worn on the chest as an amulet for divine protection. It is usually called a "prayer-box" in English. The lids are typically decorated with elaborate craftwork. *Gao* can also refer to an ornament worn by women in which the lid is sewn onto fabric in a more abstract, nearly square design. The hat worn by the chief is of a type often seen in central Tibet, known as a *mokril amcho chen* (རྨོག་རིལ་ཨ་མཆོག་ཅན་ *rmog ril a mchog can*), literally "round hat with earflaps." The style typically worn today is a bit taller and resembles a bucket.

[Reproduction 38] Pen, 25.4 × 20.1 cm

[Original 38] Sven Hedin, 1908, Pencil and Pen, 25.4 × 20.1 cm

A modern monk wearing sneakers with iPhone in hand (Lhasa: outside Jokhang Temple Monastery) ©IKD

38 Two monks

A portrait of two men wearing monastic attire and holding long rosaries does not appear in either *Trans-Himalaya* or *Sven Hedin as Artist*. The reproduction lacks even a signature by the art student who drew it, but the original has Hedin's signature and the year 1908. The handwritten notes on the reproduction and the original are both difficult to decipher because of the poorly rendered cursive script. The caption under the turbaned monk on the left appears to be a name, something like Lopsang (*blo bzang*), age 16. The name and age are usually followed by the place of the drawing or the subject's origin, but here the text is illegible. The caption under the monk on the right with a wide cloth slung diagonally over his left shoulder appears to be the name Chöwang (ཆོས་དབང་ *chos dbang*), age 27, but here again, the text that follows is illegible. I welcome further analysis.

[Reproduction 39] Nishikawa Junji, Pencil and Pen, 25.4 × 20.7 cm

[Original 39] Sven Hedin, 1908, Pencil and Pen, 25.5 × 20.5 cm

39 Tibetan man

This picture does not appear in either *Trans-Himalaya* or *Sven Hedin as Artist*. On both the reproduction and the original, the subject's name and age 22, as well as a place name, are handwritten at the bottom right. The original also has Hedin's signature and the year 1908. The Tibetan spelling of the personal name, Punsuk Jontän, is probably ཕུན་ཚོགས་ཡོན་ཏན་ (*phun tshogs yon tan*). The place name, Bitju, cannot be found on Hedin's route map. The "tju" as written by Hedin may stand for the Tibetan ཆུ (*chu*), meaning "river" and normally romanized in English as "chu." The bulge of clothing at the subject's waist appears to be a long outer garment rolled up above the belt, into which he has stuffed various personal items, using the extra space as a pocket. Hedin explains this distinctive way of wearing a garment: "They tie a belt round the waist and then pull up the sheepskin so that it hangs round the entire waist like a bulging bag. In this way they get a space that serves them instead of pockets, and is, moreover, stuffed with all sorts of small articles, amongst other things a supply of food and tobacco. The Tibetans also gain another advantage by drawing up their sheepskins in this fashion: the coats become so short that they scarcely reach to the knees, and thus do not hinder them when they walk" (*As Artist*, p. 45). The items dangling from his hip appear to be a knife and a fire-striking sickle.

[Reproduction 40] Nishikawa Junji, Pencil, 25.3 × 17.4 cm

[Original 40] Sven Hedin, 1907, Pencil, 25.0 × 17.4 cm

40 Portrait

This picture does not appear in either *Trans-Himalaya* or *Sven Hedin as Artist*. On both the reproduction and the original, the subject's name and age 19, as well as a place name, are handwritten at the top right. The original also has Hedin's signature and the year 1907 at the bottom right, but they appear to have been added in ink after the inscription in pencil at the top. The Tibetan spelling of the personal name, Sumtjuk, is probably བསམ་མཆོག་ (*bsam mchog*). The place name, Setung, cannot be found on Hedin's route map. What might be a corresponding name on the map, Sadung, appears on the opposite side of the Yarlung-tsangpo River not far from Shigatse, but the Tibetan spelling is unknown. In contemporary Chinese-character transliteration, the same place name is given as 色定 (seding). None of Hedin's works contain a mention of either a personal or a place name that might be related to this picture, so nothing is known about the subject.

[Reproduction 41] Adachi Itarō, Pencil and Black-and-white Color, 20.2×12.4 cm

Tibetans

[Original 41] Sven Hedin, 1908, Pencil and Black-and-white Color, 20.2 × 12.4 cm

41 Portrait of a Tibetan

This picture does not appear in either *Trans-Himalaya* or *Sven Hedin as Artist*. On both the reproduction and the original, a personal name, a place name, and an age 37, are handwritten at the bottom. The writing on the reproduction is in pencil, but on the original, the pencil inscription has been overwritten in ink; moreover, this has been done in conspicuous block capital letters that make the caption stand out like a title for the picture. The original also has Hedin's signature and the year 1908. Whereas the signature also appears to be overwritten in ink over pencil, the year seems to have been added for the first time in ink. The Tibetan spelling of the personal name Gova Tjöta may be དགའ་བ་ཆོས་གྲགས་ (*dga' ba chos grags*). The place name, Selipuk, appears in *Sven Hedin as Artist*: "Selipuk Gompa at the salt lake Nganglaring Tso is white-washed and its walls are painted red up near the roof" (*As Artist*, p. 47). According to Hedin's route map, lake Nganglaring-tso (ངང་ལྷ་རིང་མཚོ་ *ngang lha ring mthso*, 昂拉仁错) is in the Bongba region of the central Changtang Plateau, and this monastery name appears at the site of Camp 440 on the lakeshore. However, there is no record in Hedin's writings of the identity of the subject of the picture, so nothing further is known about this individual.

[Reproduction 42] Ishida Kinzō, Pen and Water Color, 25.6 × 20.8 cm

[Original 42] Sven Hedin, 1908, Pen and Water Color, 25.2 × 20.2 cm

42 Attire of a nomadic woman A

The penciled inscription on both the reproduction and the original reads "Hansam" and "age 18;" the name in Tibetan may be ལྷ་འཛོམས་ (lha 'dzoms). The place name Kjangjang is in the province of Bongba and is found on Hedin's route map near Camp 441. The original has Hedin's signature and the year 1908 written in ink. This picture does not appear in either *Trans-Himalaya* or *Sven Hedin as Artist*. The subject wears a head ornament known as a *go gyän* (མགོ་རྒྱན་ mgo rgyan) and has a long rosary known as a *trheng gyü* (ཕྲེང་རྒྱུད་ phreng rgyud) hanging from her neck. She bares one shoulder. Hedin writes: "A generally current usage in Tibet, especially in summer-time or at home in the tent, is to have the right arm and the right side of the trunk bare, exposing the beautifully bronze-brown and weather-bitten skin" (*As Artist*, p. 45). The deep shadowing of the face suggests that the drawing was made under bright sunlight.

[Reproduction 43] Adachi Itarō, Pen and Water Color, 25.4 × 20.2 cm

| 43 | **Attire of a nomadic woman B**

Though the original of this picture is lost, it appears in *Trans-Himalaya* II as one of the color illustrations 362. The reproduction bears a penciled inscription consisting of the subject's name, the place name Kjangjang, and the age 27. The subject's name appears to be spelled "Dålma Tsesän"; the corresponding Tibetan would be སྒྲོལ་མ་ཚེ་བརྟན་ (*sgrol ma tshe brtan*). The caption for Illustration 362 in *Trans-Himalaya* II reads "Holiday costumes and ornaments of Tibetan women of Kyangrang in the Trans-Himalaya." On Hedin's route map, the place names Kyangyang (Camp 443) and Kyangrang (Camp 444) are in the area between 31° and 32° north latitude and 81° and 82° east longitude, midway along the route over Ding-la pass to Lake Manasarovar

Contemporary Tibetan woman: a local worshipper (precincts of Tashi Lhunpo Monastery, Shigatse)

Sven Hedin (*Trans-Himalaya* II, Illustration 362)

Contemporary Tibetan woman: pilgrim from the countryside (precincts of Pelkor Chode, Gyantse)

from Nganglaring-tso (ངང་ལྷ་རིང་མཚོ་ *ngang lha ring mthso*, 昂拉仁错), the lake where the Selipuk Gompa (Camp 440) is located. On current maps, there is a village named 亚热镇 (yarezhen) in this vicinity, but no place name can be found that could be transliterated to something like Kyangyang or Kyangrang. The picture shows the attire of a woman wearing a bright red headdress and a long rosary around her neck. She has removed her dark-blue outer garment from her right shoulder.

[Reproduction 44] Nishikawa Junji, Pen and Water Color, 25.4 × 20.1 cm

Sven Hedin (*Trans-Himalaya* II, Illustration 362)

44 Attire of a nomadic woman C

This picture, too, appears in *Trans-Himalaya* II as one of the color illustrations 362, but the original is lost. The caption for Illustrations 362 reads "Holiday costumes and ornaments of Tibetan women of Kyangrang in the Trans-Himalaya," but there is no further information. At the bottom left of the reproduction is a written inscription with a name, the age 28, and the place name Kjangjang. The name is difficult to decipher; it could be "Chimi" (འཆི་མེད་ *'chi med*) or "Jikme" (འཇིགས་མེད་ *'jig med*). See the description of the previous figure (Reproduction 43) for a discussion of place names written as Kjangjang on the reproduction or Kyangrang in the caption for Illustrations 362 in *Trans-Himalaya* II. The picture shows a woman wearing a very fancy *gogyän* (headdress) and several rings on her left hand. The blue beads on the headdress are probably made of turquoise, and the red beads of coral.

[Reproduction 45] Adachi Itarō, Pen and Water Color, 25.4 × 20.3 cm

45 Woman in blue Tibetan attire

This picture does not appear in either *Trans-Himalaya* or *Sven Hedin as Artist*, and the original is lost. The only information on the reproduction is the place name Taktje, written in pencil at the bottom left. Though it seems likely to be a place in the province of Bongba, there is no such name (Taktje or, in typical English romanization, Takche) on Hedin's route map or in *Trans-Himalaya*. The only place on Hedin's route with a name having a similar pronunciation is Tokchen, a bit to the east of Lake Manasarovar, but there is no way of knowing if it is related. There are two other pictures in which the place name Taktje is written on the reproduction. In both pictures – Reproduction 47, an ink and watercolor work showing a woman in green Tibetan attire, and Reproduction 48, a line drawing of a child – the clothing suggests that both subjects are local nomads.

[Reproduction 46] Nishikawa Junji, Pen and Water Color, 25.2 × 20.2 cm

[Original 46] Sven Hedin, 1908, Pen and Water Color, 25.2 × 20.2 cm

46 Woman in violet Tibetan attire

A penciled note onto both the reproduction and the original mentions the place name Kjangjang without any other information. Regarding the place name, see the description of Reproduction 43 above. This picture was included in color Illustrations 362 in *Trans-Himalaya* II. This is the upper left of the four watercolor paintings in Illustrations 362. The caption for all four images reads simply "Holiday costumes and ornaments of Tibetan women of Kyangrang in the Trans-Himalaya." While the originals also bear Hedin's signature and the year 1908, from the fact that the year notation cannot be seen in the illustration in *Trans-Himalaya* II, we know that this was something added to the paintings later. The painting depicts the figure of a woman wearing an elaborate adornment called a *tra lung* (སྐྲ་ལུང་ *skra lung*) binding her hair and hanging down her back that has been studded with ornamental Buddhist amulet boxes known as *gao* (གའུ་ *ga'u*). On the original, Hedin has written some kind of abbreviation in pencil for each part of the picture. It seems likely that these were memos about the color of paint for each part. In Hedin's commentary in this chapter, his statement that "These I have coloured – not to produce anything that might deserve to be called a water-colour, but only to give some notion of the glaring colour characterizing their costumes" (*Sven Hedin as Artist*, p. 45) seems to suggest a picture in which he inserted a memo about the name of the color in the initial line drawing and then added color later on. This kind of annotation of what seems to be a memo concerning color names can also be seen in Chapter 5, in Reproduction 59. This was probably an instance where the opportunity to add colors having been missed, the picture would have been left as a line drawing.

[Reproduction 47] Ishida Kinzō, Pencil, Pen, and Water Color, 25.6 × 20.3 cm

[Original 47] Sven Hedin, 1908, Pencil, Pen, and Water Color, 25.2 × 20.0 cm

A souvenir photo model wearing a nomadic costume seen at a local tourist destination (Lhasa: Chakpori Lookout)

47 Woman in green Tibetan attire

According to the penciled note on the reproduction and the original, this is Angmo, age 28. The corresponding Tibetan name may be དབང་མོ (dbang mo). Nothing is known about the place name Taktje (see the discussion of Reproduction 45 above). This picture appears in color in *Trans-Himalaya* II as one of the four watercolors comprising Illustrations 362. However, whereas the other three are all inscribed with the place name Kjangjang, this one alone gives the woman's place of origin as Taktje. From this, we may surmise that Kjangjang and Taktje were located close enough to one another for the subjects to be treated as part of the same group. The original also bears Hedin's signature and the year 1908, but while the signature is written with pen and ink traced over pencil, the year does not appear in Illustrations 362 in *Trans-Himalaya* II, indicating that it was added later. Closer inspection reveals more vivid coloring and contrast in the original than in the comparatively lightly-drawn copy. Illustrations 362 also shows a light touch close to that of the copy, suggesting that coloring was added later to the original. In his description in *Sven Hedin as Artist*, Hedin writes: "These I have coloured – not to produce anything that might deserve to be called a water-colour, but only to give some notion of the glaring colour characterizing their costumes" (*As Artist*, p. 45–46). Hedin presumably wrote this in reference to coloring he added to the pictures after returning from his expedition, owing to a need to highlight contrasts and so on for inclusion in the book.

[Reproduction 48] Nishikawa Junji, Pencil and Pen, 25.5 × 20.2 cm

Tibetans

[Original 48] Sven Hedin, 1907, Pencil and Pen, 25.3 × 20.2 cm

Tibetan women and children living in the Tsangpo basin (*Trans-Himalaya* II, Illustration 237)

48 Nomad child

This portrait appears to be of a child of nomads living on the Changtang Plateau. Because it is not included as an illustration in any of Hedin's books, it has remained virtually unknown until now. According to the note in pencil at the bottom left on both the reproduction and the original, the child's name is Tashi (བཀྲ་ཤིས་ *bkra shis* in Tibetan, meaning "auspicious"), age 10. The note also contains the place name Taktje. The original bears Hedin's signature and the year 1907 at the bottom right. If the year is correct, then Hedin drew it after his sojourn in Shigatse on the way back to Ladakh, before he embarked once more to explore the Bongba region. But there is no mention of Taktje either on Hedin's route map or in *Trans-Himalaya*. The only place name with a similar pronunciation is Tokchen, a bit to the east of Lake Manasarovar. If he drew this picture in Tokchen, it would accord with his itinerary. However, Hedin also passed through Tokchen toward the end of his third expedition after exploring Bongba, so it is conceivable that he drew it at a different time from the watercolors.

Chapter 5: Tibetan Temple Monasteries

TIBETAN TEMPLE MONASTERIES

A large group of drawings from Tibet are of a number of temple monasteries from the Tsangpo valley, the Transhimalayas, the sacred lake and the upper reaches of Sutlej [Reproduction 51]. Selipuk Gompa at the salt lake Nganglaring Tso is white-washed and its walls are painted red up near the roof. The monastery presents a festive sight, and as its innumerable streamers flutter in the wind it bears a certain resemblance to a ship decorated with flags.[1] On each of them the sacred formula is written. The monks believe that when the prayer streamers are smacking and slapping in the wind these mystic words fraught with blessing are borne over mountains and valleys to the ears of the gods.

How often did I not find the temple interiors completely irresistible with their droll effects of lighting and colour! From the sunlight outside and from the vestibule protected by the four spirit-kings [Reproduction 54] one nearly always enters a room so dark that it takes quite a time for the eye to become accustomed to the meagre light [Reproduction 55].

But soon the details emerge. Through a square impluvium the daylight falls in over the images of gods on the altar table. Chief among them sits Buddha himself, unattained and smiling mysteriously, with dreaming eyes and long pendulous ears [Reproduction 57].

Along the walls one often sees other pictures, draped in silk mantles and each placed in a cabinet with gay, motley carvings [Reproduction 58].

On inbuilt book-shelves lie the parchment leaves of the sacred texts between two loose wooden covers wrapped around with leather bands [Reproduction 56]. From the beading of the impluvium are suspended neatly painted *tankas* [Reproduction 55].

On special tables before the gods brass vessels are set out for sacrificial tributes, and oil wicks burn with smoky yellow flames which struggle vainly against the mystical twilight.

In the monasteries around Manasarowar one sees representations of the lake-god, sometimes in the form of a mask peeping forth between draperies, sacrificial cloths and drums [see *Trans-Himalaya* II 251].

The most beautiful light effects arise in the temple halls where the ceiling is supported by red-lacquered columns with originally carved capitals. Through the sky-light in the roof the daylight falls in over the columns and makes them stand out in bold relief against the compact darkness in the background. When sunlight finds its way into such a temple hall the columns gleam like glowing rubies, and one imagines oneself transported to a fairy grotto. In their red togas the lamas form silent and dignified groups.

An amusing type was Namgjal Dortje, an aristocratic lama from Tokchu, who during my stay in Selipuk left the monastery to complete his pilgrimage to the sacred lake. He was wearing a magnificent costume of yellow and red, had a rosary round his neck, a yellow wooden hat on his head, and on his nose a pair of Chinese spectacles which only made him appear the more comical.

The Tibetans were always friendly and willing when I asked them to pose for me. The sittings were generally arranged in such a way that I sat on a chest at the entrance to my tent while the model sat on another chest or sack of maize out in the sunshine. The onlookers sat down on the ground round about, observed my work and now and then made little remarks that aroused merriment.

For me it was always a pleasure and a profit to get a closer contact with the Tibetans in this way and get some insights into their life and modes of thought. Quite without intention this drawing of portraits turned out to be a way of gaining their confidence. Well might they wonder what I meant with this drawing, but they soon found that it was on the whole a rather harmless occupation.

In the meantime I got them to tell me what they knew about the country round about and its roads or paths, and also about their own peregrinations with herds and tents in different seasons. They could peep into my tent and see that I lay on the ground as they did themselves, and that the furniture was for the rest simpler than in their own airy dwellings. No images of gods, no burning lamps, a *peling*,[2] a heathen, who did not believe in the transmigration of souls and who would never go to sleep in the Nirvana which lured their imagination.

SVEN HEDIN AS ARTIST p.47–48

Brass cups for placing offerings (Gyantse:Pelkor Chode)

Notes

1 A watercolor of the monastery of Selipuk Templeon on the lakeshore of Nganglaring-tso is included as Illustration 361 in *Trans-Himalaya* II. The painting vividly captures the fluttering of a great many *tarcho* (དར་ཆོག་ *dar chog*) prayer flags. Unfortunately, no reproduction of this picture has been left behind.

2 At several points, Hedin's *Trans-Himalaya* describes local Tibetans referring to Europeans as "Peling," or else discovering that he was in fact a Peling. This term in the Tibetan language is ཕྱི་གླིང་པ་ *phi gling pa*, i.e., foreigner, and is particularly used in reference to Westerners. I think the sound of the final *pa* (a suffix indicating "people") might not be recognized, since it is an unaccented syllable.

Trans-Himalaya II, Illustration 361

[Reproduction 49] Adachi Itarō, Pen and Water Color, 9.9 × 32.3 cm

Ascetic monks engaged in religious catechism (Shigatse: Tashi Lhunpo Monastery) ©IKD

Tibetan Temple Monasteries

Sven Hedin (*Trans-Himalaya* II, Illustration 360)

49 White-walled brick monastery and monks

According to the handwritten note on the reproduction, the name of the temple is Mendong. Though the original is lost, this picture appears in color as Illustration 360 in *Trans-Himalaya* II with the caption "Mendong monastery west of the Teri-nam-tso." Aside from this picture, unfortunately, there are no reproductions to be found of sketches or panoramas of Terinam Lake or its environs, Hedin's praise of the lake's beauty notwithstanding. A group of monks dressed in red robes gather in front of an outer wall of white-painted brick. Perhaps they are engaged in one of the religious debates that are part of the monastic training of Tibetan Buddhists. These are heated dialogues that offer no quarter as the monks test one another's knowledge and pounce on their opponents' logical inconsistencies in a style akin to martial arts. The photo shows debates taking place in the central courtyard in front of the Kyikang Dratsang or Exoteric Buddhist Seminary (དཀྱིལ་ཁང་གྲྭ་ཚང་ *dkyilkhang grwa tshang* [lit. Central College]) at Tashi Lhunpo in Shigatse.

[Reproduction 50] Pen, 20.4 × 25.4 cm

50 Four people resting at an entrance: smoking break

The reproduction has no handwriting on it, while the original bears only Hedin's signature and the year 1908. As the sketch does not appear in *Trans-Himalaya* or *Sven Hedin as Artist*, this is unfortunately all the information we have about it. Four people – men and women who appear to be pilgrims – are resting in front of a doorway. The door opens inward to an interior in deep shadow, in contrast to the bright sunlight outside. A woman with a cloth wrapped around her head sits in front of the door, and the person sitting in front of her smokes a long pipe. The traces of paint lines on the walls suggest that they have been plastered. A long curtain normally suspended over the door has been tied up and back with a rope to expose the entrance. The layout of this entrance closely resembles the entrance to Mendong monastery shown in the previous picture (Reproduction 49). In that scene, too, the door stands open in bright sunlight while the interior is in shadow, and a long curtain over the doorway is tied back with a rope. It seems likely that Hedin sketched four pilgrims he saw resting at the entrance to this monastery.

[Original 50] Sven Hedin, 1908, Pencil and Pen, 20.2 × 25.4 cm

A group of pilgrims from Chamdo in the Kham region (Lhasa: Drepung Monastery)

A woman spinning wool at the entrance to a house (Nakartse: near Yamdrok Lake) ©IKD

The Four Great Heavenly Kings, painted on a temple entrance at Drepung Monastery in Lhasa. From the top, the illustrations show *Vaiśravaṇa*, a mongoose held in Vaiśravaṇa's hand, *Virūḍhaka*, and *Dhṛtarāṣṭra*. The fourth king, *Virūpākṣa*, appears with Reproduction 4.

Commentary
The Four Great Kings in Tibetan Buddhism

In the entrance halls of temples in the Tibetan Buddhist tradition, magnificent painted murals can sometimes be seen depicting the Four Great Heavenly Kings (Skt. *caturmahārāja*) of Buddhism. In the Tibetan Buddhist tradition, these Four Great Kings are the guardians of the Dharma, who protect the four directions of the world. In the Tibetan language, they are called Gyälchen rikshi (རྒྱལ་ཆེན་རིགས་བཞི་ *rgyal chen rigs bzhi*), and their aspects and worldly countenances are painted beside the entrances to halls of study and mausolea in Tibetan temples in order that evil will not enter within. These guardians were originally venerated as deities watching over gates opening in each of the four directions from the Palace of the *Trāyastriṃśa* Heaven, the home of the Buddhist guardian deity Indra (also known as *Śakra*) at the summit of the mythical Mount Sumeru. Having devoted themselves to Buddhism after hearing the teachings of the Buddha, they are believed to have been entrusted with the protection of the Dharma after the death of the Buddha.

Chief among the Four Great Kings is *Vaiśravaṇa*, derived from the Skt. root *vi-śru* "hear distinctly," the guardian of the north and of winter whose name means "he who hears everything." In the Tibetan language, he is called Nam thö sä (རྣམ་ཐོས་སྲས་ *rnam thos sras*) and is often portrayed with a yellow face. The gem in the maw of a mongoose held in his left hand symbolizes wealth, and by waving the banner, known as a *dhvaja* (རྒྱལ་མཚན་ *rgyal mtshan*) held in his right, he is said to impart that wealth to the multitudes.

The guardian of the south and of summer is *Virūḍhaka*, whose name means "he who causes to grow;" he battles ignorance and protects the roots of humanity's inherent goodness. In Tibetan, he is called Phak kye po (འཕགས་སྐྱེས་པོ་ *'phags skyes po*), and is depicted with a blue face, often wearing a helmet fashioned from an elephant's head and brandishing a sword drawn from its sheath. Virūḍhaka's sword is said to signify his protection of the Dharma from all who would go against it.

The guardian of the east and of spring is *Dhṛtarāṣṭra*, as suggested by his name, which means "he who upholds the realm," he is the protector of the nation. In Tibetan, he is called Yül khor sung (ཡུལ་འཁོར་སྲུང་ *yul 'khor srung*) and is depicted with a white face holding a dram nyän (སྒྲ་སྙན་ *sgra snyan*), a kind of Himalayan lute. When Dhṛtarāṣṭra plays his dram nyän, its timbre is said to protect the entire world.

The guardian of the west and of autumn is *Virūpākṣa*, "he who sees all," and is often depicted girded for battle, standing atop a rock or devil. In Tibetan, he is called Chän mi zang (སྤྱན་མི་བཟང་ *spyan mi bzang*); he has a red face and holds a stupa and serpent in his two hands.

It should also be noted that while the cardinal directions watched over by these Four Heavenly Kings is predetermined, differences in directions arising from the layout of temple buildings mean that the order and arrangement of the positions in which the guardians are depicted on the walls of entrances is not fixed. Since it is normally the case that two guardians must be depicted on each of the walls to either side of a temple's front entrance, even attempts to uphold the principle will always encounter some contradiction or another.

Tibetan Temple Monasteries

[Reproduction 51] Adachi Itarō, Pencil, 25.5 × 40.9 cm

Vista over the Yarlung Tsangpo River Basin (along the road from Lhasa to Shigatse)

51 Terrain of the Sutlej River valley and Kyunglung Gompa

The note on the reproduction reads "Kjung-lung-gompa, Camp 463." "Gompa" means "temple" or "monastery" in Tibetan. Though the original is lost and its whereabouts unknown, this picture appears in *Trans-Himalaya* III as Illustration 95 with the caption "Kyung-lung-gompa and the Sutlej." Camp 463 was located on the Sutlej River about 80 kilometers downstream toward India from Langa-tso or Lake Rakshastal (ལག་ངར་མཚོ་ *lag ngar mtsho* 拉昂错). The Sutlej has its source at Lake Manasarovar and Lake Rakshastal, which are located near the sacred Mount Kailash in the Himalaya range in the southwest corner of Tibet. From there the river flows west, cuts through the Himalaya range, turns southwest along the border of Pakistan and northern India, crosses the Punjab Plain, joins the Chenab River in central Pakistan, and flows from there into the Indus. It is about 1,400 kilometers long. One of the greatest achievements of Hedin's third central Asia expedition was his confirmation of the source of the Sutlej. In the final stage of that expedition, Hedin left Bongba province via Lake Manasarovar and followed the Sutlej downriver to Simla, India.

[Reproduction 52 (left half)] Nishikawa Junji, Pen, 25.6 × 40.5 cm

52,53 Daba monastery atop a hill

The reproduction was divided down the middle and preserved as two separate sheets. Both halves carry the inscription "reproduced by Junji Nishikawa" at the bottom left. The original is a single long panorama on sheets glued together into one continuous piece. However, the presence of Hedin's signature and the year 1908 in two places – at the bottom center and the bottom right – indicates that it was originally divided down the middle into two sheets in the same manner as the reproduction; also, each of these sheets was further folded in half. For purposes of display in this book, the two halves of the reproduction have been combined into one sheet resembling the original. Both the reproduction and original bear the handwritten place name "Dava" in the same general area at the lower left. The picture appears as Illustration 105 in *Trans-Himalaya* III with the caption "Lama dwellings in Daba-gompa." Daba (མདའ་བ་ *mda' ba* 達巴, pronounced as *dawa* or *daba*) is located near Camp 469 at around 31.2° north latitude, 79.9° east longitude on the Sutlej River about 80 kilometers further downstream from the Kyunglung Gompa at Camp 463 portrayed in the line drawing above (Reproduction 51). According to an entry in *Trans-Himalaya* II (p. 416), Hedin visited this monastery sometime between August 1 and 13, 1908.

[Original 52 (left half)] Sven Hedin, 1908, Pencil and Pen, 25.4 × 40.5 cm

Tibetan Temple Monasteries

[Reproduction 53 (right half)] Nishikawa Junji, Pen, 25.3 x 40.3 cm

[Original 53 (right half)] Sven Hedin, 1908, Pencil and Pen, 25.4 × 40.5 cm

[Reproduction 54] Nishikawa Junji, Pencil and Water Color, 25.4 × 40.3 cm

[Original 54] Sven Hedin, 1908, Pencil, Pen, and Water Color, 25.3 × 40.3 cm

54 Deva King paintings at a temple entrance (Daba monastery)

The picture shows a temple exterior to the left of its entrance. What appear to be two of the Four Deva Kings are painted on the wall, but the mural is crumbling, exposing bare bricks underneath. Ritual implements and banners are piled up haphazardly in front. In the handwritten inscription that appears on both the reproduction and the original, the first word appears to be "Gältjen," referring to the (Four) Heavenly Kings, or རྒྱལ་ཆེན་ (རིགས་བཞི་) *rgyal chen (rigs bzhi)*. What follows is difficult to decipher, but it could be an attempt to write "three directions of the picture for the (Four) Heavenly Kings" (རྒྱལ་ཆེན་བྲིས་སྐུའི་སུམ་ཕྱོགས་ *srgyal chen bris sku'i gsum phyogs*). The word "Dava" at the end of the inscription indicates that this is the entrance to a temple at Daba monastery. The original bears Hedin's signature and the year 1908. The picture does not appear in either *Trans-Himalaya* or *Sven Hedin as Artist*, so unfortunately, this is all we know about it.

Tibetan Temple Monasteries

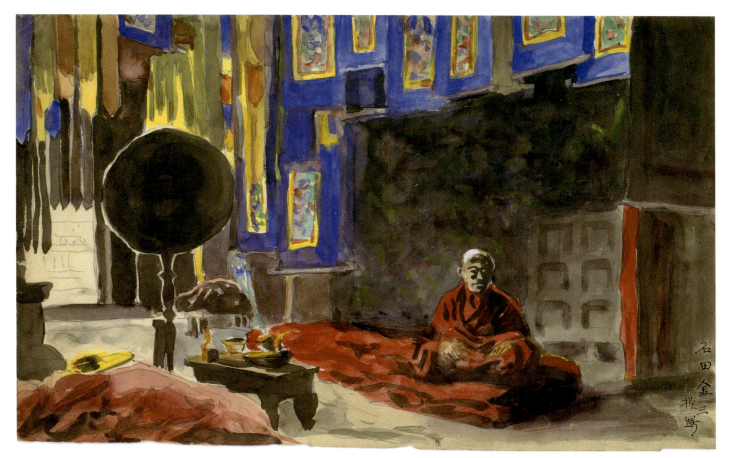

[Reproduction 55] Ishida Kinzō, Pencil and Water Color, 25.4 × 39.8 cm

55 Monk sitting in a temple with a large drum

A monk sits in a temple chamber with a large drum in silhouette and many *thangka* (scroll-like Buddhist paintings) hanging from the ceiling. The picture does not appear in either *Trans-Himalaya* or *Sven Hedin as Artist*, the original is lost, and the reproduction contains no inscription, so there is no way to identify the temple. It may be unrelated to Daba monastery, but I have inserted this picture here to illustrate the following commentary by Hedin about Tibetan temple interiors in *Sven Hedin as Artist*: "From the sunlight outside and from the vestibule protected by the four spirit-kings one nearly always enters a room so dark that it takes quite a time for the eye to become accustomed to the meagre light. [...] From the beading of the impluvium are suspended neatly painted tankas" (*As Artist* p. 47). The painting vividly depicts the blue of the *thangka* backing and the red of the monk's robe, which glow in the sunlight that shines in from the entrance at left. The contrast with the dark space behind the monk where the light does not reach, and the large black silhouette of the backlit drum, brilliantly expresses the shades of color in a temple interior that receives minimal light.

Interior of a brightly colored temple equipped with large drums (Gyantse: Pelkor Chode)

[Reproduction 56] Ishida Kinzō, Pen, 26.7 × 38.7 cm

56 Altar and scripture case (Daba monastery)

The writing on both the reproduction and the original is not clear, but appears to read "Lama lagang Dava." "Lama lagang" probably means (བླ་མ་ལྷ་ཁང་ *bla ma lha khang*), or "Lama's temple," while "Dava" is a place name, in this case, the name of the monastery. The picture appears as Illustration 111 in *Trans-Himalaya* III with the caption "In the temple of Daba-gompa. To the left a case with the holy books." In Hedin's commentary in *Sven Hedin as Artist*, he writes: "On inbuilt book-shelves lie the parchment leaves of the sacred texts between two loose wooden covers wrapped around with leather bands" (*As Artist* p. 47). However, Tibetans have traditionally produced their own indigenous paper, not parchment, for printing scriptures. When the Japanese Buddhist monk and scholar Tada Tōkan 多田等観 commissioned the printing of the Dérgé edition of the Tibetan Buddhist Canon, which he had brought back to Japan, it is said that he procured high-quality paper from Bhutan. However, the tradition of Tibetan-style papermaking no longer survives in Bhutan today, and while paper is still made from local grasses in Dérgé (Sichuan province), home of the Sutra Printing House, it is a thick paper for Buddhist paintings, and the thinner, uniform-quality paper required for printing scriptures is factory-made. From the seventeenth century on, translated sutras and commentaries were actively compiled and printed in various parts of Tibet to produce the Tibetan Buddhist Canon, of which the eighteenth-century Dérgé edition is representative. The Canon is divided into two parts, the Kangyur (བཀའ་འགྱུར་ *bka' 'gyur* 甘珠尔) or "Words (of the Buddha)," a compilation of scriptural texts, and the Tängyur (བསྟན་འགྱུར་ *bstan 'gyur* 丹珠尔) or "Treatises," a compilation of treatises and commentaries. The scriptures are printed horizontally on both sides of long sheets of paper, 7 to 10 lines on each side, with the top and bottom reversed. These sheets are stacked unbound to form a volume, which is

Tibetan Temple Monasteries

[Original 56] Sven Hedin, 1908, Pencil and Pen, 25.4 × 40.4 cm

wrapped in cloth and placed between two boards for storage. A label with the volume number is affixed to the edge. The texts shown in Hedin's sketch appear to be for daily use in recitations and are stored on the shelves in a haphazard manner. However, as most of the Canon record the venerated words of the Buddha, the texts are more commonly stored carefully on shelves in the back of the lecture hall, where they are treated as objects of worship and offerings of flowers and incense are made.

The Tibetan Buddhist Canon stored on a dedicated shelf (Gyantse: Pelkor Chode, Assembly Hall)

[Reproduction 57] Adachi Itarō, Pencil, 25.2 × 17.6 cm

Tibetan Temple Monasteries

[Original 57] Sven Hedin, 1907, Pencil, 25.0 × 17.6 cm

The thin white fabric that can be seen in front of the statue of Maitreya Bodhisattva in the photograph is an offering of khata (silk gauze). Only recently has it become common to see orange-colored khata hanging from the hands of the figures of bodhisattva (Gyantse: Pelkor Chode, Assembly Hall) ©IKD

57 Seated image of the Bodhisattva Maitreya

Though the original of this picture survives, it does not appear in *Trans-Himalaya* or *Sven Hedin as Artist*. There is no written note on the reproduction, and the original has only the word "Tjomba" – most likely a transliteration of the Tibetan *champa* (བྱམས་པ་ *byams pa*), i.e., the Bodhisattva Maitreya. The figure appears to be in a sitting position, a characteristic portrayal of Maitreya. Tibetan Buddha images tend to have upper eyelids that are curved slightly downward, a way of expressing the Buddha's compassion as he gazes down on all sentient beings. Hedin describes this as "dreaming eyes." Maitreya is a Bodhisattva (a Buddha in training) who is destined to become the next Buddha following the present-day Buddha Gautama (Shakyamuni). He is to appear in this world 5,670,000,000 years after Gautama's death, whereupon he will achieve enlightenment and save humanity. Until then, he resides and trains or preaches in Tusita, one of the Buddhist heavens where all future Buddhas dwell. The world's largest statue of a sitting Maitreya can be found at Tashi Lhunpo monastery. Built in 1914 by the [6th] Panchen Lama IX, with whom Hedin had an audience, it did not yet exist when Hedin visited Tashi Lhunpo in 1907. Hence, this sketch is not a depiction of the Maitreya statue that is a principal image at Tashi Lhunpo. Hedin's signature and the year 1907 are written in the bottom right corner of the original, but unfortunately, there are no other notes or mentions about this picture, making it difficult to identify the temple where it was drawn.

[Reproduction 58] Nishikawa Junji, Pencil, Pen, and Water Color, 25.2 × 40.2 cm

In the center of the photo, the Maitreya Bodhisattva stands behind Je Tsongkhapa, who stands behind a statue of the [7th] Panchen Lama X in the very front (Shigatse: Tashi Lhunpo Monastery, Kangyur Lhakang)

[Original 58] Sven Hedin, 1907, Pencil, Pen, and Water Color, 25.2 × 40.4 cm

58 Altar with Buddhist statuary at Mangnang monastery

The reproduction carries no inscription at all, while the original has only a signature and the year 1907 in the bottom right corner (an error: the year should be 1908, indicating that this date was probably added later). The picture appears in color as Illustration 382 in *Trans-Himalaya* II with the caption "Altar table with images of gods in Mangnang-gompa." Other than this picture, there is no description of Mangnang Gompa. But the name Mangnang appears in a passage in *Trans-Himalaya* II on page 416: "We parted with floods of tears on August 1 and my party travelled past the three monasteries, Dongbo, Dava, and Mangnang (Illust. 382), and came to Totling-gompa on the 13th, …" enabling us to determine that it was the monastery Hedin visited after Daba as he retreated down the Sutlej River toward Simla. As the picture shows, altars in Tibetan temples often have arrayed before them small statues of various venerable figures of the Buddhist pantheon. The sitting and standing figures in the middle of the array are mostly saints who accrued merit by saving sentient beings in this world. The larger statues tend to be those of Bodhisattva and higher rank.

[Reproduction 59] Nishikawa Junji, Pencil, 25.4 × 40.1 cm

59 Monk sitting in a temple with a large drum

The reproduction and original both bear the handwritten inscription "Döltja-gompa" at the bottom left, while the original also has Hedin's signature and the year 1908. *Gompa* is a Tibetan word for monastery. The year 1908 indicates that this sketch was made en route down the Sutlej River to Simla toward the end of Hedin's third central Asia expedition, after he had explored the Bongba region in the south-central part of the Changtang Plateau. Hedin's route map, though, does not include any place name corresponding to Döltja Gompa, so the actual location is unknown. This picture does not appear in *Trans-Himalaya* or *Sven Hedin as Artist*, nor is this monastery mentioned in the text of *Trans-Himalaya*. Unfortunately, we have no further information about it. The drawing shows a monk sitting next to a large drum inside a temple. There is another picture of a large drum in a temple, the watercolor described earlier (Reproduction 55), but we do not know where that temple is located, either. Although the composition of the two pictures is similar, they differ in the arrangement of ritual implements and the shape of the drum, so the locations are clearly different.

Tibetan Temple Monasteries

[Original 59] Sven Hedin, 1908, Pencil, 25.0 × 35.1 cm

Large drum placed in a temple supported by a red lacquered pillar
(Gyantse: Pelkor Chode, Assembly Hall) ©IKD

[Reproduction 60] Nishikawa Junji, Pencil, 27.4 × 21.3 cm

[Original 60] Sven Hedin, 1906, Pencil, 25.4 × 20.4cm

60 Entrance to the palace in Leh (Ladakh)

Of the extant reproductions, only this one is of a picture drawn in Leh, Ladakh in 1906, just before the departure of the third central Asia expedition. It appears as Figure 95 in *Sven Hedin as Artist* with the caption "Main gateway in Leh. Ladak 1906" and as Illustration 33 in *Trans-Himalaya* I with the caption "Portal of the palace in Leh." In *Trans-Himalaya*, Hedin describes the palace: "The old palace of Leh stands on its rock like a gigantic monument of vanished greatness." Hedin goes on to describe the view of the town of Leh from the roof: "The portal of the palace with its pillars has a very picturesque effect. Through this portal, you enter a long, dark, paved entrance and then pass up a stone staircase and through gloomy passages and corridors, with small offshoots running up to balcony windows; in the interior, however, you roam about through halls all equally dark. No one currently dwells now in this phantom castle, which fancy might easily make the scene of the most extravagant ghost stories. Only pigeons, which remain forever young among the old time-worn monuments, coo out their contentment and cheerfulness" (passages abridged from *Trans-Himalaya* I, p. 58). Leh in Ladakh is the westernmost community within the Tibetan cultural sphere. The distinctive design of the columns at the entrance to the palace has something in common with the columns and lion-head carvings visible at the entrances to the mausoleums of Tashi Lhunpo, far to the east in central Tibet.

Epilogue

Although Sven Hedin had aimed for Lhasa on his second central Asia expedition in 1901, his advance was blocked in Nakchukha, about 300 km north of Lhasa, whence he was forced to withdraw without crossing the Nyenchen Tanglha Mountains. As an initial objective on his third expedition, as well, he had planned to arrive in Lhasa, but along the way, he was blocked by Hlaje Tsering, the Governor of Naktsang. He decided to change his route to go to Shigatse, the location of the Tashi Lhunpo Monastery, seat of the Panchen Lama. From Hedin's perspective, a number of foreigners had already entered Lhasa, and the situation in the areas around Lhasa and to the east (the Ü region) was relatively well known. At the time of Hedin's departure for the third expedition in 1906, the plateau area extending north of the Yarlung Tsangpo and west of Lhasa was unexplored, a blank area on a map; the main goal of this expedition was to clarify the geography of the area. Therefore, Hedin likely would not have worried much about making it to Lhasa in the end.

Years earlier, in 1903, Great Britain had sent an armed delegation into Tibet under the command of Col. Francis Younghusband. Just before the British forces reached Lhasa, the 13th Dalai Lama had gone into exile, fleeing Lhasa for Urga in Mongolia (now Ulaanbaatar), where he stayed for over a year before traveling through Qinghai to arrive in Peking in September 1908. However, he was given a cold welcome by the Qing Dynasty, which wanted to colonize Tibet. He returned to Lhasa at the end of 1909 after staying in China for just over a year. In 1907, the year that Hedin visited Tibet on his third expedition, the 13th Dalai Lama was away from Tibet. Due to this contingent circumstance, the [6th] Panchen Lama IX acted as the representative of Tibet and extended his hospitality to Hedin, who was familiar with the international situation.

When he left Shigatse, Hedin traveled west along the Yarlung Tsangpo, and then returned temporarily to Leh in Ladakh by way of Mount Kailash and Lake Manasarovar to resupply his party. He then set out once again diagonally across the Changtang Plateau and explored the mountainous region of Western Tibet that spreads out north of the Yarlung Tsangpo until the first part of the next year before making his way from Lake Manasarovar along the Sutlej River to Shimla in India, where he brought the third expedition to an end. Then, responding to an invitation from Japan before his return home, he carried his sketches of the field with him to Japan.

Sven Hedin never saw Lhasa's Potala Palace, once home to the Dalai Lamas, and a symbolic presence in Tibet today.

Supplementary Table
List of Reproductions, Original Artworks, and Illustrations in Hedin's Books, etc.
Ikeda Takumi and Tanaka Kazuko

Figure no.	Painter's name — Upper row: Reproduction / Lower row: Original by Hedin	Object of artwork	Notes attached	Year written on original artwork	Place/camp where work was created	Pencil/pen watercolor black and white	Height x width (cm)	Illustrations and sketches in Hedin's books	Organisation holding materials: ID — Upper row: KU (Kyoto University) / Lower row: EM (Etnografiska Museet)
1	Adachi Itarō	View of Tashi Lhunpo	No	—	Shigatse	Pencil	25.1 × 35.4	*Trans-Himalaya*, Vol. I (1910), Illustration 118; *Sven Hedin as Artist* (1964), No. 110	KU:I-5
	—		No	1907		Pencil and pen	25.1 × 35.4		EM: A:1 VI:542
2	Nishikawa Junji	Tashi Lhunpo Monastery: Façade of the Labrang	Yes	—	Shigatse	Pencil, pen, and watercolor	25.0 × 35.2	—	KU:I-13
	—		Yes	08		Pencil, pen, and watercolor	25.1 × 35.4		EM: Shelf A:2 VI:574
3	Nishikawa Junji	Staircase to the Mausoleum of the [5th] Panchen Lama VIII	Yes	—	Shigatse	Pencil	25.5 × 35.3	*Trans-Himalaya*, Vol. I (1910), Illustration 133.	KU:I-3
	—		Yes	07		Pencil and pen	25.0 × 35.3		EM: Shelf A:1 VI: 547
4	Tanaka Zennosuke	Four Deva Kings Outside a Mausoleum Entrance	No	—	Shigatse	Watercolor	25.4 × 35.2	*Trans-Himalaya*, Vol. III (1913), frontispiece. (black-and-white)	KU:I-21
	—		No	1907		Watercolor	25.0 × 35.3		EM: Shelf A:1 VI:558
5	Nishikawa Junji	Monk opening the door to the Mausoleum of the [5th] Panchen Lama VIII	No	—	Shigatse	Pen and watercolor	24.9 × 35.1	*Trans-Himalaya*, Vol. I (1910), Illustration 132.	KU:I-22
	—		No	07		Pen and watercolor	25.2 × 40.1		EM: A:1 VI:556
6	Nishikawa Junji	Altar before the Stupa of the [5th] Panchen Lama VIII	Yes	—	Shigatse	Pen	35.2 × 25.2	*Trans-Himalaya*, Vol. I (1910), Illustration 126; *Sven Hedin as Artist* (1964), No. 113	KU:I-18
	—		Yes	1907		Pen	35.3 × 25.1		EM: A:1 VI:548
7	Nishikawa Junji	Stupa of a Panchen Lama	No	—	Shigatse	Pen and Black-and white Color	35.3 × 24.8	*Trans-Himalaya*, Vol. I (1910), Illustration 125	KU:I-7
	—		No	1907		Pen and Black-and white Color	35.4 × 25.0		EM: A:1 VI:545
8	Adachi Itarō	Framed sign over the entrance of the Mausoleum of the [3rd] Panchen Lama VI	Yes	—	Shigatse	Pencil	35.1 × 25.1	*Trans-Himalaya*, Vol. I (1910), Illustration 128	KU:I-4
	—		Yes	07		Pencil and pen	35.3 × 25.2		EM: Shelf A:1 VI: 546

List of Reproductions, Original Artworks, and Illustrations in Hedin's Books, etc.

Figure no.	Painter's name Upper row: Reproduction Lower row: Original by Hedin	Object of artwork	Notes attached	Year written on original artwork	Place/camp where work was created	Pencil/pen watercolor black and white	Height x width (cm)	Illustrations and sketches in Hedin's books	Organisation holding materials: ID Upper row: KU (Kyoto University) Lower row: EM (Etnografiska Museet)
9	Nishikawa Junji	Double Colonnade alongside the Lecture Court	Yes	—	Shigatse	Pencil	25.0 × 35.2	*Trans-Himalaya*, Vol. I (1910), Illustration 142	KU:I-15
	—		Yes	1907		Pencil	25.0 x 35.4		EM: Shelf A:1 VI:543
10	Tanaka Zennosuke	Trainee Monks Reading Scriptures	No	—	Shigatse	Pencil	25.1 × 35.2	*Trans-Himalaya*, Vol. I (1910), Illustration 154; *Sven Hedin as Artist* (1964), No. 114.	KU:I-23
	—		No	1907		Pencil	25.0 x 35.3		EM: Shelf A:1 VI:537
11	Adachi Itarō	Trainee Monks Reading Scriptures	Yes	—	Shigatse	Pencil	25.1 × 35.4	*Trans-Himalaya*, Vol. I (1910), Illustration 127; *Sven Hedin as Artist* (1964), No. 115.	KU:I-25
(Original is missing)	—		—	—		—	—		EM: Not found
12	Adachi Itarō	Statue of Tsongkhapa in the Namgyal-lhakang	No	—	Shigatse	Pencil and watercolor	25.2 × 17.5	*Trans-Himalaya*, Vol. I (1910), Illustration 129	KU:I-8
	—		No	1907		Pencil and watercolor	25.1 x 17.5		EM: B:11 VI:373
13	Tanaka Zennosuke	Statue of Tsongkhapa in the Namgyal-lhakang	No	—	—	Pencil	25.1 × 35.6	—	KU:I-19
	—		No	1907		Pencil and pen	25.0 x 35.4		EM: Shelf A:1 VI:550
14	Adachi Itarō	Shigatse Dzong	Yes	—	Shigatse	Pencil	25.1 × 35.8	*Sven Hedin as Artist* (1964), No. 107	KU:I-6
	—		Yes	1907		Pencil	25.1 x 35.3		EM: Shelf A:1 VI: 552
15	Nishikawa Junji	Mendicant Monk with a Prayer Wheel	Yes	—	Shigatse	Pencil	25.2 × 17.6	*Trans-Himalaya*, Vol. III (1913), Illustration 84; *Sven Hedin as Artist* (1964), No. 133.	KU:II-32
	—		Yes	1907		Pencil	25.0 x 17.5		EM: B:9 VI:132
16	Adachi Itarō	Woman of Shigatse with a Headdress	No	—	Shigatse	Pencil	35.7 × 25.6	*Trans-Himalaya*, Vol. I (1910), Illustration 158; *Sven Hedin as Artist* (1964), No. 134	KU:I-9
(Original is missing)	—		—	—		—	—		EM: Not found
17	Nishikawa Junji	Girl of Shigatse with a Headdress	Yes	—	Shigatse	Pencil	33.3 × 25.3	—	KUD:I-12
	—		Yes	1907		Pencil	35.4 x 25.1		EM: A:1 VI:512
18	Nishikawa Junji	Four People in Front of a Temple Entrance	No	—	—	Pencil	25.2 × 17.6	—	KU:II-8
	—		No	1907		Pencil	25.1 x 17.5		EM: B:11 VI:364

Figure no.	Painter's name Upper row: Reproduction Lower row: Original by Hedin	Object of artwork	Notes attached	Year written on original artwork	Place/camp where work was created	Pencil/pen watercolor black and white	Height x width (cm)	Illustrations and sketches in Hedin's books	Organisation holding materials: ID Upper row: KU (Kyoto University) Lower row: EM (Etnografiska Museet)
19	Ishida Kinzō	Landscape with People Resting by a Lake and a Cairn	Yes	—	C302	Pencil and watercolor	8.0×25.2	*Southern Tibet* (1917), Vol. III, p.316 (Illustration on the upper row).	KUD:II-4
(Original is missing)	—		—	—		—	—		EM: Not found
20	Nishikawa Junji	View of Mountains on the Changtang Plateau	Yes	—	C304	Pencil and watercolor	9.9 × 25.1	*Southern Tibet* (1917), Vol. IV, p.221 (Illustration on the lower row).	KU:II-5
	—		Yes	1908		Pencil and watercolor	9.9 x 25.0		EM: B:11 VI:384
21	Ishida Kinzō	Lake and Mountains in the Moonlight	No	—	C310	Watercolor	9.6 × 25.1	—	KU:II-6
(Original is missing)	—		—	—		—	—		EM: Not found
22	Nishikawa Junji	Snowy Mountains in the Setting Sun	Yes	—	C320	Pencil and watercolor	7.9 × 25.1	—	KU:II-2
	—		Yes	06		Pencil and watercolor	7.8 x 25.1		EM: C:8 VI:464
23	Ishida Kinzō	Mountain Landscape in the Bongba District	Yes	—	C422	Pen	21.0 × 63.5	*Trans-Himalaya*, Vol. II (1910), Illustration 299; *Southern Tibet* (1917), Vol. III, p.353 (Illustration on the lower row).	KU:II-3
	—		Yes	1907		Pen	21.4 x 64.6 (28.5 x 70.0)		EM: Shelf No Reference Number
24	Adachi Itarō	Portrait of the Bodyguard Nima Tashi	Yes	—	Saga	Pencil	32.0 × 21.3	*Sven Hedin as Artist* (1964), No. 146.	KU:II-24
	—		Yes	1908		Pencil	32.2 x 20.1		EM: B:10 VI:219
25	Adachi Itarō	Standing Figure of the Bodyguard Nima Tashi	Yes	—	En route to Teri-nam-tso	Pencil and watercolor	25.4 × 20.2	*Trans-Himalaya*, Vol. II (1910), Illustration 353.	KU:II-21
	—		Yes	1908		Pencil and watercolor	25.4 x 20.1		EM: B:10 VI:315
26	Adachi Itarō	Young Militia Boy with a Rifle	No	—	—	Pen and watercolor	25.4 × 20.3	—	KU:II-14
(Original is missing)	—		—	—	—	—	—		EM: Not found
27	Nishikawa Junji	Bodyguard Riding a Yak	No	—	—	Pencil and pen	20.4 × 25.2	*Trans-Himalaya*, Vol. II (1910), Illustration 348.	KU:II-30
	—		No	1908		Pencil and pen	20.2 x 25.4		EM: B:11 VI:405
28	Nishikawa Junji	Young Shepherd of Bongba	Yes	—	Vicinity of C420	Pencil and pen	25.3×20.2	*Trans-Himalaya*, Vol. II (1910), Illustration 350.	KU:II-34
	—		Yes	1908		Pencil and pen	25.3 x 20.1		EM: B:10 VI:266
29	Not written	Two Guides from Bongba	Yes	—	—	Pen	25.5 × 20.1	*Trans-Himalaya*, Vol. II (1910), Illustration 363.	KU:II-17
	—		Yes	1908		Pencil and pen	25.3 x 20.0		EM: B:10 VI:287

List of Reproductions, Original Artworks, and Illustrations in Hedin's Books, etc.

Figure no.	Painter's name — Upper row: Reproduction / Lower row: Original by Hedin	Object of artwork	Notes attached	Year written on original artwork	Place/camp where work was created	Pencil/pen watercolor black and white	Height x width (cm)	Illustrations and sketches in Hedin's books	Organisation holding materials: ID — Upper row: KU (Kyoto University) / Lower row: EM (Etnografiska Museet)
30	Nishikawa Junji	Young Man Wearing a Broad-brimmed Hat	Yes	—	—	Pen	25.6 × 20.0	*Trans-Himalaya*, Vol. II (1910), Illustration 324.	KU:II-33
	—		Yes	1908		Pencil and pen	25.4 x 20.1		EM: C:7 VI:461
31	Nishikawa Junji	Militia Man with a Spear and Long Sword	Yes	—	—	Pen	25.5 × 20.2	*Trans-Himalaya*, Vol. II (1910), Illustration 346.	KU:II-19
	—		Yes	1908		Pencil and pen	25.4 x 20.1		EM: B:10 VI:317
32	Nishikawa Junji	Standing Militia Man with a Rifle on his Back	Yes	—	—	Pencil and pen	25.3 × 20.2	*Trans-Himalaya*, Vol. III (1913), Illustration 63 (people in the middle of three soldiers).	KU:II-27
	—		Yes	1908		Pencil and pen	25.2 x 20.1		EM: B:10 VI:294
33	Nishikawa Junji	Standing Militia Man Holding a Rifle	Yes	—	Saga	Pencil and pen	25.4 × 20.1	*Trans-Himalaya*, Vol. II (1910), Illustration 344.	KU:II-26
	—		Yes	1908		Pencil and pen	25.3 x 20.1		EM: B:10 VI:295
34	Nishikawa Junji	Militia Man Holding a Rifle	Yes	—	—	Pen	25.5 × 20.0	—	KU:II-31
	—		Yes	1908		Pencil and pen	25.4 x 20.3		EM: B:10 VI:302
35	Ishida Kinzō	Dorche Tsuen, Governor of Saga in Profile	Yes	—	Saga	Pencil	34.0×23.3	*Trans-Himalaya*, Vol. II (1910), Illustration 327	KU:I-11
	—		Yes	1908		Pencil	30.2 x 20.3		EM: B:10 VI:217
36	Tanaka Zennosuke	Official of Saga: Portrait of Ngavang	Yes	—	Shigatse	Pencil	32.4 × 21.2	*Trans-Himalaya*, Vol. III (1913), Illustration 78; *Sven Hedin as Artist* (1964), No. 135.	KU:II-15
	—		Yes	1907		Pencil	32.1 x 21.2		EM: B:9 VI:119
37	Nishikawa Junji	Portrait of Local Chief Tagla Tsering	Yes	—	Teri-nam-tso	Pen	32.3 × 21.3	*Trans-Himalaya*, Vol. II (1910), Illustration 329; *Sven Hedin as Artist* (1964), No. 144	KU:I-10
	—		Yes	08		Pencil and pen	32.3 x 21.4		EM: B:10 VI:216
38	Not written	Two Monks	Yes	—	—	Pen	25.4 × 20.1	—	KU:II-18
	—		Yes	1908		Pencil and pen	25.4 x 20.1		EM: B:10 VI:306
39	Nishikawa Junji	Tibetan Man	Yes	—	—	Pencil and pen	25.4 × 20.7	—	KU:II-28
	—		Yes	1908		Pencil and pen	25.5 x 20.5		EM: B:10 VI:305
40	Nishikawa Junji	Portrait	Yes	—	—	Pencil	25.3 × 17.4	—	KU:II-35
	—		Yes	07		Pencil	25.0 x 17.4		EM: B:9 VI:168

Figure no.	Painter's name — Upper row: Reproduction / Lower row: Original by Hedin	Object of artwork	Notes attached	Year written on original artwork	Place/camp where work was created	Pencil/pen watercolor black and white	Height x width (cm)	Illustrations and sketches in Hedin's books	Organisation holding materials: ID — Upper row: KU (Kyoto University) / Lower row: EM (Etnografiska Museet)
41	Adachi Itarō	Portrait of a Tibetan	Yes	—	C440	Pencil and Black-and-white Color	20.2 × 12.4	—	KU:II-11
	—		Yes	1908		Pencil and Black-and-white Color	20.2 × 12.4		EM: C:7 VI:452
42	Ishida Kinzō	Attire of a Nomadic Woman A	Yes	—	Vicinity of C441	Pen and watercolor	25.6 × 20.8	—	KU:II-22
	—		Yes	1908		Pen and watercolor	25.2 × 20.2		EM: B:10 VI:250
43	Adachi Itarō	Attire of a Nomadic Woman B	Yes	—	Vicinity of C442	Pen and watercolor	25.4 × 20.2	Trans-Himalaya, Vol. II (1910), Illustration 362.	KU:II-20
(Original is missing)	—	—	—	—	—	—	—		EM: Not found
44	Nishikawa Junji	Attire of a Nomadic Woman C	No	—	Vicinity of C442	Pen and watercolor	25.4 × 20.1	Trans-Himalaya, Vol. II (1910), Illustration 362.	KU:II-12
(Original is missing)	—	—	—	—	—	—	—		EM: Not found
45	Adachi Itarō	Women in Blue Tibetan Attire	Yes	—	—	Pen and watercolor	25.4 × 20.3	—	KU:II-10
(Original is missing)	—	—	—	—	—	—	—		EM: Not found
46	Nishikawa Junji	Women in Violet Tibetan Attire	Yes	—	Vicinity of C441	Pen and watercolor	25.2 × 20.2	Trans-Himalaya, Vol. II (1910), Illustration 362.	KU:II-13
	—		Yes	1908		Pen and watercolor	25.2 × 20.2		EM: B:11 VI:391
47	Ishida Kinzō	Women in Green Tibetan Attire	Yes	—	—	Pencil, pen, and watercolor	25.6 × 20.3	Trans-Himalaya, Vol. II (1910), Illustration 362.	KU:II-16
	—		Yes	1908		Pencil, pen, and watercolor	25.2 × 20.0		EM: B:10 VI:286
48	Nishikawa Junji	Nomad Child	Yes	—	—	Pencil and pen	25.5 × 20.2	—	KUD:II-23
	—		Yes	1907		Pencil and pen	25.3 × 20.2		EM: B:9 VI:181
49	Adachi Itarō	White-walled Brick Monastery and Monks	Yes	—	West of Teri-nam-tso	Pen and watercolor	9.9 × 32.3	Trans-Himalaya, Vol. II (1910), Illustration 360.	KU:II-7
(Original is missing)	—	—	—	—	—	—	—		EM: Not found
50	Not written	Four People Resting at an Entrance: Smoking Break	No	—	—	Pen	20.4 × 25.4	—	KU:II-9
	—		No	1908		Pencil and pen	20.2 × 25.4		EM: B:11 VI:374

List of Reproductions, Original Artworks, and Illustrations in Hedin's Books, etc.

Figure no.	Painter's name Upper row: Reproduction Lower row: Original by Hedin	Object of artwork	Notes attached	Year written on original artwork	Place/camp where work was created	Pencil/pen watercolor black and white	Height x width (cm)	Illustrations and sketches in Hedin's books	Organisation holding materials: ID Upper row: KU (Kyoto University) Lower row: EM (Etnografiska Museet)
51	Adachi Itarō	Terrain of the Sutlej River Valley and Kyunglung Gompa	Yes	—	C463	Pencil	25.5 × 40.9	*Trans-Himalaya*, Vol. III (1913), Illustration 95.	KU:I-2
(Original is missing)	—		—	—		—	—		EM: Not found
52 (left half)	Nishikawa Junji	Daba Monastery atop a Hill	Yes	—	—	Pen	25.6 × 40.5	*Trans-Himalaya*, Vol. III (1913), Left half of Illustration 105	KU:I-24
	—		Yes	08		Pencil and pen	25.4 x 40.5		EM: Shelf A:2 VI:572
53 (right half)	Nishikawa Junji	Daba Monastery atop a Hill	Yes	—	—	Pen	25.3×40.3	*Trans-Himalaya*, Vol. III (1913), Right half of Illustration 105	KU:I-17
	—		Yes	1908		Pencil and pen	25.4 x 40.5		EM: Shelf A:2 VI:568
54	Nishikawa Junji	Deva King Paintings at a Temple Entrance (Daba Monastery)	Yes	—		Pencil and watercolor	25.4 × 40.3	—	KU:I-14
	—		Yes	1908		Pencil, pen, and watercolor	25.3 x 40.3		EM: A:2 VI:561
55	Ishida Kinzō	Monk Sitting in a Temple with a Large Drum	No	—	—	Pencil and watercolor	25.4 × 39.8	—	KU:I-20
(Original is missing)	—		—	—		—	—		EM: Not found
56	Ishida Kinzō	Altar and Scripture Case (Daba Monastery)	Yes	—	—	Pen	26.7 × 38.7	*Trans-Himalaya*, Vol. III (1913), Illustration 111.	KU:I-26
	—		Yes	1908		Pencil and pen	25.4 x 40.4		EM: Shelf A:2 VI:567
57	Adachi Itarō	Seated Image of the Bodhisattva Maitreya	No	—	—	Pencil	25.2 × 17.6	—	KU:II-29
	—		No	1907		Pencil	25.0 x 17.6		EM: B:9 VI:203
58	Nishikawa Junji	Altar with Buddhist Statuary at Mangnang Monastery	No	—		Pencil, pen, and watercolor	25.2 × 40.2	*Trans-Himalaya*, Vol. II (1910), Illustration 382.	KU:I-27
	—		No	1907		Pencil, pen, and watercolor	25.2 x 40.4		EM: A:1 VI:557
59	Nishikawa Junji	Monk Sitting in a Temple with a Large Drum	Yes	—	—	Pencil	25.4 × 40.1	—	KU:I-16
	—		Yes	1908		Pencil	25.0 x 35.1		EM: Shelf A:2 VI:566
60	Nishikawa Junji	Entrance to the Palace in Leh (Ladakh)	No	—	Leh (Ladakh)	Pencil	27.4×21.3	*Trans-Himalaya*, Vol. I (1910), Illustration 33; *Sven Hedin as Artist* (1964), No. 95.	KU:II-25
	—		No	1906		Pencil	25.4 x 20.4		EM: B:11 VI:326

Section II

Reports: Hedin's Tibetan Expedition and Modern Japan

1 The Headwaters of the "Exploration University"

YAMAGIWA Juichi

Kyoto Imperial University, founded in 1897, consisted of four colleges: Law, Medicine, Letters, and Science and Engineering. It did not yet have an anthropology department at the time of Hedin's visit in 1908. Records show that Hedin's lecture on November 29 was attended by more faculty from the College of Science and Engineering (40 people) than from the College of Letters (17 people), although the address appears to have been principally oriented toward a liberal arts audience which included prominent individuals, such as Naitō Torajirō (aka Naitō Konan), the historian who had been a central force in arranging Hedin's visit. It seems likely that the audience was more interested in the documents and materials that Hedin had collected, and the drawings he had made, than in the expedition *per se*.

By comparison, Tokyo Imperial University, which Hedin had visited earlier, did have an anthropology department. Hedin had been welcomed by the eminent anthropologist Tsuboi Shōgorō, then known for his thesis positing the existence of a pre-Ainu society known as the Koro-pok-guru. He also met Torii Ryūzō, who had done fieldwork in the Kuril Islands, the Kamchatka Peninsula, Taiwan, and the Korean Peninsula, and had published a monograph about the northern Kurils, establishing the legendary basis of the Koro-pok-guru thesis, in 1903. Torii subsequently conducted field studies in physical anthropology, folklore, and archaeology in Manchuria and Mongolia from 1906 to 1907, indicative of the growing tendency for anthropological researchers to conduct fieldwork-based academic studies. In this context, one can easily imagine that Hedin was welcomed as a pioneer. The expansion of Japan's military power over the next few years, though, redirected most exploration away from scholarly curiosity and towards the practical instrument of colonial rule. Despite Torii's continuing commitment to academic fieldwork that ranged widely across Manchuria, Siberia, and South America, dwindling government support would ultimately lead to the marginalization of fieldwork from the mainstream academy.

Kyoto University's own Age of Exploration was somewhat out of sync with these broader political and academic trends. It began in 1931 with the formation of the Academic Alpine Club of Kyoto (AACK), a mountaineering society. A central figure in this context was Imanishi Kinji (1902–1992), who was only six years old at the time of Hedin's visit to Japan. Although Imanishi may have seen records or heard of Hedin while studying at Kyoto Imperial University, there is no mention of Hedin in his writings. Imanishi had demonstrated himself to be an accomplished alpinist touring the Kitayama Mountains of Kyoto as a student at Kyoto Prefecture's First Middle School and Third Higher School. Determined to be the first to reach the as yet unconquered summits, he climbed a series of virgin peaks in Japan before setting his sights on the Himalayas. Before and after World War II, he journeyed on foot to Mount Paektu, the Greater Khingan Range, Sakhalin, Inner Mongolia, and the island of Ponape. While his interest was not only in mountaineering, but also in advancing the scholarly understanding of these places through studies in geology, botany, zoology, and ethnology, his objective was always to learn about a world "never yet seen, never yet experienced." This spirit was gradually ensconced in the academic traditions of Kyoto University, spreading beyond mountaineering to encompass the entirety of the unknown world and stir the hearts of faculty and students to prize creativity and originality.

While I am unable here to look back over the history of AACK in detail, the breadth of its purview is noteworthy. Kuwabara Takeo and Nishibori Eizaburō, who founded AACK with Imanishi, specialized in French literature and inorganic chemistry, respectively, while Imanishi would go on to make his name as an ecologist. Each of these men met acclaim as alpinists, and Nishibori served as captain of the overwintering party on the first Japanese Antarctic Research Expedition (JARE I). Imanishi's pupils, including Fujita Kazuo (geology), Morishita Masaaki (ecology), Kira Tatsuo (plant ecology), Umesao Tadao (ethnology), Nakao Sasuke (ethnobotany), and Itani Jun'ichirō (primatology), would go on to find success across the academy, each conducting academic explorations to develop original theories in their respective disciplines. These pupils all seem to have inherited the trailblazing ambition and applied it to open new areas in their respective disciplines. Although Imanishi and AACK did not follow a single track, they helped to define the explorer's path, sharing the aspiration to "seek out unclimbed peaks" even as they went their disparate ways.

In this context, I would like to try to elaborate on how this ethos of exploration served to shape primatology, the field with which I have been particularly concerned.

During World War II, Imanishi was appointed to direct the Seihoku Laboratory established by the government of Mongolia. What left the strongest impression on him during this time was his encounter with Przewalski's horse, a native subspecies of wild horse. After the war, he immediately set out for Toimisaki (Cape Toi) in Miyazaki Prefecture to undertake a field survey of semi-wild horses. To substantiate a theory that organisms other than human beings had societies, one that he had advanced in his 1941 treatise on *Seibutsu no Sekai* (The world of living things) prior to joining the military, he focused first on equine society. However, after two students participating in this survey in 1948 – Kawamura Shunzō and Itani Jun'ichirō – witnessed a troop of wild Japanese macaques (snow monkeys), Imanishi intuited their advanced sociality and subsequently turned the focus of his research to monkeys. Beginning with feeding monkeys at Kōjima near Cape Toi and Takasakiyama in Ōita Prefecture, as well as elucidating the characteristics and structures of Japanese macaque society, these researchers began to build a research framework for studying primates worldwide. Here, Imanishi's experience as an alpinist had a tremendous influence.

Imanishi adopted what is known as the "polar method," the Antarctic exploration practice of securing the equipment and operation at a base camp from which to deploy teams. The polar method is indispensable when assailing unclimbed peaks. Imanishi negotiated with Ōita city to create a wild monkey park in Takasakiyama, securing external funding to establish a long-term research facility. Then, in 1956, with the backing of the Nagoya Railway Company, he founded the Japan Monkey Centre in the Aichi Prefecture city of Inuyama. Hearkening to the voices of residents lamenting the disappearance of Japanese macaques during the war, he captured and transplanted Japanese macaques from Yakushima to begin creating the wild monkey park in Inuyama. Imanishi's influence can be seen in the appointments of Shibusawa Keizō, a former Governor of the Bank of Japan, and Tamura Tsuyoshi, chairman of National Park Association of Japan, as president and chairman respectively of the Monkey Centre. He was clearly aware that the behind-the-scenes clout of financiers and politicians would be necessary for developing primatology worldwide. The following year, in 1957, *Primates* was launched as the first international academic journal of primatology, with an English edition made possible with funding from the Rockefeller Foundation. After establishing a museum in the Monkey Centre he conceived of a world monkey park, gathering various species of monkeys from around the world. This set the stage for the ape survey expedition to Africa in 1958. With all this activity, though, Imanishi never forgot the mountains. In 1952, he explored Nepal as the advance team leader for an ascent of Manaslu by the Japanese Alpine Club, and in 1955, was part of an expedition as the Karakoram team leader for the Kyoto University Scientific Expedition to the Karakoram and Hindu Kush. In sum, he was a leading figure in both academia and mountaineering.

Before it was discontinued, the ape survey deployed Imanishi and Itani to Africa in 1958, Kawai Masao and Mizuhara Hiroki in 1959, and Itani in 1960. Imanishi toured Uganda, the Democratic Republic of the Congo (hereafter simply "the Congo"), Cameroon, and tropical rainforest gorilla habitats, as well as visiting Western countries to meet with anthropologists and primatologists. Imanishi, who at the time was seeking the origins of the human family in gorilla society, was ultimately forced to suspend his investigations because of the Congo Crisis in 1960. After meeting the English primatologist Jane Goodall, who was conducting a survey of chimpanzees in Gombe on the shores of Lake Tanganyika, Itani, who had given up his work in the Congo, decided that chimpanzees provided a perfect subject for exploring humanity's evolution. Imanishi and Itani subsequently established a base at Kabogo on the shores of Lake Tanganyika, where it was determined that the Japanese ape survey would shift its primary course to the study of chimpanzees.

In 1961, Imanishi began a two-pronged study involving an ape team and a human team. In Kabogo, he established a durable long-term facility using a prefab steel frame donated by Sekisui House, a Japanese housing manufacturer, carrying multiple freight car loads of materials overland by rail from Dar es Salaam. The human team established a base on the savannah near Lake Eyasi, where Tomikawa Morimichi, Umesao Tadao, Wazaki Yōichi and their colleagues began an ethnological survey of the pastoralist Datoga and hunter-gatherer Hadza peoples. Taking over from Imanishi, however, Itani soon encountered a difficulty, namely that it was hard to get a handle on the formation of chimpanzee troops, which had a strong tendency towards fission and fusion. Exasperated, Itani sent three students to different locations, assigning each to approach the survey using a separate methodology. He also decided to leave the Kabogo base, to travel on foot over the plains. Abandoning Imanishi's polar method, he devised a new approach for conducting extensive surveys with small, nimble research teams. Reminiscing on this experience afterwards, Itani says

The Headwaters of the "Exploration University"

It was around 1964 that I had three porters each carrying twenty-five-kilogram loads, for myself carrying a fifteen-kilogram rucksack and a rifle, to complete preparations for being able to spend a week or so in the desolate wilderness. Rice was our main staple, using dried sardines (*dagaa*) from the lake as our protein. I was always at the head of the party, while they walked in single file behind me through the Miombo woodlands, like freight cars pulled along by a steam locomotive. (Itani 1991)

Later, he adds that

my greatest weapon was that I was willing to set foot into unknown territory; my sole objective was to describe everything I observed and the natural surroundings in the field notebook I kept in my pocket. For survey instruments, I had binoculars and a small camera, as well as camping equipment, but even so, lighter was better.

From this time forward, the African ape survey was conducted using Itani's method. Not only did this method make it easier to change research location at a moment's notice, it also kept costs to a minimum.

When I began studying gorillas in the Congo in 1978, I also adopted Itani's fieldwork methods. Hiring two or three Twa hunter-gatherers as guides and another as a porter, I, too, would carry a pack as our small group spent a week or so traipsing around the forests and mountains in search of gorillas. As my surveys were carried out exclusively within the boundaries of a national park, I could not carry a rifle as Itani had, and our protein came from canned sardines or mackerel,

Figure 1.2: Turkana tribesman (sketch by Itani)

Figure 1.1: Chimpanzee (sketch by Itani)

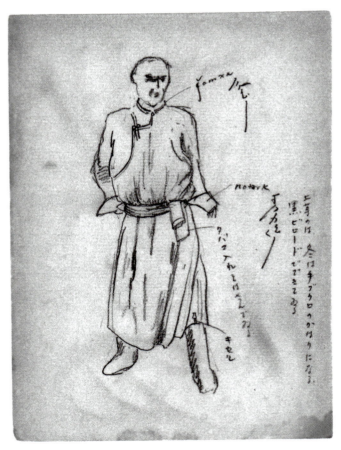

Figure 1.3: How to hold a smoking implement (sketch by Umesao Tadao, from Umesao Tadao's Mongolian Fieldwork Sketchbook). Courtesy of the National Museum of Ethnology, Japan

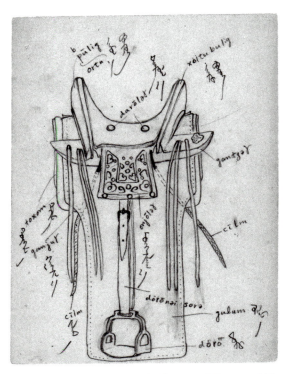

Figure 1.4: Structure of a horse-riding saddle (sketch by Umesao Tadao, from Umesao Tadao's Mongolian Fieldwork Sketchbook) Courtesy of the National Museum of Ethnology, Japan

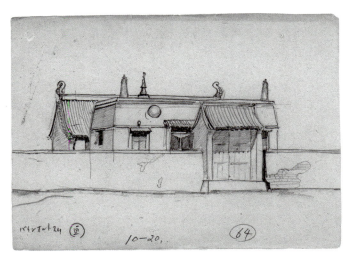

Figure 1.5: Lamasery (sketch by Wazaki Yōichi, from Umesao Tadao's Mongolian Fieldwork Sketchbook) Courtesy of the National Museum of Ethnology, Japan

or fish we caught in the river. For surveys that would last several months, I would put together caravans of around thirty porters, trying to keep the numbers in the camp to a minimum. I never set up a permanent base, endeavoring instead to be able to pull up stakes and withdraw at a moment's notice.

It seems to me that such large-scale projects – academic expeditions, if you like – were a mainstream research practice until the 1980s. Once particular troops of chimpanzees and gorillas, as well as bonobos in the inner reaches of the Congo Basin, had become sufficiently accustomed to the presence of humans to allow for close-up observation of individual behavior, it was possible to fix research sites for longer-term observations. Research technologies changed, as well. When I first entered the field, everyone filled field notebooks with text and pictures. Many researchers drew sketches as accomplished as Hedin's. Itani and Umesao, for example, left behind marvelous sketches.

However, as photographic and recording technologies advanced, researchers who eschewed the use of notebooks also began to appear. In 2001, when I visited Nishida Toshisada, who played a central role in chimpanzee research in Mahale, Tanzania, he recorded a spoken description of chimpanzee behavior while filming with a small handheld video camera. Another method, used for monkeys, involves capturing animals and attaching a small GPS (Global Positioning System) transmitter so that researchers can track their movements. More recently, setting camera traps along animal trails to analyze behavior and frequency of appearance has become a popular practice, as has the use of aerial drones for observation. Another new method involves extracting DNA from feces to estimate properties such as group composition and breeding practices. Methods involving direct contact with animals and the researcher's immersion in their milieu are gradually being replaced.

What has changed even more is the reaction of the local populace where such expeditions are undertaken. When I began investigating gorillas in the 1970s and 1980s, researchers were tolerated, admittedly as somewhat odd characters, regardless of their interests. However, as conservation activities and studies of wild animals have grown in popularity in various places, researchers now labor under the expectation that they will generate opportunities for employment. Local governments have begun charging stiffly for permission to conduct surveys even while making the inclusion of local researchers or the supervision of local students a condition of that permission. In other words, researchers are now expected to make contributions that are locally and immediately visible. Wandering the world's unexplored regions and producing accounts only in the researcher's own language for the sole benefit of her/his academic community is no longer acceptable. We must now strive to explain the outlines of our research and involve local scholars and students, to share the credit for our findings, and share the benefits of the research by producing reports in local languages.

Lands once unexplored were shaped by the history and practices of particular cultures. Globalism would have us homogenize them all, assessing the objects of exploration from a global perspective. There are very few remaining unexplored lands today, except perhaps in the depths of the ocean or outer space. But, there remain countless unexplored areas to be illuminated through academic endeavors. Science and technology are our greatest tools for contributing to new discoveries, although future explorations are likely to begin in unexpected places. Ultimately, though, such explorations, now as of old, are driven by the aspiration to "seek out unclimbed peaks."

References

Itani Jun'ichiro (1991): *Saru-Hito-Africa watasi no rirekisho* (Monkey-human-Africa, My resume). Nihon Keizai Shinnbunnsha.

Saito Kiyoaki (2014): *Imanishi Kinji Den, "Sumiwake" kara "Shizenngaku" he* (Biography of Kinji Imanishi: from "Habitat Segregation" to "Study of Nature"). Mineruva shobo.

2 Hedin's Reception in Kyoto, 1908

TANAKA Kazuko

Sven Anders Hedin (1865–1952) was a Swedish explorer of Central Asia. As a young man, he was inspired by the feats of Nils Adolf Erik Nordenskiöld, who had returned to Stockholm following the first successful navigation of the Northeast Passage in the Arctic Ocean in 1879. To the end of his life, Hedin regarded himself as a pupil of Nordenskiöld. Hedin's choice to explore Asia, rather than the Arctic, though, was largely due to the influence of Ferdinand Freiherr von Richthofen, under whom Hedin studied geography at the Friedrich Wilhelm University of Berlin. Richthofen was a pioneer in the scientific study of China and is widely noted for coining the term "Seidenstraße" (translated into English as the "Silk Road" or "Silk Route"). Encouraged by these two great teachers, Hedin would complete five expeditions to Central Asia between 1893 and 1937.Among his most notable achievements are the discovery of the ruins of Loulan, a full survey of the Trans-Himalaya mountain range, and determining the periodic movement of Lop Nur, which he famously named "Den Vandrande Sjön" (The Wandering Lake).

Hedin visited Japan on two occasions, in 1908 and 1923. His first visit to Japan was immediately after the conclusion of his Third Central Asia Expedition. On the first trip Japan, he described the day he set out from Kobe to Yokohama as follows:

> Morgen geht es los. Das wird ein harter Feldzug werden, aber ich werde ihn schon aushalten. Ich liebe Japan; Japan ist ein Teil von Asien, und Asien is ein Teil meines eigenen Lebens. (Morning, departure. This will be a tough campaign. But I will endure it. I love Japan. Japan is a part of Asia; Asia is a part of my own life.)
> (Alma Hedin 1925: 268)

Hedin was about to be received into a whirlwind of receptions, luncheons and events where he would be showered by exuberant hospitality.

In addition to the detailed reports by the Tokyo Geographical Society (1909a, 1909b), the circumstances of the welcome Hedin received in Japan in 1908 upon his arrival and during his stay has been studied from various perspectives, including works by Kaneko Tamio (1972, 1986), an expert on Hedin, as well as works by Shirasu Jōshin (2014) and Kōmoto Yasuko (2014), who considered the significance of Hedin's visit to Japan in the context of international politics regarding Tibet. These studies, though, have focused on the numerous receptions held in Hedin's honor in Tokyo and his relationship with Ōtani Kōzui and the Ōtani Expedition; the latter part of Hedin's visit and the welcome he received in Kyoto had been largely overlooked when I began this research (e.g., Tanaka 2015).

In this chapter, I examine the characteristics and significance of Hedin's welcome in Kyoto, especially his reception as a distinguished guest of Kyoto Imperial University. In doing so, I focus on two aspects. First, the differences in the receptions Hedin received at Tokyo Imperial University and Kyoto Imperial University; second, the exhibition of materials that was held in conjunction with his lecture. I consider how the College of Letters and the Society of Historical Research became involved in a large-scale exhibition – an exhibition that was not part of Hedin's lectures to the Tokyo Geographical Society or elsewhere – from the perspective of their aspirations for the field of Oriental Studies.

Hedin's visit to Japan: The official welcome in Tokyo

A series of events centered on the Tokyo Geographical Society

In August 1908, in India, on the heels of the successful conclusion of his Third Central Asia Expedition, Sven Hedin was inundated with invitations from around the world to lecture on his exploits. On the recommendation of Gustaf Oscar Wallenberg, the Swedish Envoy to Japan, and encouraged by a telegram from Abbot Ōtani Kōzui of Nishi Hongan-ji Temple, Hedin accepted the invitation of the Tokyo Geographical Society to visit Japan (Alma Hedin 1925: 259). On November 4, Hori Ken'yū met Hedin in Shanghai. Hori had been directed by Ōtani to serve as the explorer's interpreter and attendant. They arrived in Nagasaki on November 7, and after a brief stay in Kobe, arrived in Yokohama on November 12. The first half of his one-month visit was to be based in Tokyo and Yokohama, and the second in Kyoto.

In Tokyo, he was a guest in the Yokohama residence of the Swedish Envoy and the Swedish Legation in Tsukiji. Of the events held in Hedin's honor in Tokyo (Table 2.1), the most prominent are the award of the Grand

Table 2.1: Hedin's reception in Tokyo (November 13–27, 1908)

Tokyo Geographical Society	Politicians, bureaucrats, diplomats	The imperial household, imperial family, nobility	Universities	Military	Nishi Hongan-ji	Tours, etc.
(11/13) Visits with Society and officials	(11/13) Banquet hosted by the Swedish Envoy	(11/13) Visit with Prince Kan'in Kotohito			(11/13) Kimono fitting in Minitsukoshi (gift from Ōtani Kōzui)	
		(11/14) Chrysanthemum-viewing reception at Akasaka Imperial Palace				(11/14) Kabuki theater performance
(11/15) Welcome reception						
	(11/16) Banquet hosted by the Foreign Minister		(11/16) Lecture at Tokyo Imperial University		(11/16) Visit to Nishi Hongan-ji Betsuin	(11/16) Luncheon hosted by the Kōjunsha Club
	(11/17) Banquet and evening reception hosted by the British Ambassador		(11/17) Lectures at Waseda University and Tokyo Imperial University			(11/17) Luncheon hosted by Shiga Shigetaka; Visit with Ōkuma Shigenobu; Tour of Zōjō-ji Temple, Shiba, and the Ōkura Museum of Art
	(11/18) Banquet hosted by the Swedish Envoy	(11/18) Visit to Nanki Bunko Library; Luncheon hosted by Tokugawa Yorimichi	(11/18) Lecture at Keiō University			
(11/19) Lecture	(11/19) Luncheon and tea reception hosted by the Swedish Envoy					
						(11/20-21) Visit to Nikkō Tōshō-gū Shrine
	(11/22) Banquet hosted by the Swedish Envoy	(11/22) Lecture, luncheon, and refreshments hosted at Prince Kan'in Kotohito's residence				
	(11/23) Banquet hosted by the Deputy Minister of Education		(11/23) Lecture to the Imperial Educational Society			(11/23) Luncheon hosted by Wada Tsunashirō; Visit to the Yūshūkan at Yasukuni Shrine, Kudan, and viewing of the Ministry of Education Fine Arts Exhibition
(11/24) Tea party and farewell reception			(11/24) Inspection tour of the College of Science and Botanical Gardens at Tokyo Imperial University, followed by luncheon; lecture and martial arts demonstration at Tokyo Higher Normal School			
	(11/25) Awarded the Grand Cordon of the Order of the Sacred Treasure	(11/25) Lecture at the Peer's Club, banquet hosted by Tokugawa Iesato		(11/25) Visit with Nogi Maresuke and Tōgō Heihachirō; Luncheon hosted by the Imperial Japanese Army General Staff Office		
		(11/26) Audience with Emperor Meiji at Imperial Palace				
						(11/27) Visits with various officials

Source: Tokyo Geographical Society 1909a "Dokutoru Suwen Fuon Hedin-shi kangei hōkoku (Report on the welcome given to Dr. Sven Hedin)," *Chigaku Zasshi*, 21(6).

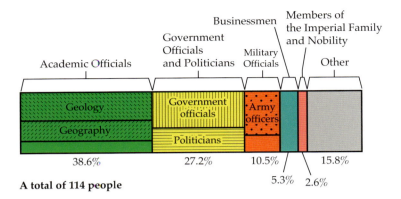

Figure 2.1: Professional fields of the people involved in the welcome reception given to Hedin by the Tokyo Geographical Society.

Sources: Tokyo Geographical Society 1909a "Dokutoru Suwen Fuon Hedin-shi kangei hōkoku (Report on the Welcome Given to Dr. Sven Hedin)" *Chigaku Zasshi* 21(6); Furubayashi Kamejirō, ed. 1912. *Gendai jinmei jiten* (Contemporary Japan biographical encyclopedia); Nichigai Associates, ed. 2011. *Meiji Taishō jinbutsu jiten* (Biographical encyclopedia of Meiji and Taishō era Japan); Geological Survey of Japan, ed. 1982. *Chishitsu chōsajo hyakunenshi* (Centennial history of the Geological Survey of Japan), etc.

Cordon of the Order of the Sacred Treasure and Hedin's audience with Emperor Meiji. The welcome ceremony, the conferral of a gold medal award, the lecture given at the Tokyo Geographical Society, which had invited him to Japan, as well as the luncheon hosted by Prince Kan'in Kotohito, who served as the Society's president, were also important occasions. The sheer volume of official functions in Tokyo – including the many luncheons and banquets – were held by ambassadors, envoys, and government officials. It is evident that Hedin's information on the latest Tibetan situation had attracted a strong political interest. Other functions were hosted by members of the imperial family, nobility, and the business community, including a chrysanthemum-viewing reception at Akasaka Imperial Palace, a visit to Nanki Bunko Library, and a luncheon at the Kōjunsha Club. University-related functions included visits and lectures at Tokyo Imperial University, Waseda University, Keiō University, and the Tokyo Higher Normal School. While an overnight trip to Nikkō and tours of places of interest such as Zōjō-ji Temple and the Ōkura Museum of Art provided moments of respite from Hedin's exhausting schedule, the majority of events were official receptions and lectures. The events associated with Nishi Hongan-ji Temple are noteworthy. One of these is a kimono fitting visit arranged on the instruction of Ōtani Kōzui,[1] while another is a visit to the temple's branch (*betsuin*) in Tokyo. While Kōzui was attentive to Hedin, as in sending Hori Ken'yū to greet Hedin in Shanghai, it seems that Hedin also held Nishi Hongan-ji in some esteem. In Nagoya, furthermore, despite the brevity of his visit, Hedin delivered a lecture at the local Nishi Hongan-ji Temple.

The characteristics of the many receptions in Tokyo can be deduced from examining the persons involved. According to reports by the Tokyo Geographical Society, in addition to the twenty-one people on the welcome committee commissioned by the Society, there were a total of 114 individuals who participated in the Society's four main functions (the welcome reception, welcome gala, luncheon with Prince Kan'in Kotohito, and farewell reception), or made financial contributions for Hedin's welcome (leaving aside officials with the Swedish Legation and journalists, and excluding duplicates; Tokyo Geographical Society 1909a). While more than a few of them were involved in multiple fields, their various affiliations can be roughly classified as in Figure 2.1. Slightly less than forty percent are from academic fields, more than half of whom are involved in fields related to geology, with geography accounting for a quarter. Most of the former are associated with Japan's Imperial Geological Survey. Other names include professors at Tokyo Imperial University in Western history, oriental history, economics, medicine, physics, and chemistry, while scholars of literature are poorly represented. Government officials and politicians (mainly members of the House of Peers) also account for slightly less than forty percent of the total, many with responsibilities in foreign affairs, education, and the Imperial Court. The Imperial Japanese Army was well-represented. As well as businessmen such as Mitsui Hachirōemon, Iwasaki Hisaya, and Shibusawa Ei'ichi, other participants included Kojima Kyūta (Usui) and Takatō Shoku (also known as Takatō Jinbee) from the Japanese Alpine Club, founded in 1905. This who's who of interested parties offers a good reflection of the character of the Tokyo Geographical Society, which was founded in 1879, with Prince Kitashirakawa Yoshihisa as its first president, in the mold of the Royal Geographical Society in London and the Austrian Geographical Society in Vienna. The membership at the time included many nobles, politicians, diplomats, military officers, businessmen, university professors and others. Rather than a site for purely academic exchange, the Society was regarded as a kind of salon where prominent figures shared stories of their travels, accounts of their explorations, and information on matters such as foreign affairs.

---

1 According to the *Kyoto Shimbun* (December 3, 1908), the price of a fitted Japanese kimono at Tokyo's Mitsukoshi kimono store was 300 yen at the time. The Japanese kimono that Hedin subsequently wore to lectures and banquets and when posing for photographs was presumably this outfit, tailored for him at Mitsukoshi.

Another notable feature of the receptions in Tokyo was the frequent contact with officers from the Imperial Japanese Army. For example, Oku Yasukata and Fukushima Yasumasa, respectively the Chief and Deputy Chief of the Imperial Japanese Army General Staff, and Ōkubo Noriaki, Director of the General Staff Land Survey (Tokyo Geographical Society 1909a: 20–21), attended the gathering at Prince Kan'in Kotohito's residence. Oku Yasukata also sponsored the luncheon in honor of Hedin's being awarded the Grand Cordon, which Hedin later described as "Um 12 Uhr desselben Tag gaben zwölf Generale ein Fest (At 12 o'clock on the same day, twelve generals had a celebratory banquet)" (Alma Hedin 1925: 273). Hedin also visited with Generals Nogi Maresuke and Tōgō Heihachirō separately. All of this attention from high-ranking military officers suggests that Hedin's information and knowledge about the Asian interior was of great military interest (Abe 2014: 115–120). Such direct involvement with the military and state was characteristic of the Tokyo Geographical Society, though.

Hedin's lecture and tour of Tokyo Imperial University

It is somewhat surprising that Tokyo Imperial University was involved in so few of the receptions honoring Hedin during his stay in Tokyo. Aside from a series of lectures held over two days, there is no record of a formal welcome by the university administration, and the time was limited, permitting only a tour of the College of Science, a luncheon at the botanical gardens, and the presentation of a set of vases as a commemorative gift (Table 2.1). Although this is a deeper engagement than he had with other universities, it remains a remarkably small role in Hedin's time in Tokyo. Of course, the sheer number of official functions may have left little room in Hedin's schedule for much else.

Furthermore, Hedin's reception at Tokyo Imperial University was quite scientifically focused, as the Tokyo Geographical Society reception had been. This comes across clearly in the fact that only the College of Science was toured: the departments of seismology, anthropology, geology, and botany, as well as the botanical gardens. Faculty from across the university may have participated in the luncheon or other aspects of the visit, but it does not appear that they had any involvement in the formal arrangements.

Kyoto Imperial University and Nishi Hongan-ji Temple

Hedin's schedule in Kansai (Table 2.2) featured fewer lectures and events relating to the Imperial Court, government, and diplomats than he had experienced in Tokyo, but included many opportunities for shopping, tours, and sightseeing. The overall arrangements for Hedin's visit to Kansai were made by Kyoto Imperial University. The university stationed a staff member as liaison at the Sawabun Ryokan, where Hedin was lodging, and arrangements for events were made by Kyoto Imperial University as a whole.[2] In sum, the Swedish envoy had been the primary host during his stay in Tokyo, and Kyoto Imperial University served that role in Kyoto.

Kyoto Imperial University's *Gaikoku meishi shōtai kankei shorui* (Archive Documents Relating to Invitations to Celebrated Foreign Nationals)[3] contains a wealth of documents detailing Hedin's welcome, from the banquet menu to the seating arrangements for Hedin's lecture, including telegraph messages concerning freight shipments and more. From Hedin's arrival in Kyoto on the evening of November 28 until December 5, Kyoto Imperial University treated Hedin as a distinguished academic guest, arranging an itinerary that included: campus lectures, guided tours of historical sites and museums in the city, a visit to Nisshō Elementary School, and outings to Osaka and Nara (Sakaguchi 2013). For his tours of the Imperial Museums of Kyoto and Nara, as well as sites such as Tōdai-ji Temple, the Katsura Imperial Villa, and the Kyoto Imperial Palace, Hedin was given guided tours by individuals such as Kubota Kanae (Director of the Kyoto and Nara Imperial Museums), the temple conservator and restoration specialist Kameoka Suekichi (a technician in Kyoto Prefecture), and Amanuma Shun'ichi and Kagoya Yūtarō (technicians from Nara Prefecture), suggesting an academic approach to the presentation of traditional Japanese culture.[4] Nisshō Elementary School was regularly visited by observers from around Japan and overseas as an example of advanced educational technique; its selection as a site of interest was probably intended to showcase Japan's high level of education.[5]

Important receptions in Kyoto were held by Kyoto Imperial University and Nishi Hongan-ji Temple. The largest function hosted by the university was held on

---

2 The *Osaka jiji Shimpō* newspaper reported that "for this Doctor who has such esteem for Japanese pursuits, the inn has set aside Room No. 4 as a drawing room, Room No. 3 as an office for a member of the university staff, and the entirety of the ten tatami-mat salon in Room No. 2 as living quarters." (November 29, 1908)

3 *Gaikoku meishi shōtai kankei shorui* (documents for 1908–1912), materials held in the Kyoto University Archives (ID: 01A19469). The documents of the year 1908 in this volume are exclusively related to Hedin's visit.

4 According to *Gaikoku meishi shōtai kankei shorui* (documents for 1908–1912), materials held in the Kyoto University Archives (ID: 01A19469) and articles in the *Kyoto Hinode Shimbun* newspaper and others.

5 Another reason for visiting Nisshō Elementary School may have been that the school had incorporated Swedish calisthenics into its curriculum. Hedin gave a demonstration of Latin calligraphy at the school and posed for a commemorative photograph (*Nisshō hyaku-nenshi henshū iinkai* 1971: 99, 123, 150–152).

Table 2.2: Hedin's reception in Kyoto (November 28 to December 12, 1908)

Kyoto Imperial University	Nishi Hongan-ji	Military	Politics and business	Tours, sightseeing, other
				(11/27) Tour of Nagoya Castle and the studio of the Ando Cloisonné Company
	(11/28) Lecture at the Nishi Hongan-ji branch temple in Nagoya			
(11/29) Luncheon; lecture (with exhibition); welcome banquet				
	(11/30) Banquet and overnight stay at the Sanya-so Inn			(11/30) Tour of Kasuga Taisha Shrine, Nara Prefectural Public Hall, Nara Imperial Museum, Mikazuki-tei teahouse, Tōdai-ji Temple, and Nara Prefecture Products Display Center (now the Research Center for Buddhist Art Materials of Nara National Museum)
				(12/1) Tour of Ōbaku-san Manpuku-ji Temple and Byōdō-in Temple in Uji, Kangetsukyō, Kemari (the Kyoto branch of the Peer's Club); Kabuki performance at Minami-za Theater
	(12/2) Visit to Nishi Hongan-ji; discussion with Ōtani Kōzui; lecture, luncheon and banquet; Noh and Kyōgen performance, etc.; overnight stay			
	(12/3) Commemorative photograph with the Ōtani family			(12/3) Tour of Katsura Imperial Villa, Kyō-ō-gokoku-ji (Tō-ji) Temple, Higashi Hongan-ji, Kikoku-tei Estate (Shōsei-en Garden), and Kyoto Imperial Museum
(12/4) Luncheon hosted by faculty members			(12/4) Visit to Kyoto Prefectural Office and Kyoto Municipal Office	(12/4) Tour of Kyoto Imperial Palace, Nijō Castle, Chion-in Temple, Heian Jingū Shrine, and Butoku-kai (martial arts demonstration)
(12/5) Luncheon hosted by President		(12/5) Visit to Murin-an Garden; interview with Yamagata Aritomo	(12/5) Lecture and banquet co-hosted by Kyoto city and Kyoto Chamber of Commerce	(12/5) Visit to Nisshō Elementary School
(12/6) President visits the Sawabun Ryokan; presentation of commemorative gifts		(12/6) Visit by Yamagata Aritomo to the Sawabun Ryokan		(12/6) Commemorative Photograph; shopping at Iida Trading Co. (Takashimaya) and S. Ikeda & Co. Antiques
			(12/7) Welcome party hosted by Osaka city and the Osaka branches of four major newspapers (*Osaka Asahi*, *Osaka Mainichi*, *Osaka Jiji Shimpo*, and *Osaka Shimpo*)	(12/7) Tour of Osaka Castle and Shitennō-ji Temple
				(12/8) Tour of Hōryū-ji and Chūgū-ji Temples
				(12/9) Shopping at Takashimaya
	(12/10) Visit to Nishi Hongan-ji; discussion with Ōtani Kōzui			(12/10) Shopping at S. Ikeda & Co. Antiques and Sanpōdō Buddhist Altar Store
				(12/11) Shopping.

Sources: Tokyo Geographical Society 1909b, "Hedin hakase tairaku kiji (Dr. Hedin in Kyoto)," *Chigaku Zasshi* 21(6); issues of the *Kyoto Hinode Shimbun* for November and December 1908; articles in *Kyōkai Ichiran*, especially no. 445; and newspaper articles collected in "Sven Hedin in Japan" (a scrapbook of articles related to Hedin held in the collection of the Etnografiska Museet in Stockholm), etc.

November 29, the day after Hedin's arrival in Kyoto. The day's events began with a luncheon hosted by the regents of the university, followed by a public lecture to an audience from across the university's colleges and other institutions of higher education in Kyoto in conjunction with an exhibition of related materials. This was followed by a welcoming party attended by public officials including the prefectural governor and the mayor of Kyoto. The largest function hosted by the temple was held over two days on December 2 and 3 at

Nishi Hongan-ji Temple. Beginning with a personal talk between Hedin and Ōtani Kōzui, with whom Hedin had a deep and long-standing friendship, and who had collaborated on Hedin's expeditions, the series of events included a luncheon and banquet with Ōtani's family, a Noh and Kyōgen performance, and a lecture, after which Hedin spent the night at the temple.

Hedin's welcome by Kyoto Imperial University

According to a Tokyo Geographical Society report, chief among those who devoted themselves to Hedin's visit were Kikuchi Dairoku (President of Kyoto Imperial University) and Count Ōtani Kōzui (Abbot of Nishi Hongan-ji Temple), as well as Matsumoto Bunzaburō (Dean of the College of Letters), Ogawa Takuji (Professor in the College of Letters), Hiki Tadashi (Assistant Professor in the College of Science and Engineering), Ishikawa Hajime (Imperial University official), and Hori Ken'yū (Tokyo Geographical Society 1909b: b 2). The report also lists those involved in organizing the university lecture: Nakayama Chikakazu (Imperial University official), Yamamoto Ryōkichi (Dean of Students), and Naitō Torajirō (Konan) (Lecturer in the College of Letters). Among other things, these lists indicate that the entire institution of Kyoto Imperial University was committed to Hedin's visit.

Let us now consider what distinguished Hedin's embrace by Kyoto Imperial University from his reception by Tokyo Imperial University, and his stay in Tokyo more generally. Aside from the differences in hosting arrangements, two points stand out immediately: first, the university president took the lead in welcoming Hedin, and second, that faculty from disciplines across the university were involved in organizing and participated in the various events.

President Kikuchi Dairoku's initiative

Ogawa Takuji, a geographer like Hedin, was also appointed to Hedin's welcome contingent by the Tokyo Geographical Society. He not only took care of Hedin for the lecture and banquet, but also served as his guide in and around Kyoto, Nara, and Osaka. Kyoto Imperial University's then president, Kikuchi Dairoku, was, however, not to be outdone by Ogawa in extending a welcome to Hedin. Figure 2.2 shows a map of the sites and facilities that Hedin visited during his stay in Kyoto, marking instances where President Kikuchi met, accompanied, or retrieved Hedin during the visit. Among the sites listed, the visit to the Minami-za theater was hurriedly arranged by Ogawa Takuji and Hori Ken'yū upon learning of Hedin's desire to attend a Kabuki performance (*Osaka jiji shimpō* December 2, 1908). Figure 2.2 and Table 2.2 show Hedin's densely packed schedule, as well as President Kikuchi's high level of involvement in it. While it is unclear whether

● ■ Locations that Hedin visited or at which he stayed

• Locations where President Kikuchi accompanied or came to meet Hedin

a Peer's Club, **b** Prefectural Office, **c** Sawabun [Inn], **d** Municipal Office, **e** Nisshō Elementary School, **f** Butoku-kai, **g** Heian Jingū Shrine, **h** Murin-an, **i** Minami-za, **j** Narui Photo Studio, **k** Chion-in Temple, **l** Higashi Hongan-ji Temple, **m** Kikoku-tei Estate, **n** Imperial Museum of Kyoto, **o** Tō-ji Temple, **p** Kangetsukyō Bridge, **q** Manpuku-ji Temple, **r** Byōdō-in Temple

Dining: **A** Hyōtei, **B** Miyako Hotel, **C** Maruyama Nakamura-rō, **D** Kyoto Hotel, **E** Ki no eda

Shopping: **1** Iida Trading Co. [Takashimaya], **2** Sanpōdō Buddhist Altar Store, **3** Seisuke Ikeda & Co. Antiques, **4** Mikami Lacquerware

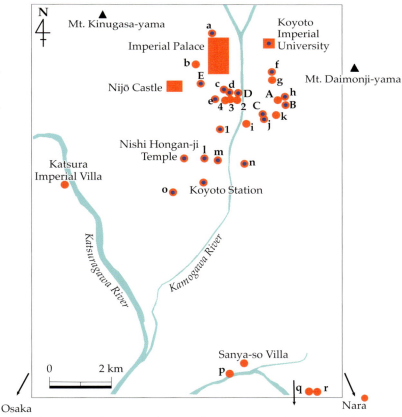

Figure 2.2: Activities of Hedin and President Kikuchi in Kyoto during Hedin's stay (November 28–December 12, 1908)
Sources: Tokyo Geographical Society 1909b, "Hedin hakase tairaku kiji (Dr. Hedin in Kyoto)," *Chigaku Zasshi*, 21(6); issues of the *Kyoto Hinode Shimbun* for November and December 1908; and newspaper articles collected in "Sven Hedin in Japan" (a scrapbook of articles related to Hedin held in the collection of the Etnografiska Museet in Stockholm), etc.

this reflected Hedin's inclinations or a desire on the part of his hosts to show him Kyoto's rich traditions, a full itinerary was prepared. Rickshaws and horse-drawn carriages were used for Hedin's movements around the city; and between his various visits and tours, he was treated to traditional Japanese cuisine, including the *yūsoku ryōri* traditionally prepared for the Imperial Court.

From the moment he greeted Hedin at Kyoto Station on November 28, President Kikuchi was present for most of the events on Hedin's itinerary, and took every opportunity to explain Japanese customs such as *kemari* – an ancient Japanese ball game – and martial arts and hosting luncheons at which Hedin met with notable figures such as Yamagata Aritomo. Hedin was keenly interested in traditional Japanese crafts and art work, especially lacquerware and the ritual implements of Buddhist practice. Toward the end of his time in Kyoto, he reportedly purchased close to 4,000 yen worth of goods at the Takashimaya store, including an embroidered folding screen and picture scroll painted by Uemura Shōen (*Shin-ishō* 1909: vol. 81, 13; *Kyoto Hinode Shimbun*, December 11, 1908). President Kikuchi accompanied Hedin on some of these shopping expeditions, along with Nakazawa Iwata (Principal of the Kyoto College of Technology). Moreover, on December 6, Kikuchi visited the Sawabun Ryokan to present Hedin with commemorative gifts on behalf of Kyoto Imperial University (a suit of samurai armor and a Japanese sword), and on December 12, bade Hedin farewell from Kyoto Station as the explorer departed for Pyongyang.

President Kikuchi was also an acting president of the Tokyo Geographical Society, because President Enomoto Takeaki suddenly passed away at the end of October 1908. It was just before Hedin's arrival to Japan. From the moment that he greeted Hedin on the pier in Yokohama on November 12 as acting president of the Tokyo Geographical Society, President Kikuchi was a ubiquitous and active presence, introducing Hedin at various events, including the welcome reception, banquet, and lecture hosted by the Society. Of course, as the President of Kyoto Imperial University, Kikuchi would have already been actively involved in making the necessary arrangements and preparations for Hedin's visit to Kyoto even during Hedin's stay in Tokyo. In other words, Kikuchi must have had the explorer's visit on his mind day and night for the entire month of Hedin's sojourn in Japan.

Collaboration and participation by faculty in diverse fields

The wide range of fields of the faculty who took part in welcoming Hedin as a guest of Kyoto Imperial University is notable for its difference to his reception in Tokyo and Tokyo Imperial University. We can begin to see this by looking at the circumstances of November 29; the day after Hedin's arrival in Kyoto was filled with a day-long series of events at Kyoto Imperial University.

The events began when Ogawa Takuji fetched Hedin from the Sawabun Ryokan and accompanied him to President Kikuchi's official residence, whence he was guided to a luncheon hosted by the Regents of the University in Sonjōdō Hall from one o'clock in the afternoon. From two o'clock, the university lecture was held in the College of Law, where Hedin spoke to an audience of 1,200 people from within and outside the university. In conjunction with the lecture, documents related to Hedin's Central Asia Expedition were exhibited in a separate room. In the evening, the university sponsored a welcome banquet at the Kyoto Hotel.

Despite the short notice of the event – it was only around November 20 that university officials asked each College or each department, as well as the hospital, the library, and others for an estimate of the number of people who would be attending the lecture and banquet – a large number of university faculty ended up participating. Table 2.3 shows the total number of participants by department. The College of Medicine had three departments with high attendance rates, with both members from each of the Departments of Pharmacy and Forensics and six of the seven members of the Department of Pathology attending.

Among the University's four constituent Colleges, the College of Science and Engineering had the highest attendance rate, followed by the College of Letters. Figures 2.3 and 2.4 summarize the respective fields of the faculty members who attended the lecture and

Table 2.3: Summary of participation in the reception for Hedin on November 29

Department name (Total number of professors, assistant professors, and lecturers)	Lecture	Banquet
College of Law (33 people)	9	5
College of Medicine (114 people)	25	13
College of Letters (39 people)	17	12
College of Science and Engineering (77 people)	42	27
Hospital	5	–
Library	11	–
Total	109	57

Note: The number of people who attended the banquet from the university hospital and library are not known, as they are not accounted for in *Gaikoku meishi shōtai kankei shorui*.
Sources: *Gaikoku meishi shōtai kankei shorui* (1908–12) and *Kyoto Teikoku Daigaku Ichiran* (1908–09).

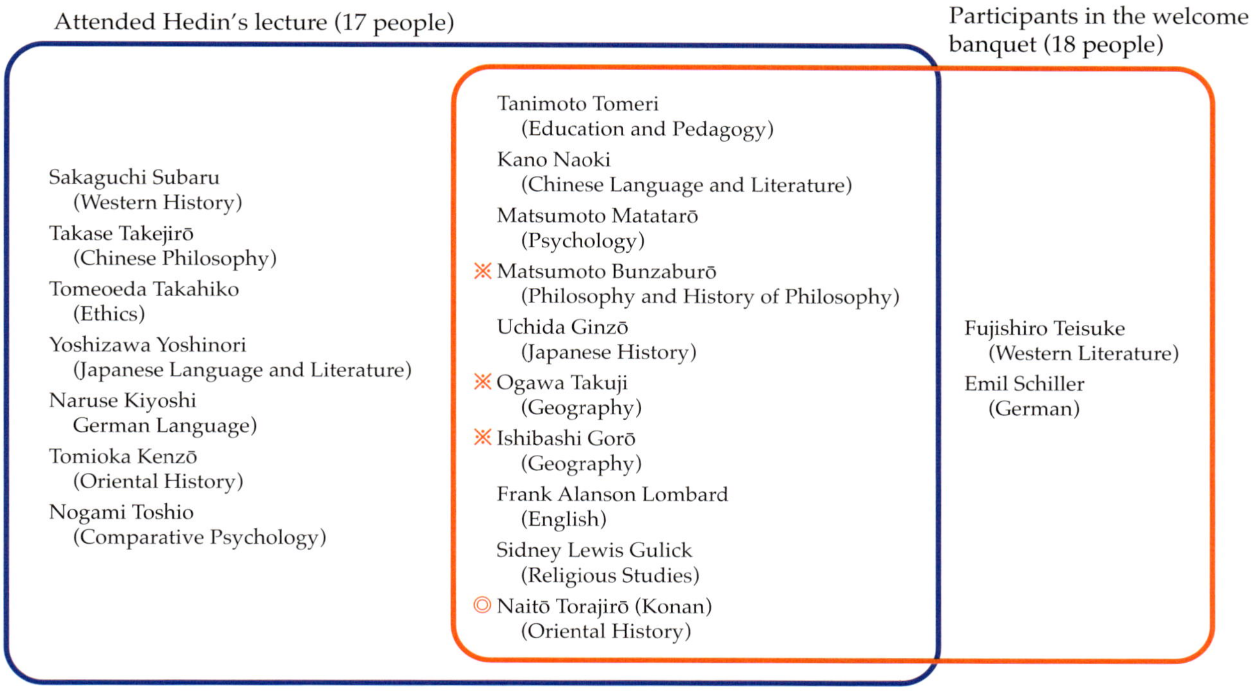

Attended Hedin's lecture (17 people)

- Sakaguchi Subaru (Western History)
- Takase Takejirō (Chinese Philosophy)
- Tomeoeda Takahiko (Ethics)
- Yoshizawa Yoshinori (Japanese Language and Literature)
- Naruse Kiyoshi German Language
- Tomioka Kenzō (Oriental History)
- Nogami Toshio (Comparative Psychology)

(Intersection — attended lecture and banquet)

- Tanimoto Tomeri (Education and Pedagogy)
- Kano Naoki (Chinese Language and Literature)
- Matsumoto Matatarō (Psychology)
- ※ Matsumoto Bunzaburō (Philosophy and History of Philosophy)
- Uchida Ginzō (Japanese History)
- ※ Ogawa Takuji (Geography)
- ※ Ishibashi Gorō (Geography)
- Frank Alanson Lombard (English)
- Sidney Lewis Gulick (Religious Studies)
- ◎ Naitō Torajirō (Konan) (Oriental History)

Participants in the welcome banquet (18 people)

- Fujishiro Teisuke (Western Literature)
- Emil Schiller (German)

※ Denotes individuals who had an important role in Hedin's welcome (as noted in a *Chigaku Zasshi* article)
◎ Denotes individuals who cooperated in Hedin's lecture (as noted in a *Chigaku Zasshi* article)

Figure 2.3: Faculty members from the College of Letters who took part in the welcome reception for Hedin on November 29
Sources: *Gaikoku meishi shōtai kankei shorui* (1908–1912) and *Kyoto Teikoku Daigaku Ichiran* (1908–1909).

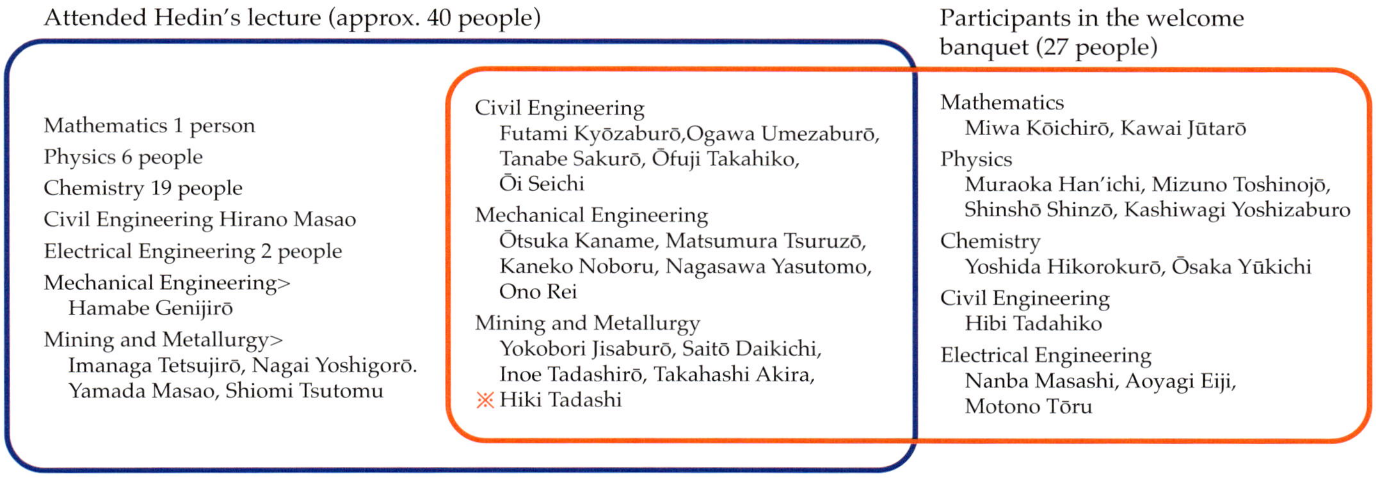

Attended Hedin's lecture (approx. 40 people)

- Mathematics 1 person
- Physics 6 people
- Chemistry 19 people
- Civil Engineering Hirano Masao
- Electrical Engineering 2 people
- Mechanical Engineering> Hamabe Genijirō
- Mining and Metallurgy> Imanaga Tetsujirō, Nagai Yoshigorō. Yamada Masao, Shiomi Tsutomu

(Intersection)

- Civil Engineering
  Futami Kyōzaburō, Ogawa Umezaburō, Tanabe Sakurō, Ōfuji Takahiko, Ōi Seichi
- Mechanical Engineering
  Ōtsuka Kaname, Matsumura Tsuruzō, Kaneko Noboru, Nagasawa Yasutomo, Ono Rei
- Mining and Metallurgy
  Yokobori Jisaburō, Saitō Daikichi, Inoe Tadashirō, Takahashi Akira, ※ Hiki Tadashi

Participants in the welcome banquet (27 people)

- Mathematics
  Miwa Kōichirō, Kawai Jūtarō
- Physics
  Muraoka Han'ichi, Mizuno Toshinojō, Shinshō Shinzō, Kashiwagi Yoshizaburo
- Chemistry
  Yoshida Hikorokurō, Ōsaka Yūkichi
- Civil Engineering
  Hibi Tadahiko
- Electrical Engineering
  Nanba Masashi, Aoyagi Eiji, Motono Tōru

※ Denotes individuals who had an important role in Hedin's welcome (as noted in a *Chigaku Zasshi* article)

Figure 2.4: Faculty members from the College of Science and Engineering who took part in the reception for Hedin on November 29
Sources: *Gaikoku meishi shōtai kankei shorui* (1908–1912) and *Kyoto Teikoku Daigaku Ichiran* (1908–1909).

the welcome banquet from these two colleges. In the College of Letters, as well as Ogawa and Ishibashi from Geography, faculty members from a variety of other fields were in attendance, including History, Oriental and Western Literature, Philosophy, and the History of Philosophy. While the College of Letters during this period had thirty-nine faculty members, including lecturers both within and outside the university, as well as several individuals studying abroad, its attendance rate was quite high, and many of these people participated in both the lecture and the banquet.

People from every department of the College of Science and Engineering participated in the lecture or the welcome banquet. Especially noteworthy were the many attendees from the Earth Sciences Department of Mining and Metallurgy. For some departments, the *Gaikoku meishi shōtai kankei shorui* records only the number of individuals. Where more details are recorded, their names and respective fields are reproduced in Figure 2.4. It is quite clear that the faculty of the College of Science and Engineering were highly interested in Hedin's presentation.

No doubt some who attended were merely interested in the celebrity of this internationally renowned explorer, whose visit to Japan had generated great fanfare. Others, perhaps, attended simply to show respect and courtesy to an honored guest of the university. However, even though their disciplines and activities are different from Hedin's, there were likely many who were academically intrigued by Hedin's explorations, by the scientific researcher Hedin, or by his geographical findings. Until his 1905–1908 expedition, Hedin had always conducted fieldwork on his own, hiring locals as porters or field escorts. In addition to the natural scientific work of observation, surveys, quantitative measurements of water depth and flow, and mineral sampling, he also conducted social and cultural surveys that involved the collection of vocabulary and the study of lifeways, religions, and customs, as well as sketching, taking photographs, and producing maps. Hedin's wide-ranging talents and activities as a geographer and explorer no doubt contributed significantly to his audience-appeal to people from so many different fields.

Exhibition of documents in conjunction with the lecture

Another distinguishing feature of Hedin's visit to Kyoto Imperial University is the exhibition of documents held in conjunction with his lecture. During Hedin's lectures to the Tokyo Geographical Society and Tokyo Imperial University, he displayed maps and pictures on the walls using a magic lantern projector, but we find no record of any of Hedin's materials being exhibited for his audiences in Tokyo (Yazawa 1989: 370). In Japan, the exhibition was exclusive to Kyoto Imperial University.

Exhibited materials

In addition to the books and materials that Hedin had personally created during the Central Asia Expedition prior to his arrival in Japan (Table 2.4), the materials on display included survey reports by Western explorers of Central Asia and Tibet (Table 2.5), Chinese geography texts (Table 2.6), Buddhist scriptures, including some which had been translated into European languages (Table 2.7), and copied inscriptions and old maps (Table 2.8). These materials are reported to have been exhibited in the Department of Geography of the College of Letters (Tokyo Geographical Society 1909b), but there is some conflicting evidence.[6] Judging by their sheer volume and the large scale of the *Honil gangni yeokdae gukdo ji do* (Kon'itsu kyōri kokuto no zu) (a medieval map of East Asia produced in Korea measuring 163 cm × 158 cm), the venue would have to have been quite spacious.

Among the documents listed in Tables 2.4 through 2.8 are books belonging to the Department of Geography, and the Departments of Oriental Studies, including Oriental History, Indian Philosophy, Chinese Philosophy, Chinese Literature, and Sanskrit. Among the European reports, we find accounts of explorations and travelogues by figures such as the French missionary Évariste Régis Huc, the explorers Francis Edward Younghusband and Marc Aurel Stein, and the Tibetologist Sarat Chandra Das. Among the Chinese texts concerning Tibet and Western Asia, the *DaQing yitong zhi* (Records of the Unity of the Great Qing), regarded as a classic work of geography, is a comprehensive gazetteer describing the entirety of the area governed by the Qing Dynasty spanning hundreds of volumes. Also noteworthy are the books concerning waterways. For example, the *Shui jing zhu* (Commentary on the Water Classic), compiled in the Northern Wei Dynasty, is a large compendium of geographical treatises respectively describing China's major river systems, while the *Shuidao tigang* (Guide to the Network of Waterways) is an excellent hydrological treatise covering the rivers of the Chinese mainland and surrounding regions based on the *Huang yu quan lan tu* (Complete Maps of the Empire). The *Xiyu shuidao*

---

6 The *Osaka Mainichi Shimbun* daily newspaper reports that "An exhibition of sketches prepared by the Doctor, including 'Local Customs,' 'Structure of a Tibetan Temple,' and 'Model of the Gobi Desert,' was staged for the benefit of the audience in the Department of Western History in the College of Letters" (November 30, 1908). The question of whether it was held in the Western History Department rather than the Geography Department, or both, remains unclear.

Table 2.4: Hedin's books and expedition materials exhibited for the university lecture

(1) Books by Dr. Hedin	Holdings in departments and libraries in the College of Letters (date of registration prior to Hedin's lecture)
1. *Through Asia*. 1898.	Oriental History
2. *Durch Asiens Wüste*. 1899.	
3. *Die geographisch-wissenschaftlichen Ergebnisse meiner Reisen in Zentral-Asien 1894–1897*. Ergänzungsband 28 zu Petermanns Mitteilungen. Gotha 1900.	
*4. *Central Asia and Tibet*. 1903.	**Geography (1908. 3. 31)**, Oriental History, Sociology
5. *Im Herzen von Asien*. 1903.	
*6. *Adventures in Tibet*. 1904.	**Geography (1908. 6. 20)**, Chinese Text
*7. *Scientific Results of a Journey in Central Asia and Tibet 1899–1902*. 1905.	**Geography (1908. 10. 10)**, Sanskrit
(2) Sketches by Dr. Hedin	
Sketches of the Tibetan mountains, lakes and marshes, temples, peoples, and sites from the Third Expedition (108 sheets)	

Note: *Denotes materials signed by Hedin (dated November 29, 1908)
Source: Tokyo Geographical Society 1909b, "Hedin hakase tairaku kiji (Dr. Hedin in Kyoto)," *Chigaku Zasshi*, 21(6).

Table 2.5: Reports on Tibet and Central Asia exhibited for Hedin's lecture

(3) Explorers' accounts of Central Asia and Tibet	Holdings in departments and libraries in the College of Letters (date of registration prior to Hedin's lecture)
1. M. Huc: *Souvenirs d'un voyage dans la Tartarie, le Tibet et la Chine*. 1853. (*Souvenirs d'un voyage dans la Tartarie et le Thibet pendant les années 1844, 1845 et 1846*)	
2. W. H. Knight: *Diary of a Pedestrian in Cashmere and Tibet*. 1863.	
3. R. Shaw: *Visits to High Tartary, Yarkand and Kashgar*. 1871.	**Oriental History (1908. 7. 10)**, Sociology
4. C. R. Markham: *Narratives of the Mission of George Bogle to Tibet, and of the Journey of Thomas Manning to Lhassa*. 1876.	Haneda Memorial Hall
5. G. Bonvalot: *Du Caucase aux Indes à travers le Pamir*. 1888.	
6. L. Dutreuil de Rhins: *L'Asie Centrale, Tibet et Régions limitrophes: texte et Atlas*. 1889.	**Oriental History (1908. 7. 25)**
7. W. W. Rockhill: *Land of the Lamas*. 1891.	Oriental History
9. H. Lansdell: *Chinese Central Asia*. 1893.	**Oriental History (1908. 7. 25)**
10. F. E. Younghusband: *Heart of a Continent*. 1896.	
11. The Earl of Dunmore: *The Pamirs*. 1894.	Oriental History, Indian Philosophy
12. A. H. S. Landor: *In the Forbidden Land*. 1898.	Geography
13. M. S. Wellby: *Through Unknown Tibet*. 1898.	Haneda Memorial Hall
14. H. H. P. Deasy: *In Tibet and Chinese Turkestan*. 1901.	Oriental History, Haneda Memorial Hall
15. Sarat Chandra Das: *Journey to Lhasa and Central Tibet*. 1902.	Geography
16. G. Sandberg: *Exploration of Tibet: its History and Particulars from 1623 to 1904*. 1904.	**Oriental History (1906. 11. 20)**
17. *Papers relating to Tibet* (presented to both Houses of Parliament by Command of His majesty) 1904.	Oriental History
18. L. A. Waddell: *Lhasa and its Mysteries*. 1905.	Buddhist Studies
19. W. J. Ottley: *With mounted Infantry in Tibet*. 1906.	**Oriental History (1908. 5. 25)**, Haneda Memorial Hall
20. Sir T. Holdich: *Tibet, the Mysterious*. 1907.	**Oriental History (1907. 6. 15)**, Geography, **(1908. 3. 31)** Haneda Memorial Hall
21. M. A. Stein: *Ancient Khotan*. 1907.	**Indian Philosophy (1908. 2. 5)**
22. N. Kuehner: *Opisanie Tibet*. 1907.	

Note: Built in 1966, Haneda Memorial Hall was named to honor the contributions made by Dr. Haneda Tōru to the development of the study of the Asian interior.
Source: Tokyo Geographical Society 1909b, "Hedin hakase tairaku kiji (Dr. Hedin in Kyoto)" *Chigaku Zasshi* 21(6).

Table 2.6: Chinese geographical materials exhibited for Hedin's lecture

(4) Chinese Writings on Central Asia			Holdings in departments and libraries in the College of Letters (date of registration prior to Hedin's lecture)
Title	(Dynasty) author or editor	No. of volumes	
1. 初刊本禹貢錐指 First Edition of *Yugong zhuizhi* (History of Changes in Water Flows since Han Dynasty, based on *Yugong* (Description of the Legendary Yu the Great and the Provinces of His Time))	(Qing) Hu Wei	10	Oriental History, Chinese Language and Literature
2. 水經注 *Shuijing zhu* (Commentary on the Water Classic)	(Later Wei) Li Daoyuan	12	History of Chinese Philosophy, Geography, Oriental History
3. 水道提綱 *Shuidao tigang* (Guide to the Network of Waterways)	(Qing) Qi Shaonan	8	History of Chinese Philosophy, Oriental History
4. 大清一統志 *Daqing yitong zhi* (Records of the Unity of the Great Qing)	(Compiled by Imperial Edict)	1 selected	**Oriental History (1907. 1. 4)**, Sociology
5. 欽定皇輿西域圖志 *Qinding Huangyu Xiyu tuzhi* (Authorized Geographical Description of the Western Regions)	(Qing) ed. Fuheng et al.; (Qing) comp. Chu Tingzhang et al.		History of Chinese Philosophy, Geography, Oriental History, Sociology
6. 小方壺齋輿地叢鈔 *Xiaofanghu-zhai yudi congchao* (Geographical Series of the Xiaofanghu Studio)	(Qing) ed. Wang Xiqi	3 selected	Geography
7. 西域考古錄 *Xiyu kaogu lu* (Archeological Records of the Western Regions)	(Qing) Yu Hao	10	Oriental History
8. 漢西域圖考 *Han Xiyu tukao* (Consideration on the Maps of the Western Regions made in Han Dynasty)	(Qing) Li Guangting	3	Geography, Oriental History
9. 西域聞見錄 *Xiyu wenjian lu* (The Travels in the Western Regions)	(Qing) Qishiyi	3	Oriental History
10. 西域水道記 *Xiyu shuidaoji* (Records of Waterways in the Western Regions)	(Qing) Xu Song	6 volumes; and 漢書西域傳補註新疆賦 *Hanshu Xiyuzhuan buzhu, Xinjiang fu*	Oriental History
11. 欽定新疆識略 *Qinding Xinjiang shilüe* (Authorized Description on the New Territory: Eastern Turkestan)	(Qing) Songyun et al.	10	Oriental History
12. 新疆要略 *Xinjiang yaolüe* (Outline of the New Territory: Eastern Turkestan)	(Qing) Qi Yunshi		Oriental History
13. 回疆誌 *Huijiang zhi* (Geography of the New Territory: Eastern Turkestan)	(Qing) Su Erde		Oriental History
(5) Chinese Books of Tibetan Geography			Holdings in departments and libraries in the College of Letters (date of registration prior to Hedin's lecture)
Title	Author or Editor	No. of Volumes	
14. 西招圖略 *Xizhao tulüe* (Description on Mountains and Rivers in Tibet)	(Qing) Songyun	2	Oriental History
15. 衛藏通志 *Weizang tongzhi* (Chorography of Ü-Tsang (Central and Western Parts of Tibet))	(Qing) Songyun	8	History of Chinese Philosophy, Geography, Oriental History, Sociology
16. 西藏紀述 *Xizang jishu* (Descriptions on Tibet)	(Qing) Zhang Hai	1	
17. 西藏記 *Xizang ji* (Book on Tibet)	Anonymous,	2	Oriental History
18. 康輶草 *Kang you cao* (Collection of Poems on a Journey to Tibet)	Chen Zhongxiang	1	
19. 得一齋雜著四種:西輶日記、印度箚記、遊歷芻言、西徼水道 (Four miscellaneous books written by Deyizhai: *Xiyou riji* (Travel Diary in the Western Region), *Yindu Zhaji* (Memoirs in India), *Youli chuyan* (Essays on Journey), *Xijiao shuideo* (Waterways in the Western Frontier)	Chen Zhongxiang	1	Oriental History
20. 西藏圖考 *Xizang tukao* (Consideration on the Maps of Tibet)	(Qing) Huang Peiqiao	4	Geography, Oriental History
21. 西藏賦 *Xizang fu* (Verses on Tibet)	(Qing) He Ning aka He Ying	1	**Oriental History (1907. 6. 10)**
22. 明代四譯館表文 *Mingdai siyiguan biaowen* (Diplomatic Documents written by Ming Dynasty's Government Office)		(Blueprint) 1	

Note: As many of the Chinese texts are available in multiple editions, it was not possible to conclusively establish if the library's holdings were reprints or the like. Also, the copy of the *Shuidao tigang* held in the department of Oriental History bears the inscription "*Bungaku hakase Naitō Torajirō kizōbon* (Book presented by Naitō Torajirō, Doctor of Letters)."
Source: Tokyo Geographical Society 1909b, "Hedin hakase tairaku kiji (Dr. Hedin in Kyoto)," *Chigaku Zasshi*, 21(6).

Table 2.7: Tibetan and Western Buddhist scriptures exhibited for the university lecture

(6) Western Chinese Buddhist scriptures, including Tibetan Buddhist teachings		
Title	No. of volumes	Contributor
23. 洛陽伽藍記 初印漢魏叢書 *Luoyang qielan ji* (Book of Temple's Old Stories and Historical Changes in Luoyang in Northern Wei era) (Han Wei congshu, First Edition)	1	Honpa Hongwan-ji Temple
24. 龍藏本佛國記 Longzang ben (Books from the Dragon Canon): *Foguo ji* (The Travel Journal of a Buddhist Monk Faxian)	10	Honpa Hongwan-ji Temple
25. 校本大唐西域記 Annotated version of *Tang Xiyu ji* (Great Tang Records on the Western Regions)	4	Honpa Hongwan-ji Temple
26. 長寬寫本大唐西域記 *Chōkan shahon Dai Tō Saiiki-ki* (Great Tang Records on the Western Regions: Manuscript Made during the Chōkan Era of Japan)	12	Ishiyama-dera Temple
27. 宋版大唐西域記 Songban DaTang xiyu ji (Great Tang Records on the Western Regions: Book Published in the Song Dynasty of China)	12	Tō-ji Temple
28. 龍藏本大唐西域記 Longzang ben (Books from the Dragon Canon): *Tang Xiyu ji* (Great Tang Records on the Western Regions)	12	Honpa Hongwan-ji Temple
29. 龍藏本慈恩寺三藏傳 Longzang ben (Books from the Dragon Canon): *Ci'en si Sanzang zhuan* (Xuanzang's Pilgrimages in the Western Regions and his Works to Translate Buddhist Scriptures into Chinese)	5	Honpa Hongwan-ji Temple
30. 龍藏本南海寄歸內法傳 Longzang ben (Books from the Dragon Canon): *Nanhai jigui neifa zhuan* (Buddhist Monk Yijing's Travels in India and Southeast Asia)	10	Honpa Hongwan-ji Temple
31. 龍藏本西域求法高法傳 Longzang ben (Books from the Dragon Canon): *Xiyu qiufa gaoseng zhuan* (Biography of Sixty Monks who Sought the Teachings of Buddha and the Way of Enlightenment in India and Southeast Asia during the Tang Dynasty)	10	Honpa Hongwan-ji Temple
32. 佛説十力經 *Foshuo shili jing* (Scripture of Buddha's Preaching on the Ten Kinds of Power Used to Save People)	10	Honpa Hongwan-ji Temple
33. 呉船錄 范成大著 *Wuchuan lu* (Voyage Notes Returning to Wu Region in the Southern Song Dynasty) written by Fan Chengda	2	Honpa Hongwan-ji Temple
34. 至元法寶勘同錄 *Zhiyuan Fabao kantong lu* (Catalog of over 1,400 Chinese Buddhist Scriptures Translated from Sanskrit, Indicating the Corresponding Tibetan and Sanskrit Titles)	1	Honpa Hongwan-ji Temple
35. 康熙板番藏經目錄 *Fanzang jing mulu* (Catalog of *Fanzang jing* Scriptures) (Kangxi version)	1	Honpa Hongwan-ji Temple
36. 西藏文藏經 *Xizang wen Zangjing* (The Integrated Classic Tibetan Buddhist Scriptures Written in Tibetan)		Honpa Hongwan-ji Temple
37. 原刻本造像量度經 *Zaoxiang liangdu jing* (Technique Guide for Tibetan Buddhist Painting) (Original version)	2	—
(7) Western Buddhist scriptures	Holdings in departments and libraries in the College of Letters (date of registration prior to Hedin's Lecture)	
38. A. Rémusat: Foĕ Kouĕ Ki, ou Relation des royaumes bouddhiques: voyage dans la Tartarie, dans l'Afghanistan et dans l'Inde, exécuté, à la fin du IVe siècle. 1836.	Sanskrit	
39. S. Julien: Mémoires sur les contrées occidentales. 1857–58.	Oriental History	
40. S. Julien: Histoire de la vie de Hiouen-Thsang et de ses voyages dans l'Inde depuis l'an 629 jusqu'en 645 par Hoeï-Li et Yen-Thsong, suivie de documents et d'éclaircissements géographiques tirés de la relation originale de Hiouen-Thsang. 1853.	Oriental History	
41. A. F. R. Hoernle: The Bower Manuscript. 1893.	Sanskrit	

Source: Tokyo Geographical Society 1909b, "Hedin hakase tairaku kiji (Dr. Hedin in Kyoto)," *Chigaku Zasshi*, 21(6).

Table 2.8: Inscriptions and old maps exhibited for Hedin's lecture

(8) Inscriptions	Reference
42. *Han Pei Cen jigong bei* (漢斐岑紀功碑 "Stele Commemorating the Victory of Pei Cen"; Han Dynasty, 137 CE), 1 scroll	
43. *Tang-Tubo huimeng bei* (唐吐蕃會盟碑 "Stele of the Tang-Tubo [Tibet] Alliance"; Tang Dynasty, 821 CE), 1 scroll	
44. *Dajianlu zangwen bei pian* (打箭爐藏文碑片 "Fragmentary Tibetan Inscription from Dangjianlu [Dartsedo]"), 1 scroll	
45. Ancient bronze mirrors: 5 "sea-horse-and-grape mirrors" attributed to the Han Dynasty, 15 mirrors attributed to the Han, Six Dynasty, and Tang eras (20 items)	
(9) Old maps	Document source
46. *Honil gangni yeokdae gukdo ji do* [Kon'itsu kyōri kokuto no zu] (混一疆理歷代國都之圖 "Map of Integrated Lands and Regions of Historical Countries and Capitals"; Map of East Asia made in Korea in 1402 CE), 1 scroll	Honpa Hongwan-ji Temple

Source: Tokyo Geographical Society 1909b, "Hedin hakase tairaku kiji (Dr. Hedin in Kyoto)," *Chigaku Zasshi*, 21(6).

ji (Records of Waterways in the Western Regions) is a geographical and historical text relating to the waterways of East Turkestan.[7] The exhibition could thus be regarded as an homage to Hedin's interests and accomplishments, recognizing the great efforts he had made in locating the sources of the major rivers of Central Asia.

Among the documents listed in Tables 2.4 through 2.8, I have listed the departmental provenance for materials now held in the library of the Graduate School of Letters and Faculty of Letters. It seems unlikely that many of the documents in the current collection are those that were exhibited during Hedin's lecture. Nevertheless, faculty members in the College of Letters at the time were clearly interested in the lands that Hedin had explored, as well as his findings, discoveries and excavations, and this tradition remains alive today. More than anything, the very fact that the faculty of the College of Letters went to such lengths to stage an exhibition of these materials in conjunction with Hedin's lecture at a venue in the college offers graphic testimony of the state of the college's academic interest in Hedin's visit.

Help from Naitō Konan and Ogawa Takuji

Among the materials in the Kyoto University Archive is a document stating that "after preparations by Lecturer Naitō on the morning of November 29, visitors were permitted entry from noon onwards (with possession of a ticket stub from the lecture)," adding that "following the Lecture, the exhibition materials are being kept in the storeroom of the new library" (Kyoto Imperial University 1909). The Lecturer Naitō referred to here was Naitō Torajirō (also known as Konan) of the College of Letters.

The exhibition had been planned and assembled during the short period between Hedin's arrival in Japan and the day of his lecture at Kyoto Imperial University. How and whence were these materials brought together? Of the documents and materials placed on display, the Western Chinese Buddhist Scriptures and old maps were borrowed from outside the University, in many cases from the collection of Nishi Hongan-ji Temple. This indicates the cooperation of Ōtani Kōzui and Nishi Hongan-ji Temple. While the *Chigaku Zasshi* articles by the Tokyo Geographical Society offer no details of the other contributing collections; most of the exhibited documents were from Naitō's personal library, as attested to in a 1911 letter to Hedin from Kikuchi Dairoku, the President of Kyoto Imperial University until 1912.[8] Other documents were perhaps provided by Ogawa Takuji. Naitō and Ogawa were both assiduous bibliophiles reputed to have amassed huge collections of Chinese texts and Western books.

Another possible source of these materials is the Imperial University library. Accordingly, I checked the documents exhibited to see which had been catalogued by the university's library prior to Hedin's lecture on November 29, 1908 and have listed the relevant catalogue dates in Tables 2.4 through 2.7. Thirteen of these documents had been catalogued prior to the lecture, three of which were Hedin's own works held in the collection of the Department of Geography, inscribed on the inside cover with Hedin's signature and the date of the university lecture (Figure 2.5). From this, it is certain that at least some of the exhibited materials were books from the collection of the College of Letters.

Hedin would surely have seen the venue where the materials from his own expedition and related documents had been put on display. Evidence for this comes from not only the signatures on his own books, but also the fact that he describes being shown the Chinese texts by Ogawa, as also noted in the aforementioned letter from Kikuchi. Ogawa translated a passage from one of these Chinese texts into English for Hedin during the latter's stay in Kyoto, which Hedin quoted from in *Trans-Himalaya*, published for a popular audience, even prior to the writing or publication of an academic report (Hedin 1910: vol. 2, 182–184). The Chinese text in question is the *Shuidao tigang* listed in Table 2.6. The passage that Ogawa translated into English is found in Book 22. In the academic report based on Hedin's third expedition, published as *Southern Tibet* (Hedin 1917–1922), Ogawa's English translation is quoted in Volume 1, Chapter 12 in two passages describing the headwaters of the Brahmaputra River and the relationship between the Sutlej River and two lakes, respectively (Hedin 1917: vol. 1, 114–116; 119–120). In Volume 8 of the same work,

---

7 Ogawa (1902) lists at least ten major examples of such Chinese texts, arguing their utility in the study of China's history and geography. Among these, the *DaQing yitong zhi*, *Shui jing zhu*, *Xiyu shuidao ji*, and *Han xiyu tu kao* (Consideration of the maps of the Western Regions made in the Han Dynasty) were displayed on November 29, 1908.

8 The letter from Kikuchi Dairoku to Hedin, dated September 17, 1911, is kept in File 417 (Correspondence by Country / Japan and Yugoslavia) in the National Archives of Sweden (Riksarkivet) in Stockholm. The letter is in response to a request from Hedin for a translation of descriptions in the Chinese texts, notifying Hedin of the state of progress and mentioning the names of three faculty members in the College of Letters (i.e., Ogawa Takuji, Naitō Torajirō, and Haneda Tōru). Naitō is referred to as follows. "As you (Hedin) may remember, he is a major authority on Chinese matters, as well as the owner of most of the books you wrote about that were put on display at that exhibition," presumably the exhibition in conjunction with Hedin's lecture on November 29, 1908.

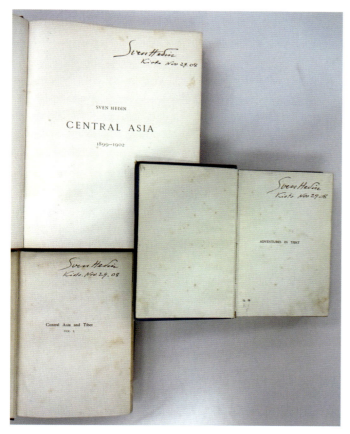

Figure 2.5: Three books autographed by Hedin: (*Central Asia and Tibet* (1903), *Adventures in Tibet* (1904), and *Scientific Results of a Journey in Central Asia and Tibet 1899–1902* (1905))

Ogawa's article is also quoted in relation to premodern Chinese cartography (Hedin 1922: vol. 8, 95). Ogawa's status as a well-known geographer and scholar versed in the Chinese classics is evident in this relationship between the two men.[9]

Hedin, the Society of Historical Research, and Oriental Studies

Lectures and exhibitions – a convention for the "Society of Historical Research"

Looking into the origins of the idea of exhibiting documents in conjunction with a lecture so that audiences might have the opportunity to view the materials, a lead can be found in the activities of the Society of Historical Research (*Shigaku kenkyūkai*), founded the previous December, predominantly comprising faculty members from the College of Letters (Society of Historical Research 1909: 176). Table 2.9 situates Hedin's lecture in the context of the Society's main activities during its first two years.

According to the first four volumes of its published Proceedings, *Shigaku kenkyūkai kōen-shū*, during the period between its inception and October 1910, the Society of Historical Research held sixteen regular meetings, three general meetings, one occasional outing, and two occasional lectures. These regular and general meetings, in most cases, featured lectures and exhibits. The themes addressed by the lectures included the municipal organization of Osaka in the Edo period (Kōda Shigetomo), the Nara period capital of Heijō-kyō (Kita Sadakichi), the scholarly legacy of the Song dynasty (Nishimura Tokitsune (Tenshū)), the topography of Mt. Paektu and the headwaters of the Songhua River (Ogawa Takuji), the *Daijō-sai* Imperial Japanese enthronement ceremony (Inokuma Asamaro), Farsi texts transmitted to Japan (Haneda Tōru), questions concerning the history of the Japanese language (Shinmura Izuru), the nobility and warrior classes (Miura Hiroyuki), inscriptions on tortoise shells excavated at Youli Castle (Tomioka Kenzō), Japan's foreign trade (Uchida Ginzō), the vernacular language of Edo (Yoshizawa Yoshinori), the Taima Mandala (Ema Tsutomu), four-sided steles of the Western Wei dynasty (Hamada Kōsaku), the period of the establishment of the Three Kingdoms of Goguryeo, Baekje, and Silla (Naitō Torajirō), the Han imperial Envoy Zhang Qian, Duke of Bowang (Kuwabara Jitsuzō), thoughts on *Aesop's Fables* (Ueda Bin), materials for the study of Indian history (Matsumoto Bunzaburō), materials for the historical study of interreligious conflict between Confucianism, Buddhism, and Daoism (Takase Takejirō), and Frederick the Great (Nakamura Zentarō). The speakers at these meetings included Society members as well as invited guests. In addition, a lecture delivered in October 1910 on "The Six Categories of the *Shuowen*" by Hoshino Hisashi (Tokyo Imperial University) was held jointly with the Society for Chinese Studies (*Shina gakkai*, established October 1907) of the College of Letters (Society of Historical Research 1908–1911).

For the exhibitions, materials in the possession of the Society's members and related organizations were displayed and subjected to commentary. The records include many documents detailing what kinds of materials were presented and by whom. Ōtani Kōzui, who was not a member of the Society, is once again a notable contributor of materials. In some cases, the lecturers would bring materials relevant to their lectures, suggesting an emphasis on seeing original materials and referring directly to the relevant documents. Among the events listed in Table 2.9, the June 1908 exhibition

---

9 I have been unable to find any details of what became of Hedin's written request for the translation, mentioned in Kikuchi's letter in note 8.

Table 2.9: Hedin's university lecture and other events in the first two years of the Society of Historical Research

Date	Event (location)	Principal content
December 1907	Society of Historical Research	Society founded
16 Feb, 1908	First Regular Meeting (College of Letters, Classroom No. 8)	Lecture (Takeda Goichi) Exhibition (Presenters: Department of Japanese History, Tomioka Kenzō, Miura Hiroyuki, Ema Tsutomu, Takeda Goichi, and Sakaguchi Subaru) Lecture (Uchida Ginzō)
22 March, 1908	Occasional Excursion	Tour of Byōdō-in Temple in Uji and environs (Guide: Takeda Goichi)
26 April, 1908	Second Regular Meeting (Kyoto Women's Normal School)	Lecture (Kōda Shigetomo) with reference books and materials Exhibition (Presenters and commentators: Naitō Torajirō, Usui Kosaburō, Tomioka Kenzō, Uchida Ginzō)
7 June, 1908	Third Regular Meeting (Kyoto Women's Normal School)	Lecture (Kita Sadakichi) Exhibition in Memoriam of Dr. Naka (Michiyo) (Presenters: Departments of Oriental History and Japanese History, Kawashima Motojirō, Naitō Torajirō, Tomioka Kenzō, Kano Naoki, Kōda Shigetomo, Haneda Tōru, Ōtani Kōzui, Shiratori Kurakichi, Masuzawa Chōkichi, Nakayama Kyūjirō, and others)
27 Sept, 1908	Fourth Regular Meeting (Kyoto Women's Normal School)	Lecture (Nishimura Tokitsune (Tenshū)) Exhibition (Presenters: Department of Japanese History, Kyoto Prefectural Library, Nishimura Tokitsune, Kamimura Kankō, and Tomioka Kenzō)
29 Nov, 1908	**Hedin Lecture** (Kyoto Imperial University)	Luncheon Lecture (Sven Hedin) Exhibition (Materials: Hedin's sketches and survey materials, related documents, old maps; Presenters: Honpa Hongwan-ji Temple et al.) Welcome banquet (Kyoto Hotel)
6 Dec, 1908	First General Meeting (Honpa Hongwan-ji Temple)	General Meeting (Bukkyō University Library) Refreshments (Count Ōtani's residence) Exhibition (Presenter: Ōtani Kōzui) Lecture (Ōtani Kōzui) Tour of the Flying Cloud Pavilion (*Hiunkaku*)
21 Feb, 1909	Fifth Regular Meeting (College of Law, Classroom No. 8)	Lecture (Kamimura Kankō; Ogawa Takuji) Exhibition (Presenters: Ogawa Takuji, Tomioka Kenzō)
23 May, 1909	Sixth Regular Meeting (First High School for Girls of Kyoto Prefecture)	Lecture (Uchida Ginzō; Inokuma Asamaro; Hara Katsurō)
20 June, 1909	Seventh Regular Meeting (College of Law, Classroom No. 8)	Lecture (Tanaka Kanbei; Kuwabara Jitsuzō)
31 Oct, 1909	Eighth Regular Meeting (College of Law, Classroom No. 8)	Lecture (Haneda Tōru; Uchida Ginzō) Exhibition (Lecture-related materials)
28 Nov, 1909	Second General Meeting (Kyoto Prefectural Library) (* The exhibition remained open to the public on November 29, attracting many visitors)	General Meeting Lecture (Shinmura Izuru) Luncheon Lecture (Miura Hiroyuki) Exhibition: Ancient paintings and calligraphic works from the Dunhuang Caves with a catalogue of related reference books (Comments: Ogawa Takuji, Naitō Torajirō, Tomioka Kenzō, Hamada Kōsaku, Haneda Tōru, Kano Naoki, Kuwabara Jitsuzō)

Sources: Society of Historical Research 1908–1910, *Shigaku kenkyūkai kōen-shū* (Lectures at Research Meetings by the Society of Historical Research), vols. 1–3. Tokyo: Fuzanbō. Tokyo Geographical Society 1909b, "*Hedin hakase tairaku kiji* (Dr. Hedin in Kyoto)" *Chigaku Zasshi* 21(6).

in Memoriam of Dr. Naka (Michiyo) and the November 1909 exhibition of ancient paintings and calligraphic works from the Dunhuang Caves and related reference books are representative of this format.

In each case, the published bulletin includes a detailed table classifying the materials on display and detailing the names of materials, their quantity, and the identity of the presenters (Society of Historical Research 1908: 165–171; Society of Historical Research 1910: 285–290). For an exhibition of ancient paintings and calligraphic works from the Dunhuang Caves, Drs. Ogawa, Naitō, and Kano each provided a commentary on the materials based on their respective fields of expertise, attesting to the cross-sectional nature of collaborative efforts in the College of Letters.

In March 1908, following a lecture by Takeda Goichi on the decorative motifs of Byōdō-in Temple, the Society took a field trip to tour the temple, with Takeda providing commentary (Society of Historical Research 1908: 147–172: Society of Historical Research 1909: 175–183).

In sum, from its inception, the Society of Historical Research had developed a custom of combining lectures with exhibitions for its meetings. Thus, when presented the opportunity to host Hedin at Kyoto Imperial University, it is hardly surprising that they should choose this format, with the College of Letters serving as the venue. Showcasing a careful selection of documents curated with a clear vision, and cooperation with off-campus partners such as Honpa Hongan-ji (Nishi Hongan-ji Temple) to source appropriate materials are both common features of the Society of Historical Research events. We must recognize the possibility that other members of the Society of Historical Research may have contributed materials for the exhibition staged for Hedin's lecture, too; and consider the guided tours of famous sites and attractions as field-based education sessions, complete with expert commentary.

Finally, we should note that shortly after Hedin's lecture, the Society's first general meeting was held at Nishi Hongan-ji while Hedin was still in Kyoto. That meeting featured a lecture by Ōtani Kōzui entitled "On the Study of Oriental History" and an exhibition of materials from the collection of Nishi Hongan-ji. In this context, Hedin's lecture and exhibition appear to be merely an extraordinary session in the Society of Historical Research's regular series of activities.

The Society of Historical Research and Oriental Studies in the College of Letters

Let us now consider the nature of the Society of Historical Research as an organization. The Society was formed by faculty members in the College of Letters in December 1907 "for the purpose of bringing together like-minded scholars to carry out research related to historiography" (Society of Historical Research 1908: 172). As well as meetings and research reports, the society launched a journal, and for its four years published summaries of its lectures in its annual Proceedings (*Shigaku kenkyūkai kōen-shū*), which, after two further incarnations, was relaunched in 1916 as the scholarly journal *Shirin* (Journal of History), which remains in print today. At the time of its inception, the Society counted 63 members, increasing to 105 four years later (116 unique members, with 10 withdrawals, and 1 death). Figure 2.6 lists its membership. Despite its name, many of its members were faculty in the College of Letters from non-historical fields such as Philosophy and Literature. There were also members from the Third Higher School and other institutions of higher education, as well as from public institutions such as the Kyoto Prefectural Library and the Imperial Museums, and newspaper publishers. In sum, the Society opened its gates wide, admitting anyone with an interest in the study of history. In Figure 2.6, members who took part in Hedin's welcome reception are marked with an asterisk (*). As many as twenty-two such participants can be identified in the Kyoto University archives (*Gaikoku meishi shōtai kankei shorui*), along with other faculty from the College of Letters and members affiliated with other educational institutions in Kyoto. Kameoka Suekichi (a technician from Kyoto) was tasked with showing Hedin around places such as the Katsura Imperial Villa.

The Society's inclusion of members from a variety of fields and institutions is consistent with its aims for conducting comprehensive and broad-based historical research. At the first regular meeting, held in February 1908, Uchida Ginzō stated that "it is my earnest desire that the study of Oriental civilization will lead to opening up new horizons here in Kyoto." After emphasizing the diversity and breadth of the historical periods and areas, matters of concern, materials, and methodologies to be subjected to historical research, Uchida argued the importance of researchers in multiple related fields sharing opinions and information to mutual stimulation (Society of Historical Research 1908: 148). Judging from the gallery of members and the themes of its lectures, it seems clear that the scope of both the "Orient" and "civilization" within Uchida's "history of Oriental civilization" were conceived in extremely broad and inclusive terms.

The orientation towards the history of Oriental civilization advocated by the Society was moreover a continuation of the founding spirit behind the College of Letters at Kyoto Imperial University. That is, the College had emphasized the development of Oriental Studies in response to insistent calls to distinguish itself from the College of Letters at Tokyo Imperial University. In line with this focus, Chinese Philosophy (previously known as "Chinese Studies"), Oriental

Higher Educational Institutions in Kyoto City			Other Higher Educational Institutions			Graduates of the College of Letters
Maekawa Kamejirō*, Nakamura Zentarō*, Yamamoto Yukinori*, Yamanouchi Shinkyō*, Nonomura Kaizō*, Itakura Tarō, Fujita Motoharu*, Masuzawa Chōkichi*, Ema Tsutomu, and others			Shigeta Teiichi, Matsumoto Hikojirō, Chō Hisayoshi, Ueki Naoichirō, and others			Terada Sada'ichi, Kiyohara Sadao, Nishida Naojirō, and others
Kyoto Imperial University College of Letters		**Geography** Ishibashi Gorō*, Ogawa Takuji*	**Oriental History** Haneda Tōru, Kuwabara Jitsuzō, Tomioka Kenzō*, Naitō Torajirō*	**Japanese History** Kōda Shigetomo, Kita Sadakichi, Miura Hiroyuki, Uchida Ginzō*	**Western History** Hara Katsurō, Sakaguchi Subaru*	**Education and Pedagogy** Tanimoto Tomeri*
<English> Shima Bunjirō*	<Archaeology> Hamada Kōsaku*					
<Linguistics> Shinmura Izuru	**Japanese Language and Literature** Yoshizawa Yoshinori*, Fujii Otoo	**Chinese Language and Literature** Kano Naoki*	**Sanskrit Language and Literature** Sakaki Ryōzaburō	**Indian Philosophy** Matsumoto Bunzaburō*	**Chinese Philosophy** Takase Takejirō*	**Aesthetics and Art History** Takeda Goichi, Taki Seiichi
Newspapers Iwai Taketoshi, Nishimura Tokitsune (Tenshū), Maki Makijirō	**Public Institutions** Kameoka Suekichi*, Kawashima Motojirō, Yuasa Kichirō, Mizuki Yōtarō, Mori Junzaburō, Fukui Rikichirō	**Nishi Hongan-ji Temple** Hori Ken'yū* Umekami Son'yū* Watanabe Tetsujō	**Other Temples** Ōtani Katsumasa, Kamimura Kankō, Tanimura Ichishige, and others	**Other** Nakanome Akira, Nagoshi Nakajirō, Usui Kosaburō, Mizoe Yaota, and many others		**College of Law** Ikebe Yoshikata

Figure 2.6: Members of the Society of Historical Research (1908–1911)

Note: Typographical errors found in names have been corrected.

* Members who attended the welcome reception for Hedin on November 29, 1908.

Sources: *Shigaku kenkyūkai kōen-shū* (Lectures at Research Meetings by the Society of Historical Research) (vols. 1–4), *Kyoto Teikoku Daigaku Ichiran* (1908–1909), *Dai-san kōtō gakkō ichiran* (September 1908 to August 1909), etc.

History, and Chinese Literature were each established as independent courses in the respective departments of Philosophy, History, and Literature, beginning with three classes for Oriental History alone (Faculty of Letters of Kyoto Imperial University 1935: 16–17). Space does not permit a history of the development of Oriental Studies in the College of Letters, but suffice to mention that the Society of Chinese Studies was created in October 1907, just over a year after the College was established, with the objective of bringing together people from outside the university around three subjects of Chinese Philosophy, Oriental History, and Chinese Language and Literature to engage in comprehensive research. The formation of the Society of Historical Research later that year, with the objective of "studying the history of Oriental civilization," was also in line with the College's policy of emphasizing Oriental Studies (Faculty of Letters of Kyoto Imperial University 1935: 34).

Another important characteristic of Oriental Studies in the College of Letters is highlighted in an article by the Tokyo Geographical Society introducing Kyoto's new Department of Geography (Tokyo Geographical Society 1908: 525). The article praises the establishment of the department in September 1907, noting that "Kyoto is seen as an historical center of geographical study of East Asia." As evidence to support this claim, the article points to the presence in Kyoto of Ōtani Kōzui at Nishi Hongan-ji as an enthusiast of geographical initiatives, his leadership of a team of Asian explorers, and his collection of documents about the Oriental world. It also mentions the Society of Historical Research exhibition in Memoriam of Dr. Naka (Michiyo), for which a valuable collection of historical materials about the geography of the Mongolian region was loaned by Naitō Konan, Tomioka Kenzō, and Ōtani Kōzui. In sum, the Department of Geography was notable for its involvement with Nishi Hongan-ji and the Society of Historical Research, and was conceptualized with an orientation towards Oriental Studies research.

Kyoto reveals itself in welcoming a distinguished guest

In this chapter, I have focused on the welcome that was arranged in Kyoto for Hedin's visit in 1908. I have explored the characteristics and significance of the reception he received as a distinguished academic guest at Kyoto Imperial University, highlighting its differences from his reception at Tokyo Imperial University, especially the exhibition of historical materials in conjunction with his lecture.

Hedin's welcomes in Tokyo and Kyoto may be seen to contrast in several ways. Firstly, in Tokyo the Tokyo Geographical Society provided the primary institutional support as the organization that had invited Hedin. In contrast, in Kyoto, Kyoto Imperial University was his main host, treating Hedin as a distinguished academic guest, arranging his itinerary and events. The University President personally took the lead in extending the university's hospitality. Second, during his brief visit to Tokyo Imperial University he met almost exclusively with faculty from the College of Science, whereas a great many faculty members from all the constituent colleges of Kyoto Imperial University participated in his events there. When this latter point is combined with the unique exhibition staged at the College of Letters, and recognizing that field-matter experts served as guides to the local attractions and historic sites, we might say that Kyoto placed scholarship and culture at the forefront. In this respect, it differed considerably from the welcome in Tokyo, at which official functions, scientific researchers, and military officers had predominated.

For the College of Letters and its associated academic societies, all newly created and attempting to develop a foundation for Oriental Studies, Hedin's visit to Kyoto was not only extremely exciting, but came at a most opportune moment. From this perspective, while the efforts of local dignitaries and institutions can all be seen as gracious expressions of hospitality, the College of Letters and the Society of Historical Research must also have sensed a unique opportunity for raising the profile of Oriental Studies research at the College of Letters in Kyoto Imperial University.

The attitude of the College of Letters and its orientation to Oriental Studies is especially evident in the exhibition of documents. The fact that no such exhibition was held for any of Hedin's other lectures in Japan can perhaps be seen as an expression of the unique character of the College of Letters. Finally, the fact that Hedin quoted Ogawa's English translation of the *Shuidao tigang*, rather than accepting it as merely a token of hospitality or friendship, is a meaningful testament to a life-long academic exchange.

References

Abe, Hirotoshi 2014. Hedin no rainichi to nihon seifu oyobi nihon no sho-kikan no taiō (Hedin's visit to Japan and the correspondence to Hedin by the Japanese Government and other institutes). In Shirasu, Jōshin. ed. *Ōtani Kōzui to Sven Hedin: Nairiku ajia tanken to kokusai seiji* (Ōtani Kōzui and Sven Hedin: Explorations of inland Asia and international politics). Tokyo: Bensei-dō Shuppan, 103–121.

Chishitsu chōsajo hen (Geological Survey of Japan, ed.) 1982. *Chishitsu chōsajo hyakunenshi* (Centennial history of the Geological Survey of Japan). Tokyo: Kōgyō-gijutsu-in chishitsu chōsajo sōritsu hyaku-shūnen kyōsan-kai.

Dai-san kōtō gakkō (The Third Higher School) 1908. *Dai-san kōtō gakkō ichiran Meiji 41-nen ku-gatsu shutu Meiji 42-nen hachi-gatu shi* (The Third Higher School Handbook from September 1908 to August 1909). Kyoto: The Third Higher School.

Furubayashi, Kamejirō 1912. *Gendai jinmei jiten* (Contemporary Japan biographical encyclopedia). Tokyo: Chūō tsūshin sha.

Hedin, Alma 1925. *Mein Bruder Sven: Nach Briefen und Erinnerungen*, Mit 61 Abbildungen (My Brother Sven: Based on Letters and Memories, with 61 Illustrations). Leipzig: F. A. Brockhaus.

Hedin, Sven 1903. *Central Asia and Tibet: Towards the holy city of Lassa*. London: Hurst and Blackett.

Hedin, Sven 1904. *Adventures in Tibet*. London: Hurst and Blackett.

Hedin, Sven 1905. *Scientific Results of a Journey in Central Asia and Tibet 1899–1902*, vol. 1–3. Stockholm: Lithographic Institute of the General Staff of the Swedish Army.

Hedin, Sven 1909–1913. *Trans-Himalaya: Discoveries and adventures in Tibet*, vol. 1–3. New York: MacMillan. (First edition issued 1909 to 1912).

Hedin, Sven 1917–1922. *Southern Tibet: Discoveries in former times compared with my own researches in 1906–1908*, vol. 1–9. Stockholm: Lithographic Institute of the General Staff of the Swedish Army.

Hinode shimbun sha 1908. He hakase futatabi kitaru (Dr. Hedin returns to Kyoto). *Kyōto Hinode Shimbun*, December 11.

Kaneko, Tamio 1972. *Hedin den – Idai na tanken-ka no shōgai* (Biography of Hedin: A great explorer's life). Tokyo: Sin jinbutsu ōrai sha.

Kaneko, Tamio 1986. *Himerareta Berlin shisetsu – Hedin no Nazi doitsu nikki* (A secret envoy to Berlin: Hedin's diary of Nazi Germany). Tokyo: Kurumi shobō.

Kōmoto, Yasuko 2014. Hedin no rainichi – kindai nihon to Hedin to Tibet (Hedin's visit to Japan: Modern Japan, Hedin, and Tibet). In Shirasu, Jōshin ed. *Ōtani Kōzui to Sven Hedin: Nairiku ajia tanken to kokusai seiji* (Ōtani Kōzui and Sven Hedin: Explorations of inland Asia and international politics). Tokyo: Bensei-dō Shuppan, 123–144.

Kyōkai Zasshi Sha 1908. *Kyōkai Ichiran*, No. 445: 17, December 12.

Kyōto shimbun sha 1908. Hongan-ji ni okeru tanken hakase (The exploration doctor staying at Hongan-ji Temple). *Kyōto Shimbun*, December 3.

Kyōto Teikoku Daigaku (Kyoto Imperial University) 1908–1912. *Gaikoku meishi shōtai kankei shorui (Ji Meiji 41-nen shi Meiji 42-nen* (Documents relating to the invitation and welcome of foreign celebrities for 1908–1909). Materials held in the Kyoto University Archives (ID: 01A19469).

Kyōto Teikoku Daigaku (Kyoto Imperial University) 1909. *Kyōto teikoku daigaku ichiran Jū Meiji 41-nen shi Meiji 42-nen* (Kyoto Imperial University Handbook 1908–1909). Kyoto: Kyoto Imperial University.

Kyōto Teikoku Daigaku Bungaku bu (Faculty of Letters of Kyoto Imperial University) 1935. *Kyōto teikoku daigaku bungaku bu sanjū shūnen shi* (The 30th-year memorial book of Faculty of Letters, Kyoto Imperial University). Kyoto: Faculty of Letters, Kyoto Imperial University.

Nichigai Associates ed. 2011. *Meiji Taishō jinbutsu jiten* (Biographical encyclopedia of Meiji and Taisho era Japan). 2 volumes, Tokyo: Kinokuniya.

Nisshō hyakunenshi henshū iinkai 1971. *Nisshō hyakunenshi* (The centennial commemorative journal of Nissho Elementary School). Kyoto: Nisshō hyakunenshi henshū iinkai.

Ogawa, Takuji 1902. Hoku-sei zakki (Dai ichi kō) (Notes on Chinese classic books of geography (Part One)). *Chigaku Zasshi* (The Journal of Geography), 14 (8): 562–565.

Ōsaka Mainichi Shimbun sha 1908. He hakase no kōen (Dr. Hedin's lecture). *Ōsaka Mainichi Shimbun*, November 30.

Osaka Jiji Shimpō sha 1908. Tanken hakase no nyūraku (The explorer doctor entered Kyoto). *Osaka Jiji Shimpō*, November 29.

Osaka Jiji Shimpō sha 1908. Tanken hakase no kangeki: Butai wa jūdan-me no Mitsuhide (The explorer doctor enjoyed watching the Kabuki performance, the program was the Ehon Taikōki's tenth stage where Akechi Mitsuhide played a hero). *Osaka Jiji Shimpō*, December 2.

Sakaguchi, Takahiro 2013. Sven Hedin no kōydai hōmon (Sven Hedin's visit to Kyoto University). *Kyōto Daigaku Bunsho-kan Dayori* (Kyoto University Archives newsletter), 25: 8.

Shigaku Kenkyū Kai (The Society of Historical Research) 1908. *Shigaku kenkyū kai kōen-shū*, dai issatu (Lectures at research meetings by the Society of Historical Research, Vol. 1), Tokyo: Fusambō.

Shigaku Kenkyū Kai (The Society of Historical Research) 1909. *Shigaku kenkyū kai kouen-shū*, dai ni-satu (Lectures at research meetings by the Society of Historical Research, Vol. 2), Tokyo: Fusambō.

Shigaku Kenkyū Kai (The Society of Historical Research) 1910. *Shigaku kenkyū kai kouen-shū*, dai san-satu (Lectures at research meetings by the Society of Historical Research, Vol. 3), Tokyo: Fusambō.

Shigaku Kenkyū Kai (The Society of Historical Research) 1911. *Shigaku kenkyū kai kouen-shū*, dai yon-satu (Lectures at research meetings by the Society of Historical Research, Vol. 4), Tokyo: Fusambō.

Shirasu, Jōshin ed. *Ōtani Kōzui to Sven Hedin: Nairiku ajia tanken to kokusai seiji* (Ōtani Kōzui and Sven Hedin: Explorations of inland Asia and international politics). Tokyo: Bensei-dō Shuppan.

Takashimaya kyōto gofuku ten. 1910. He hakase no go-raiten (Dr. Hedin enjoyed shopping at our store). *Shin-ishō*, Vol. 81: 13, January 1.

Tanaka, Kazuko 2015. Kyoto daigaku ga shozō suru Sven Hedin ni kakawaru kaiga shiryō ni tsuite (A preliminary observation of the drawings and paintings related to Sven Hedin stored at Kyoto University: A legacy of his stay in Japan in 1908). *Jimbun Chiri* (Japanese Journal of Human Geography), 67 (1): 57–70.

Tōkyō Chigaku Kyōkai (Tokyo Geographical Society) 1908. Kyōto teikoku daigaku ni okeru chirigaku (The Department of Geography at Kyoto Imperial University), *Chigaku Zasshi* (The Journal of Geography), 20 (7): 525.

Tōkyō Chigaku Kyōkai (Tokyo Geographical Society) 1909a. Dokutoru Sven Fuon Hedin shi kangei hōkoku (Report on the welcome given to Dr. Sven Hedin), *Chigaku Zasshi* (The Journal of Geography), 21 (6): a1–a31.

Tōkyō Chigaku Kyōkai (Tokyo Geographical Society) 1909b. Hedin hakase tairaku kiji (Dr. Hedin in Kyoto), *Chigaku Zasshi* (The Journal of Geography), 21 (6): b1–b12.

Yazawa, Daiji 1989. "Sven Hedin to Lou-Lan Ōukoku ten" ni omou (Exhibition of "Sven Hedin and the Kingdom of Lou-Lan" and Tokyo Geographical Society). *Chigaku Zasshi* (The Journal of Geography), 98 (3): 366–373.

3 The Legacy of Sven Hedin's Stay in Kyoto
Reproductions of Original Art by Hedin Left at Kyoto University
TANAKA Kazuko

As well as an explorer and geographer, Sven Hedin was an accomplished and talented painter. He produced a prodigious number of paintings over his lifetime, most of which are now held in a collection in Sweden's Museum of Ethnography (Etnografiska Museet) in Stockholm. And, at present, Kyoto is the only known case of the creation and preservation of reproductions of Hedin's original artwork. This chapter introduces and explores the circumstances behind the reproduction of Hedin's watercolors and sketches from Tibet during Hedin's stay in Kyoto in November and December 1908. It examines the staging of an exhibition that included classical Chinese texts and original artwork by Hedin as one of a series of events organized by Kyoto Imperial University, and considers how this exhibition occasioned the reproduction of Hedin's works. The College of Letters, whose successor is the Faculty of Letters today, made a great contribution to holding the exhibition. Behind the exhibition and the reproductions we find a web of diverse exchanges across organizational and university boundaries between the academic and artistic communities in Kyoto at the time.

Reproductions left by Hedin in the Department of Geography

Overview of the reproduced works

At the beginning of 2014, sixty sketches and watercolors were discovered in a drawer in a cabinet in the Department of Geography in the Faculty of Letters at Kyoto University, twenty-six sandwiched between two pieces of card stock labeled in calligraphic brushstrokes with the words "Ishida Kinzō, Nishimura Junji, Adachi Itarō; Reproductions; Central Asia (?) Terrain and Customs I," and thirty-four in a paper envelope also labeled in calligraphic brushstrokes "Central Asia; Terrain; Customs; Reproductions II" (Figure 3.1). A list of these works can be found in Part I of this volume (see page 140). As I have already published a detailed report on these sixty reproductions and the people who created them (Tanaka 2015), I only briefly introduce them here. Among the sixty reproductions, fifty-seven are signed with the names of their creators, Nishikawa Junji (30 pieces), Adachi Itarō (15 pieces), Ishida Kinzō (8 pieces), and Tanaka Zennosuke (4 pieces). The name "Nishimura Junji" as it is written on the card stock is a misspelling of Nishikawa.

The representations can be broadly divided into three groupings: depictions of Central Asia, especially Tibetan landscapes and outdoor vistas (e.g., mountains, ruins, monastery temple complexes, buildings and crowds, and monastery facades); depictions of temple interiors (e.g., a Buddhist altar, monks, guardian deities portrayed on an entrance wall, corridors, monks' cells, a man pushing a door, groups of monks); and human figures (upper body portraits, figures clothed in full costume, full-body portraits of figures wearing clothing and equipment). Although these works are all reproductions, they are alluring pictures, with figures, temples, and mountains that have been vividly realized. Twenty-two are sketches drawn in pencil, sixteen in pen, and the remaining twenty-two are watercolors, in some cases

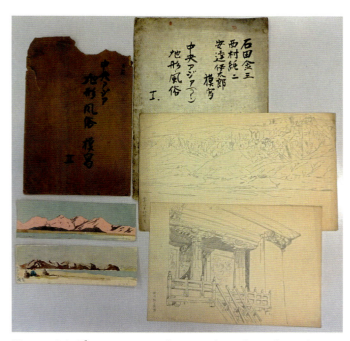

Figure 3.1: The paper envelope and card stock enclosing the sixty reproductions

Source: Department of Geography, Faculty of Letters, Kyoto University.

Figure 3.2: An example of a reproduction
Source: Department of Geography, Faculty of Letters, Kyoto University (Collection ID: KU II–7).

Figure 3.3: Original painting by Hedin
Source: Hedin, Sven 1910. *Trans-Himalaya: discoveries and adventures in Tibet, vol. 2*, Illustration 360.

Figure 3.4: An exhibition of Hedin's paintings (Shimla 1908)
Source: Hedin, Alma 1925. *Mein Bruder Sven: Nach Briefen und Erinnerungen.*

featuring both pen and pencil. The substrates are thin straw paper and cartridge paper, seemingly cut to suit the drawings in question in a variety of sizes ranging from roughly 8 cm × 25 cm at the smallest to 21 cm × 63.5 cm at the largest. Forty-two of the reproductions feature words or descriptions in one corner as a kind of memo, written in cursive alphabetical script in pencil. These reproductions were not accompanied by any descriptive materials or contextual details such as the date or purpose of the reproductions or the sequence of events by which they came to be stored in the Department of Geography.

The artists behind the reproductions

The reproductions were created by four art students from the Kansai Art Academy (Kansai Bijutsu-in) (Tanaka 2015: 59), which had been established in 1906, primarily around the figure of Asai Chū. Asai was a prominent advocate of modern Western-style painting. The Kansai Art Academy had been formed by uniting three groups which had common interest in Western-style arts: the Shōgoin Institute of Western-style Painting founded by Asai in 1903, the Kansai Art Society (Kansai Bijutsu-kai) founded in 1901, and the Twentieth Day Club (Hatsuka-kai) founded in 1902. While teaching as professor at the Kyoto Higher School of Arts and Technology, founded in 1902, Asai also served as the principal of the Kansai Art Academy until his death in 1907. Tanaka and Nishikawa were among the first cohort of students, while Adachi and Ishida were among the second (Shiga and Shimizu 2006: 195–196). Of these four student painters, we can trace the artistic careers of Tanaka (1889–1946) and Nishikawa (1896–1974).

Adachi was mentioned as a professional illustrator (*gakō*) in introductory remarks of the academic book on microscopes, whose pages feature many intricate illustrations (Suzuki 1910). To date, I have been unable to uncover any details about Ishida or his works. Tanaka, a private pupil of Asai's, exhibited his work energetically, and became a leading proponent of Kyoto's Western-style painting movement (Hoshino and Hoshino 1990). Nishikawa, a pupil of Kanokogi Takeshirō, in addition to working at Mitsukoshi in Osaka and Kyoto's Shimadzu Corporation, frequently held solo exhibitions as a painter of private houses and landscape paintings (Kyoto Municipal Museum of Art 1974). As a professional painter, he did not use his real name of "Nishikawa Junji" but "Nishikawa Jun." Kanokogi was another leading Western-style painter who played a central role with Asai in establishing the Kansai Art Academy. Later in their lives, both Tanaka and Nishikawa would serve as professors and directors at the school (Shiga and Shimizu 2006: 213–215). Given that "Nishikawa Junji" is listed as one of the painters of the reproductions, we can surmise that they were produced prior to his emergence as a full-fledged artist; that is, while he was still a student.

When were the reproductions made, and in what context?

Many of the sixty images that were reproduced – landscapes and human figures from Central Asia, especially Tibet – were published in Hedin's book *Trans-Himalaya* (1910–1913, 3 vols.), and the posthumous album *Sven Hedin As Artist* (1964) (Tanaka 2015: 60–62). The published illustrations were all original works by Hedin. Figure 3.3 shows the Hedin original for the reproduction in Figure 3.2. While the scope for published illustrations is slightly constrained, we can see that the two images are extremely similar. There are several reasons to doubt that the reproductions were based on the illustrations published in these books. First, and primarily, we know that many of the illustrations published in *Trans-Himalaya* were redrawn by Hedin specifically for this publication. Second, the dimensions of the illustrations in the book are only a few centimeters on either side and thus not conducive to precise reproductions. Third, not all of the reproductions are represented in the book. Fourth, some of the pictures published in black-and-white are vivid watercolors in the reproductions. Finally, some of the reproductions are larger in scope than the corresponding published illustration. Accordingly, it seems reasonable to conclude that the art students were referring to Hedin's original works when they created the copies. We may therefore presume that the reproductions were made during Hedin's stay in Kyoto, specifically between November 28 and December 12, 1908, based on original works that were included among the 108 of Hedin's images exhibited at Kyoto Imperial University on November 29 (Tanaka 2015: 64).

Over a lifetime of exploration, as well as taking photographs, Hedin sketched and painted people and landscapes wherever he visited, leaving a legacy of several thousand pictures. Hedin had enjoyed drawing since childhood, learning the basics from his father. His paintings, which vividly convey the landscapes and people, reportedly enjoyed considerable popularity and were frequently exhibited to the public. A photo taken during Hedin's sojourn in Shimla shortly before his visit to Japan (Figure 3.4) shows a tabular board covered in a white sheet (or paper) on which dozens of Hedin's pictures have been arrayed, which are being viewed by people standing in front of them (Alma Hedin 1925: 240). The fact that both popular accounts of his travels and his academic reports are richly illustrations with images produced by his own hand, and the posthumous publication of an album of his sketches in 1964, attest to the allure of his pictures. But to the best of our knowledge, no other reproductions of his work have been found. Hence, this collection of sixty reproductions left in the Department of Geography in the Faculty of Letters at Kyoto University is a rare and interesting event.

The people involved in creating the reproductions

Kanokogi Takeshirō and the exhibition of Hedin's original works

So how were these reproductions made? As described above, the exhibition of Hedin's materials featured a total of 108 original works, including sketches and watercolors he had produced in Tibet (Tokyo Geographical Society 1909b). Naitō Torajirō (then a Lecturer in the College of Letters) played a central role in putting this exhibition together. Would he have had a hand in displaying these original works? Was he the one who found the art students to reproduce them? But since the reproductions ended up in the Department of Geography, someone other than Naitō must have been involved, too. While Ogawa Takuji, Professor of Geography, was most likely involved, we have no evidence to tie him, personally, to the arts community. A more likely candidate – someone intimately familiar with the art world – was Kanokogi Takeshirō, who had served as Hedin's guide to the Katsura Imperial Villa and the Imperial Palace. Kanokogi, as one of modern Kyoto's leading Western-style painters at the time, served as both the principal of the Kansai Art Academy and a lecturer at the Kyoto Higher School of Arts and Technology. In a detailed diary written by Kanokogi's wife Haruko,[1] an entry dated December 3, 1908 notes that "from this morning, a host of students has come to prepare the reproductions of Dr. Hedin's pictures," revealing that the reproductions were made in the Kanokogi household. A few days earlier, the entry for November 29 reads "Husband left for a bit of business at the university this morning." Since the exhibition opened at noon that day, it is likely that Kanokogi spent the morning helping to arrange Hedin's works in the venue at Kyoto Imperial University. Mrs. Kanokogi's diary mentions "sketching in Maruyama Park in the afternoon," suggesting that Kanokogi did not attend Hedin's lecture or the welcome reception. Kanokogi was to meet Hedin on the afternoon of December 1 at a game of *kemari* at the Kyoto branch of the Peer's Club, and again on the afternoon of the 2nd, when he went to Nishi Hongan-ji Temple in connection with Hedin's welcome, as well as the 3rd and 4th when he showed Hedin around the city districts. Nishikawa Junji, one of the four students who created the reproductions, was a student of Kanokogi's. Hence, it is clear that Kanokogi introduced the art students and provided the venue for creating the reproductions.

But who came up with the idea, proposed it to Hedin, and obtained his consent? Given his many interactions with Hedin, and that he was a professor in the Department of Geography where the reproductions were found, it seems highly likely that it was Ogawa who raised the idea with Hedin. But it seems less likely that Ogawa came up with the idea of reproducing Hedin's work. And while Kanokogi met Hedin on several occasions, they were all social events attended by many others; it seems unlikely these events provided an opportunity to broach the idea of the reproductions. Further, following Hedin's lecture on November 29, Hedin's originals and the other materials were stored in the stacks of the Kyoto Imperial University Library (Kyoto Imperial University 1908–1909). When we ponder how the paintings got from the Library to Kanokogi's residence (Kobori-Fukuro chō, Gion),[2] it seems unlikely to have been either Ogawa or Kanokogi: Ogawa accompanied Hedin throughout most of his packed schedule, and Kanokogi was serving as Hedin's guide from December 1st to 4th; hence neither of them appear to have had sufficient time to transport Hedin's artworks from the university. Mrs. Kanokogi's diary makes no mention of her husband visiting the university during this period. Either they were delivered from the library stacks to the Sawabun Ryokan where Hedin stayed, and then transported to the Kanokogi residence, or delivered directly to the Kanokogi residence; in either case, whoever gave the instructions to release the artwork from the library stacks would have been associated with Kyoto Imperial University.

Conversely, for Hedin, entrusting others with invaluable artwork that he had produced to record his perilous expeditions, and especially to allow them to be reproduced, exposing them to the risk of soiling with paint or from handling, must have been a major decision. The very fact that Hedin, at the end of his expedition, had not sent his pictures back to his home in Stockholm, but

---

1 From Mrs. Kanokogi Haruko's diary for "Meiji 41, 1908." I am indebted to the good graces of Ms. Kanokogi Yoshiko, who inherited and preserved the materials of the Kanokogi household, for permitting me to consult the diary.

2 Mrs. Kanokogi Haruko's diary entry for December 31, 1908 notes an address in "Kobori-Fukuro-chō, Gion" as their fourth residence after moving from Okayama in the spring of 1904. While I cannot find this district listed in current registers, it is likely that Kobori refers to the Kobori hiromichi (now Higashi-ōji-dōri) road and Fukuro-chō refers to the area of Gion Fukuro-chō near the gates of Chion-in Temple. Kanokogi Takeshirō is known to have frequently taken his sketch pad to Maruyama Park.

had carried them with him to India and then through China to Japan, suggests that he considered these to be valuable materials that he wanted to keep close to hand in order to show them, or use them in necessary cases. The point is that neither the request to reproduce his work nor submitting the originals for reproduction would have been possible without significant trust between Hedin and the Kyoto people.

Behind the reproductions: Links across organizations and fields

Ogawa's autobiography (Ogawa 1941) only recounts events up to July 1904. The diary for 1908 of Hori Ken'yū, who attended to Hedin throughout his stay, is not extant (Hori 1987). Neither newspaper articles from the time or reports in the *Chigaku Zasshi* (The Journal of Geography) mention the reproductions. Kanokogi's autobiography (Kanokogi Takeshirō Gahaku kanreki kinen-kai 1934) only mentions his return from studying abroad in France and his reinstatement as a lecturer at the Kyoto Higher School of Arts and Technology for the year 1908. No diaries from the period or similar materials written by the art students have been found, nor is there any mention of the reproductions made in Hedin's autobiography (Hedin 1926). From documentary materials, then, it is difficult to pin down the circumstances leading to the reproduction of Hedin's original pictures.

Perhaps, though, we can find some insight by changing tack, and look instead at the ways in which people were related within and outside Kyoto Imperial University at the time of Hedin's visit. Figure 3.5 is a schematic representation identifying contemporary figures affiliated with Kyoto Imperial University, the Kyoto Higher School of Arts and Technology, and the Kansai Art Academy who were closely involved with both the painting community and Hedin's reception. In the figure, the Futaba-kai was a Western-style painting appreciation society directed by Asai Chū and comprised of staff and students of Kyoto Imperial University, the Third Higher School, and the Kyoto Higher School of Arts and Technology, while the Kansai Art Society, one of organizational antecedents of the Kansai Art Academy, had been founded under the leadership of Nakazawa Iwata in 1901 (Murakami 1903: 1–2). Figure 3.5 highlights overlapping interpersonal connections that cut across organizational boundaries. Nakazawa Iwata, Takeda Goichi, and Ishikawa Hajime were each associated with Kyoto Imperial University, the Kyoto Higher School of Arts and Technology, and the Kansai Art Academy or Kansai Art Society. Furthermore, Shima Bunjirō, Hibi Tadahiko, and Suzuki Buntarō from Kyoto Imperial University each occasionally taught at or loaned materials to the Kansai Art Society or Kansai Art Academy.

As noted earlier, Kanokogi Takeshirō held concurrent posts as lecturer at the Kyoto Higher School of Arts and Technology and as principal of the Kansai Art Academy. The Futaba-kai brought together aficionados of Western-style painting from these three institutions under the direction of Asai Chū. Although Asai, a leading Western-style artist in Meiji Japan, had died a year before Hedin's visit, we can nevertheless see his presence as the primary point of contact between the individuals involved in the reproductions and those involved in Hedin's welcome.

Following Asai's death, the memorial society formed by his colleagues to publish his manuscripts and erect a tombstone in his memory (named the "Mokugo-kai" in reference to a pseudonym Asai had favored) included Nakazawa, Takeda, Ishikawa, Kanokogi, Ogawa, and Shima – all shown in Figure 3.5 – as well as Asai's erstwhile pupil Tanaka (Chiba Prefectural Museum of Art 1981: 52–58). From the Mokugo-kai membership, we can see the interactions mediated by Asai between Western-style painting circles and university officials.

Let us now look more closely at personal connections. Nakazawa Iwata, who with President Kikuchi had accompanied Hedin on his shopping expedition, was the Dean of the College of Science and Engineering at Kyoto Imperial University, and was also dedicated to the Kyoto Higher School of Arts and Technology, where he had been appointed principal in 1902, when the school first opened. Asai Chū, who had been appointed as a professor at the Kyoto Higher School of Arts and Technology with Nakazawa's sponsorship, created the Shōgoin Institute of Western-style Painting at his home in Shōgoin, near Kyoto Imperial University in 1903. Then, in 1906, he also became the founding principal of the Kansai Art Academy, which he had established in collaboration with the Kansai Art Society founded in 1901 and the Twentieth Day Club founded in 1902. After Asai's death in December 1907, Nakazawa succeeded him as principal of the Art Academy. Ishikawa Hajime, a university administrator who had overseen Hedin's itinerary, had been teaching ethics at the Kyoto Higher School of Arts and Technology since the school's establishment. He was also an accomplished painter, praised as an equal, even by professionals; he had submitted works to Kansai Art Society exhibitions, and on occasion, had won prizes in the Society's competitions (Kuroda 2006: 114–115; Shimada 1995: 87–88). Kanokogi was also involved, through Asai, with both the Kyoto Higher School of Arts and Technology and the Kansai Art Academy. In 1904, having returned from a period of study in Paris, Kanokogi became a lecturer at the Kyoto Higher School of Arts and Technology on Asai's recommendation. He was later reinstated to the post after a second study trip to France from February 1906 to January 1908. In June 1908, he was appointed to replace Nakazawa as the prin-

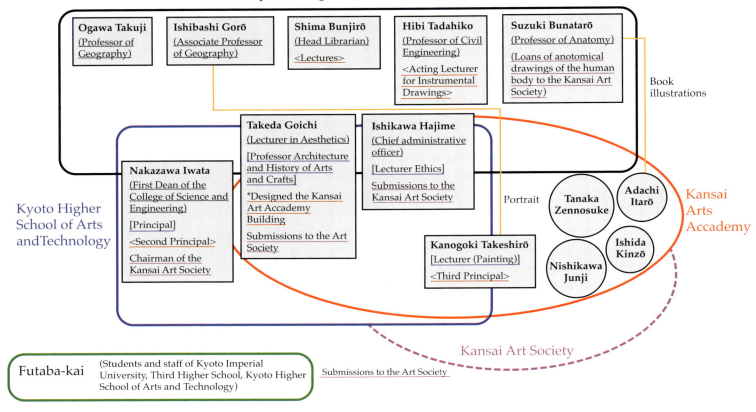

Figure 3.5: Links between people closely involved in Hedin's reception

Sources: Murakami Kanbē 1903. *Kansai bijutsu-in tenrankai shuppin mokuroku Meiji 36-nen* (Catalogue of submissions to the 1903 Kansai Art Academy Exhibition); Kyoto Higher School of Arts and Technology 1908. *Kyōto kōtō kōgei gakkō ichiran ji Meiji 41 shi 42-nen* (Handbook of Kyoto Higher School of Arts and Technology, 1908–1909); Suzuki Buntarō 1910. *Kenbikyō oyobi kyōsajutsushiki* (Microscopes and Microscopy); *Shōwa 11-nen 1-gatsu Ishibashi Hakushi kanreki kinen ehagaki* (Picture postcards in honor of Dr. Ishibashi's 60th birthday, January 1936); Kyoto Prefectural Library and Archives 1972. "Kansai bijutsu-in in'nai nisshi Meiji 39-nen–Meiji 44-nen (Kansai Art Academy daily record for 1906 to 1911)"; Chiba Prefectural Museum of Art 1981. *Asai Chū to Kyōto yōga-dan no hitobito* (Asai Chū and his circle: Kyoto's Western-style painters); Shimada Yasuhiro 1995. *Meiji no yōga: Asai Chū to Kyōto yōga-dan* (Meiji Western-style painting: Asai Chū and the Western-style painters of Kyoto); Kuroda Jūtarō 2006. *Kyōto yōga no reimeiki* (The very early days of Western-style painting in Kyoto), revised edition, etc.

cipal of the Kansai Art Academy. Takeda Goichi, who became a professor at the Kyoto Higher School of Arts and Technology upon his return from studies in France, also delivered lectures on aesthetics at the College of Letters (Kyoto Higher School of Arts and Technology 1908). Takeda had been responsible for designing the building for the Kansai Art Academy; like Ishikawa, he also exhibited and won awards at the Kansai Art Society (Shimada 1995: 62, 88). At the Kansai Art Academy, Hibi was responsible for teaching technical drawing (i.e., perspectival representation), while Shima was invited to give a lecture on December 10, 1908 (Kyoto Prefectural Library and Archives 1972: 1–2). Both Hibi and Shima Bunjirō participated in Hedin's reception (see Chapter II-2 of this volume).

Suzuki, a professor in the Department of Anatomy, had also attended the feast to welcome Hedin. The Department of Anatomy, in turn, had collaborated on an exhibition with the Kansai Art Society in 1903 lending human anatomical diagrams and other materials kept in the department (Murakami 1903: 10). For Suzuki's 1910 book on microscopes (Suzuki 1910), Adachi Itarō, one of the art students who had created the reproductions, was employed as a professional illustrator (*gakō*). Suzuki also appears to have had an interest in painting, as evidenced by his collaboration on a book concerning techniques for depicting the human body (entitled *Bijutsu kaibō-gaku* (Art Anatomy); Suzuki and Kurata 1908) and had worked as a lecturer at the Kyoto Municipal School of Painting. While I have been unable to establish precisely how Suzuki came to recruit Adachi for his book, this link between the two is suggestive. Likewise, how Kanokogi was enlisted to act as Hedin's guide is unknown, it seems likely that he was recommended by someone well-versed in art who was also fluent in both English and French – perhaps Nakazawa or Ishikawa. Figure 3.5 depicts how these mutual interactions repeatedly overlapped and intermingled; in these circumstances, a recommendation or introduction would not be unusual. Compared with these intricate relationships, Ogawa's and Ishibashi's (the Department of Geography's) connections to the painting world seem rather faint. But a portrait of Ishibashi Gorō painted by Kanokogi (Figure 3.6) printed as postcards to commemorate Ishibashi's 60th birthday in 1936, almost thirty years after Hedin's visit to Japan,[3] reveals a friendship between the two men which continued for many years.

The relationships traced in this section reveal that the art world and the academic world in Kyoto at the time of Hedin's visit to Japan significantly overlapped, to the extent that many people, including Ogawa, would have been in a position to have come up with the idea of reproducing Hedin's artwork and collaborating to make it happen. It seems safe to assume that this was the background to the reproduction of Hedin's pictures. The absence of any written records about them leaves us wondering why reproductions were made, rather than, for example, simply photographing them. Perhaps it was to preserve the allure of Hedin's pictures, as a memorial of his visit. Or perhaps they were intended to aid in geographical education and research into the landscapes and customs of Tibet, a land that was exceedingly difficult to visit, much less explore. Perhaps the exercise was merely intended to train the art students in the techniques of Western-style paintings? Any of these suggestions are plausible, and none are compelling. It is of course possible that all served as motivations. In light of the close connections between scholars and artists in Kyoto at the time, it is likely that artistic and scholarly motivations overlapped, creating an environment which would ferment a collective inspiration to ask Hedin to allow them to reproduce his artwork. This environment was also highly conducive to role-sharing and collaboration among the individuals who asked Hedin for permission, those who introduced the art students, those who arranged for transportation of the originals to Kanokogi's residence, and those who would later find a home for the reproductions.

Did Hedin see the reproductions?

The original pictures that had been taken to Kanokogi's residence for copying were returned to Hedin before he departed from Kyoto. As we have seen, the reproduction work began on December 3, and Hedin departed Kyoto on December 12. In the interim, Hedin was extremely busy, giving a speech and enjoying a feast sponsored by

---

3   The wrapping paper enclosing the picture postcards reads "Commemorating Dr. Ishibashi's 60th Birthday, January 1936," and features two portraits, one depicting its subject wearing a suit, and the other in formal dress. Both are labeled as works by Kanokogi Takeshirō.

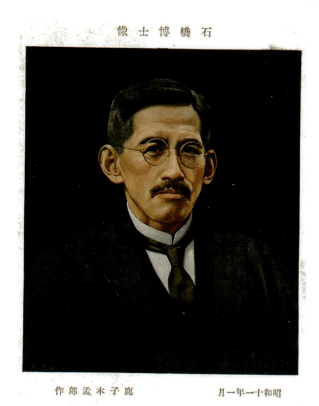

Figure 3.6: Portrait of Ishibashi Gorō. Painted by Kanokogi Takeshiro, January 1936.
Source: Department of Geography, Faculty of Letters, Kyoto University.

Kyoto's Chamber of Commerce and Industry (December 5), as well as touring Kyoto's historic sites and attractions, making excursions to Osaka and Nara (December 7–8), visiting with Abbot Ōtani Kōzui at Nishi Hongan-ji Temple (December 10), and squeezing in some personal shopping on December 6 and the few days from December 9–11 (Tokyo Geographical Society 1909b). The reproduction work no doubt took several days. Even split among four artists, the time required to make sixty reproductions would have been considerable. Hence, it seems reasonable to assume that the original works were not returned to Hedin until the end of his stay.

But who would have done so? And would they have brought the reproductions to show Hedin? Once again, the absence of documentary evidence makes it difficult to pin down answers. One clue, though, can be found in the memos penciled on the reproductions. Among the annotations are the Swedish word "år" ("year") and words that appear to be the Tibetan place names "Selipuk" and "Dava." It is conceivable that these markings had been copied from the originals. This raises two questions: namely whether the same information written on the reproductions was inscribed on the originals; and the identity of the person who annotated the reproductions.

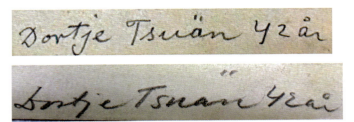

Figure 3.7: Sample handwritten annotations (top: reproduction; bottom: original)

Source: Reproduction held by the Department of Geography, Faculty of Letters, Kyoto University (Collection ID: KU I–11) and original work by Hedin held by Sweden's Museum of Ethnography (Etnografiska Museet) (Collection ID: EM B10 VI 216).

Figure 3.8: Sample handwritten annotations (top: reproduction; bottom: original)

Source: Reproduction held by the Department of Geography, Faculty of Letters, Kyoto University (Collection ID: KU II–11), and original work by Hedin held by Sweden's Museum of Ethnography (Collection ID: EM C 7 VI 452).

We sought answers to the first question in a November 2015 survey, which determined that forty-nine of the reproductions correspond to original works kept in the Museum of Ethnography in Stockholm.[4] Comparing these originals with the corresponding reproductions led to the following discoveries.

The annotations on the originals and the reproductions are largely identical. The word orders on the originals have been faithfully reproduced on the copies, and there are no transcription errors. The handwriting, however, despite some similarities, is characteristically distinct in several respects. First, there are clear differences in the alphabetical script for the letters D, K, L, and T, as well as for the numerals 2, 3, and 4, among others. Thus, while it is not definitive, it seems unlikely that the reproductions were annotated by Hedin himself. Figure 3.7 provides a sample of text written on an original with the corresponding annotation on the reproduction. A slightly stranger exception is presented in the annotation in Figure 3.8. On the original, Hedin has later, presumably after returning to Stockholm, written a new annotation in pen and ink

---

4 While some of the reproductions are annotated to indicate dates and others are not, such annotations were found on all forty-nine of the corresponding originals. However, where years have been appended on Hedin's originals in ink beside signatures in pencil, these were probably added later by Hedin.

over the note penciled during his exploration. However, the penciled annotation remains visible under the inked annotation, and the first two words appear to have been transposed. While Hedin penciled memos on his art works in his fields, he added or corrected the information in pen and ink at his home in Stockholm. This can be inferred to have been his usual way, according to careful observation of many of his works. The annotation on the reproduction, however, is as per the overwritten inked one on the original. Why does the annotation on the reproduction (Figure 3.8) reflect the later-revised annotation on the original? There are at least two possibilities. That is, it was either written by Hedin himself or in accordance with his spoken instructions in Kyoto. Given that the numeral 7 on the reproduction is missing the oblique line usually used by Hedin, the latter scenario is more likely.

Assuming that the annotations on the reproductions were written by someone other than Hedin, then who was it? Either the art students transcribed the annotations while preparing the reproductions, or else Ogawa, Kanokogi, or someone else did so either before returning the originals to Hedin or while comparing them against the reproductions as they were being returned. Given the difference in the thickness of the penciled lines in the annotations on the reproductions from those used for the signatures of the students who created them, it may be that the person who wrote the annotations was someone other than the students who copied the pictures, using a different pencil. Also, since some of the annotations appear to feature different handwriting, there is also the possibility that they were written by more than one person. Whoever made the annotations on the reproductions, and whenever they might have done so, a reversal of word order like the one shown in Figure 3.8 could only have occurred if Hedin had seen the reproductions. It seems quite plausible that when the originals were returned to Hedin, the reproductions were brought along with them. Hedin's reaction to seeing the reproductions, and whether it was communicated to the art students, must be left to the imagination.

Encounters between art and academia: Paris and Shimogamo

An overseas encounter: The Exposition Universelle de Paris, 1900

Expanding our perspective beyond Kyoto and looking at interactions overseas, we discover further links between the people involved with Hedin's reception in Kyoto. One notable example is L'Exposition Universelle de Paris, the World's Fair held in Paris, France in 1900. Ogawa Takuji was dispatched from Japan's Imperial Geological Survey to the Paris Exposition, setting sail from Yokohama in March. In Paris, he was introduced to Asai Chū, who at that time was studying in France, and the two men enjoyed excursions to the southern banlieues of Paris that autumn (Ogawa 1941: 130–131). Ogawa stayed in Europe, and participated in the International Geological Congress held in Vienna in January 1901. On this occasion, he joined the party of Ōtani Kōzui on visits to the city's suburbs along with Yamasaki Naomasa (then Professor of Geography at the Second Higher School and studying abroad in Europe),[5] and Albrecht Penck, Professor of Geography at the University of Vienna (Ogawa 1941: 133; Katayama 2004:46).[6] Returning from Vienna to Paris, Ogawa was dissuaded from returning immediately to Japan by Asai, who insisted that he should stay to see the Carnaval de Paris. In March, he left Paris for a brief visit to London (Ogawa 1941: 149). There, he rejoined Ōtani Kōzui, who took him for a tour of the Royal Geographical Society. Ogawa also met Hori Ken'yū and seems to have been interested in the plans for the Central Asia Expedition sponsored by Nishi Hongan-ji Temple (Ogawa 1941: 152; Katayama 2004: 48). At the time, Hori was studying geography – primarily cartography – at University of Oxford (Shinozaki 2001: 1–2). Meanwhile, Nakazawa Iwata also attended the Paris Exposition in the summer of 1900, and upon encountering Asai in Paris, asked him to join the staff of the Kyoto Higher School of Arts and Technology (Shimada 1995: 86; Kuroda 2006: 104). Although missing the Paris Exposition, Kanokogi Takeshirō set out from Japan in November 1900 and arrived in Paris in June 1901 after visiting the USA and Great Britain. He, too, became acquainted with Asai, on whose ardent recommendation he ended up remaining in Paris for two and a half years, earnestly studying Western painting (Kanokogi Takeshirō Gahaku kanreki kinen-kai 1934: 5–7). It was through his connection with Asai that Kanokogi came to live in Kyoto after returning to Japan in the spring of 1904. Thus, we see that Ōtani Kōzui, Ogawa Takuji, and many other people who would later be involved in Hedin's visit in Kyoto had encountered each other in Paris around 1900.

In Japan during the Meiji and Taishō periods, studying in Western countries was actively pursued in both academic and art fields; many of the figures mentioned in the previous section, including Takeda, Hibi, Suzuki, Nakazawa, Ishibashi, Shima, and Ishikawa, as well as Asai and Kanokogi, had studied overseas. In their rare encounters and exchanges with Japanese compatriots, these men created strong friendships that continued in Japan on more than a few occasions.

We can also find strong evidence of connections between painters and the university by examining the portraits alluded to earlier. For example, for the 60th anniversary of the Kyoto University Library, its reading room was decorated with portraits of the University's past presidents. As well as a portrait of Kinoshita Hiroji, the university's founding president, painted by Asai Chū, the collection featured portraits of Konishi Shigenao and Matsui Motooki (both by Kanokogi Takeshirō), Hamada Kōsaku (by Ōta Kijirō), Torigai Risaburō and Hattori Shunjirō (both by Suda Kunitarō), and Takikawa Yukitoki (by Oguri Yoshiji); the atmosphere was reportedly that of a gallery showcasing the heavyweights of the Kyoto painting community (Kyoto University Library 1961: 71–72). The portrait of Kinoshita Hiroji signed "1907 C. Asai" was one of Asai Chū's final works. As well as university presidents, there is no shortage of commissioned portraits hanging in the departments and classrooms of the university's constituent colleges, like the one of Ishibashi Gorō in the Department of Geography.

Exchanges centered on Kanokogi: Shimogamo

Finally, I would like to look at the friends and relationships centered on Kanokogi, an instructor of the art students who created the reproductions. I do so with reference to his own *Chijin meibo* (Name book of friends and acquaintances).[7] This address book, covering the period from approximately 1915 to 1933, consists of about 315 pages of names in alphabetical order from A to Y, along with about another 80 pages listing names associated with the Kansai Art Academy, painting schools, and similar groups. Moreover, filled as it is with the names of individuals who attended celebrations, farewell parties, lectures, and other events, the address book has also been affixed with numerous loose-leaf pages, booklets, and other addenda. Among those listed as friends and acquaintances are colleagues and students from the Art Society, gallery and department store officials, newspaper journalists, and patrons. Some names have been stricken out, while others have been rewritten several times owing to changes of address. In total, there are more than 3,000 individual listings, including duplications.

---

5 Following his return to Japan in 1901, Yamasaki Naomasa became Professor at the Tokyo Higher Normal School. When Hedin visited Japan in 1908, Yamasaki assisted in the welcome arrangements as a member of Tokyo Geographical Society (Tokyo Geographical Society 1909a).

6 Professor Albrecht Penck visited Kyoto Imperial University in 1909. According to records kept by Kyoto University (Kyoto Imperial University 1908–1912), he was the next international scholar of note to be welcomed after Hedin.

7 I am indebted to the good graces of Ms. Kanokogi Yoshiko, who has inherited and preserved the materials of the Kanokogi household, for permitting me to consult Kanokogi's *Chijin meibo*.

Table 3.1: Faculty members from Kyoto Imperial University listed in Kanokogi Takeshirō's *Chijin meibo* (Name book of friends and acquaintances), (1915 to 1933)

Department	Faculty members at Kyoto Imperial University (as of 1908)	Faculty members at Kyoto Imperial University (after 1908)
College of Law	Senga Tsurutarō*; Oda Yorozu; Tajima Kinji; Atobe Sadajirō*; Suehiro Shigeo*; Kanbe Masao; Ichimura Mitsue; Takarabe Seiji; Takeda Shō; Kawakami Hajime*	Ugaya Shikayoshi
College of Medicine	Araki Torasaburō*; Kamon Keitarō*; Nakanishi Kametarō*; Kaya Ryūkichi; Watsuji Shunji; Imamura Shinkichi*	Kominami Mataichirō
College of Letters	Matsumoto Bunzaburō*; Kano Naoki*; Fujishiro Teisuke*; Ogawa Takuji*; Shinmura Izuru; Ishibashi Gorō*; Takeda Goichi; Matsumoto Matatarō*; Nogami Toshio*	Ishida Kenji; Fukada Yasukazu; Ueda Bin; Taki Sei'ichi
College of Science and Engineering	Shinjō Shinzō*; Ōsaka Yūkichi*; Yoshikawa Kamejirō*; Chikashige Masumi; Tanabe Sakurō*; Ōfuji Takahiko*; Kaneko Noboru*; Saitō Daikichi*	Imanishi Kinji; Ishino Matakichi; Miyata Michio; Nishibori Eizaburō; Sekiguchi Eitarō
Library	Shima Bunjirō*	

Note: Some names may be missing owing to the difficulty of deciphering the original, a result of stains and damage.
* Indicates attendance at the welcome reception for Hedin hosted on November 29, 1908.
Sources: Documents kept by the Kanokogi household; Kyoto Imperial University 1909. *Kyoto Teikoku Daigaku ichiran* (1908–1909), etc.

Table 3.1 lists faculty members at Kyoto Imperial University at the time of Hedin's visit whose names are listed in Kanokogi's address book. The list runs to over thirty names. Of these names, those who attended the lecture or welcome feast held at Kyoto Imperial University on November 29, 1908 are marked with an asterisk. Since Kanokogi's address book postdates Hedin's visit, we must accept that some of those he knew at the time might not be included, due to death or moving away, in which case this list of more than thirty faculty members is incomplete. Table 3.1 also lists staff who joined Kyoto Imperial University after 1908. From science to the humanities, we can see that Kanokogi maintained friendly relationships with faculty from a broad spectrum of fields. The book also includes faculty at universities outside Kyoto, including Tokyo Imperial University, Kyushu Imperial University, and Kobe Higher Commercial School. One of these, Tanaka Kaoru of the Kobe Higher Commercial School, was taken at the age of ten to hear one of Hedin's lectures by his father, Viscount Tanaka Akamaro, who was given responsibility by the Tokyo Geographical Society for seeing to Hedin's amusement (Tanaka 1969: 202). Of course, in a book listing more than 3,000 names, the proportion of university staff is quite small, but it is nevertheless noteworthy that academics are so well represented. Indeed, from a different perspective, given that the total faculty at Kyoto Imperial University around 1908 was fewer than 300 people, the fact that Kanokogi was acquainted with more than 10% of them is remarkable (Kyoto Imperial University 1908–1910). From scholars in the College of Letters like Kano Naoki in Oriental studies, Ogawa and Ishibashi in geography, and Fukada Yasukazu in aesthetics, to their colleagues in the Colleges of Law, Medicine, and Science and Engineering, the address book includes names from a wide variety of academic fields. Some of them may have had patronage relationships through portrait commissions and the like, while others may have been interested in Kanokogi's paintings out of a personal enthusiasm for painting or art, or perhaps from having sent their children to study at his painting school. In some cases, friendships may have grown out of acquaintances made when they were studying or stationed overseas, as had happened between Ogawa Takuji and Asai Chū after meeting in Paris.

Another factor to consider is connections between fellow community residents. Shimogamo, where Kanokogi settled upon returning from his third study tour in 1918, had just begun to develop as a residential suburb following its incorporation that same year into the wider Kyoto municipality. A notable characteristic of those who were moving to Shimogamo was the high concentration of scholars and artists. Many of the scholars were employed at Kyoto Imperial University or the Third Higher School. For 1918, we can identify ten names, including Oda Yorozu, Senga Tsurutarō, Fukada Yasukazu, and Atobe Sadajirō (all listed in Kanokogi's address book), increasing to twenty-two in 1931, by which time the area already had a reputation as a "Scholars' Village" (Ishida 2000: 253–254; *Kyoto Hinode Shimbun* for March 6, 1918). As for the painters, after Kanokogi settled near Shimogamo Shrine, many other artists began moving into the area, which soon came to be known as the "Barbizon of Japan." One stretch along the Kamogawa River to the west of Shimogamo Shrine seems to have had a particularly high density of resident scholars and artists.

Another kind of relationship runs even deeper than that between neighbors. Kanokogi's address book also includes Imanishi Kinji, known for his studies in ecology and anthropology, as well as Imanishi's mountain-climbing partner, Nishibori Eizaburō. Nishibori married Imanishi's younger sister in 1927, and the following year, Imanishi married Kanokogi's eldest daughter, a close friend of Imanishi's youngest sister. Kanokogi became Imanishi's father-in-law (Saitō 1994: 29–30) and Nishibori his brother-in-law. Hence, these were the relationships of families and children, of relatives. And when we include other relationships, such as those to a home village or school ties, the exchanges between people seem to have been diverse, extending far beyond workplace and discipline. It is unclear whether such extensive connections with the academic sphere was unique to Kanokogi or was common for painters and artists of the day. Nevertheless, the conception – already prevalent at the time of Hedin's visit – that the art world and the academic world in Kyoto were somehow interconnected in various settings – sometimes casually, sometimes intimately – seems to be well supported in Kanokogi's case. Hedin's lecture and welcome feast brought together people from various fields in the university, including, of course, those who were directly interested in Hedin's work in geography and the history of Central Asia, but also people from fields as diverse as philology, geology, and mineralogy. It seems clear that these interdisciplinary connections extended beyond the professional activities of the University into the private lives of families, friendships and community.

The reproductions as a legacy of Hedin's visit to Kyoto

What was the purpose behind reproducing Hedin's work? While it might have been a valuable opportunity for the art students training in Western-style painting, the intention might have been to use the reproductions as reference materials for studying the topography and customs of Central Asia and Tibet in the Department of Geography. Unfortunately, we have found no clear evidence in support of either hypothesis.

Nevertheless, we might, at the very least, find meaning in the fact that the reproductions were made and preserved. The stimulus for the reproductions was the exhibition of Hedin's original works together with the Chinese texts and other related documents. The public exhibition was part of a series of events organized by Kyoto Imperial University as a whole, and this type of event was unique to Kyoto Imperial University; nothing similar was arranged by either Tokyo Imperial University or the Tokyo Geographical Society. Also, in contrast with Tokyo, where successive events had been attended primarily by academics in scientific fields such as geography and geology, the contribution made to the exhibition by the College of Letters was a significant characteristic of the Kyoto welcome. In this chapter, I have clarified the overlapping and cross-cutting connections between the individuals involved in Hedin's welcome reception, both within and outside Kyoto Imperial University, such as Ogawa Takuji, Ishikawa Hajime, Kanokogi Takeshirō, and Nakazawa Iwata, as well as organizations such as Kyoto Imperial University, the Kyoto Higher School of Arts and Technology, and the Kansai Art Academy. I have also pointed out that these connections overlapped with a variety of friendships and relationships, including residence-based ties focused in Shimogamo and those formed from overseas encounters, and thus in many ways transcended the fields of art or academic research. From this perspective, the reproductions can be seen as a manifestation of Kyoto's particular culture. Of course, both Hedin "the man" and his explorations and exploits had strong and wide appeal, and thus his visit provided great opportunities for interdisciplinary exchanges and collaborations between scholars and artists. It is also, of course, possible that it was Hedin himself who suggested the reproductions, in response to his experience of Kyoto and its interconnected arts/academic community; or the idea of the reproduction may have arisen organically as "an interesting prospect" in this rich context. It is also clear that the production process required the involvement and cooperation of quite a few people. Thus, in reflecting on the background conditions, we find that these reproductions of Hedin's original works, left for so long in the Department of Geography in the Faculty of Letters at Kyoto University, can be seen as evidence of the creative energy of the countless exchanges taking place between the worlds of art and academia in Kyoto and Kyoto Imperial University at the time. In that sense, these sixty reproductions are a true legacy of Hedin's visit to Kyoto in 1908.

References

Chiba kenritsu bijutsu-kan (Chiba Prefectural Museum of Art) 1981. *Asai Chū to Kyōto yōga-dan no hitobito* (Asai Chū and his circle: Kyoto's Western-style painters). Chiba: Chiba Prefectural Museum of Art.

Hedin, Alma 1925. *Mein Bruder Sven: Nach Briefen und Erinnerungen*, Mit 61 Abbildungen (My brother Sven: Based on letters and memories, with 61 illustrations). Leipzig: F. A. Brockhaus.

Hedin, Sven 1926. *Mein Leben als Entdecker* (My life as an explorer). Leipzig: F. A. Brockhous.

Hedin, Sven 1909–1913. *Trans-Himalaya: Discoveries and*

Adventures in Tibet, vol. 1–3. New York: MacMillan. (First Edition was issued from 1909 to 1912).

Hedin, Sven. 1964. *Sven Hedin as Artist: for the Centenary of Sven Hedin's Birth*. Revised and with supplement by Gösta Montell; and essay by Folke Holmér; translated by Donald Burton. Stockholm: Sven Hedins Stiftelse, Statens Etnografiska Museum.

Hori, Ken'yū (revised by Mizuno, Tsutomu) 1987. *Ōtani tanken-tai saiiki ryokō nikki* (Ōtani expedition: Travel journal in Central Asia). Tokyo: Hakusui sha.

Hoshino, Keizō and Hoshino, Mamiko 1990. *Seitan 101-nen Tanaka Zennosuke ten* (Exhibition commemorating the 101st year from the birth of Tanaka Zennosuke). Kyoto: Hoshino Art Gallery.

Ishida, Jun'ichirō. 2000. Kitashirakawa, Shimogamo / Kyōto – Kyōto no kindai ga motometa kyojū-kūkan (Kitashirakawa and Shimogamo in Kyoto: Required residential areas in modern Kyoto). In Katagi, Atsushi et al. eds. *Kindai nihon no kougai jūtakuchi* (Suburban residential areas in modern Japan). Tokyo: Kajima shuppan kai, 245–260.

Kanokogi Takeshirō Gahaku kanreki kinen-kai 1934. *Kanokogi Takeshirō gashū: Futō Sanjin* (Book of paintings by Kanokogi Takeshirō, Futō Sanjin [another name used by the artist]). Kyoto: Kanokogi Takeshirō Gahaku kanreki kinen-kai, 5–7.

Katayama, Akio. ed. 2004. *Yo tamatama eikoku London ni ari: Ōa ōkan nishi-hongan-ji ryūgakusei, Ōtani tanken-tai no hyaku nen* (I happened to be in London, England: Students sent by Nishi Hongan-ji Temple to Europe, who returned to Japan after completing their study, and one hundred years of Ōtani Expedition). Beppu: Ōtani kinen kan.

Kyōto daigaku fuzoku toshokan hen (Kyoto University Library ed.) 1961. *Kyōto daigaku fuzoku toshokan rokujū-nen shi* (The 60th-year memorial book of Kyoto University Library). Kyoto: Kyoto University Library.

Kyōto furitsu sōgō shiryō kan (Kyoto Prefectural Library and Archives) 1972. Kansai bijutsu-in innai nisshi Meiji 39-nen – Meiji 44-nen (Diary of Kansai Art Academy from 1906 to 1911). In Kyōto furitsu sōgō shiryō kan (Kyoto Prefectural Library and Archives) *Kyōto fu hyaku nen no shiryō. Hachi, Bijutu-kōgei hen* (Documents collected by Kyoto Prefecture for one hundred years (Part 8) arts and technology). Kyoto: Kyoto Prefectural Office.

Kyōto Hinode Simbun 1918. Shin shigai (6) Shimogamo mura (jō) (New urban areas (part 6) Shimogamo Mura Village (First half article)), *Kyōto Hinode Simbun*, March 6.

Kyōto Kōtō Kōgei Gakkō (Kyoto Higher School of Arts and Technology) 1908. *Kyōto kōtō kōgei gakkō ichiran ji Meiji 41 shi 42-nen* (Handbook of Kyoto Higher School of Arts and Technology, 1908–1909). Kyoto: Kyoto Higher School of Arts and Technology.

Kyōto Shi Bijutu-kan (Kyoto Municipal Museum of Art) 1974. (Fuhō) Nishikawa Jun (News of Death of Nishikawa Jun). *Kyōto shi bijutu-kan nempō* (Annual Report of Kyoto Municipal Museum of Art), 49: 45.

Kyōto Teikoku Daigaku (Kyoto Imperial University) 1908–1912. *Gaikoku meishi shōtai kankei shorui (Ji Meiji 41-nen shi Meiji 42-nen* (Documents relating to the invitation and welcome of foreign celebrities for 1908–1912). Materials held in the Kyoto University Archives (ID: 01A19469).

Kyōto Teikoku Daigaku (Kyoto Imperial University) 1909. *Kyōto teikoku daigaku ichiran jū Meiji 41-nen shi Meiji 42-nen* (Kyoto Imperial University handbook 1908–1909). Kyoto: Kyoto Imperial University.

Kuroda, Jūtarō 2006. *Kyōto yōga-dan no reimei-ki* (The very early days of Western-style painting in Kyoto), revised edition. Kyoto: Yamazaki shoten, 114–115.

Murakami, Kanbē 1903. *Kansai bijutu-in tenrankai shuppin mokuroku Meiji 36-nen* (Catalogue of submissions to 1903 Kansai Art Academy Exhibition). Kyoto: Yamada unsō dō.

Ogawa, Takuji. 1941. *Ichi chiri-gakusha no shōgai* (A geographer's life). Kyoto: Ogawa Yoshiki.

Saitō, Kiyoaki 1994. Imanishi Kinji nenpu (Imanishi Kinji's chronological records). In Imanishi, Kinji and Saitō, Kiyoaki. *Imanishi Kinji zenshū bekkann* (Imanishi Kinji's complete works, separate volume), augmented version. Tokyo: Kōdan sha, 1–140.

Shiga, Hidetaka and Shimizu, Sahoko eds. 2006. *Asai Chū to Kansai Bijutu-in ten* (Exhibition on Asai Chū and Kansai Art Academy). Fuchū Municipal Museum of Art, Kyoto Municipal Museum of Art, and the Kyoto Shimbun.

Shimada, Yasuhiro 1995. *Meiji no yōga: Asai Chū to kyōto yōga-dan* (Meiji Western-style painting: Asai Chu and the Western-style painters of Kyoto). Tokyo: Shibun dō, 86–91.

Shinozaki, Yōko 2001. Hori Ken'yū shi (M. Hori) jikihitsu eibun siryō "The Lob-Nor. N. Przhevalysky & S. Hedin." (Oxford, 9. June 02.) ni tsuite. (A study of the autographed English documents of M. Hori, "The Lob-Nor. N. Przhevalsky & S. Hedin." (Oxford, 9. June 02.)). *Ryūkoku shidan*, 115: 1–35.

Suzuki, Buntarō 1910. *Kenbi-kyō oyobi kyōsajutsusiki* (Microscope and microscopy). Tokyo: Maruzen.

Suzuki, Buntarō and Kurata, Teizō 1908. *Bijutsu kaibō-gaku* (Art anatomy). Kyoto: Suzuki Buntarō.

Tanaka, Kaoru 1969. Tōkyo chigaku kyōkai to chichi to watasi (The Tokyo Geographical Society, my father, and myself). *Chigaku zasshi* (The Journal of Geography), 78: 200–203.

Tanaka Kazuko 2015. Kyoto daigaku ga shozō suru Sven Hedin ni kakawaru kaiga shiryō ni tsuite (A preliminary observation of the drawings and paintings related to Sven Hedin stored at Kyoto University: A legacy of his stay in Japan in 1908). *Jimbun Chiri* (Japanese Journal of Human Geography), 67 (1): 57–70.

Tōkyo Chigaku Kyōkai (Tokyo Geographical Society) 1909a. Dokutoru Sven Hedin shi kangei hōkoku (Report on the welcome given to Dr. Sven Hedin), *Chigaku Zasshi* (The Journal of Geography), 21 (6): a1–a31.

Tōkyo Chigaku Kyōkai (Tokyo Geographical Society) 1909b. Hedin hakase tairaku kiji (Dr. Hedin in Kyoto), *Chigaku Zasshi* (The Journal of Geography), 21 (6): b1–b12.

4 Exploration, Science, and Understanding Others
Thinking Through Hedin's Trajectory
Matsuda Motoji

Intolerance of difference in the contemporary world

In this time of globalization, the influx of large numbers of foreign and heretofore unfamiliar people to become new or perhaps temporary members of established societies has become an everyday occurrence. For people whose differences range from religious beliefs and sense of humanistic values to dress and dietary customs to coexist with and live as neighbors in the same society will inevitably occasion certain kinds of surprise and aversion, of sentiments and reaction. "Coexistence and conviviality with the other" could well be the greatest challenge facing the contemporary world.

In this chapter, as a way of engaging with this challenge, I focus on the experience of explorers in the so-called Age of Exploration that lasted from the nineteenth century into the first half of the twentieth century, men who for the first time in human history encountered and built intensive relationships with utterly foreign others on a global scale. My objective in doing so is to find clues for approaching this contemporary challenge through the trajectory of Sven Hedin, the Swedish explorer of Central Asia.

A dominant trend in today's world, rather than giving further guarantees for the coexistence of disparate entities by "respecting differences" of nationality and racial or ethnic origin, gender, sexual orientation, and religion as was proclaimed at the dawn of the twenty-first century, seems on the contrary to be a "return" to what was historically the mainstream in such societies, an ongoing transition in the direction of "intolerance of difference." This intolerance, in practice, leads to the exclusion of that which is – and those who are – different, sometimes by violent means.

In Europe, the tolerant attitude once shown by the EU toward refugees from the Middle East and Africa has dropped off sharply, to the point of becoming a hot issue dividing populations along political lines, as seen in the UK's "Brexit" from the EU and France's recent presidential election. Most apparent has been the "othering" of Islamic immigrant communities, including the children of immigrants who have already settled and acquired citizenship in their host countries and the emergence of movements that are seizing on such people as targets for social hatred and ostracism. When attempting to exclude the scarves and bathing costumes of Islamic women from public spaces as "religious" markers, as a matter of course, the Christian costumes and accessories worn by mainstream women and clerics are not subjected to condemnation on the same grounds. Such "Islamophobia" is growing more and more blatant in the context of a nascent populism in mainstream society.[1]

Nor is "intolerance of difference" unique to contemporary Europe. Even in the context of the new South Africa, a society that threw off the ruling regime of apartheid, which had sought to persecute and eliminate difference using the most systematic and violent methods, exclusionism and violent attacks rooted in national and cultural differences repeatedly target African migrant laborers arriving with their families in large numbers in search of steady work from neighboring countries such as Zimbabwe and Mozambique. This has become the new problem of "xenophobia" in the post-apartheid era. Here, as in so many cases, we can observe the tragedy of those who were victims of persecution rooted in racial difference becoming the new perpetrators of such persecution.[2] Japanese society is no exception when it comes to exclusion of difference, either. The negative history of having once engaged in colonial rule and political and cultural persecution has been dismissed as a "masochistic view of history," justifying the institutional discrimination and exclusion of Zainichi

---

1 In the wake of terrorism carried out by "Islamic extremists" in countries like France, Belgium, and the UK, social solidarity has strengthened among that portion of the populace marked by sentiments of hatred and wariness against Islam, people who are fundamentally skeptical of values such as "multicultural coexistence," "acknowledgment of difference," and "political correctness." The political forces rooted in this consciousness and working to incite and mobilize it further have gained an unprecedented level of support. See e.g., Mori (2016), Brubaker (2015), Todd (2015).

2 As for the ostracism (xenophobia) targeting foreign migrants and migrant workers in contemporary South African society, the view that this cannot simply be interpreted or understood to stem from frustrations on the part of impoverished black South Africans over being deprived of work by foreign migrants, and which suggests instead a pathogenesis at the heart of post-apartheid society has been advanced by commentators such as Michael Neocosmos (2010) and Francis Nyamnjoh (2006).

Koreans[3] living in Japan. Hate speech by organizations like the Zaitokukai,[4] which advocates "killing the Koreans" and "driving out the Koreans" and violent attacks against Korean schools are more serious in that they provide support for such socially pervasive exclusionary awareness.

Legal remedies are of course important measures for addressing intolerance and its exclusionary and ostracizing tendencies that seem increasingly present in our contemporary world. However, rather than formal methods for addressing social issues, it is necessary to begin by thinking at a more fundamental level about strategies for mutual recognition, about ways of interacting when encountering and existing alongside difference. I would like to attempt a deeper consideration of this task in this chapter.

Encounters with others who live in cultures, value systems, social milieu, and environments different from one's own – from our own – have been ubiquitous in the migrations and wanderings that characterize human history. Encountering these unknown others, we have forged relationships (whether of trade, of marriage exchange, or of war). At such times, considering the attitudes we adopt toward these others (this difference) and the nature of the perception (or regard) toward others in which these are rooted can provide an important hint for thinking of strategies to overcome "intolerance of difference" in our contemporary world. When considering encounters with as-yet-unknown others in historical terms, setting aside natural (i.e., everyday) contact with neighboring others to focus on cases of encounters made against the backdrop of unequal power relations (as in the present day) with those from whom we are completely different, then from a global perspective, the period when such encounters took place in the most systematic and concentrated fashion was that of the nineteenth and early twentieth centuries, when European powers were attempting to gain knowledge and mastery of the world. Even earlier than the era of colonial rule in Africa and Central Asia, the age of exploration and adventure which had attempted to subsume other worlds and other peoples into the European intellectual world represents in itself a useful source for considering the attitudes that characterize the cross-cultural encounter.

Exploration and science

The period from the latter half of the nineteenth century to the beginning of the twentieth century, when Europe was attempting to secure its knowledge of the entire world, bore witness to a tremendous number of cross-cultural encounters. At this time, Europeans who were encountering other cultures came to adopt two mutually overlapping yet opposing attitudes toward other cultures. The first focused on what was novel about other cultures and placed paramount value on "discovery." Novel "discoveries" brought back to Europe came to be seen as the highest achievement and was a means of acquiring wealth and fame. This was supported by a crude, unvarnished curiosity toward novelty and the unknown. During this period, a great many explorers and adventurers set out seeking "discoveries"[5] on the "frontiers" of the globe, where they "discovered" lakes and cataracts, mountains and rivers. The Scottish missionary and explorer David Livingstone, who had "discovered" the waterfalls that the local people knew affectionately as the "river of mists" named this natural feature "Victoria Falls" after the reigning Queen of Great Britain and reported this honor back to his native country.

The second was an attitude that sought to find a way to understand different societies and cultures. This activity of understanding was also an act of epistemic domination which positioned its object according to its own epistemic standards, assigning meanings and perceiving it within the context of its own epistemic universe. This task found support in the (modern) sciences. In accordance with this attitude, the peoples encountered in Africa and their societies and cultures were categorized as savage blacks belonging to the lowest-ranked primitive societies (in evolutionary terms, for example) and then scientifically perceived and acknowledged as such.

---

3 *Zainichi* literally means those foreigners living in Japan, but typically refers to Korean living in Japan with the status of special permanent residents. Their population in 2017 was approximately half a million. Historically "Zainichi Koreans" refers to Koreans who had moved to Japan during the Japanese colonial occupation over Korea, or the upheavals following Liberation and Korean War of 1945–1953, and their descendants. They have been marginalized in postwar Japanese society as Other. They have been discriminated against in employment, political participation, marriage, social welfare and education.

4 *Zaitokukai* (*zainichi tokken wo yurusanai shimin no kai* can be literally translated as "the citizens group to protest privileges of Zainichi") is a militant xenophobic group of ultra-right nationalists. It was organized in 2007 and extended its influence in the early 2010s, with membership over 10,000.

Its main target is Zainichi Koreans and their community. They organized anti-Korean demonstrations in Tokyo and Osaka shouting "Kill Koreans" and raided a Korean school in Kyoto. Their hateful speeches and acts were found to be hate crime by the Japanese courts, including the Supreme Court.

5 No doubt those mountains, rivers and falls which were "discovered" by European explorers were already well-known and part of the lived experience of the local inhabitants.

In encounters with the unknown, the curiosity-driven attitude toward "discovery" and the scientific attitude toward "perception and understanding" were typical modes of interaction demonstrated by Europe throughout world history. Those who led the former were the explorers and adventurers who rushed from Europe into the world beyond, while those who led the latter were the ethnologists and geographers who emerged from the ranks of those same explorers and adventurers. Seen in terms of global history, expeditions and ethnology were established simultaneously in the context of these encounters with the other.

It was only natural that the political role and objectivist slant of expeditions and explorers grounded in the two attitudes became subject to powerful criticism. Explorers were principal protagonists of the Berlin Conference of major European powers who in 1884–85 unilaterally divided Africa among themselves, and their "discoveries" and "scientific reports" constituted important resources for colonial rule. In a real sense, they played the role of political and military "agents" for the colonization of Africa by Europe. Moreover, as "field directors" of the task of incorporating Africa into the epistemic universe constituted by modern Europe and engendering its unilateral understanding and perception, they advanced Europe's epistemic domination of Africa.

How these explorers depicted the Africans they encountered as foreign others from strange lands is palpably expressed by Samuel Baker, one of the most prominent explorers of this period, and one of many involved in the competition to discover the source of the Nile.[6] He writes:

> The black man is a curious anomaly, the good and bad points of human nature bursting forth without any arrangement, like the flowers and thorns of his own wilderness. A creature of impulse, seldom actuated by reflection, the black man astounds by his complete obtuseness, and as suddenly confounds you by an unexpected exhibition of sympathy. From a long experience with African savages, I think it is as absurd to condemn the negro in toto, as it is preposterous to compare his intellectual capacity with that of the white man (Baker 1866: 181).

This view was shared by other explorers of the day, including "true" explorers like the humanitarian Livingstone and the geologist Joseph Thomson, who differed from the "amateur" explorers driven purely by curiosity.

While those who situated these others (and the world of the other) as utterly foreign and by a process of epistemic incorporation unilaterally understood and perceived them within the context of their own Eurocentric world (the world of the self) accounted for an overwhelming majority of these explorers, there were also a few whose attitude was diametrically opposed to that of their peers. Hints for overcoming "intolerance of difference" in the context of our contemporary world can be found in the attitudes and behaviors of this handful of explorers. One was the Swedish explorer of Central Asia, Sven Hedin. Where explorers like Hedin differed utterly from the majority was in the way they established links between the world of the self and that of the other. Stated briefly, the difference was whether they conceived of these two worlds as being disconnected from one another or as being connected. This was the difference between conceiving of the human populations, societies, and cultures of Asia and Africa that they took as their object as worlds apart from (and usually inferior to) their own (i.e., the Eurocentric world) and conceiving of these as worlds that, while differently imagined, were contiguous with their own and inhabited by human beings like them. When we compare images of Africans from Livingstone's journals with Hedin's sketches of the young women he encountered on his expeditions in Central Asia, for example, the difference between these two perspectives is quite clear.

In this attitude toward and regard for the other held by those explorers who conceive of contiguity between the worlds of the self and the other, we may find hints for exploring the coexistence with alterity that we now seek.

Sven Hedin's world

Given this understanding of the problem, I turn now to approach Sven Hedin's thoughts and practices. While the details of Hedin's arrival in Japan and sojourn in Kyoto are discussed by Tanaka Kazuko elsewhere in this volume, I would like to consider Hedin here as an exemplar of the kind of thought and practice that links the worlds of exploration and cross-cultural understanding (i.e., ethnology), of curiosity and science.

---

6 Samuel Baker (1821–1893) was an eminent explorer of Africa in the late nineteenth century, distinguished from his contemporaries in that he was given the rank of Pasha (Major-General) by the Ottoman Turkish authorities who ruled Egypt at the time, and governed the state of Equatoria in the upper reaches of the Nile in what is now South Sudan. He is known for his "discovery" of Lake Albert, the source of the Nile (the "Albert Nile"). Among his contemporaries, he is also known for his frank prejudice toward Africans, as illustrated by his view that "When the horse and the ass shall be found to match in double harness, the white man and the African black will pull together under the same regime. It is the grand error of equalizing that which is unequal, that has lowered the negro character, and made the black man a reproach" (Baker 1866: 181).

The enthusiasm shown by both officials and the populace suggest that Hedin's visit to Kyoto in 1908 was a grand political drama for Japan, having recently joined the ranks of the world's foremost powers with its victory in the Russo-Japanese War. Hedin's arrival affirmed Japan's identity as a nation–state that would welcome global explorers. At the time, however, Hedin was still struggling with the initial stages of linking the two worlds of exploration and scholarship (i.e., science).

Håkan Wahlquist, an ethnologist with the Hedin Foundation, proposes the we understand the development of Hedin's expeditions and scholarship in three stages. The first stage as "quasi-archaeology," when the explorer discovers and unearths surprising mysteries about the past but has not yet begun systematic and professional archaeological surveys.[7] Hedin discovered clusters of ancient dwellings on his first expedition, from 1893 to 1897, across the Taklamakan Desert from the Pamir Mountain southwest of the Tarim Basin. Four years later, these ruins were identified as the site known locally as Dandan Uilik (meaning "the houses with ivory") by Aurel Stein. Further, in the process of surveying the Tarim Basin and Tarim River on his second expedition from 1899 to 1901, Hedin discovered fragmentary Chinese manuscripts that spoke of the ruined city of Loulan. These prominent archaeological discoveries earned Hedin renown around the world. But Hedin lacked archaeological knowledge and qualifications, and Wahlquist notes that the "amateurish" quality of Hedin's "quick and dirty" survey methods is readily apparent in his survey of the ruins of Loulan.

Those who move on to the second stage begin to acquire the systematic knowledge of the professional archaeologist and to approach his object in a scientific manner. Wahlquist calls this stage "earnest archaeology." While the explorer is not himself a professional archaeologist, but rather an amateur scientist, or a professional in a different scientific discipline (e.g., geography and geology, ethnology and linguistics), he conducts excavations and analysis by learning the systematic knowledge of the professional archaeologist. Although Hedin had studied geography and geology under Professor Ferdinand von Richthofen at the University of Berlin in Germany, he actively acquired archaeological knowledge and skills through his repeated explorations.

The third and final stage is that of "professional archaeology" or "scientific archaeology," a stage in which surveys are conducted of sites and artifacts excavated and discovered by a professional who has mastered the basics of systematic archaeology. In Hedin's case, this corresponds to the fourth expedition from 1927 to 1935. Utterly unlike any of the first three "expeditions" he had completed on his own, this expedition involved a multinational team of researchers (mostly Chinese) from a variety of different fields whose legacy includes, so to speak, a "comprehensive plan for fieldwork" (Wahlquist 2001: 32). Thus, Hedin's development as an explorer might be seen as a process of transitioning from one rooted in the "curiosity of the strong" that pervaded Europe in the late nineteenth century toward that of a scholarly practitioner of knowledge which transcends nationality, ethnicity, and culture.

An important factor in Hedin's development was the international esteem of Ferdinand von Richthofen, Hedin's teacher and mentor. Richthofen's name is familiar to some as the man who coined the term "Silk Road." He was a China specialist as well as a global authority on geology and geography in the latter half of the nineteenth century. He travelled to Japan twice, first at the end of the Edo period and then again in the early Meiji period. On his first visit, in 1860, he came as a member of the Prussian trade and diplomatic mission led by Count Friedrich Albrecht zu Eulenburg. On his second visit, 10 years later, he remained in Japan for an extended period to avoid the new exclusionist sentiment that had broken out in Qing China (which ended in the Tianjin massacre). Richthofen kept detailed journals of his visits to Japan, and his cross-cultural perspective is clearly expressed in the encounters he describes with the Japanese people and culture.[8] His entry for the day

---

7 Although Wahlquist elucidates the sense of "wonder" that the geographically and politically isolated Swedish explorer and scientist bestowed upon the development of the archaeology of Western China, in his three-stage theory, he offers Hedin as a representative contributor to the first stage, citing the example of Hedin's survey of Loulan. He points out that during the period that corresponds to this first stage of exploratory surveys, Hedin became a "skilled field geologist" through the hands-on development of a basic knowledge of geology and paleontology that he had learned in Sweden and Germany. In this sense, Hedin was also a representative contributor to the second stage of Wahlquist's scheme (Wahlquist 2001: 4–35).

8 Although the shogunal authorities did not authorize Richthofen to stay anywhere other than Edo, Yokohama, or Nagasaki on his first visit to Japan, which lasted for five months, his cool cross-cultural descriptions stand out as being quite unlike those of contemporary missionaries and merchants. Among other things, he left behind a written account of a Yokohama brothel. On his second visit, after traveling from Tokyo via Kofu, Matsumoto, Nagoya, Kyoto, and Osaka to Kobe, he sailed to Nagasaki and toured Kagoshima and Kumamoto, with a stop in the Amakusa Islands. His account of these travels includes a particularly detailed description of Japan's silver mines. When Richthofen reached Peking after his first visit to Japan, he found that the government had prohibited academic surveys by foreign nationals, and decided to continue his journey, leading him to the United States via Southeast Asia. In 1868, he returned to China, where he spent the next three years pursuing his studies and traveling through

he arrived in Japan on October 20, 1860 describes his encounter with a French couple with whom he had a heated conversation about the perceived uniqueness of the Japanese character (what today would be described as an example of *Nihonjinron*):

> The *madame* stated that the Japanese are filthy and detestable, that their character is utterly odious, is discomfiting and has an air of deception. Afterwards, these odious qualities were spelled out in detail by this young Parisienne.

However, Richthofen took a cool, analytical view of such attitudes, writing that "herein was reflected a pathological vanity and an unsated appetite for gaiety". He was criticizing "narrow views" like that of the young woman as judging the object of their regard "according to their own situation and perennially lacking in any comprehension of spiritual content."

The shogunate, which had been forced to abandon its long-standing policy of national isolation (*sakoku*) and open the country to outsiders, restricted the movement and settlement of foreign nationals and routinely monitored their activities, which in turn stirred resentment among foreigners in Japan. However, Richthofen states that "while there is a certain justification for finding them [i.e., the Japanese officials] extremely detestable, such judgments should always consider that some responsibility also appertains to those Westerners that aroused such disservice," thereby avoiding reducing the Japanese people and Japanese culture to any sort of generalized stereotypes.

In this way, he seems to operate through an inclusive perceptual framework that is qualitatively distinct from a perspective that makes decisions about its object unilaterally and arbitrarily, seeing the worlds of self and other as disconnected; Richthofen, conversely, joins these two worlds as contiguous. This age of history was one in which Europe expanded out into the world, in which explorers and adventurers, missionaries, merchants, and military men made extensive encounters with other cultures, whom they dominated for the ostensible purpose of "civilizing" them, and whom they "understood" by fixing them as subordinates within their own perception of the world. In this context, attitudes like Richthofen's stand out in their defiance of such perception. It is safe to say that Hedin's attitude, effervescing with a sense of contiguity with other cultures, is a more developed and evolved form of Richthofen's.

The Age of Explorers

The world of nineteenth-century exploration

Our consideration of Hedin's approach, based in a "sense of contiguity" with other cultures, requires that we examine the era in which he was operating, namely the "Age of Explorers" of the latter half of the nineteenth century. What society looked for from the explorers of this period – beyond natural resources and cheap labor to enrich European society, regardless of the cost to the locals – was novel and unusual discoveries on the world's frontiers about unknown peoples, things, societies, and cultures. Nor was this of course all that was sought after. There was also an audience for tales of the "adventures" that these explorers underwent while making their discoveries (especially tales in which the protagonists barely escaped with their lives from hellish wilderness or wild savages). On this point, as Claude Levi-Strauss (2012: 41) sardonically notes:

> Society shows complete indifference to what might be called the rational outcome of such adventures... What counts is the attempt in itself, not any possible aim. For example, a young man who lives outside his social group for a few weeks or months, so as to expose himself to an extreme situation, comes back endowed with a power which finds expression in the writing of newspaper articles and bestsellers and in lecturing to packed halls.

As he explains,

> The fact is that these primitive peoples, the briefest contact with whom can sanctify the traveler, these icy summits, deep caverns and impenetrable forests – all of them august settings for noble and profitable revelations – are all, in their different ways, enemies of our society. (ibid.)

The "cross-cultural" element desired for such adventure stories was the world of a primitive and savage "them" that lay beyond the experience of and was absolutely different in character from that of their readers, the world of the self, "us", which was aligned with civilization. For explorers to present a cross-cultural perspective was also a powerful social desideratum. To comprehensively survey this heterogeneity and conceptualize the whole (in a hierarchical and self-referential manner) was at that time the "royal road" to cross-cultural understanding. The World's Fairs that appeared in the late nineteenth

---

the countryside, subsequently publishing a report of his researches. These efforts helped Richthofen secure a worldwide reputation as a China scholar and an authority in the field of geography (Kamimura 2013: v–vii).

century for public consumption were a grand apparatus for achieving this end.[9] Beginning with the Great Exhibition in London in 1851, World's Fairs were held five times in Paris, as well as Vienna (1873), Antwerp (1885), Barcelona (1888), and Chicago (1893). Through the synoptic overview these events provided of the different cultures of the world, the World's Fairs served as public affirmations and celebrations of Europe's hegemony – cultural and epistemic as well as political and economic – over the rest of the world. Over 48 million people attended the 1900 Exposition Universelle in Paris. From the beginning, the exhibition of other cultures was one of the star attractions of such events; artefacts were displayed from the indigenous societies of India, Ceylon, Gambia, Cape Colony, as well as Canada and Australia. The accounts of the explorers were among the most celebrated works of the time.

Behind the dispatching of these explorers and subsuming their "discoveries" within the epistemic framework of a European perception of the world were the geographical societies that had been established in a number of countries. In the French case, the *Société de géographie*, although established in 1821, had to some extent grown out of the *Société des observateurs de l'homme* (the "Society of Observers of Man"), a learned society founded in 1799 based on Enlightenment ideas which had been involved in organizing an expedition to the South Seas. Beginning with less than 200 members when the *Société de géographie* was first convened in Paris, by the end of the nineteenth century, there were as many as 30 separate societies boasting a combined membership of close to 20,000 members in France. These geographical societies all sent expeditions to Africa and Oceania and, when the explorers returned, awarded medals and conferred social honors in recognition of their accomplishments. The geographical societies were a driving force behind the European encounter with other cultures in the latter half of the nineteenth century, as well as the inventors and purveyors of a unilateral perception of other cultures as disconnected from their own world. As contributors to the inherent violence of this scientific perception of other cultures, worlds, and peoples, however, these geographical societies were far from alone. In the case of France, with the organization of the *Société ethnologique de Paris* in 1839, the one-sided "discoveries" and "facts" produced in a fragmentary manner by explorers and missionaries were ranked and positioned in the context of the epistemic universe. Following the birth of the *Société d'anthropologie de Paris* in 1859, foreign people (and races) living in foreign cultures came to be scientifically positioned within the hierarchy of biological evolution. The brain capacity of the "civilized races" was considered to be larger than those of the "savage races," thereby providing a basis for the discovery of their relative inferiority and superiority as biological organisms.

This systematic and institutionalized framework for looking at other cultures at a societal, psychic, and scientific level was established during the European Age of Explorers into which Hedin was born. The difficulty and significance of renouncing or opposing this framework cannot be over-emphasized.

Even in Japan, which was racing to catch up with Europe on the road to civilization and modernization, the systems and institutions that Europe had built for engaging with other cultures were emulated. Copying the World's Fairs and imitating the exhibition of other cultures and races took this game into extra innings, so to speak. When Hedin came to Japan, it was a matter of course that the Tokyo Geographical Society would be institutional base for disseminating his academic findings. At the time, the Tokyo Anthropological Society (*Tokyo jinruigakkai*; now the *Nihon jinruigakkai*, The Anthropological Society of Nippon) was already 20 old. Like their European models, these academic societies were perpetuating a one-sided perception of other cultures and races.

Explorers and the encounter with other cultures

The historical mentality of the "Age of Explorers" that emerged in Europe in the late nineteenth century is aptly depicted by the "5 Cs": Civilization, Christianity, Colonization, Commerce, and Curiosity (Hugon 1993: 35–36). Certainly, the explorers of this period included missionaries sent by Christian evangelical organizations to proselytize and conduct missionary work among the peoples of Africa, speculators exploring the commercial opportunities availed by rare materials, and curious adventurers sponsored by geographical societies and other organizations seeking to make their names by exploring unknown lands. Colonial rule would soon follow.

As mentioned, most of these explorers, at the most fundamental level, did not conceive of the local people, societies, and cultures as being in any way contiguous with themselves or their own societies and cultures. By "contiguous" I mean an attitude and perceptual framework that tries to perceive cross-cultural "others" in the worlds of others with the same attitude as the regard

---

9 For Japanese perspectives on the significance of the political and cultural apparatus represented by the World Fairs (Universal Expositions) that appeared in nineteenth-century Europe, and the historical conditions and zeitgeist that gave birth to them, see, e.g., Yoshida (1986), Yoshimi (1992), Unno (2013) and Matsuda (2003).

with which we apprehend and perceive "ourselves" and "others" in the world of the self. Yet the idea of such contiguity was one that in the Age of Explorers remained beyond even the likes David Livingstone, who was perhaps the most acclaimed African explorer among the "civilized" societies of his day.

Livingstone's eminence, for example, is attested to by the fact that in 1856, he was awarded a gold medal by the Royal Geographical Society, the same medal, incidentally, that years later was awarded to Sven Hedin. Herein, the "5 Cs" are studded as medals, honoring him as a traveler, geographer, naturalist, astronomer, doctor, missionary, commercial pioneer, and humanitarian warrior. Also, after his death in Africa in 1873, his remains were brought to London for burial, in order that he could be interred in Westminster Abbey as a national hero. Another prominent explorer, Henry Morton Stanley, who led the *New York Herald's* Livingstone Relief Expedition, esteemed Livingstone's sublime character when he wrote that "I grant he is not an angel, but he approaches to that being as near as the nature of a living man will allow" (Stanley 1872: 430).

While Stanley's intense and discriminatory attitudes to other cultures and peoples (in this case, Africans) are obvious from the published accounts of his explorations, similar sentiments are also found in Livingstone's accounts. In Stanley's account of *How I Found Livingstone: Travels, Adventures, and Discoveries in Central Africa* (London 1872),[10] he describes how several Africans caught attempting to abscond from his caravan when they could no longer endure the harsh conditions "were well flogged and chained, to secure them against further temptation" (Stanley 1872: 318). He also notes that, on another occasion, involving a woman who had lapsed into hysterics, "there remained nothing else for me to do but to try the virtue of my whip over her shoulders […] she desisted before the tenth blow and became silent," meekly accepting her punishment (Stanley 1872: 398–399). Similarly, although certainly less violent, we can also ascertain Livingstone's own non-contiguous perception of Africans and their customs. For instance, on observing an African with "twenty or thirty charms hung round his neck," Livingstone, after rejecting his beliefs, calls him "cautious and timid" and takes pity on his kind, lamenting, "How painful is the contrast between this inward gloom and the brightness of the outer world – between the undefined terrors of the spirit, and the peace and beauty that pervade the scenes around us!" (Livingstone 1861: 292) Livingstone's depiction of Africa is shot through with this conception of Africans as "little children" to be educated and guided.

Cross-cultural encounters of this type were faithfully reproduced by modern Japan. From the beginning of the Meiji period, the Empire of Japan, which, was quite unabashed about its territorial interests in the surrounding region, deployed numerous explorers, motivated by four of the "5 Cs" (sans Christianity). At the top of this list was the anthropologist, Torii Ryūzō.[11] Heading for Taiwan immediately after the First Sino-Japanese War (1894–1895), Torii would conduct four separate research expeditions by 1900. Traversing Taiwan's Central Mountain Range, he encountered ethnic minorities in the mountainous regions where, as well as collecting biometric measurements of the local inhabitants, he also conducted ethnological surveys on various topics, including pottery techniques and vocabulary. In his reports, Torii demonstrates that he has inherited a mentality, shared with the Age of Explorers of the nineteenth century, that emphasizes and exaggerates benightedness and savagery (and conversely his own "civilized" nature). For example he writes "the shrine at Danan has now taken three severed heads and can now stage its grand festival; I am greatly afraid that if I am now delayed by a day or two, my own head will also be added to the collection." Torii went on to record cross-cultural encounters on his voyages to Korea, Manchukuo, and Mongolia. Of course, in this, he was the advance reconnaissance for another of the

---

10 From 1840 until his death in 1873, Livingstone continued his explorations almost unceasingly, from southern Africa to central and eastern Africa, while evangelizing Western civilization and the Christian Gospel. He was accompanied by his family for some time, until the death of one of his children. After contact with Livingstone was lost in 1868, the publisher of the *New York Herald* delegated a mission to find and rescue him to its correspondent, Henry Morton Stanley. Stanley, with a quickly assembling and massive caravan of 350 people, eventually found Livingstone recuperating from ill health in the town of Ujiji on the shores of Lake Tanganyika on November 10, 1871. While this "discovery" made Stanley's reputation as a star explorer, Livingstone continued his explorations, dying two years later in the village of Chief Chitambo in what is now Chitambo District, Central Province, Zambia.

11 In Taiwan, which Japan had acquired from Qing-dynasty China by dint of its victory in the First Sino-Japanese War, backlash toward the Han Chinese residents was on the rise, and the "pacification" and "enlightenment" of the indigenous peoples of the mountain interior were becoming important challenges to governing the island territory. To this end, specialized scholars from Tokyo Imperial University were dispatched to conduct field surveys in anthropology, geology, zoology, and botany. At this time, Torii, who had surveyed the Liaodong Peninsula, which had been occupied by the Japanese military during the war, was appointed to head the anthropological survey. Torii's encounters with other worlds, cultures, and peoples were to be deeply implicated in Japan's colonial rule and military ascendancy from the earliest days of Japan's colonial project (Sakano 2005: 228–235).

"Cs", namely colonization. By the time Hedin visited Japan, this perspective was firmly established in both Europe and Japan.

Hedin's praxis

Central Asia expedition

Before approaching Hedin's cross-cultural perspective, that is, his basic attitudes and perceptual framework for engaging with others, I would first like to outline Hedin's praxis as an explorer. Among the ultimate goals of exploring the Arctic, the Antarctic, and the Himalayas, the objects of adventurers' ambitions at the time of his youth, Hedin set his sights on crossing the Himalayas to explore the expanses of Central Asia, which were unknown lands for Europeans. His inspiration for this choice was Richthofen, with whom he studied at the University of Berlin. Before commencing his exploration activities in earnest, he traveled through Persia and Mesopotamia, and a few years later, visited Samarkand and Kashgar.

Hedin's first expedition, which began in 1893, was a four-year trek from Orenburg in Russia over the Ural Mountains, through the Pamir Mountains, across the southern edge of the Taklamakan Desert, and finally to Peking via Qinghai and Zhangjiakou. Sparing no time for rest, Hedin began his second expedition in 1899. This time, he trekked across the Tarim Basin and the northern margins of the lake region of Central Tibet. Along the way, in 1900, he discovered the dry lakebed of Lop Nur and the ruins of the ancient city of Loulan. While the lake was dry at that time, it later came to be known as the "Wandering Lake." On this second expedition, Hedin also "discovered" a trove of Chinese texts and relics in the vicinity of the ruins that, to this day, remains a valuable source for unraveling the ancient history of the local area. Then Hedin crossed the Karakoram Range before returning home to Sweden through Russia by way of Kashgar. He arrived home in 1902, after an expedition that had spanned three years.

Then, after three years of preparation, Hedin's third expedition continued from 1905 until immediately prior to his arrival in Japan in 1908. This expedition included his attempt to illegally enter Tibet under the veil of secrecy (Tibet at that time prohibited the entry of foreigners). Around this time, a complex political situation was developing in this area with the extension of Russia's sphere of influence from the north and that of Great Britain from India in the south, further complicated by the Qing dynasty's claims to suzerainty. Hedin, while on one hand receiving patronage and support from the Russian Emperor Nicholas II, whom he had known since before he ascended to the throne, was on the other hand seeking support from the British government through the Indian colonial administration.

Hedin traveled first to Persia, entering India from there, whereupon he started to make his way into Central Tibet. After initially entering the northwestern part of Tibet, Hedin explored the lake region of Central Tibet and surveyed the headwaters of India's major rivers, including the Indus, its tributary the Sutlej, as well as the Brahmaputra, a tributary of the Ganges. Then, after a stay in Shigatse, he "discovered" a "new" mountain range connected with the Karakoram Range to the north of the Himalayan Range. These were the Trans-Himalayas, which later sparked a variety of debate.

Hedin's fourth expedition was continued for more than eight years from 1927, almost 20 years after the third expedition. Hedin's earlier explorations had all been "solo" (he, of course, travelled in caravans that included guides and camel drivers for carrying baggage, but he was the sole explorer). On this occasion, however, he set up a systematic interdisciplinary and international organization in the form of a scientific survey team comprised of Swedish, German, and Chinese academics (the Northwest Scientific Expedition). This signaled a shift from the third stage of exploration mentioned earlier to full-fledged scientific surveying. This expedition attempted to cover a vast territory, extending from the Rehe region in the eastern reaches of Mongolia, to what is now the Xinjiang Uygur Autonomous Region, in the south to northern Tibet, and in the north to the Tian Shan Range. In the vastness of Central Asia, specialists in a variety of fields, including geography, geology, biology, archaeology, meteorology, ethnology and anthropology, attempted to work together to carry out surveys. Even though the expedition was unable to achieve all of its goals, owing to the turmoil in Xinjiang and the global instability in the lead-up to the Second World War, for Hedin, it had been a new challenge that had required fundamentally changing his previous style.

Hedin's representations of other cultures

In contrast to this total transformation of his research methods over the course of four expeditions and four decades, his attitude to other worlds, cultures, and peoples encountered along the way remain remarkably consistent in the style of description and the respect derived from seeing them as contiguous. While I discuss his specific approaches to writing and drawing below, by simply accepting the ways that other cultures and peoples were different from himself (while assuming that they are, in fact, different), he developed interpersonal relationships through engaging with others with much the same attitude that he brought to engaging with intellectuals and peers in Europe. The way he built relationships by immersing himself in the local scene was completely unlike the attitude of those who see the world of others as disconnected from the world of the self. In this, he differed fundamentally from the earlier explorers who had been active in the Age of Explorers and the prevailing mentality of the European zeitgeist in which their consciousness had been steeped. This mentality severed "us" and "them" by treating the latter as absolute others, radically different to the worlds of the self. Its inherent structure was one in which the subject looking at "them" was always the plural "us" and never the singular "I." Hence, when encountering "uncivilized" or "savage" others, interlocutors were always treated as a collective "them," never as individuals. The utter erasure of the "I" was a characteristic of this perspective. By contrast, Hedin's attitude, inserted an "I" into every encounter, thus opening the possibility of overcoming this dichotomy between "us" and "them."

To better understand Hedin's approach, it is illustrative to compare it with the cross-cultural perspective of another explorer working in the same area at around the same time. Kawaguchi Ekai, a Japanese monk of the Ōbaku school of Zen, was an explorer who smuggled himself into Tibet at around the same time as Hedin. Around the time of Hedin's first expedition, Japan was experiencing a "Tibetan fever" – a heightened enthusiasm for knowledge about Tibet. During this period (the late 1880s and 1890s), Western scholars of Buddhism and Oriental studies were repeatedly publishing arguments that the Buddhism that had come to Japan via China did not faithfully reflect the teachings of the Buddha. Hence, Japan's Buddhist community was eager to acquire a copy of a compendium of Buddhist scripture (*issai zōkyō*) written in Sanskrit in Tibet, which was held to have faithfully inherited the teachings of the Buddha (sutras) in order to prove that the teachings of Japanese Buddhism were the same. Explorers, adventurers, and religious adherents were therefore trying to infiltrate Tibet.

Kawaguchi made two attempts to smuggle himself into Tibet, the second of which was successful. His initial attempt lasted from 1897 to 1903, during which time, he traveled to Nepal from India. From Kathmandu, although he reached Mustang in western central Nepal, he was unable to enter Tibet. However, the following year, he tried again to enter Tibet, successfully smuggling himself into the country in 1914 and continuing his explorations until 1915. He published an autobiographical account of his journey as *Chibetto ryokō-ki* (1904), which was published in his own English translation as *Three Years in Tibet* (1909).

Kawaguchi excelled in the art of the cross-cultural encounter. His approach was quite distinct from the dominant European perspective, which had been emulated by Japanese explorers like Torii. Unlike the violent understanding by which other peoples and cultures in the encounter are regarded as inferior, Kawaguchi's stance is in some ways recognizable as an incipient form of the kind of cultural relativism that was to become the dominant paradigm in the social sciences in the late twentieth century. For example, polyandry, the distinctive form of marriage observed in Tibetan society wherein several men – particularly brothers – share a wife in common, is inconceivable for those who live in parts of the world that do not have this practice. Generally, such practices are presented as symbols of promiscuity and backwardness when reported to the observers' home world. However, while Kawaguchi expresses this astonishment when he writes that "it is generally known that a peculiar system of marriage prevails in Tibet – a plurality not of wives but of husbands" (Kawaguchi 1909: 352), he calmly grasps the facts of the matter, continuing: "They are quite insensible to the shame of this dissolute condition of matrimonial relations […]; and yet there do exist some restrictions: marriage of brothers with sisters, or between cousins, is not only censured by the public as immoral, but also prohibited by the law as criminal." Noting that this custom of "Polyandry flourishes in Tibet even at the present time, and it is considered by the general public to be the right thing to follow" (1909: 372), he emphasizes that family institutions are considered "normal" as long as they adhere to the familial norms of the society in question. Yet, while expressing this incipient cultural relativist perspective, Kawaguchi's perspective on other cultures nevertheless differs markedly from Hedin's in his use of a style which, after completely disconnecting the world of the self from the world of the other, the "I" is effaced as the subject of cross-cultural description and replaced with an unconsciously and unconditionally assumed "we." For example, in his accounts of both of his journeys to Tibet, one characteristic he emphasizes about the Tibetan people and culture is their "filthiness" and "uncleanliness."[12] Furthermore, his account of his first visit repeatedly emphasizes their difference from his world (i.e., the "civilized" world):

---

12 Kawaguchi's examples of the height of "uncleanliness" include his observations that "the Tibetan […] does not even wash or wipe himself after the calls of nature," that cups used to serve Tibetan butter tea would not be washed, no matter how rancid they were with butter from the previous day, and that when "I asked a servant to wash my cup, it was wiped with his sleeve, which might be quite wet and dirty from being used as a handkerchief" – indeed, "they think nothing of making a cup of tea for you with the same fingers with which they have just blown their nose" (Kawaguchi 1909: 53, 264; cf. 1904: 56–57, 306–307).

> In point of uncleanliness, Tibetans stand very high among the inhabitants of the earth, but I think the natives of Tsarang go still higher in this respect [than the folk of Lhasa]. [...] I have no courage to dwell here on their many other doings, which are altogether beyond imagination for those who have not seen them done, and are too loathsome, even unto sickening, to recall to mind. (Kawaguchi 1909: 52–53)

In the account of his second journey, he repeats this point, offering a comparison with Black Africans in which he concludes that "while the blackness of the African natives, being the natural blackness of their skin, does not produce any sense of squalor, a mere glimpse of the blackness of Tibetan women, glistening darkly with grime, dust, and oil, is sufficient to induce nausea" (Kawaguchi 1981: 240). Here we see an observer exaggerating the difference between his own culture and the other's, disconnecting these two worlds; and, again, this process effaces the observing self so that judgment is performed not by the "I" but by the "we."

An approach that, as Hedin did, clearly interposes the self (the "I") in the perception of other worlds and other peoples that are encountered in other cultures can lead to a bilateral cross-cultural understanding, not violent and fixed but fluid and versatile – one that is not caught up by the dichotomy between "us" and "them."

In the next section, I want to inspect this more concretely along with Hedin's approach to cross-cultural representation.

Ways of representing the other

Writing

When explorers encounter another culture, they apprehend (understand) these as objects (other worlds, other cultures, other peoples) in accordance with perceptual frameworks already embedded in their own minds. Then, as they have perceived and understood these objects, the explorers in turn represent them to the inhabitants of their own worlds (including themselves). Objectivizing description is perhaps the most typical method by which this representational circuit is actuated – that is, in the act of "writing (other) cultures."

While the enterprise of "writing (other) cultures" in ethnology and cultural anthropology equates to the act of "writing ethnography," since the 1980s, this process has been continuously subjected to fundamental critique. The flashpoint for this critique was the publication of *Writing Culture* (Clifford and Marcus 1986), an edited volume of essays that instantly sent shockwaves through anthropologists, ethnologists, and ethnographers the world over.[13] In the wake of this *Writing Culture* "shock," the proud accomplishments that had until then been seen as contributing to cross-cultural understanding were suddenly subjected to critique and even doubt as to whether these were in fact fictions created by anthropologists making deft use of the politics and poetics wrapped up in the act of "writing culture." While the fundamental problem raised in anthropology, ethnology, and ethnography by the reflexive turn that *Writing Culture* triggered was the incisive interrogation of issues that the contemporary enterprise of "cross-cultural representations" had covered and concealed, with the turn of the twenty-first century, these issues came to be carefully avoided and ultimately forgotten in favor of emphasizing the practicality, utility, and public nature of field-based scholarship. However, the importance of extracting and examining the perceptual frameworks and rhetorical techniques that – sometimes naively, sometimes cleverly – lay submerged and concealed within the process of "writing (other) cultures" remains the same now as ever.

In this section, I want to try comparing the cross-cultural perspectives expressed naïvely in naked form in the cross-cultural representations written by observers in the "Age of Explorers" with those found in Hedin's writings.

First, let us consider two heroes of the Age of Exploration that we have already encountered. Stanley and Livingstone constitute twin poles among the explorers of this era. One embodied the peculiar qualities of commercialism and the adventurer's allure, while the other was prominent as a proselytizer of humanitarianism and civilization. Although these two were in many respects diametrically opposed, as we have seen, a glimpse of what they have in common can be seen in the basic regard they had for other cultures. Theirs is a style that depicts the ignorance of the natives of other cultures with "smiles" and "laughter" from their own higher ground of "civilization." This is a posture of derision toward the gap between "civilization" and "savagery," quite unlike the "humor" that laughs at the gaps between oneself and an equal other. This posture also pervades contemporary Japanese society, which

---

13 The publication of *Writing Culture* fundamentally altered the subsequent work of anthropologists around the world, especially in terms of modes of ethnographic description. While the 1990s saw an efflorescence of so-called "experimental ethnographies" that sought to acknowledge and address the critique leveled by *Writing Culture* within the ethnographic description, a counter-tendency also appeared, of anthropologists suspending thought to stop short of such critique, or opposing, ignoring, or disparaging it as vacuous idealism while kneeling before the altar of "empirical reality" (Matsuda 1996: 23–48).

"laughs" at the "surprise" shown by the "indigenous people" of the African "hinterland" upon seeing the advanced technologies and skyscrapers of advanced "civilized" countries. Something like the root of such depictions can be found in the writings of both Stanley and Livingstone.

For example, Stanley, after whipping the locals who had tried to escape from the caravan, subjected their compatriots to yet other humiliation.

> I next produced a bottle of concentrated ammonia, which as I explained was for snake bites, and headaches [...]. The effect was magical, for he fell back as if shot, and such contortions as his features underwent are indescribable. His chiefs roared with laughter, and clapped their hands, pinched each other, snapped their fingers, and committed many other ludicrous things. (Stanley 1872: 334–335)

Rather than laughing at their individual ignorance, this is a style that laughs condescendingly from atop the disparity between "civilization" and "savagery." In a likewise fashion, on occasions when his caravans approached their villages, the humanitarian Dr. Livingstone describes the behavior of panic-stricken villagers as follows:

> [...] we met a woman with a little child, and a girl, wending their way home with loads of manioc. The sight of a white man always infuses a tremor into their dark bosoms [...]. In the villages the dogs run away with their tails between their legs, as if they had seen a lion. The women peer from behind the walls till he comes near them, and then hastily dash into the house. When a little child, unconscious of danger, meets you in the street, he sets up a scream at the apparition, and conveys the impression that he is not far from going into fits. Among the Bechuanas I have been obliged to reprove the women for making a hobgoblin of the white man, and telling their children that they would send for him to bite them. (Livingstone 1857: 465)

When "writing" his bemusement at such ignorance, he does not consider whether the villagers are afraid of attacks by groups of slavers from outside the area, or what they've experienced at the hands of other white men. His account simply reproduces the cross-cultural representations of base matters such as cannibalism and the benighted ignorance of the Africans. Or, when he encounters an African who refuses to let Livingstone pass through his territory, he has no intention of paying for right of passage, declaring that "I would never have it said that a white man had paid tribute to a black, and that I should cross the Kasai in spite of him" (Livingstone 1857: 469–470), before brandishing a revolver to force his way across the river.

My point is not to criticize the details of this episode but consider the structure in which such a representation (way of writing) is accepted in the description of a cross-cultural encounter; it is the fixed, hierarchical dichotomy between "us" and "them." In this sense, it was not Livingstone the individual brandishing the revolver to cross the river, but rather the society and people he identifies as "us."

Hedin's writing style is quite different. In his case, the people of other cultures are distanced by the dichotomy of "civilization" ("us") and "savagery" ("them"), but are always included through "I"; respectful exchanges between specific individuals. This can be seen in his depictions of a dancer he encountered during his third expedition and of an attendant who died on their journey:

> My heart beat faster as a girl floated between me and the flame and her graceful form became silhouetted against the illuminated background. (Hedin 1935: 1)

> Aldat was good-looking and young, but as quiet and reserved as a dreamer. He gave the impression of suffering under the memory of an ineradicable sorrow, avoided the society of his fellow-humans, and spoke, when induced to do so, only in short and measured terms. (Hedin 1935: 72)

When mourning the young man's death, Hedin considers the perspective of the other culture and the world in which the deceased had lived.

> When a person dies and his body has been laid out for wolves and vultures to devour, the soul wanders about in strange places and dim regions to seek a new body for its habitation. (Hedin 1935: 53)

This writing style is markedly different from the supposedly "objective" cross-cultural depictions typical of the "Age of Explorers."

Also, in contrast to the pistol-brandishing Dr. Livingstone, consider Hedin's account of an interaction with a Tibetan whom he had asked for assistance in his plans to illegally enter Tibet. No handgun was drawn here. Hedin was pondering disguising himself as a lama and then sneaking into Tibet in the company of another Tibetan lama. To this end, he asked a lama he had come to know on his journey to go along with him. This request was not framed as a coercive order that ignored the needs and wishes of the other. "Shereb Lama, you have full liberty to choose the way you wish to take. [...] You must understand that I will in no wise try to coerce you." The lama rejected Hedin's overture, demurring, "I cannot go with you, sir; I would justly be regarded as an apostate and traitor if I showed the way to Lhasa to a European." Hearing this, Hedin suggested to the lama, "Well, then, let me propose that you remain in the camp, while I [...] start out upon the forbidden way," to which the lama surprisingly responded "No, no, that will not do. How can I desert you, sir, when you most need me?" Hedin describes this situation by observing that Shereb Lama "had a hard struggle between his duty as a Lama and his desire to render me faithful service" (Hedin 1935: 83–84). Here we see the structure of an exchange based on a "You" and "I" approach that developed over the course of a journey through a mutual respect that transcends the self-other dichotomy. Of course, it does not annihilate or efface the respective worlds of the two men, but is rather an attempt to connect the two worlds while recognizing their differences. In this regard, Hedin's cross-cultural perspective might contain hints for overcoming the challenges that have been recognized in cross-cultural description in the wake of the reflexive turn heralded by *Writing Culture.*

Drawing

Drawing is another typical method of representing other cultures. In the consumption and rendering of other cultures into entertainment, the social impact of drawing is even greater than that of writing. Travelers' and explorers' accounts of cross-cultural encounters typically feature illustrations that vividly visualize the descriptions given in the text, in some cases determining the popularity of the explorers' accounts. How to draw other cultures, and the other people who live in them, is an important clue for understanding cross-cultural perspectives.

Here, again, let us bring back our two heroes from the Age of Exploration – Stanley and Dr. Livingstone. What is expressed by the illustrations of their accounts of African explorations is a regard that distinguishes sharply between civilization ("us") and savagery ("them"). In Stanley's account of *How I Found Livingstone* and Livingstone's own autobiographical descriptions, explorers are typically depicted striking dignified poses, gun in hand, facing their interlocutors (other explorers) (e.g., Figure 4.1). By contrast, indigenous Africans are shown kneeling beside the explorers, or else thronging or milling about in confusion. Absent here is any conscious attempt to capture the humanity of individual Africans from a stance of contiguity (Figure 4.2). In contrast, the sketches that Hedin made of his encounters with other cultures and peoples in the field, such as those he brought to Japan, are based on a diametrically opposed point of view than found in the African illustrations. We see that rather than drawing other people from other cultures lumped together as a collective and indistinguishable "them," he draws them presenting as individual human beings, people with selves, like "us" (Figures 4.3 and 4.4). As we can see, Hedin's cross-cultural perspective diverges from the dichotomy between "us" and "them"; when faced with other cultures and peoples, he does not efface the "I" but works to highlight it in the encounter.

In lieu of a conclusion: Hedin's contemporary significance

A creative synthesis of scholarship and exploration

Hedin's significance in the history of the study of cross-cultural understanding lies in the fact that against the backdrop of Europe's vast political, economic, and military predominance and claims to epistemic and moral superiority, he operated from a perspective different to the dichotomy between "us" and "them" – a dichotomy that symbolized the Age of Exploration in the latter half of the nineteenth century, when other cultures were being encountered around the globe. Of course, in today's debates over the understanding and perception of other cultures, cross-cultural perspectives based in such clear hierarchies of relative superiority and inferiority are rejected in principle as "politically incorrect." Even so, the dichotomizing perspective and the ensuing invisibility of the "I" is an issue problematized by the reflexive turn of the 1980s, and still today, it is difficult to argue that a resolution has been found to the chronic problems of cross-cultural perspectives and representations. Hedin's approach to cross-cultural perspectives goes beyond the dimension of merely perceiving the relative superiority or inferiority of other cultures to raising important ideas for addressing this contemporary challenge.

Before expanding on this point, however, I would first like to look at how, in his fourth expedition, Hedin transformed and created the praxeological form of the expedition. As mentioned, Hedin changed many practices with this expedition. The result of these formal innovations – from his previous solo format to a new organizationally-based structure, from exploration to interdisciplinary academic surveying, from single-nation endeavor to multi-national collaboration, and from an exploitative to a recuperative relationship with the local community – was an expedition organized with most of the basic features found in academic surveys today. In this context, the survey was to be conducted on the basis of official partnership among China's academic societies, materials acquired in the course of the survey were to be administered by China's museums and educational

Exploration, Science, and Understanding Others

Figure 4.1: The white explorer grapples with the beast as Africans flee in terror
Credit: "David Livingstone being attacked by lion during expedition in Africa" / De Agostini Picture Library / Bridgeman Images; from *The Life and Explorations of David Livingstone, LLD, Carefully Compiled from Reliable Sources* (London & Newcastle on Tyne: Adam and Co. for John R. Haslam, Nottingham, n.d. [c. 1878]).

Figure 4.2: A native African kneels
Credit: "The Meeting of Stanley and Livingstone" / Mary Evans Picture Library; from *The Life and Explorations of David Livingstone, LLD, Carefully Compiled from Reliable Sources* (London & Newcastle on Tyne: Adam and Co. for John G. Murdoch, London, n.d. [c. 1878]).

Figure 4.3: Sketch by Hedin ("Young Woman")

Figure 4.4: Sketch by Hedin ("Young Man")

research institutes, and in the event that these were brought back to European research agencies, permission would be sought and any materials returned after use. This was a strikingly different relationship than that typical of the Age of Exploration.[14] The languages spoken in this interdisciplinary international organization included Swedish, German, French, English, Chinese, Danish, Mongolian, Russian, and Eastern Turki (Uyghur), its members switching freely between languages as necessary. This Northwest Scientific Expedition was called a "peripatetic university" and became fertile soil for educating young Chinese researchers interested in various fields.

This synthesis of scholarship and exploration was of course not Hedin's invention. During this period, Japan was also beginning attempts that aspired to a similar synthesis of scholarship and exploration in China. At the center of these attempts were scholars from Kyoto Imperial University, especially researchers around Imanishi Kinji, who had organized the Kyoto Society for Exploration and Geography. Imanishi and his colleagues had organized the Kyoto Imperial University Expedition to Mount Paektu in 1935, the Kyoto Imperial University Mongolian Academic Survey Expedition in 1938, and the Trans-Daxing'anling Expedition in 1942. During the war, these academics worked to apply their exploration and scholarship to national policy, based at the Institute of Ethnology and the Northwest Research Institute. In 1944, the Northwest Research Institute, established in Zhangjiakou, was engaged in ecological and ethnographic surveys of Manchuria and Mongolia; Imanishi had been appointed as director, overseeing young researchers who were to become intellectual leaders in Japan after the war, including Umesao Tadao, Iwamura Shinobu, Fujisawa Akira, and Nakao Sasuke.

---

14 Although Hedin remained the effective leader of the Expedition on this occasion, in organizational terms, supreme authority was vested in the director of the Chinese Ministry of Railways. Hedin was officially there in an advisory capacity. In total, ten Chinese scholars and university students were part of this "peripatetic university." Hedin also " volunteered to hand over later, after their European staffs had carried out series of observations over at least a year, the meteorological stations, together with the whole of their instrumental equipment, as a present to the Chinese Government" (Hedin 1931: 55). He explains his motive was so "the Chinese would enjoy the same rights as the Europeans. The Chinese, moreover, were in their own country, at home; we, on the other hand, were guests" (Hedin 1931: 7).

Nevertheless, this approach to synthesizing exploration and scholarship differed in important ways from Hedin's "peripatetic university." One was that it did not see the Chinese as any sort of collaborator, but merely a part of the "world" to be surveyed. Another was that this synthesis was a matter of Japanese "national policy" in the Japanese – not Chinese – "national interest."[15] The director of the Institute of Ethnology was Takata Yasuma from Kyoto Imperial University, who was also responsible for "ethnographic, ethnohistorical, and ethnic policy research associated with ethnic strategy" within the Japanese military's sphere of influence.[16] The "1944 Annual Report of Activities" of the Ethnological Association (*Minzokugaku kyōkai*), an academic organization engaged in cross-cultural research, describes "conducting a fact-finding study of a Mengjiang lamasery and lamaist monks in partnership with the Northwest Research Institute in association with the Mongolia Garrison Army, the Mengjiang United Autonomous Government, the Japanese Embassy."

The explorers and scientists of Japan who in Hedin's day carried out their academic studies while exploring Mengjiang and Xizang (Tibet) did not necessarily face up to or perceive other worlds and other cultures except in the dichotomous terms "us" and "them" that Hedin was attempting to overcome. Theirs was an attempt at synthesizing exploration and scholarship in the context of more involuted and nationally focused divisions of the world. In this sense, the synthesis of exploration and scholarship that Hedin practiced on his fourth expedition could be described as a unique and creative union.

Re-evaluating Hedin's attempt within the history of research

Finally, let us return to the question posed at the beginning of this chapter of how we might be able to overcome the "intolerance of difference" that pervades the contemporary world. After Hedin's "debut" as an explorer in the Age of Exploration at the end of the nineteenth century, he began encountering and forging his perceptual framework (regard) for other cultures at a time when the praxeological significances of his own activities was changing from exploration to scholarship (science). In doing so, he established a view that departed from the dichotomy between civilization ("us") and savagery ("them") that at the time had been the dominant framework of cross-cultural perspectives. As mentioned, Hedin's significance for contemporary cross-cultural perspectives does not lie in the fact that he does not see a disconnect between the worlds of self and other into humanistic (ethical, moral, or epistemic) categories according to their relative superiority or inferiority. Rather, it lies in the fact that in addition to escaping the perspective of relative categories, he is attempting to overcome the dichotomy between "us" and "them," between his own and other cultures. Moreover, it lies in the fact that, to this end, when representing other worlds, his practice is to position the "I" (self) as observing subject in the context of a mutual face-to-face relationship. This also differs from the strategy of first- or second-person ethnographies that appeared among the raft of experimental ethnographies that appeared in the 1990s after the *Writing Culture* shock. This is because Hedin's perceptual framework is furnished with a composition in which the worlds of "us" on one hand and "them" on the other become contiguous on an axis of "you" and "I."

So how can this perceptual framework of Hedin's contribute a solution to the problem of today's intolerance? Needless to say, at the foundation of the perceptual framework that supports this contemporary problem is a way of thinking that disconnects our own world from the others'. The "intolerance of others" is configured when

---

15 Imanishi was an outstanding explorer, organizer, and scholar, and was instrumental in establishing the Kyoto Society for Exploration and Geography around 1939. However, the Society's first large scholarly expedition in 1941 was to the South Pacific island of Ponape (Pohnpei), underwritten by Nan'yō Kōhatsu, the "South Seas Development Company," which was one of the primary engines of colonial rule for the Empire of Japan, to the degree that it was known as the "Mantetsu of the Sea" (the railway company that was deeply implicated in Japan's development of Manchuria in continental Asia, itself known as "Japan's East India Company in China"). Similarly, the Daxing'anling Expedition mounted the following year was effectively dictated by a request from the Kwantung Army (with advice and support from the Manchukuo Security Department). See Nakao (2016: 394–404).

16 At the request of the Kwantung Army, the Institute of Ethnology actively collaborated with not only colonial rule, but also military operations, such as investigating anti-Japanese sentiments throughout Manchuria in preparation for the possibility of Soviet invasion. Egami Namio, a member of the Institute who would later find fame for propounding the "horse-rider thesis" of Japanese ethnogenesis, in order to break the stalemate in the Burmese theater and achieve the withdrawal of Japanese forces, counselled the Imperial Army's General Staff "to dispatch about a platoon of soldiers to Lhasa by airplane, land them on a frozen lake, and persuade the Dalai Lama to declare Tibetan independence with assurances of support from Japan. Doing so would weaken the attacking force at the Burmese border by splitting the British forces engaged in the Burmese theater, drawing them off to provide border security in Tibet, during which time the Japanese troops should withdraw" (Nakao 2016: 364–365).

a political, social, or historical animosity or exclusion is mobilized or elicited on top of the preexisting perception of a dichotomous disconnect from the world of others (other peoples). The root of this is the dichotomy between "us" and "them" – a dichotomy in which the subjective "I" is always effaced in favor of the "we." Accordingly, the existential foundation of intolerance can be modified by changing the root perception of others.

However, the perception of dichotomous others is not something that can be taught, but rather is a mode of perception rooted in our everyday consciousness. A scenario in which we were to perceive and address "one and all as individually different people" by individualizing all human beings is also something that would be difficult to achieve in practice. This is due to the fact that by categorizing people according to certain criteria and setting boundaries between our own worlds and those of others, we comprehend each other and build up mutual relationships. Accordingly, the burial of the dichotomous perceptual framework is in itself not what we should be aiming for. In this regard, Hedin's praxis will be subject to reevaluation in terms of its contemporary significance. Hedin's ideas and praxis of relativizing the dichotomy "us" and "them" while contiguously linking these two worlds through mediating "I" is increasingly important in perceiving and coming face-to-face with other cultures in our contemporary world. For it is beyond this that may be glimpsed the possibility of finally overcoming our own "intolerance of difference."

References

Baker, S. W., 1866 *The Albert N'Yanza Great Basin of the Nile and Explorations of the Nile Sources*, London: Macmillan and Co.

Brubaker, R., 2015 *Grounds for Difference*, Cambridge, Mass.: Harvard University Press.

Clifford, J. & G. E. Marcus eds., 1986 *Writing Culture: The Poetics and Politics of Ethnography*, Berkeley: University of California Press.

Hedin, S., 1931 *Across the Gobi Desert*, London: Routledge.

Hedin, S., 1935 *A Conquest of Tibet*. (translated from Swedish by Julius Lincoln) London: Macmillan.

Hedin, S., 1938 *The Silk Road* (translated from Swedish by F.H. Lyon) London: G. Routledge.

Hedin, S., 1940 *The Wandering Lake* (translated from Swedish by F.H. Lyon) London: Routledge & Sons.

Hugon, A., 1991 *L'Afrique des explorateurs*. Paris: Éditions Gallimard.

5 Sven Hedin as Artist and Photographer
Extending the Techniques of Cartography and Illustration at the Turn of the Last Century
Håkan Wahlquist

Maps and illustrations

Extending our knowledge of the world in all its geographical, geological, natural, social and cultural complexity requires techniques first to record data in the field, then convey the results to fellow scientists, get these discoveries accepted, and eventually disseminate new knowledge to a wider audience.

Words have rarely been sufficient for this endeavor. Early reports of visits to distant places before the nineteenth century often contained references to things that scientists had neither seen nor recorded and written about before. At that time there might not even have been the words necessary to accurately describe them. Conveying a foreign landscape, a new bird, or a foreign culture, is, as we know, very much a matter of translation, sometimes requiring the creation of new scientific terms, sometimes expanding the meanings of existing words, and sometimes the introduction of foreign words.[1]

To meet the demand for ever more advanced scientific fieldwork, there were continuous innovations in techniques and research methods, such as the development of increasingly sophisticated instruments for accurately determining positions, distances and heights, more reliable meteorological observations and improved sample collection methods. Accordingly, increasingly refined techniques, instruments and representational conventions were developed for map-making, for both in the field and later. Specimens of mammals, birds, fish, insects, flowers and what-not collected in the field, were with various techniques carefully skinned and mounted, dried and fixed on paper, secured with pins and sorted in boxes or stored in glass-bottles filled with spirits, enabling them to be brought "home" for systematic study in the future, as were geological and soil samples.

Artefacts and archaeological objects were also collected in early expeditions, but it was not until the nineteenth century that they were collected for explicitly scientific purposes, of a kind we would recognize today.[2]

Until the end of the nineteenth, and indeed well into the twentieth century, the scientist in the field was often a solo explorer carrying out research, accumulating information and samples.[3]

This increasing flow of material, sometimes quickly displayed in exhibitions, was inadequate to convey the setting in which it had been collected; the landscape which had been captured on maps, the peoples encountered and described in the texts and what the flowers looked like before they were dried and fixed on paper. A visual supplement was required for the descriptions printed in books or verbally conveyed in lectures.

Photography entered the scene in the latter nineteenth century and was immediately embraced as a way to fill this gap. For many years, however, executed in the field during arduous expeditions, its use was constrained by severe limitations. For a start, cameras were large and heavy and glass negatives were alarmingly fragile.

Taking exposures was neither quick nor easy, especially in poor light conditions. The early versions of film negatives from the 1880s were prone to curl, especially in hot and humid or cool and dry weather conditions, making them less durable and difficult to use. It was a long time before color negatives would be practical in the field.[4]

---

1 Translation into numerical, as well as graphical, representations is of course also an alternative.

2 There is an ever-growing literature about the development of collecting, arranging and studying the collections as well as the ideas behind such endeavors, from early private "Kunstkammers" to modern museums, and from Medieval Italy to the world today.

3 The most common exceptions were expeditions carried by ships, which could accommodate more men, and thus also scientists, such as the Cook expeditions in the late eighteenth century or the Nordenskiöld circumnavigation of Asia and "conquest" of the North-east passage in the late nineteenth century.

4 Hedin never experimented with color photos. Some lantern slides made for his public lectures, copied from his glass negatives, were however tinted. During his final expedition, his geophysicist, Nils Ambolt used autochromes to document his research in West Turkestan/Xinjiang and north-west Tibet.

Figure 5.1: Sounding the depth of Little Kara Kul, Pamir, September 1894

Figure 5.2: Sounding the depth of Little Kara Kul, Pamir, September 1894

Figure 5.3: The Potala Palace in Lhasa and its surroundings as depicted in Athanasii Kircheri: "China Monumentiis," 1667. (From the Sven Hedin Library)

Sven Hedin (1865–1952) used glass negatives during his first three expeditions into Central Asia between 1893 and 1908, and most of them have survived.[5]

They are still generally in fine condition, and their large surface areas carry an enviable amount of information. Transporting them, however, required a fair share of the horses, mules, yaks or camels constituting his caravans, which, due to the hardships encountered, continuously decreased in numbers.[6]

Furthermore, in the early years, transferring photos to a printed medium was a major challenge. Photos often had to be redrawn with ink before they could be reproduced with the desired clarity. Hedin occasionally did so himself (Figure 5.1 & 5.2).

This combination of factors ensured that early techniques of visual representation, including drawing/sketching with pencil and ink and painting with brush and colors, survived well into the twentieth century.[7]

Sven Hedin was familiar with the illustrations in old texts about the Asia he was interested in. He knew that artists were often attached to embassies in foreign countries to convey the impressions of their emissaries, like William Alexander (1767–1816), who accompanied Lord Georg MacCartney (1737–1806) to China in 1793 in his attempt to reach a diplomatic breakthrough with Emperor Qianlong (1711–1799). However, such illustrations could be quite fanciful indeed. An illustration in Athanasii Kircheri's "China Monumentis" from 1667, for example, incorporates numerous European elements in a scene depicting the newly extended Potala Palace in Lhasa (Figure 5.3).

In this respect Hedin was highly influenced by his predecessors in the natural sciences, foremost among them German explorers cum scientists like Alexander von Humboldt (1769–1859) and the Schlagintweit brothers; Hermann (1826–1882), Adolf (1829–1857), Robert (1833–1885) and Emil (1831–1860), whom Humboldt had actively supported and encouraged.[8] Their lavishly illustrated publications can be found in Sven Hedin's library[9] (Figure 5.4).

---

5 Before then, during his first two ventures into Asia (1886–1887 in the Caucasus and Persia and 1890–1891 to Persia and Central Asia), he had to rely on photos bought from Turkic, Persian and Russian sources, and on his own drawing skills.

6 Towards the end of the Tibetan leg of Hedin's third expedition (1906–1908), the stock of glass negatives ran low and he had to break them into several plates to take the number of photos he required.

7 For a recent publication on this topic, see Lewis-Jones & Herbert 2017.

8 Körner 1982: 63 and Kick 1982.

9 Primarily Humboldt 1814–1819, 1837–1842, 1844; Schlagintweit, Hermann, Adolph and Robert 1861–1866; Schlagintweit-Sakünlünski, Herman 1869–1880.

In contrast to Ferdinand von Richthofen (1833–1905), Adolf Erik Nordenskiöld (1832–1901), Nikolay Mikhaylovich Przhevalsky (1839–1888) and Ármin (Hermann) Vámbéry (1832–1913), von Humboldt and the Schlagintweit brothers have only rarely been mentioned among the role-models who influenced Sven Hedin's choice of career. But there are such obvious links between the German geographical tradition they represent and Hedin's methods for planning and conducting expeditions that the connections should be acknowledged.

Humboldt, late in life, long after his American explorations at the turn of the nineteenth century, aspired to go to Tibet. In 1829, with Russian collaboration, as Hedin would later do, he crossed Central Asia from the West reaching the Chinese border. Humboldt, though, never reached Tibet.

The Schlagintweit brothers were dependent on British support, as was Sven Hedin for his Tibetan explorations 1906–1908. For their research in South and Central Asia between 1854 and 1857, they were employed by the East India Company. Inspired by Humboldt's quest to understand the mountain-systems of Asia, the "orography" of the continent, they paid special attention to the relationship between the Himalayan, Karakorum and Kun Lun mountains.[10] This issue was to be central to Hedin's research, after he had carefully studied his predecessors' achievements.[11]

The broad multi-disciplinary character of the Humboldt and the Schlagintweit expeditions is evident in the way Hedin planned and finished his scientific expeditions. He carried or sent notebooks and letters to Sweden with observations of all kinds, route maps and sketches, as well as crates filled to the brim with specimens and objects related to natural as well as human sciences, just as his forerunners had done.[12]

The Schlagintweit brothers' main task for the British, though, was to establish a triangulated and astronomically fixed network of points for magnetic observations.[13] Hedin only partly replicated this, only making astronomical observations to fix positions on his route maps. During his last expedition, 1927–1935, however, triangulation was consistently done for mapmaking. Careful astronomical observations were also taken, as were measurements of gravitation.[14]

They also shared numerous other scientific interests, like meteorology and climatology, and related studies of

Figure 5.4: The Salt Lake Tso Mitbál, in Pangkóng, Tibet. Aquarelle painted by Hermann de Schlagintweit, June 1856. (From the Sven Hedin Library)

glaciers, coupled with attempts to climb high mountains. In 1802 Humboldt, in a famous attempt, had tried to scale the volcano Chimborazo in Ecuador, but according to estimates he and his party had to turn back at an elevation of 5878 meters. The Sclagintweit brothers were more successful. They carefully measured not less than 63 glaciers in the Himalayas, and in 1855, in an attempt on what they believed to be Kamet (7756 meters) they followed the Ibi-Gamin glacier to a height of 6766 meters,[15] which remained an altitude record for a long time. In 1890, Hedin successfully scaled Damavand (5610 meters) in Iran, but was less successful in 1894 on Mustagh Ata (7509 meters). Despite repeated attempts he had to turn back at an estimated altitude of 6300 meters.

Humboldt and the Schlagintweit brothers, furthermore, made great efforts to visually record their observations in the form of drawings and paintings. Hermann and Adolf Schlagintweit excelled in this art. They were true artists with their pencils, charcoals, water- and oil colors. Humboldt had drawn panoramas of the landscapes he witnessed. This technique was subsequently developed and widely employed by the Schlagintweit brothers. Their collections contain 743 sketches of landscapes, including panoramas of up to 4 meters long.[16] Like Hedin they reproduced them for publications but also displayed them in numerous public lectures.

---

10 Körner 1982.
11 Hedin 1916–1922.
12 Körner 1982: 67 for some details on the extent of the Schlagintweit collections.
13 Polter 1982.
14 Ambolt 1938 and 1948.

15 Körner 1982: 64.
16 Körner 1982: 67.

The Schlagintweit brothers, in particular Robert, were early pioneers of photography in the field. Some 50 exposures seem to have survived, all of them from 1856, depicting people encountered in India. The chemicals required for the photographic process were then lost in an accident.[17] For the remainder of their journey, like Hedin in the latter part of his first expedition (1893–1897), they had to rely on their skills as artists.

Sven Hedin – an explorer's background

In a way, Hedin thus belonged to the last of the classical explorers of the seventeenth to nineteenth centuries; persons who in the field did everything or almost everything on their own, not only pursuing the natural sciences, charting routes and describing life around them, but also being competent artists/draftsmen.[18]

To Hedin's credit it should be mentioned that in addition to being one of the last "classical" explorers, he can also be considered to be one of the first "modern" ones. The Sino-Swedish Expedition that he negotiated, organized, supplied and directed between 1927 and 1935 was an interdisciplinary and international undertaking with participants from several different countries, each a specialist in their respective field, spanning the natural and human sciences.[19]

During this expedition other members of the team took care of most of the map-making as well as the cameras. Some of them also produced drawings/watercolors.[20] Hedin continued to make drawings as well, but largely for his own amusement and recreation. Still, some of them found their way into his publications, both popular and scientific.

But let us return to Sven Hedin's three early expeditions, when he not only drew and compiled all route maps, securing positions with astronomical observations, but also took all the photographs, drew all the sketches and panoramas and occasionally painted watercolors, in addition to writing diaries, keeping all field notes and meteorological records, and collecting geological, botanical, zoological and paleontological samples.

How does one prepare for something like that? First you should of course have an aptitude for ceaseless work in the field, as well as the equally ceaseless work at your desk at home writing articles, books and scientific reports, delivering lectures and participating in public life. Sven Hedin was a "late bloomer."[21] His school performance was mediocre, even weak. The turning point came in his early 20s when he was exposed to the world outside Sweden, which until then he had only read about in books and scientific journals.

In Baku, and during a long journey through Persia, he met and was caught by "Asia", its nature and its people.[22] Earlier dreams of following in the footsteps of a succession of Swedish Polar researchers were abandoned for Persia and Central Asia.

However, his almost unbelievable work ethic,[23] which was to become one of his greatest assets in life,[24] would not have been enough, at least not to launch him on his career, if he had not had a loving, encouraging and supportive family behind him.

It should be noted that "supportive" did not mean financially. The Hedin family was by no means wealthy. Socially they belonged to what one could call the upper-middle class, very much the result of the efforts of Sven Hedin's father, Ludvig Hedin (1826–1917) (Figure 5.5). Ludvig Hedin had risen from a situation of very restricted means, when he and his siblings, while still small, were orphaned to be taken care of by their eldest twin sisters and a relative overlooking their meagre finances. Hedin's father initially trained to become a bricklayer. An undeniable artistic skill, revealed in small delicate paintings of land- and townscapes, prompted him to enter the Royal Academy of Arts, where he was educated to become an architect. A skilled draftsman, he was sent around Sweden to design and inspect churches and other places of importance. He was the gifted archi-

---

17 Lindgren 1982.
18 In order to enhance the appeal of his earliest travelogues, Hedin and his foremost Swedish publisher, Albert Bonnier, commissioned a number of well-known Swedish artists to paint scenes from his early expeditions, based on Hedin's instructions and sketches. His later books, though, include only his own works.
19 Cf. Romgard 2013. The Sino-Swedish Expedition was furthermore conducted in accordance with agreements signed with relevant Chinese authorities, something that Western scholars until then, with the exception of Johan Gunnar Andersson (1874–1960), had consistently avoided.
20 Like Hans Eduard Dettman (1891–1969) and Birger Bohlin (1898–1990).

21 His early work with a hand-drawn atlas, mentioned later, foreshadowed this character trait.
22 Hedin 1886 and 1887.
23 Sven Hedin's incredible, tireless working capacity and productivity, in the field and elsewhere, has often been commented upon, but perhaps with best understanding by some of his close colleagues (Wegener 1935; Haack 1941). Coupled to this, he had an enviable memory, which some of his friends described as almost unbelievable (cf. Stolpe 1974).
24 This was in addition to many other gifts such as a flair to pick up and use languages and social skills allowing him to master any situation he might find himself in. At the same time, he held on to a geopolitical interpretation of world politics and history, which included categorical support of Germany, irrespective of the policies pursued by its leaders and governments.

tect of many rural churches, mansions and lighthouses as well as countless residential and other buildings in towns, foremost in Stockholm (Figure 5.6).

This was in the late nineteenth century, when Stockholm began to change from a small, dirty and reportedly very unhealthy town mostly of wooden houses to the well-built city with multistoried houses constructed of stone and brick recognized today.

Ludvig Hedin was very much a part of this transformation, and as a result the Hedin family became well placed in society, enjoying wide-ranging and important social networks and cultural contacts, reaching as far as the Royal family. Sven Hedin's formidable career, nationally and internationally, vastly extended these networks.

In previous generations, there was an intellectual tradition in the family, and on Sven Hedin's paternal grandmother's side, also some substantial wealth to be remembered. Sven Hedin's great grandfather, Sven Anders Hedin (1750–1821), was an important intellectual and medical scientist at the turn of the nineteenth century. He was a pupil of Carl von Linnaeus and an influential member of the Royal Swedish Academy of Sciences. Sven Hedin's maternal grandfather, Christian Gissel Berlin (1800–1863), was a reader in mathematics who became a prominent clergyman of the Swedish Church and a member of the old parliament, which was based on the four stands. The family line can be traced back to eighteenth century Jewish immigration to Sweden, a heritage that was never denied, even though Jewish customs had no place in the Hedin home.

Except for Sven Hedin himself, his immediate, natal family had no real academic ambitions. Hedin was showered with honorary doctoral titles and memberships in learned societies and academies, but never accepted a professorial appointment. He preferred to remain an independent scholar. His uncles pursued careers in government service, with the post and customs. One uncle, however, was a celebrated actor of his times employed by the Dramatic Theatre in Stockholm, specializing in comic roles and with unusual friends. Sven Hedin's siblings pursued a variety of humbler careers. His youngest sister, Alma, however, was a social entrepreneur with important housing projects directed at poor people, especially women, to her credit. The family, though staunchly conservative with the monarchy, church and country as the three pillars of life, also demonstrated an undeniable social concern for society's less fortunate.

Family life was all important, and even though theatres, restaurants, and occasionally the opera were visited, it was carried out at home, in summer residences in the archipelago, and in the homes of close relatives and friends. Family occasions were intensely observed. A specialty of the Hedin family was to

Figure 5.5: Ludvig Hedin at work together with his wife Anna, Stockholm 1890s

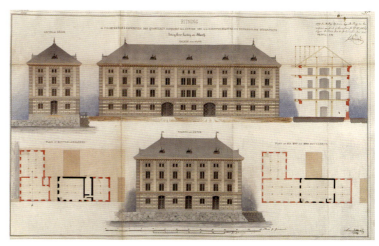

Figure 5.6: Ludvig Hedin 1859; architectural drawing for the front of "Eldkvarn" in Stockholm. (From the Stockholm City Archives)

write long, and in the case of his father, often exalted and admonishing poems to be read aloud. Sometimes, especially when accompanying the presentation of Christmas gifts, the poems turned witty. They could be richly illustrated, and they were always kept so that they would be remembered. Sven Hedin was an eager participant of this family ritual, and thus from early on he began developing his skills in writing, making illustrations and appearing in front of people.

Only one of his six siblings married. The others, Sven Hedin included, remained with their parents, forming what one could call a devoted secretariat for him while in the field, on tour and at home in Stockholm. This

Figure 5.7: The Hedin family in their summer home 1898

Figure 5.8: Sven Hedin surrounded by his remaining siblings 1948

arrangement continued throughout their lives (Figure 5.7 & 5.8).

A self-taught and productive artist: Portraits and panoramas for science

The Hedin family also provided a setting in which necessary skills and talents could be nourished. There was a saying in the family that money should not be spared when it was for Sven's books or the children's teeth. For instance, he was allowed to subscribe to *Petermanns Geographische Mitteilungen*, the foremost German geographical journal of its time, filled with maps and information on what was going on in the field of geography and exploration. His library thus began to grow.

Sven Hedin, as a child and youth, could surely have followed and been inspired by his father's work. The family bible, with Doré's famous illustrations, provided another source of inspiration, as did the often burlesque illustrations offered by the artist F. W. Scholander (1816–1881), a close friend of the family, and an important Swedish architect.

Those were the kind of illustrations that Sven Hedin as a schoolboy tried to transfer to his own fantasy world.[25] However, they hardly influenced his later production, which only occasionally allowed for that kind of free creativity.

There was one trait of his father's work that must have made a lasting impression on him: the attention to precision and exactitude. Sven Hedin left some texts behind in which he informs the reader about the ideas guiding his work as an artist.[26] The most important one is a small book published in 1920[27] in which he stresses that he at all times strived to depict exactly what he had seen in front of him be it a mountain ridge, a lake, a monastery exterior or interior, or a person.

Making a drawing or creating a watercolor was thus another way to write notes, or like taking a photograph. In doing so he could invest special attention in details not easily captured by other techniques. Photographing a landscape, with the sharpness of distant objects that his camera lenses could offer, often did not capture the details of far-off side valleys, ravines mountain crests and glacial fields. In his drawings he could carefully render and locate these features.

The monumental work that he carried out during the Tibetan part of his third expedition (1906–1908) in drawing exact panoramas of the surrounding landscape with its mountains[28] resulted in an unbroken chain of carefully executed views, with bearings taken to all prominent topographical features. The cartographer,

---

25 Well described in Wennerholm 1978: 28 ff.
26 It should be noted that he had no formal schooling in drawing, apart from some summer-weeks as a schoolboy, when he was offered training in drawing portraits by "Miss Kerstin Cardon"; Kristina Mathilda Cardon (1843–1924).
27 Hedin 1920. Its Swedish title *En Levnads Teckning* has a double meaning. It refers both to the biographical outline of the text, from his first journey to the East in 1885 to his experiences on the battlefields during the Great War and his journey to the Middle East in the 1910s; it also provides a reference to a life filled with artistic work. The text was republished for the centenary of Sven Hedin's birth, in both Swedish and English (Hedin 1964a & b), and was probably translated into German and published in Munich as early as 1926. The text was certainly published in the early 1930s in Berlin and was republished for the Hedin Centenary, then with all illustrations (Hedin 1933 and 1965). For the English edition the title was translated as *Sketches of a Life Time*. In a German interview he also talked about his life as an artist (Hedin 1936).
28 Published in Hedin 1917 (Col. Herman Byström had redrawn the panoramas with ink for publication.) The panoramas were primarily captured from camp-sites and passes.

Sven Hedin as Artist and Photographer

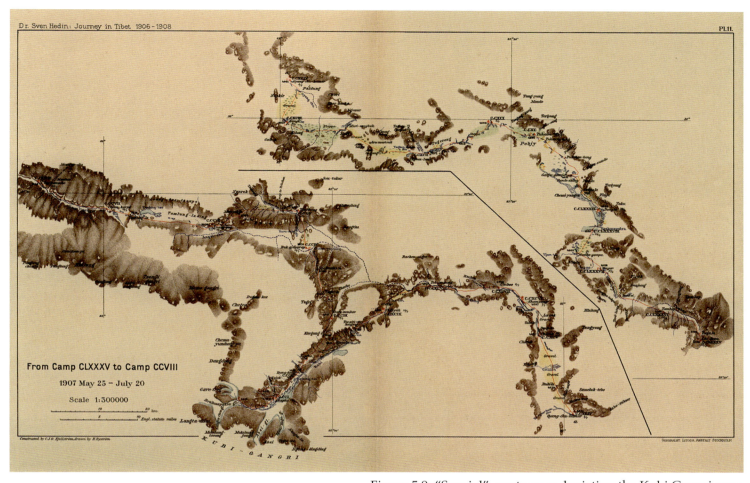

Figure 5.9: "Special", route map depicting the Kubi Gangri area, where Sven Hedin argued that the source of Yarlung Tsangpo/Brahmaputra can be found 1907

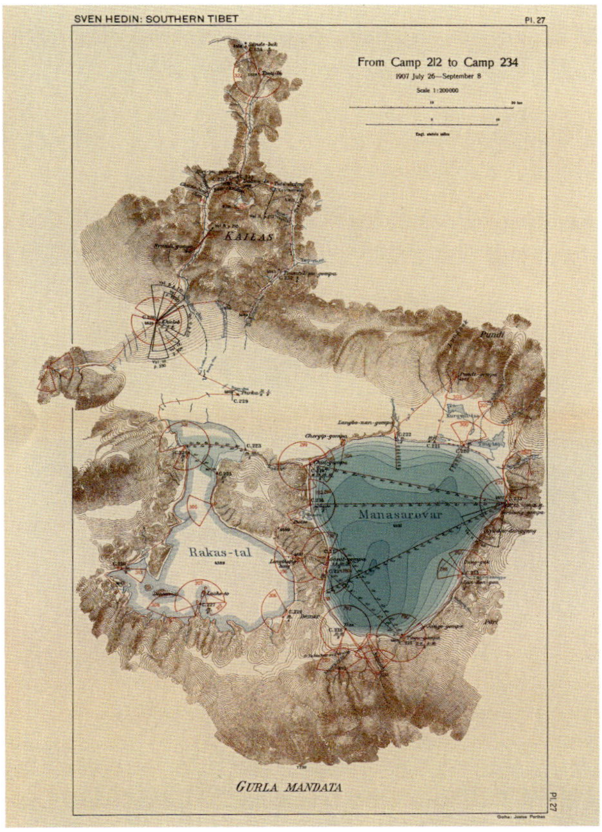

Figure 5.10: Hypsometrical map of the Kailash-Manasarowar area. Red circles indicate the panoramas drawn by Sven Hedin. Black circles indicate his photographic panoramas. The soundings of the Manasarowar Lake also detailed 1907

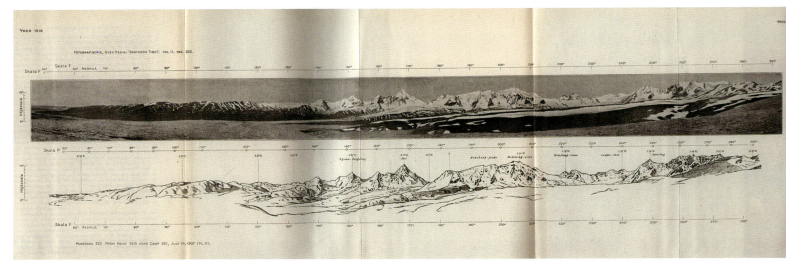

Figure 5.11: The photographic and hand-drawn panoramas of the sources of the Brahmaputra at Kubi Gangri compared. Sven Hedin 1907 (From Dahlgren et al. 1920)

Figure 5.12: Sven Hedin levelling the Lop Desert between the dried-up basin in the north and the basin in the south, then receiving the water of the Tarim River system 1901

who transferred Hedin's field notes to printed maps,[29] could then use these to construct a set of route maps, "hypsometrical" ones, an alternative set to the set of "special" maps based on his original route maps, drawn in the field.[30] The latter were produced with a difficult but efficient technique which will be described later

A famous example of Hedin's panoramas, also chosen for its detailed calculation and review,[31] was the one covering the mountain range East and South of Kubi Gangri's uppermost catchment area in Southwest Tibet with its prominent glaciers, which Hedin considered to contain the source of Yarlung Tsangpo/Brahmaputra. The reviewers found that the vertical and horizontal differences between Hedin's drawn panorama and the photographed one were negligible, and furthermore, almost constant from one panorama to another[32] (Figure 5.11).

One may well wonder from where Sven Hedin got the idea of using this arduous technique[33] of drawing panoramas. It seems to have developed over time through

---

29 Colonel Axel Herman Byström (1858–1933) and Lieutenant Otto Kjellström (1855–1913).
30 Hedin n.d. Special maps in 26 sheets; scale 1:300.000; Hedin 1922 Hypsometrical maps in 52 sheets, scale 1:200.000. The location and direction of each panorama, the photographic as well as the drawn ones, are carefully inserted on the hypsometrical maps.
31 Dahlgren et al. 1918.
32 "As for the accuracy of this investigation of panorama 262 it has become clear that within the area (of the panorama) studied…the mean deviation of the azimuth and height are ± 0°,5 and ± 0°,4, respectively. When these figures are transferred to the original drawings…it can be ascertained that Hedin, on two sheets of drawings, with a total length of 115 cm and a height of the actual drawing of 8 cm, made a mistake of only 5 mm vertically and 4 mm horizontally. This incredible sharpness of the observations should, we believe, attract the interest of students of human physiology. It is not only a question of the eyes to determine correct measurements, but also of orientation, since drawing the panorama required the draughtsman to turn 120°." (Dahlgren et al. 1918: 146–147, my translation from Swedish). In two articles (Bergwik 2018a & b). the author discusses Hedin's use of panoramas. Bergwik "reads Hedin's geographic images and texts through a broader nineteenth century history of the panorama and indicates how his panoramic visions were part of a broader media culture of the century" (Bergwik 2018b).
33 It should be noted that Hedin's panoramas were most often drawn under taxing conditions in Tibet, on top of windy and cold passes, at early or late campsites, during winter conditions and at great heights. Drawings could also be executed during conditions when photography would not produce any useful results. It could take up to 4 hours to finish a single panorama. He drew no less than 1736 separate sheets of panoramas, which in turn could be combined into 552 complete panoramas, from two to six sheets each. Hedin excelled in numerically calculating the extent of his achievements. Adding up the lengths of all his panoramas, he finds that together they have a total length of 875,3 meters. (Hedin 1910)

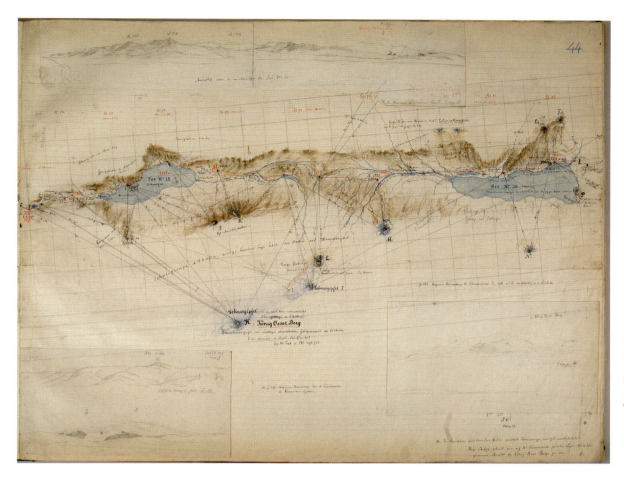

Figure 5.13: Bruno Hassenstein's second-generation map 1898, of an area in north-east Tibet, based on Sven Hedin's route maps of 1897, with inserted panoramas.

a desire to truthfully capture the landscape around him. He could manage the horizontal plane well with the technique he used for map-making, and he could fairly well calculate the altitude of his position from the boiling point of water. As for determining his position he first used a sextant, then a theodolite.[34] However, the vertical plane posed problems that he could not overcome with the instruments available to him at the time. He could not produce material that could be interpreted photogrammetrically,[35] so he had to use his eyes and meticulously transfer the landscape and mountains toward the horizon to his panoramas which sometimes covered the entire 360° around him[36] (Figure 5.12).

Small panoramas first appeared in a second generation set of maps from his first expedition, drawn by his German cartographer Bruno Hassenstein (1839–1902) at Perthes Geographisches Anstalt (Geographical Institute) in Gotha, who constructed the maps from this expedition.[37] In the sheet covering a section of Hedin's route through north-eastern Tibet, Bruno Hassenstein inserted small panoramas by Hedin indicating the bearings to a number of mountains needed to construct the map (Figure 5.13).

---

34 Cf. Hedin 1927: 6 ff. Hedin's chief geologist and cartographer during his last expedition (1927–1935), Erik Norin (1895–1982), notes that during the Tibetan campaigns of 1906–1908 Hedin's eyesight had deteriorated to such an extent that he had to refrain from observing the stars at night, instead going for less reliable measurements of the altitude of the sun. Norin later checked the latitudes and longitudes given by Hedin for five camp-sites in Aksai China and the Tarim Basin, the former determined with the instruments mentioned, the latter chronometrically, with those arrived at with much higher precision by Nils Ambolt (1900–1969), Hedin's geophysicist during the Sino-Swedish expedition. Norin finds them to be remarkably good. (Norin 1954: 21 and Amboldt 1938).

35 Hedin 1916: xvi.

36 Ulla Ehrensvärd (1927–2015) calls Hedin's method a "merger between photogrammetrical construction and topographical reconnaissance" (Ehrensvärd 1990: 95) (my translation). This complicated technique involves rendering the elevation of mountains and successive altitudes of the landscape. Several methods were available, while a transfer to modern contour lines, which Hedin would have preferred, required a very different quality of basic data than the kind Hedin could provide. He used so-called back strokes in the field, a technique developed in Germany in the late eighteenth century. For publication, these were either retained or used together with a shading technique (Ehrensvärd 1990).

37 Cf. Smits 2004 for a comprehensive history of map-making and map-makers at Justus Perthes Geographischen Anstalt in Gotha published in *Petermanns Geographische Mitteilungen*. Cf. Weber 2012 for the Hedin collection of maps at Gotha. For Bruno Hassenstein see Smits 2004:40–41.

Figure 5.14: Campsite in Tibet Sven Hedin 1901

Nearing the end of his second expedition (1899–1902), when crossing the Tibetan plateau, Chang Tang, he became increasingly aware that he lacked the means to uninterruptedly depict the types of landscape that he passed, preserving them in the form of images. He continued to take photos, but that was not enough[38] (Figure 5.14). Thus, he started to occasionally make drawings or even panoramas of the landscapes surrounding him. However, they did not connect to one another to form unbroken documentation. Rather they would leave the observer in the dark as to what the landscape looked like to the right and left of the panorama.[39]

It was during his third, Tibetan expedition (1906–1908) that Sven Hedin turned this technique into the concerted effort that resulted in the outcome just explained. During his Persian campaign (1905–1906), which preceded the Tibetan one, he also drew panoramas, but not ones that formed an unbroken picture of the landscape, such as those in Tibet. Those panoramas were then often executed in color, as were indeed quite a few panoramas painted later in Tibet. To work in watercolor was a conscious choice made by Hedin because those panoramas were also meant to capture the geology of the mountains in front of him, with their strata in different colors. Panoramas containing lakes on the Tibetan plateau supported Hedin's conclusion that it was undergoing desiccation, demonstrated by the receding shorelines clearly depicted in his paintings (Figure 5.15). Parallel to the drawn panoramas he also took carefully executed photographic panoramas, often in several exposures that he could then stitch together. Many of the panoramas thus produced are quite beautiful[40] (Figure 5.16). The limited number of glass negatives, however, precluded using this technique to consistently capture the landscape.

Hedin knew about earlier examples of the technique of using panorama drawings or "small-scale relief representations."[41] During the formative months spent in Berlin attending his mentor Ferdinand von Richthofen's lectures and seminars around 1890 Hedin became firmly anchored in the German school of geography and cartography. Carl Ritter (1779–1859), its dominant figure in the first half of the nineteenth century, used such representations of the landscape to support his two-dimensional maps and, as noted, Humboldt and the Schlagintweit brothers used it in the field.[42] But Hedin put it to a much more determined use as a field technique, making it an important tool for map-making.

Another source of inspiration might have been the nautical charts constructed to ease the entry of ships into harbors. They could be accompanied by clear sketches of the entry to the harbor, indicating the exact contours of the coastline with its islands, straits and open waters. Adolf Erik Nordenskiöld, as well as being a renowned Polar researcher, was a prominent scholar of nautical and early cartography.[43] Sven Hedin was a schoolmate of Nordenskiöld's youngest son Gustaf, allowing him to visit Dalbyö, south of Stockholm, where Adolf Erik Nordenskiöld resided, surrounded by his fabulous collection of maps and books, among many other things.[44]

The route maps executed in the field were always finished when brought back to Sweden. In the evenings at campsite in his tent, as a part of going through and completing the records made during the day, he saw that was the case.

---

38 The number of photos he could take was restricted by the number of glass-negatives he had packed (cf. note 6.).
39 Hedin 1927: 133.
40 In 2016 some of them were included in an exhibition in Landskrona, Sweden (cf. Forsberg, Lars and Janne Jönsson (eds.) 2016).
41 Smits 2004: 12.
42 Ulla Ehrensvärd notes that Sven Hedin had a slightly ambivalent view of the value of his panoramas, being well aware of using a cartographic technique that could be regarded as dated. The influential German geographer Carl Ritter (1779–1859) and his contemporaries used to "anchor the two-dimensional map with the help of panoramas" (my translation). And, furthermore, the technique had then become too closely associated with mountaineering (Ehrensvärd 1990:93).
43 Nordenskiöld 1897. For his collection of antique maps see Nordenskiöld 1889. Both of these publications can be found in the Sven Hedin Library. Nordenskiöld's collection of maps and his huge library can be found in the University Library in Helsinki/Helsingfors.
44 It should be noted that Hedin also became a prominent scholar of historical maps, following in the footsteps of his mentor. Hedin's great work *Southern Tibet* is to a large extent a treatise on the early maps of Asia and Tibet, and the Hedin Library and Archives contain a nice collection of unique maps of Asia.

Figure 5.15: Panorama across Shemen Tso, Tibet. Sven Hedin watercolors. From Camp 320, 6 February 1908

Figure 5.16: Photographic panorama of the mountain ridge south of "Lake Lighten" in the Aksai Chin Area of northwest Tibet. Sven Hedin from Camp 15 at an altitude of 5095 meters. 18 September 1906

As for his drawings and watercolors he had a slightly different idea. Hedin maintained that a drawing made in the field should not be improved upon or redrawn later, not even the same evening. In fact, he regretted having done so. "Original drawings are both better and more valuable", Hedin argued.[45]

It should be a record of that very moment in the field, not based on later memories. Indeed, many of his works appear to have that quality of immediacy. Quite often they even appear to be left unfinished, either intentionally or unintentionally. His attention was focused on capturing the essentials of what was in front of him, well worked out and placed towards the center of the image. Drawings and watercolors typically become sketchier towards their margins.[46] He then quickly moved on to the next motif.

However, there were also many works that were carefully finished at the time they were executed: most of the watercolors, the panoramas and many of the portraits. Hedin made many detailed studies of his beloved Bactrian camels and drew still lifes of wild yaks (Figure 5.17). Furthermore, as we have seen, we know of many paintings that were transferred from pencil or photo to ink, work executed at home in Stockholm while preparing a publication.

Hedin further claims that he had no aspiration to be regarded as an artist. "It would be ridiculous to judge my drawings from an artistic point of view", he argues.[47] But no doubt he was rather flattered whenever being reviewed as an artist. When his works from Tibet were displayed in Kyoto in 1908 it apparently pleased him to show them as works of art. In addition, there have been a few exhibitions of his works in conjunction with other exhibitions or in their own right.[48]

Hedin probably never sold any of his drawings or paintings for personal financial gain. The ones that

---

45 Hedin 1920: 17 and 1964b: 14.
46 Cf. his perhaps best-known watercolor, the one depicting a monk entering the mausoleum of the Fifth Panchen Lama in Tashi Lunpo, Shigatse, reproduced in this book, is partly unfinished. In the foreword to his book *Transhimalaya* he defensively writes, "I claim not the slightest artistic merit for my drawings, and my watercolours are extremely defective in both drawing and colouring. One of the pictures, the lama opening the door of a mausoleum, I left unfinished in my haste; it has been thrown in with the others, with the wall-paintings and shading incomplete." (Hedin 1909

Vol I: viii). Actually, many of Hedin's works are in this way "unfinished", which did not seem to bother him in any other context.
47 Hedin 1920: 6.
48 There was an exhibition at the National Museum in Stockholm in 1969 (Magnusson 1969) and another at the Museum of Ethnography, also in Stockholm in 1990 (Wahlquist 1990).

Figure 5.17: Drawings of Bactrian camels Sven Hedin 1896.

Figure 5.18: Sven Hedin sketching the portrait of a Mongolian woman 1927

occasionally turn up on the market are there for various reasons. He might have presented them to friends or colleagues, or they may have been offered for sale at a fund raiser for some charitable cause. His book *En Levnads Teckning* was published for an exhibition of his works in Stockholm in 1920, in support of a school for children affected by the recently ended war. A few years later, some works were offered for sale via an auction house in Stockholm, but again this was to raise money for charity.

During the Century of Progress Exhibition in Chicago (1933–1934) a fully furnished copy of the so-called Golden Temple from Chengde/Jehol was exhibited by Sven Hedin and the Sino-Swedish Expedition.[49] Hedin then quickly produced a lot of small rather sketchy ink drawings, depicting scenes recalled from previous drawings. The idea was to sell them during the exhibition to raise funds for the Expedition, which was then in great need of additional financing. However, sales of the drawings fell short of Hedin's hopes.[50] Hedin never parted with them and left thousands of drawings and watercolors behind,

neatly catalogued by his brother Carl Hedin (1872–1964). Most of them can be found in the Hedin archives.

Even though Hedin used his pencils, ink pot and paint box for scientific purposes, drawing and painting also presented him with moments of relaxation, doing something that he really enjoyed. If he was stuck somewhere and had to stay there longer than planned, he sent his men around to recruit people willing to sit to have their portraits drawn (Figure 5.18).

Perhaps his best drawings, especially among the portraits, were made during the latter part of his first expedition (1895–1897). During the so-called "death march" into the Taklamakan Desert in 1895 he lost not only some of his men and most of his camels but also most of his equipment. Having lost his cameras and glass negatives during the rest of the expedition he had to fully resort to making drawings (Figure 5.19).

In the scientific publications comprising the results of his second expedition (1899–1902)[51] he turned his drawings to a different purpose than those noted above. He compiled one entire part of a multivolume work containing the portraits that he had drawn, primarily during his previous journeys into Asia (1885–1897). This signals that there may have been an early scientific intention behind his drawing activities, or at least his use of them, to collect a portrait gallery of all the ethnic groups he was in contact with during his journeys. Evidently, when publishing them, he believed that they would reveal characteristic racial/ethnic features

---

49 Montell 1932.
50 The same kind of small drawings were also produced to illustrate his popular books.

51 Hedin 1904–1907.

Figure 5.19: Mohamed Togda Bek, 66 years old, resident of Kapa, Xinjiang. Sven Hedin 1896

Figure 5.20: Men constructing a ger, sketched by Sven Hedin in Inner Mongolia 1927, later redrawn with ink.

typical of the groups he had encountered, a practice not uncommon at that time.[52]

During his last ventures into the field (1927–1928 and 1933–1935), not being tied down by map-making, there are many examples of his works that are less constrained than the earlier ones. For instance, he sometimes caught people in motion with a restricted number of strokes, displaying a more "reporter-like" approach (Figure 5.20).

It was a long development from his childhood drawings executed in a style still recognizable in his first attempts to document his journey to Baku in 1885. But that was the start of a concerted effort to train his eyes and improve his technique. This runs right through his life culminating in an almost photographic rendering of the Tibetan landscape in 1906–1908, realized in color images catching the splendor of the Grand Canyon in 1923 and exhibited in playful scenes from his last years in Central Asia in 1933–1934.

One should remember that while in the field Hedin was already planning his next travelogue, which was important for his finances. His letters to his family, were at the same time his diaries, which constituted the first draft of a book. His photos and drawings, as well as supporting his memory, were also intended to illustrate his immediately published popular works, making them more attractive, and as evidence in his scientific works.[53]

Sven Hedin – the cartographer

An underlying argument of this paper is that there is a close connection between Sven Hedin the "artist" and Sven Hedin the "cartographer."[54] When discussing his artistic talent one is at the same time invoking an important factor in his success as a cartographer. He was following a long line of explorers and cartographers, who preceded him.

However, we have also noted that the Sino-Swedish Expedition (1927–1935), which he masterminded and led,[55] was an undertaking with participants from many countries and scientific fields collaborating and complementing one another in a decidedly modern way.[56] Cartography was then executed with modern means, and drawings were no longer an indispensable scientific tool.

---

52 Hedin 1907.
53 The scientific account of his first expedition (1893–1897) contains no photos, only his drawings (Hedin 1900).
54 Ulla Ehrensvärd remarks that the way Hedin describes his activities is more that of an artist than a scientist (Ehrensvärd 1990: 91).
55 Which is not to diminish the vital contributions of his Chinese co-leaders.
56 Philippe Forêt has argued that around 1910, Hedin participated in a debate that contributed to professionalizing geography, moving geography from discoveries and exploration to science (Forêt 2000).

We have also noted that he became a formidable field cartographer, probably individually charting larger areas than anyone before or since. The quality of his work has been confirmed by most reviewers.[57]

An investigation of his formal training in cartography reveals very little; only a brief course offered for military officers in 1885, by Colonel Nils Selander (1845–1922). Beyond this, he was self-taught, and the quality of his map-making noticeably improves with each expedition. The 550 sheets from his first expedition were on paper of various sizes and at different scales, creating difficulties for the cartographer entrusted handling them, who admonished Hedin to be better organized next time.[58] Hedin understood this point. The 1149 drawings of the second expedition (1899–1902) were produced on uniform sheets and consistent scales (1:30,000 and 1:40,000). The 232 drawings from Persia (1906) and the 880 from Tibet (1906–1908) were likewise produced on paper of the same size (25 x 31,5 cm) and a consistent scale (1:40.000).[59]

We have mentioned that as a schoolboy, Hedin engrossed himself in the best maps of his time, especially those produced at Justus Perthes in Gotha,[60] an institute that he was to collaborate with to produce the maps from his first expedition (1893–1897) as well as for the atlas that became one of the main outcomes of the Sino-Swedish Expedition (1927–1935).[61]

In 1881, at 16 years of age, he began a project that was somewhat indicative of what was to come. He embarked on an undertaking that would take him a couple of years to complete; drawing and coloring maps of the world around us and the starry sky above us, and of European and Scandinavian geology, palaeontology and ornithology. Basing his work on existing material the idea was truly his own. In a biographical note he describes it as an expression of "megalomania."[62] When the six volumes were finished, they were so neatly and

Figure 5.21: Sven Hedin delivering a lecture on his Tibetan expedition, in front of a quickly constructed map, Simla, 1908

exactly executed, including the text, that it is almost impossible to see that they are not printed.[63]

Sven Hedin's atlas became known to people in the right circles, among them Adolf Erik Nordenskiöld (1832–1901), mentioned above. After "conquering" the Northeast Passage and being the first person to circumnavigate Eurasia, he was a celebrity in Sweden, as well as an important source of inspiration and support for Hedin as previously discussed. National heroes in those days were chosen among those who combined being adventurous explorers and recognized scientists.[64]

A lecture was to be delivered in front of the Swedish Society for Anthropology and Geography on the Central Asian expeditions of Nikolay Mikhaylovich Przhevalsky (1839–1888), another important role model for Hedin. Przhevalsky was to be awarded the Vega Medal by the Society. Hedin was asked to produce the large map needed for a lecture on the topic. After seriously studying what was known about Central Asia's geography, he did so. This was in 1884, and Nordenskiöld was reportedly impressed by the cartographic skills exhibited by the young man[65] (Figure 5.21).

---

57 Ulla Ehrensvärd notes that considering the formidable area mapped by Hedin one should be skeptical as to the quality of the finished work. But she also admits that independent scholarly reviews of his maps attest to their remarkably high and consistent quality (Ehrensvärd 1991: 86) Cf. Dahlgren et al. 1918 and Norin 1954: 20–24. Recent comparisons of Hedin's maps with satellite-based maps have confirmed this.
58 Hassenstein 1900.
59 On the Sino-Swedish Expedition, most of the members were expected to produce route maps, which were then collected and collated. The technique and equipment had then improved; plain tables were used, and trigonometrical networks were aimed at.
60 Cf. Smets 2004 for many examples of the maps that inspired him.
61 Norin (ed.) 1969.
62 Hedin 1920: 10.

63 These were not his first maps, however. At the age of 13 years, if not earlier, he had already drawn maps of similar quality (Montell 1961: 480).
64 It should be noted that on the way home in 1879, on-board his ship Vega, Nordenskiöld and his crew stayed in Japan for almost 2 months, September-October, while the ship was repaired. He and his crew were received with full honors, including an audience with Emperor Meiji.
65 Some years later, Hedin translated and condensed the travelogues and scientific reports from Przhevalsky's four expeditions from Russian and French and published them in Swedish (Hedin 1891).

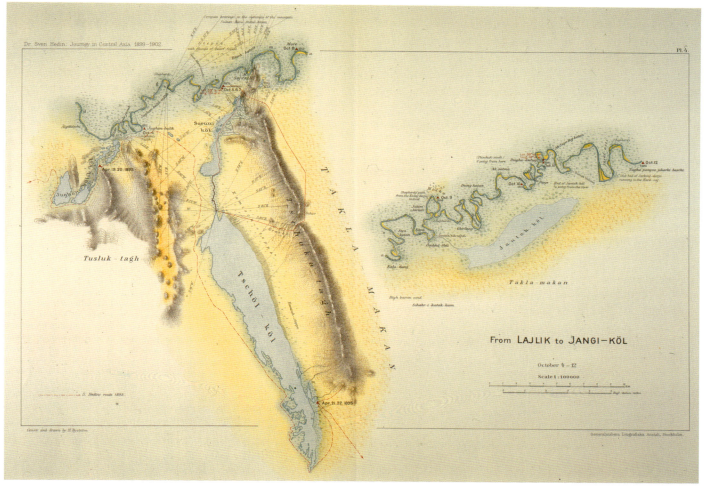

Figure 5.22: By Otto Kjellström and Herman Byström, compiled map of the area around the Northern Mazar Tagh, Tarim Basin, based on Sven Hedin's route maps from his first and second expeditions

Hedin's map-making in the field was as simple as it was efficient. Nevertheless, if executed with the same precision and attention day in and day out, month after month, never allowing a gap in the series of maps and observations, it must have been an exceedingly strenuous task, especially mentally. During his first three expeditions, he did it all himself, never complaining. The standard of his work never slipped, even though over the years, as we have noted, it improved with each successive expedition. Adding one sheet of paper after another to his collection was obviously rewarding enough. Amassing material and building evidence out of exact observations was Hedin's way to scientifically argue and prove his points. He was not a builder of general, grand theories, but he did formulate particular theories, the best known being the theory of oscillating lakes, accounting for the changing positions of Lop Nor, the terminal lake of the Tarim river system. As a scientist he kept close to the ground.

Hedin has a few times explained how he went about mapping.[66] Distances were measured by the number of paces and the time taken by his camel, horse, mule or yak to cover a certain distance (150 meters) over different kinds of terrain. This formula had to be regularly checked, as the terrain and altitude changed and the condition of his animal deteriorated.

This method proved to be astonishingly accurate,[67] especially when his mount was a Bactrian camel. Sitting

---

66 Hedin 1927 provides the most concise account of his methodology. Also cf. Hedin 1931 and Montell 1961.
67 Erik Norin carefully tested this technique, also using it in the field during the Sino-Swedish Expedition, finding it to be surprisingly reliable. He made comparisons with distances ascertained from his own work with the plain table and from measurements gained with a cyclometer (Norin 1954: 20–21). Dahlgren and colleagues (Dahlgren et al. 1918) also found that the technique stood up to experience from other sources.

on his animal provided a good view of the surrounding landscape. The chronometer and his rectangular compass, his only two instruments at the time, were in constant use to determine every change of direction and every distance gained. Prominent features in the landscape and distant peaks were provided bearings from different distances along the route. The maps of previous explorers of the area were kept at hand to avoid following in their footsteps. When their routes crossed comparisons of positions could be made.

His original route maps may look simple and sometimes untidy but are filled with long series of bearings securing the map, the result of his work with the compass.[68] Every day he could take up to 200 bearings. Eric Norin praises Hedin's work not only for its precision but also for its lack of generalizations, not adding anything that he could not observe. "They contain observed facts only, and nothing else" (my translation). He could have extrapolated the landscape from what he saw but refrained from doing so. Norin also thanks him for consistently adding information on vegetation, allowing Norin to find grazing grounds for his own caravan.[69]

From route maps to printed maps

The route maps we see in Hedin's books and scientific reports are, however, not the original ones, even though such maps are occasionally reproduced. Once back in Sweden, Hedin left it to professional map-makers to turn his route maps into the beautiful maps we can see today as the result of his labor in the field.

Before our era of aerial photos, satellites and computers, these maps were hand-drawn and hand-colored. The masters who made them, and their teams, were not only technical craftsmen, but artists of a kind.

For his first set of maps, from the expedition of 1893–1897 he turned to *Justus Perthes* Geographisches Anstalt in Gotha. Its most famous cartographer at the end of the nineteenth century, Bruno Hassenstein (1839–1902), turned Hedin's route maps into six large-scale maps covering the Tarim Basin and the northern flank of the Tibetan plateau. Hedin's routes and the new geographical discoveries that he had made were inserted into a larger setting based on existing maps.[70] The maps, along with his scientific account of the expedition, were published as a supplement to the journal of the Institute.[71]

When Hedin returned from his second expedition (1899–1902) his social position was quite changed; he was turned into the national hero that Sweden, or at least its conservative forces, required.[72] Producing maps and publishing scientific reports from his latest expedition were considered matters of national importance and pride and were financially supported by the government. The maps were handed over to the Swedish Army Map Service where Major (later Colonel) Axel Herman Byström (1856–1933) and Lieutenant Otto Kjellström (1855–1913) took care of them. As already noted, Hedin's competence as a fieldworker had improved since his first expedition, which in many ways was a learning exercise, and the resultant maps are often quite beautiful and informative (Figure 5.22). His original route maps were turned into multi-colored maps covering all his routes travelled, totaling 84 sheets providing plentiful details, such as land cover.

The maps from Hedin's third expedition, which consisted of two parts, covering the Kavir deserts of Eastern Persia/Iran (1905–1906) and south-western Tibet (1906–1908), were delayed for many years, primarily because of the First World War. They were initially executed by the same couple, but after Kjellström's death in 1913 they were finished by Colonel Byström and his staff at the Army Map Service. In eight sheets the Kavir maps covered the entire area traversed by Hedin. The Tibetan maps were published in the same way as the maps from the expedition 1899–1902, i.e. as complete route maps.[73] As previously mentioned they were worked out in two sets: one set of "special" maps and another set of "hypsometrical" maps.

Hedin never saw the final publication of the maps from the Sino-Swedish Expedition. He could admire the four sheets produced at Gotha,[74] but was never able to see what ultimately happened to the material when the project was taken over by the American Army Map Service, following the defeat of Germany in the Second World War. Erik Norin worked closely with the Americans and in 1969 a box with 13 sheets of the Hedin Central Asia Atlas was published as volume 47 in a series of reports from the Sino-Swedish Expedition,[75] to which Sven Hedin had devoted many of his final years.

---

68 Examples of his original route-maps are published in Hedin 1904–1907 and 1918–1927.
69 Norin 1954: 22–23.
70 Hassenstein 1900.
71 Hedin 1900.

---

72 Sweden was fundamentally changing at the time, through urbanization and industrialization, heavy emigration to America and the dissolution of the union with Norway.
73 The maps from the 1899–1902 expedition also included the route maps from the last leg of Hedin's previous expedition (1893–1897), when he mapped the northern fringe of the Tibetan plateau. Byström managed to produce them based on Hedin's original maps from the field, something that Hassenstein never attempted.
74 Haak 1941.
75 Norin (ed.) 1969; Ambolt & Norin 1967; Faraquhar, Jarring & Norin 1967; Bergman, Bexell, Bohlin, Chen, Hedin, Hörner & Norin 1980; Norin 1982.

References

Ambolt, Nils 1938, "Latitude and Longitude Determinations in Eastern Turkistan and Northern Tibet derived from Astronomical Observations." *Reports from the Scientific Expedition to the North-western Provinces of China under the leadership of Dr. Sven Hedin*, Vol. 6 Stockholm.

―――― 1948, "Relative Schwerkraftsbestimmungen mit Pendeln in Zentralasien." *Reports from the Scientific Expedition to the North-western Provinces of China under the leadership of Dr. Sven Hedin*, Vol. 30 Stockholm.

Ambolt, Nils & Erik Norin, 1967, "Records on Surveys. Sven Hedin Central Asia Atlas". *Reports from the Scientific Expedition to the North-western Provinces of China under the leadership of Dr. Sven Hedin*, Vol. 48, *Sven Hedin Central Asia Atlas. Memoir of Maps* Vol I. Stockholm.

Bergman, Folke, Gerhard Bexell, Birger Bohlin, Parker Chen, Sven Hedin, Nils Hörner & Erik Norin, 1980, "The Kansu-Hohsi Corridor and the Suloho-Ochinah Drainage Regions." *Reports from the Scientific Expedition to the North-western Provinces of China under the leadership of Dr. Sven Hedin*, Vol. 50, *Sven Hedin Central Asia Atlas. Memoir of maps* Vol III fasc. 3. (wrongly printed as Vol I:3), Stockholm.

Bergwik, Staffan 2018a, "Panoramic visions: Sven Hedin in 'Transhimalaya' 1906–1909, The power of the In-between". In: Sara Callahan, Magdalena Holdar, Christer Johansson & Sonya Pettersson (eds.): *Intermediality as a tool for Aesthetics Analysis and Critical Reflection*, Stockholm University Press, Stockholm.

―――― 2018b, "Det hopklistrade panoramat" In: Johan Kärnfelt, Karl Grandin & Solveig Jülich (eds.) *Kunskaper i rörelse: Vetenskapsakademien i det moderna Sverige*, Makadam, Göteborg.

Czibulka, A. von 1933, "Berühmte Weltfahrer von Marco Polo bis Sven Hedin", Drei Masken-Verlag Berlin.

Dahlgren, E.W., Karl D. P. Rosén and H. W:son Ahlman, 1918, "Sven Hedins Forskningar i Södra Tibet 1906–1908" *Ymer* 1918 H.2: 8–186.

Ehrensvärd, Ulla, 1989, "Sven Hedin – Der Kartenmacher" *Meddelanden från Krigsarkivet* XII: 157–180. Stockholm.

―――― 1990, "Kartan mellan kod och verklighet" In: *Bilden som källa till vetenskaplig information*, Konferens 23: 85–104. Kungl. Vitterhets Historie och Antikvitets Akademien, Stockholm.

Faraquhar, Gunnar Jarring, Erik Norin, 1967, "Index of Geographical Names". *Reports from the Scientific Expedition to the North-western Provinces of China under the leadership of Dr. Sven Hedin*, Vol. 49, *Sven Hedin Central Asia Atlas. Memoir of Maps* Vol II Stockholm.

Forêt, Philippe, 2000, *La véritable histoire d'une montagne plus grand que l'Himalaya Les résultats scientifiques inattendus d'un voyage au Tibet (1906–08) et la quarelle du Transhimalaya*. Éditions Bréal, Paris.

Forsberg, Lars and Janne Jönsson (eds.), 2016, *AgNO3 Histories of Science and Photography in Sweden*, Historiska Media & Landskrona Foto Museum, Lund & Landskrona.

Haack, Hermann, 1941, "Sven Hedins Zentralasien-Atlas" *Petermanns Geographische Mitteilungen* 87 Jahrgang 1941 1. Heft: 2–7.

Hassenstein, Bruno, 1900, "Begleitworte zu den Karten" *Petermanns Mitteilungen*, Ergänzungsheft No. 131: 378–399. Justus Perthes, Gotha.

Hedin, Sven, 1886, "Om Baku och Apscheronska halfön" *Ymer*: 337–350.

―――― 1887, *Genom Persien, Mesopotamien och Kaukasus. Reseminnen*. Albert Bonniers Förlag, Stockholm.

―――― 1891, *General Prschevalskij's forkningsresor i Centralasien*. Albert Bonniers Förlag, Stockholm.

―――― 1900, "Die geographisch-wissenschaftlichen Ergebnisse meiner Reisen in Zentralasien 1894–1897" *Petermanns Mitteilungen*, Ergänzungsheft No.131. Justus Perthes, Gotha.

―――― 1904–1907, *Scientific results of a journey in Central Asia 1899–1902* (6+2 vols.) Generalstabens Litografiska Anstalt, Stockholm.

―――― 1907, "Racial types from Western and Central Asia drawn by Sven Hedin" *Scientific results of a journey in Central Asia 1899–1902*, vol. 6: Part 3 Generalstabens Litografiska Anstalt, Stockholm.

―――― 1909, 1912, *Transhimalaya. Upptäckter och äfventyr i Tibet* (3 vols.) Albert Bonniers förlag, Stockholm.

―――― 1910, "Die wissenschaftlichen Ergebnisse meiner Reise in Tibet 1906–1908", *Petermanns Geographische Mitteilungen* 2: 1–6. Justus Perthes, Gotha.

―――― 1916–1922, "Southern Tibet. Discoveries in former times compared with my own researches in 1906–1908" (9+3 vols.) Generalstabens litografiska anstalt, Stockholm and F.A. Brockhaus, Leipzig.

―――― 1916, "Lake Manasarovar and the Sources of the Great Indian Rivers. From the remotest antiquity to the end of the eighteenth century." *Southern Tibet – Discoveries in former times compared with my own researches in 1906–1908* Vol I. Generalstabens litografiska anstalt, Stockholm.

―――― n.d. "Special maps of Dr. Sven Hedin's Route through Tibet 1906–1908. 26 sheets, by O. Kjellström and H. Byström, 1:300000." *Southern Tibet Discoveries in former times compared with my own researches in 1906–1908*. Maps Vol. I set 4 Generalstabens litografiska anstalt, Stockholm.

―――― 1917, "Atlas of Tibetan Panoramas" *Southern Tibet Discoveries in former times compared with my own researches in 1906–1908* Generalstabens litografiska anstalt, Stockholm.

―――― 1918–1927, *Eine Routenaufnahme durch Ostpersien* Band I–II + Karten. Generalstabens Litografiska Anstalt, Stockholm.

―――― 1920, *En Levnads Teckning*, Albert Bonniers Förlag, Stockholm.

―――― 1922, "Hypsometrical maps in 52 sheets with special use of Dr. Sven Hedin's Panoramas constructed and drawn by Colonel H. Byström. 1:150000". *Southern Tibet Discoveries in former times compared with my own researches in 1906–1908*: Maps Vol. II Generalstabens litografiska anstalt, Stockholm.

―――― 1927, *Eine Routenaufnahme durch Ostpersien Zweiter Band*, Generalstabens litografiska anstalt, Stockholm.

―――― 1931, "Kartläggning under mina resor i Asien," *Globen* 10: 55–62.

―――― 1933, "Meine Reise durch Asien vom Standpunkt eines Zeichners und Malers," In: A. von Czibulka 1933: *Berühmte Weltfahrer von Marco Polo bis Sven Hedin*: 450–483, Drei Masken-Verlag Berlin.

―――― 1936, "Sven Hedin über seine Bilder", *Velhagen & Klasings Monatshefte*: 81–88, Berlin.

―――― 1964a, "Sven Hedin som tecknare" *Sven Hedin Life and Letters* Part II, Generalstabens litografiska anstalt, Stockholm.

―――― 1964b, "Sven Hedin as Artist" *Sven Hedin Life and Letters* Part II, Generalstabens litografiska anstalt, Stockholm.

―――― 1965, *Sven Hedin als Zeichner*, F.A. Brockhaus, Wiesbaden.

Humboldt, Alexander von, 1844, *Central-Asien: Untersuchungen über die Gebirgsketten und die vergleichende Klimatologie* 2 vols. Berlin.

Humboldt, Alexander von (ed.) and Aimé Bonpland, 1814–1819, *Voyage aux régions équinoxiales du nouveau continent fait en 1799, 1800, 1801, 1802, 1803 et 1804* (2 vols.), Paris.

Humboldt, Alexander von, G. Ehrenberg and G. Rose, 1837–1842, *Reise nach dem Ural, dem Altai und dem Kaspischen Meere. Auf Befehl Sr. Majestät des Kaisers von Russland im Jahre 1829 ausgeführt* (2 vols.), Berlin.

Kircheri, Athanasii, 1667, *China Monumentis: qua Sacris quà Profanis nec non variis Naturæ & Artis spectaculis, Aliarumque rerum memorabilium Argumentis Illustrata. Apud Jacobum à Meurs*, Amsterdam.

Körner, Hans, 1982, "Die Brüder Schlagintweit – Hermann, Adolph, Robert und Emil, Familie, Forschungsreise in Indien und Hochasien, Werke, Sammlungen und Nachlaß, Bibliographie," In: Müller und Raunig *Der Weg zum Dach der Welt*, Pinguin, Innsbruck and Frankfurt/Main.

Lewis-Jones, Huw & Kari Herbert, 2017, *Explorers' Sketchbook: The Art of Discovery & Adventure*, Thames and Hudson, London.

Lindgren, Uta, 1982, "Die Naturwissenschaftlichen Forschungen der Brüder Schlagintweit in Hochasien," In: Müller und Raunig *Der Weg zum Dach der Welt*, Pinguin, Innsbruck and Frankfurt/Main.

Magnusson, Börje (ed.) 1978, *Sven Hedin Teckningar*, Nationalmusei utställningskatalog 416, Stockholm.

Montell, Gösta, 1932, *The Chinese Lama Temple*, Potala of Jehol Century of Progress Exposition, Chicago.

——— 1961, "Sven Hedin's Mapping in Asia," *The Bulletin of the Geological Institutions of the University of Uppsala*, Vol XL: 479–484, Uppsala.

Müller, Claudius C. und Walter Raunig (eds.), 1982, *Der Weg zum Dach der Welt*, Pinguin, Innsbruck and Frankfurt/Main.

Nordenskiöld, Adolf Erik, 1889, *Facsimile-Atlas to the early history of cartography with reproductions of the most important maps printed in the XV and XVI centuries*. Stockholm.

——— 1897, *Periplus, Utkast till sjökortens och sjöböckernas historia, med talrika afbildningar av sjökort och kartor*. Stockholm.

Norin, Erik, 1954, "Sven Hedins Forskningsresor i Centralasien och Tibet,' *Geografiska Annaler* Årg. XXXVI: 9–39, Svenska Sällskapet för Antropologi och Geografi, Stockholm.

——— 1982, "The Pamirs, K'unlun, Karakoram and Chang T'ang Regions. Sven Hedin Central Asia Atlas. Memoir on Maps. Vol III, fasc. 1." *Reports from the Scientific Expedition to the North-western Provinces of China under the leadership of Dr. Sven Hedin*, Vol. 54 Memoir of Maps Vol. I Stockholm.

Norin, Erik (ed.), 1969, "Sven Hedin Central Asia Atlas." 13 sheets 1:1000000, 1 special map 1:500000, 5 Reconnaissance Triangulation Charts: *Reports from the Scientific Expedition to the North-western Provinces of China under the leadership of Dr. Sven Hedin*, Vol. 47 Stockholm.

Polter, Stefan B. 1982, "Nadelshau in Hochasien: Englische Magnetforschung und die Brüder Schlagintweit," In: Müller und Raunig *Der Weg zum Dach der Welt*, Pinguin, Innsbruck and Frankfurt/Main.

Romgard, Jan, 2013, *Embracing Science: Sino-Swedish Collaborations in the Field Sciences, 1902–1935*, Department of Oriental Languages Stockholm University, Stockholm.

Schlagintweit, Hermann, Adolph and Robert, 1861–1866, *Results of a scientific Mission to India and High Asia*, undertaken between the years MDCCCLIV–MDCCCLVIII by order of the Court of Directors of the Honourable East India Company. Trübner, London and F.A. Brockhaus, Leipzig.

Schalgintweit-Sakünlünski, Herman von, 1869–1880, *Reisen in Indien und Hochasien. Eine Darstellung der Landschaft, der Cultur und Sitten der Bewohner, in Verbindung mit klimatischen und geologischen Verhältnisse. Basiert auf die Resultate der wissenschaftlichen Mission von Hermann, Adolph und Robert von Schlagintweit*. H. Costenoble, Jena.

Smits, Jan, 2004, "Petermann's Maps Carto-bibliography of the maps in *Petermanns Geographische Mitteilungen* 1855–1945", *Utrechtse Historisch-Kartographische Studien* 3, Hes & de Graff Publishers BV, 'tGov-Houten.

Stolpe, Sven, 1974, "Sven Hedin och hans minne." In: *Tål ni höra mer Minnen och Anekdoter*: 20–30, Askild & Kärnekull, Stockholm.

Wahlquist, Håkan, 1990, *Sven Hedin – tecknaren Med papper och penna i Centralasien*, Folkens Museum Etnografiska & Sven Hedins Stiftelse, Stockholm.

Weber, Matthias, 2012, "Die Erkundung Zentralasiens - der Nachlass Sven Hedins in der 'Sammlung Perthes Gotha'," *Cartographica Helvetica* Heft 46: 25–37.

Wegener, Georg, 1935, "Das Künstlerische in Sven Hedin", In: *Hyllningsskrift tillägnad Sven Hedin Geografiska Annaler* Vol. 17 :463–469.

Wennerholm, Eric, 1978, *Sven Hedin: En biografi*, Bonniers, Stockholm.

6 Hedin and Classic Chinese Texts

Kizu Yuko
Tanaka Kazuko

In his lecture to Kyoto Imperial University on November 29, 1908, Sven Hedin spoke about the Third Central Asia Expedition that he had completed just prior to coming to Japan. In conjunction with his lecture, on the same day, in a separate venue, an exhibition of related documents was held, including a collection of sketches drawn by Hedin's own hand. As described in a report of the welcome activities, this documentary exhibition owed much to the considerable efforts of Naitō Torajirō (Konan), a lecturer in the College of Letters (Tokyo Geographical Society 1909).

One of the Classic Chinese texts (*kanseki*) displayed on this occasion was "水道提綱 *Shuidao tigang*" (Guide to the Network of Waterways). During Hedin's stay in Kyoto, a passage from Volume 22 of this text, on "*Xizang* (i.e., Tibet)" was translated into English for Hedin by Ogawa Takuji, a Professor in the College of Letters (Tanaka 2015). Hedin incorporated Ogawa's translation without alteration into two of his later works, namely *Trans-Himalaya* (1909–1913) and *Southern Tibet* (1917–1922). That Hedin, himself unable to read these Chinese texts, came to incorporate the contents of the *Shuidao tigang* into his own works suggests the considerable background efforts by Ogawa, Naitō and their colleagues at the College of Letters.

Håkan Wahlquist (2001) points out that Hedin had a keen interest in "Oriental geographical treatises" – including those of China. However, we find that the relationship between Hedin and Chinese texts has yet to receive any detailed consideration. To that end, in this chapter, we explore Hedin's approach to Chinese texts from the perspective of his exchanges with members of the faculty of the College of Letters during his visit to Kyoto. The goal of this chapter is to clarify the influence on Hedin of Oriental studies scholarship coming out of Kyoto at that time.

The challenge taken up in this paper entails the following three tasks. The first is to show how the description in the *Shuidao tigang* relates to Hedin's findings on his Third Central Asia Expedition (1906–1908). The second is to present the collection of Chinese texts that Hedin would have seen at the exhibition and highlight the features of the material in order to better understand the nature of the *Shuidao tigang* as a text. The third is to clarify how Hedin's interest in such Chinese texts was piqued through his explorations and studies, as well as the significance of his visit to Kyoto in the process of his approach to Oriental studies.

In addition, we consider the passage from the *Shuidao tigang* that Hedin considered to be so significant and how it was translated by Ogawa by looking at each with reference to the original text.

Hedin's citation of Ogawa's translation of the *Shuidao tigang* in his own scientific report could be regarded as a collaboration between the so-called "deskwork" of text-based studies and the "fieldwork" of exploration. Our hope in engaging with the challenge noted above is to clarify the contemporary significance of the exchange between Hedin and the members of the College of Letters as an event that provided impetus for such a collaboration.

It should also be noted that in this chapter, Kizu has assumed responsibility for Section 2 and Appendix 2 (the passage in question from Volume 22 of the *Shuidao tigang* and its related annotation), while Tanaka was responsible for all other sections and Appendix 1 (the English text from Chapter 12 of Volume 1 of *Southern Tibet*, Ogawa's English translation and related annotation). Please also refer to Appendix 3 for place names and Appendix 4 for major water systems and mountains in the Brahmaputra and Sutlej headwater regions.

The *Shuidao tigang* and the findings of the third central Asia expedition

Discovery of the sources of the Brahmaputra and Sutlej rivers

To begin, let us consider the geographical findings achieved by Hedin's Third Central Asia Expedition (1906–1908).

Yamasaki Naomasa, a Japanese geographer who played an active role in arranging Hedin's invitation and welcome to Japan, delivered a lecture prior to Hedin's arrival introducing Hedin and his accomplishments. As a major geographical finding, Yamasaki first cited Hedin's discovery of what the explorer had dubbed the "Trans-Himalaya," namely the range of mountains running parallel to the north of the Himalayas that connected with the Karakoram. Next, he applauded and underlined the significance of Hedin's feat in clarifying and clearly mapping the source of the Indus, as well as those of the Brahmaputra and Sutlej, which until then had been among major rivers of Asia whose headwaters remained a mystery (Yamasaki 1908: 777–780).

In his lecture to the Tokyo Geographical Society, having noted the discovery of the Trans-Himalaya as his most important accomplishment, Hedin described his survey of the source of the Indus and his discovery of the sources of the Brahmaputra and Sutlej. The sources of the two great rivers of the Brahmaputra and the Sutlej are in fact located very close to one another. Hedin first traced the Brahmaputra upriver to the northwest, and after identifying the Kubi-tsangpo as having the highest volume of flow among the five tributaries flowing into the river's upper reaches, traced the Kubi-tsangpo upstream where he identified its source, confirming its flow from the meltwaters of three glaciers perched atop the mountain known as Kubi-gangri. Moreover, he determined that a stream called the Tage-tsangpo, which flows west from the western side of the watershed of the Brahmaputra's westernmost tributary, gradually gained breadth as it flowed via Lake Manasarovar and Lake Rakastal (Rakshastal) to become the Sutlej River (Tokyo Geographical Society 1908: 55–62, 81–874, 91–92).[1]

Hedin reported on his explorations in two types of publications, namely the popular account of his explorations for the general reader that was issued as *Trans-Himalaya* (3 vols., 1909–1913) and the scientific report published as *Southern Tibet* (9 vols. with atlases, 1917–1922). The end of the second volume of *Trans-Himalaya* – which went to publication first – includes a series of three maps, consisting of "A Map of Tibet showing Dr. Sven Hedin's Routes 1906–1908," "The Sources of the Brahmaputra, Sutlej, and Indus," and "A Map of the Trans-Himalaya by Dr. Sven Hedin." It is clear that, for Hedin, the discovery of the sources of the rivers was an important accomplishment that ranked alongside his discovery of the Trans-Himalaya.

The *Shuidao tigang*, a classic Chinese text quoted in Hedin's works

In the second volume of *Trans-Himalaya*, Hedin devotes individual chapters to the surveys of the sources of each of the three great rivers: Chapter 42 "In Search of the Source of the Brahmaputra" (pp. 89–98), Chapter 43 "The Source of the Sacred River – A Departure" (pp. 99–109), and Chapter 50 "The Source of the Sutlej" (pp. 178–188). Ogawa's translation of the description in the *Shuidao tigang* of the headwaters of the Sutlej is quoted in Chapter 50. Regarding the particulars of the quoted text, Hedin notes that the *Shuidao tigang* was one book in a collection of Chinese texts that he was shown during a stay in Kyoto in 1908, and that Ogawa translated the passage for him from Volume 22 (Hedin 1910: 182–183). Hedin states further that "This description of the position of the source of the Sutlej is of such extraordinary interest that I do not like to reserve it for my scientific work" (Hedin 1910, Vol. 2: 184).

The description in the *Shuidao tigang* contains passages that concern not only the source of the Sutlej, but also that of the Brahmaputra. In *Southern Tibet*, Hedin also quotes Ogawa's English translation faithfully. Having done so, he closely examines the details of the description in the *Shuidao tigang* while comparing them with maps produced by explorers, thereby clarifying the significance of his own discovery of the sources of the Brahmaputra and Sutlej (Hedin 1917–1922, Vol. 1: Chapter 12).

The description quoted from the *Shuidao tigang* for both the Brahmaputra and the Sutlej concern their uppermost headwaters. Each contains a detailed description of the vicinity of the source, the mountains that are the sources of the tributaries flowing into the main stream and the directions of flow, and the length and curvature of the course of these main streams. However, Ogawa has not translated the entirety of the passage regarding the two rivers, but only an excerpt.

For details written in the *Shuidao tigang* concerning the sources of the two great rivers, how Ogawa translated these, and the nature of the additional consideration that Hedin carried out based on Ogawa's translation, please see Appendices 1 and 2 in this volume. For interested readers, a reference list of relevant toponyms and a map of the vicinity of the river sources have also been provided (Appendices 3 and 4).

As mentioned earlier, the focus of this chapter is to clarify Hedin's link with Chinese texts in terms of the involvement of the faculty members at the College of Letters who welcomed him in Kyoto. Accordingly, we will investigate descriptions concerning matters such as the locations of the sources of the Brahmaputra and Sutlej, their routes, and associated toponyms in another paper, and not go into them here.

In the next section, we introduce readers to the nature of *Shuidao tigang* as a text. In addition, we present readers with an idea of the collection of Chinese texts that served as the inspiration for Hedin's quotation of the *Shuidao tigang*.

---

1 Toponyms in the text follow those used by Hedin in the second volume of his *Trans-Himalaya* (Hedin 1909–1913).

The *Shuidao tigang* and other Chinese texts seen by Hedin

The *Shuidao tigang* compiled by Qi Shaonan

The *Shuidao tigang* (Guide to the Network of Waterways) is a geographical treatise compiled during the Qianlong era (1736–1795) of China's Qing Dynasty. Spanning twenty-eight volumes, the work offers a detailed accounting of the topography of China's territories on the basis of its water courses. Its authorship is attributed to Qi Shaonan (1703–1768), a native of Tiantai in Zhejiang Province, of whom a biography may be found in volume 305 of the *Qingshi gao* (Draft History of the Qing). The *Siku tiyao* (Catalogue of the Complete Library in the Four Branches of Literature) records his appointment to take part in the compilation of the *DaQing yitong zhi* (Records of the Unity of the Great Qing) at the time of his service as an editor at the Hanlin Academy. Having been charged with responsibility for the geography of the "territories of the outer feudatory Mongols" (*waifan Menggu zongbu*), Qi became quite well-versed with the topography of northwestern China – being able to browse the maps of various regions in the collection of the Bureau of Books is noted as having been of great help in the compilation of the *Shuidao tigang*.[2]

The *locus classicus* for the kind of geographical treatise that describes topography with reference to hydrography is of course the *Shuijing zhu* (Commentary on the Water Classic) authored by Li Daoyuan (469–527) of Northern Wei. However, over the millennium and more between Li's day and the Qing era, not only had China's river systems themselves changed as natural features with the passage of time, but also knowledge of China's ethnic and dynastic boundaries had been considerably transformed. Despite these facts, however, no systematic geographical treatises appeared to address the changes over this time. Of course a tradition did exist of comprehensively recording national censuses that went so far as to include even individuals and sites of scenic beauty, as in the case of the *Taiping huanyu ji* (Record of the World in the Taiping Era) compiled in the latter tenth century by Yue Shi (930–1007) during the Song Dynasty and the *DaMing yitong zhi* (Comprehensive Gazetteer of the Great Ming) (1461) compiled by Ming Dynasty officials, both based on localized geographical texts. From the time of the Yuan dynasty, in particular, knowledge of geography was accumulating in forms that included detailed maps of cities, rivers, and geographical features for the various regions, as well as at the national level.

The Qing Dynasty, established with the Manchus' entry into Beijing (in 1644), until the arrival of the Qianlong era (1736–1795), was for the most part embroiled in repeated border conflicts in the Western Regions (Xiyu), where maintaining control over the frontier remained an extremely sensitive military problem. It was for this reason that the custom arose for the first order of business among Investigating Censors appointed to remote areas to be the creation of maps of their jurisdictional area for submission to the Court. This is also clear from the fact that the collection of maps known as the *Shanxi bianyuan tu* (Maps of the Region Along the Great Wall in Shanxi) in the collection of the National Palace Museum (Taipei) were submitted to the Court in 1645, 1647, 1649, and 1658 – namely, with each appointment of a new censor during the reign of the Shunzhi Emperor. Moreover, because two censors were appointed in rapid succession in the span of a single year in 1649, maps of a similar flavor were presented twice.[3]

Qi Shaonan was also involved in the editing of the *DaQing yitong zhi* compiled by imperial edict. This work reflects the history of the frequent fluctuations of the boundaries of the Qing Dynasty. The gazetteer, whose compilation began in the Kangxi era (1662–1722), was published in 1744 in a first, provisional edition of 360 volumes. During the compilation process, however, and even after it was printed, the Qing dynasty's western borders were continually fluctuating, as when the Qing Dynasty held back the powerful opposing forces of the Dzungar Khanate in Tibet during the Yongzheng era (1723–1735) and then pacified the residual forces in the Uyghur district of Ili in 1755. Then, in 1763, in response to the fact that "Xinjiang" would finally be incorporated into the Qing map as a new territory, an imperial edict to substantially expand the geographical listings in the existing edition of the *DaQing yitong zhi* was handed down in 1764. In response to this order, a revised edition of the *DaQing yitong zhi* known as the "1764 Edict Edition" running to 424 volumes was completed in 1784. And while the *DaQing yitong zhi* would go on to receive yet another, third round of extensive revisions in the Jiaqing era (1796–1820), this is not relevant to our discussion here.

Qi Shaonan is believed to have been at the Bureau of Books with the *DaQing yitong zhi* until 1744 (Hummel

---

2 The original Chinese text reads as follows: 召南官翰林時，預修大清一統志. 外藩蒙古諸部, 是所分校. 故於西北地形, 多能考驗. 且天下輿圖, 備於書局, 又得以博考旁稽, 乃參以耳目見聞, 互相鉤校, 以成是編. (*Shi bu* 25, *Dili lei* 2)

3 The term *bianyuan* ("near the ramparts") is a reference to the Great Wall defining the boundary with the northern territories inhabited by ethnically foreign peoples. For a detailed discussion of this series of maps, see Tanaka and Kizu (2011).

1990: 106), and to have retired from the Court and returned to his home district after an injury resulting from a fall from a horse in 1749. In other words, he had no direct involvement in the editorial revisions that produced the 1764 Edict Edition. After retiring to his home district, Qi Shaonan devoted himself to his own writing, completing the *Shuidao tigang* in 1761.[4] Nevertheless, here, comparing Volume 22 of the *Shuidao tigang* (on "Xizang (Tibet)") with Volume 413 of the 1764 Edict Edition of the *DaQing yitong zhi* (on the same region), we were strongly impressed by the similarities between the two texts. Whether the latter was created with reference to the former, or whether both texts were based on common source material, in either case, we have been able to conclude that the *Shuidao tigang* is an extremely reliable text that was closely based on the latest and most important documents of its time.

The following discussion summarizes the characteristic features of Qi Shaonan's *Shuidao tigang* and its scholarly significance based on Chen Ruiping's "Shuidao tigang tiyao (Summary of the 'Guide to the Network of Waterways')" (cited below as Chen Ruiping 1995), which is included in the *Zhongguo kexue jishu dianji tonghui, Dixue juan* (General Introduction to Comprehensive Compendium of Materials and Sources on Chinese Science and Technology: Vol. 5 Geography) (edited by Tang Xiren, Henan jiaoyu chuban she, 1995).

First, we should note that the *Shuidao tigang* is the first geographical treatise to systematically present a method for describing "waterways" (*shuidao*). The organization of the book follows the Chinese tradition of conceiving of matters in terms of *gang* (literally, "ropes", "outlines"; figuratively, "essential principles") and *mu* (literally, "eyes", "items"; figuratively, "categorical divisions"). The preface of each volume repeats the idea that in a given water system, the source is considered *gang* and its tributaries *mu*, that regarding the relative sizes of rivers, larger rivers are *gang* and smaller rivers *mu*, and the very sea into which all rivers flow and mingle is *gang* among *gang*. In addition, as when he proposed the idea that, with respect to major rivers that have many tributaries, "*gang* are present in *mu* and *mu* are present in *gang*", Qi can be seen to have flexibly and substantively grasped the mutual interrelationships of waterways (Chen Ruiping 1995: 644).

Certainly, Volume 22 on "Xizang (Tibet)" adheres to this principle consistently. While readers are invited to consult the translations in the appendices for further detail, a very precise description is developed over the entire work concerning the catchment basins of important rivers, beginning from their sources and inquiring how far and in which direction they flow before they absorb other rivers, where the sources of these other rivers are located and from which direction they flow, whether any change in the direction of the main stream occurs in association with the confluence of the tributary, and how the tributaries joining the stream are interrelated with other tributaries. Although reading these descriptions gives one the impression that Qi Shaonan must have carried out measurements in the field, as a coastal native from Tiantai in Zhejiang Province and an editor with the Hanlin Academy, he had never journeyed beyond the Great Wall. Also, the following anecdote is included among the collection of epitaphs compiled by Yuan Mei (1716–1797) ("Yuan ren libu shilang Qi gong muzhiming (Epitaph for Master Qi, Former Deputy Minister in the Ministry of Rites)" included in *Xiaocang shanfang wenji* (Anthology of Prose and Poetry from the Cottage at Xiaocang shan), vol. 25).

> …moreover, all of the officials who were going out as envoys to that land now that Ili had been newly incorporated into the territories[5] went first of all to visit Deputy Minister Qi (i.e., Qi Shaonan) to ask about the route they would take to get there, whereupon he would give them each a book and tell them to mind this-or-that signpost, stop at this-or-that road station, where to lodge, the amount of provisions they should carry with them, giving instructions about lands beyond the Wall tens of thousands of *li* away as though tracing the palm of his hand. Nor was there any hint of confusion therein. When one fellow asked him if he had ever gone beyond the Wall himself, Master Qi replied that he had not, whereupon when asked how he had become so well-versed in the geography of those northern territories, he answered that it was solely on account of his familiarity with the "*Dili zhi* (Treatise on Geography)" in the *Han shu* (Book of Han).[6]

It is immediately obvious that the knowledge contained in the *Shuidao tigang* far surpasses the extent of that in the "*Dili zhi*" in the *Han shu*. This epitaph might be viewed as an attempt to give special honor to the

---

4 Publication was delayed until after his death, when it was printed in a woodblock edition by his son Qi Shiqian in 1775.

5 A reference to the Ili region in Uyghur Xinjiang. Following its pacification of Dzungar resistance in the area in 1755, the Qing Dynasty dispatched officials to fill the office of "Imperial Resident in Ili" (*Zhufang Yili dachen*) in 1758, and then, in 1762, established additional posts, including General of Ili (*Zongguan Yili dengchu jiangjun*), Minister Consultant for Ili (*Yili canzan dachen*), and Minister Superintendent for Ili (*Yili lingdui dachen*). Cf. the *Qingshi gao*, volume 12, "Gaozong benji."

6 The original Chinese text reads as follows: …有新開伊犁, 諸臣奉使者輒先詣齊侍郎家問路. 公與一冊, 某墩某驛, 應宿何所, 需若干糧數. 萬里外, 若掌上螺紋, 毫忽無訛. 或聞, 曾出塞外乎. 曰, 未也. 然則何由知之. 曰, 不過漢書地理志熟耳.

respectful attitude demonstrated by Qi Shaonan – the author of texts that included *Shangshu zhushu kaozheng* (Edited Commentary and Evidential Study of the *Book of Documents*), *Liji zhushu kaozheng* (Edited Commentary and Evidential Study of the *Book of Rites*), and *Lidai diwang nianbiao* (An Imperial Chronology) – toward the "*Dili zhi*" in the *Han shu* as being the *fons et origo* of Chinese geographical texts.

It is also worth noting that no details are known regarding the specific text on which Ogawa Takuji based his translation of the *Shuidao tigang* for Hedin. Incidentally, the list of Chinese texts displayed on the occasion of Dr. Hedin's lecture (detailed in the next section) lists "8 volumes" of the *Shuidao tigang*. However, while the university currently holds two editions of the book – namely a four-volume edition (Chuanjing shuwu, 1776) and a six-volume edition (Hongda-tang, 1879) that has been stamped as having been "Presented as a Gift by Naitō Torajirō" – neither of the editions matches the volume count on the exhibition list. Also, while much of the former library belonging to Naitō Konan is now held as the "Naitō Bunko" in the Kansai University Library, since Book 8 of the *Shuidao tigang* (Qianlong edition) may be found in this collection, it is also possible that this was the book provided for the exhibition.

The collection of Chinese texts seen by Hedin

As mentioned, Dr. Hedin's lecture at Kyoto Imperial University was accompanied by an exhibition of numerous Chinese texts from the College of Letters (currently the Faculty of Letters) as documentary sources relevant to Central Asia and Tibet. The tables below are lists of the Chinese texts and Buddhist scriptures, excerpted from the complete list published in *Chigaku zasshi* (Journal of Geography).[7] The texts selected and presented by the College of Letters correspond to the two sections described as "(4) Chinese Geographical Treatises on Central Asia" (Table 6.1) and "(5) Chinese Writings on Tibetan Geography" (Table 6.2). The third table "(6) Western Chinese Buddhist Scriptures, including Tibetan Buddhist Scriptures" (Table 6.3) lists books described variously as "Presented by Honpa Hongan-ji" or "Presented by Ishiyama-dera," which suggests that these were high-quality (*zenpon*) manuscripts of Chinese texts and Buddhist scripture on loan from the collections of temples around Kyoto. Supposedly, this collection had been brought together through the sponsorship of Ōtani Kōzui, the Hongan-ji Abbot, who had exercised considerable influence in arranging Hedin's invitation. Based on these lists, we will touch on a few matters that we can infer from each. The *Chigaku zasshi* list presents the data in three columns: A to C. In the tables below, information in parentheses () is our own supplementary annotations, while comments are added in column D.

With the exception of books like the *Shuijing zhu*, *DaQing yitong zhi,* and *Xiaofanghu-zhai yudi congchao* (Little Square Vase Studio Anthology of Geographical Inscriptions), all of which seek to provide a national conspectus of China's geography and topography, the majority of the titles listed as "Table 6.1: (4) Chinese Geographical Treatises on Central Asia" are concerned with what from China's perspective were the "Western Regions" including *Qinding Huangyu Xiyu tuzhi* (Imperially Commissioned Cartographical Treatise on the Western Regions), *Xiyu kaogu lu* (Archaeological Report of the Western Regions), *Xiyu wenjian lu* (Record of Matters Witnessed and Heard in the Western Regions), and *Xiyu shuidao ji* (Waterways of the Western Regions).

The nomenclature "中央亜細亜 *Chūō Ajia* (Central Asia)" for the area traditionally denoted in China as "*Xiyu* (Western Regions)" is believed to have first been used by the naturalist and explorer Alexander von Humboldt in his monograph *Central-Asien: Untersuchungen über die Gebirgsketten und die vergleichende Klimatologie* (Central Asia: Studies of Mountain Chains and Comparative Climatology) (Berlin: Verlag von Carl. J. Klemann, 1844).[8] It is not known when this nomenclature first came to be used in the Japanese context, but the term 中央亜細亜 *Chūō Ajia* (Central Asia) is found in *Bankoku sangyō ibun* (Curios episodes of World sericultures), an 1884 survey of sericulture (Kikuchi 1884: 35), while an 1888 textbook of intermediate geography lectures by Alexander Keith Johnston and Fujitani Takao (*Joshi chiri kyōkasho: Chūtō kyōiku*, folio 2, volume 2) includes a chapter on "露領中央亜細亜 *Ro-ryō Chūō Ajia*" (The Russian Territories in Central Asia) (Fujitani 1888: 406). Additionally, the synonymous term "中亜細亜 *Chū Ajia* (Central Asia)" seems to have come into use around the same time; the first chapter of the same textbook (entitled "*Shina teikokuki* (An Account of Imperial China)") includes a passage concerning the Chinese province of Gansu stating that "Concerning Gansu (…) the northwestern part of its jurisdiction extends far beyond the Great Wall into the Central Asia Plateau, where it touches the eastern boundary of the Northern Route from East Turkestan to Tianshan, which is to say the eastern end of Tianshan" (ibid.: 334). The term was also used in the title of Nishi Tokujirō's *Chū-Ajia kiji* (Chronicle of Central Asia) (1886). While the textbook mentioned above was a translation, the 1895 publication of the second volume of Matsushima Gō's

---

7 *Chigaku zasshi* 246 (1909) Supplement, pp. 9–12.

8 The text "Paris, im Monat Februar 1843 (Paris, in the month of February 1843)" in the author's note on the inside of the front cover dates the book's authorship to 1843.

Table 6.1: (4) Chinese Geographical Treatises on Central Asia

A: Title	B: Author (editor)	C: No. of volumes	D: Notes
初刊本禹貢錐指 Yugong zhuizhi (1st. edition)	Hu Wei	10	The Graduate School of Letters in the present Kyoto University holds the 1705 (Qing Dynasty) Shuliu-xuan edition, a complete set of 10 volumes.
水経注 Shuijing zhu	(Northern Wei) Li Daoyuan	12	Complete sets of 12 volumes were issued variously by Wuying-dian and Chongwen shuju. Kyoto University's collection holds both editions.
水道提綱 Shuidao tigang	Qi Shaonan	8	Published 1775 (Qing Dynasty); the 8-volume Shiwanjuan-lou edition is held in the Naitō Bunko Collection at Kansai University.
大清一統志 DaQing yitong zhi	(Compiled by Imperial Edict)	1 selected volume	
欽定皇輿西域図志 Qinding Huangyu Xiyu tuzhi	(Compiled by Chu Tingzhang et al.)		Published 1782; maybe by Wuying-dian in Beijing.
小方壺斎輿地叢鈔 Xiaofanghu-zhai yudi congchao	(Edited by Wang Xiqi)	3 selected volumes	Published 1891; Part of series: Nanqinghe Wang-shi suoji shu.
西域考古録 Xiyu kaogu lu	Yu Hao	10	Published 1847; complete sets of the current edition such as the Haiyue-tang zazhu edition held by Kyoto University, run to 12 volumes.
漢西域図考 Han Xiyu tukao	Li Guangting	3	Published 1870; the current edition runs to 4 volumes.
西域聞見録 Xiyu wenjian lu	Qishiyi	3	Published 1777; the 3-volume edition may be the one printed in 1801 by Suharaya Mohee.
西域水道記附漢書 西域伝補註新疆賦 Xiyu shuidaoji, and Hanshu xiyuzhuan buzhu, Xinjiang fu	Xu Song	6	Published 1823 (Introduction); Kyoto University holds 4-, 5-, and 8-volume sets. No details are known about a 6-volume set.
欽定新疆識略 Qinding Xinjiang shilüe		10	Published 1821; maybe by Wuying-dian in Beijing.
新疆要略 Xinjiang yaolüe	Qi Yunshi		Published 1903; Third collection in the Huangchao fanshu yudi congshu series.
回疆誌 Huijiang zhi	Su Erde		Published 1857; while a printed edition of the Introduction exists, the only versions that exist in Japan are excerpts.

Table 6.2: (5) Chinese Writings on Tibetan Geography

A: Title	B: Author	C: No. of volumes	D: Notes
西招図略 Xizhao tulüe	Songyun	2	The 2-volume edition may be the 1847 Wang shidao reprinting.
衛藏通志 Weizang tongzhi	Songyun	8	The 8-volume edition may be the 1896 Jianxicun-she printing.
西蔵紀述 Xizang jishu	Zhang Hai	1	1894 Zhenqi-tang congshu edition
西蔵記 Xizang ji	Authorship unknown	2	The 2-volume edition may be the 1794 Longwei mishu edition.
康輶草 Kang you cao	Chen Zhongxiang	1	1860, anthologized in the Quyuan chuji wu zhong and Yiyin-zhai shichao; the edition held in the Naitō Bunko collection at Kansai University is the only known copy in Japan.
得一斎雑著四種: 西輶日記、印度箚記、遊歴芻言、西徼水道 Deyi-zhai zazhu sizhong: Xiyou riji, Yindu Zhaji, Youli chuyan, Xijiao shuidao	Huang Maocai		The 1878 Xinyang Zhao-shi printing is held by Kyoto University.
西蔵図考 Xizang tukao	Huang Peiqiao	4	4-volume editions include the 1886 DianNan Li shi printing.
西蔵賦 Xizang fu	(He Ning aka He Ying)	1	1797 Ba printing; the edition held by Kyoto University is a manuscript copy.
明代四訳館表文 Mingdai siyiguan biaowen		1 indigo-printed volume	

Table 6.3: (6) Western Chinese Buddhist Scriptures, including Tibetan Buddhist Scriptures

A: Title	B: Author	C: Volumes
洛陽伽藍記　翻印漢魏叢書 Luoyang qielan ji (Fanyin HanWei congshu version)	Presented by Honpa Hongwan-ji	1
龍蔵本仏国記 Foguo ji (Books from the Dragon Canon: Longzang ben)	Same as above	10
校本大唐西域記 Annotated DaTang Xiyu ji	Same as above	4
長寛写本大唐西域記 *Chōkan shahon Dai Tō Saiikiki*	Presented by Ishiyama-dera	12
宋版大唐西域記 Songban DaTang xiyu ji	Presented by Tō-ji	12
龍蔵本大唐西域記 DaTang xiyu ji (Books from the Dragon Canon: Longzang ben)	Presented by Honpa Hongwan-ji	12
龍蔵本慈恩寺三蔵伝 Ci'en-si Sanzang zhuan (Books from the Dragon Canon: Longzang ben)	Same as above	5
龍蔵本南海寄帰内法伝 Nanhai jigui neifa zhuan (Books from the Dragon Canon: Longzang ben)	Same as above	10
龍蔵本西域求法高僧伝 Xiyu qiufa gaoseng zhuan (Books from the Dragon Canon: Longzang ben)	Same as above	10
仏説十力経 Foshuo shili jing	Same as above	10
呉船録　范成大著 Wuchuan lu, by Fan Chengda	Same as above	2
至元法宝勘同録 Zhiyuan Fabao kantong lu	Same as above	1
康熙板番蔵経目録 Fanzang jing mulu (Kangxi version)	Same as above	1
西蔵文蔵経 Xizang wen Zangjing	Same as above	2
原刻本造像量度経 Zaoxiang liangdu jing (original version)	Same as above	

Note: For the Chinese characters in Tables 6.1, 6.2 and 6.3, please refer to Tables 2.6 and 2.7 of the present volume.

Shin chirigaku (New Geography) on foreign geography includes a map of "印度及中央亜細亜 Indo oyobi Chūō Ajia (India and Central Asia)" (Matsushima 1895: Map 6). In sum, it is clear that this geographical terminology was widely used in educational settings by the end of the nineteenth century.[9]

Conversely, however, there was never a tradition in either China or Japan of using the geographical concept of "Central Asia" in the classification of Chinese texts – a state that remains unchanged. In this sense, the fact that the exhibition staged in 1908 of these Chinese texts used the geographical classification of "Central Asia" rather than the conventional "Western Regions" is somewhat unique. To understand this, we should consider the role of Ogawa Takuji (1870–1941), the Professor of Geography in the College of Letters at Kyoto Imperial University who was instrumental in the activities that took place during Hedin's stay in Kyoto and was also closely involved in the planning of the exhibition. Although Ogawa was a scholar with a profound knowledge of Chinese texts, having been schooled in the practice of recitation by his father, a Confucian scholar, and finishing a reading of the *Zizhi Tongjian* (Comprehensive Mirror in Aid of Governance) as a middle-school student,[10] as a student at Tokyo Imperial University in 1896, he had contributed a brief note to the "Miscellaneous" section of *Chishitsugaku*

---

9 This bibliographic information reflects information searched and accessed using the "National Diet Library Digital Collections" (http://dl.ndl.go.jp/; database searches were conducted over August and September 2017).

10 At the risk of being superfluous, it may be noted that three of Ogawa's sons also went on to become professors at Kyoto University, namely Kaizuka Shigeki (Oriental History), Yukawa Hideki (Physics), and Ogawa Tamaki (Chinese Language and Literature).

zasshi (the Journal of Geology) (issue 3-33), entitled "Chūō Ajia no sōi ni tsuite (On the Stratigraphy of Central Asia),"[11] which introduced the findings from a Russian field survey of geological strata in Central Asia with his own critical commentary. Hence, it appears that Ogawa had no compunction about incorporating this new territorial concept into the classification of Chinese texts, in contrast to most sinologists. In this way, the heading used in the exhibition of "Chinese Geographical Treatises on Central Asia," as well as referring to a selection of books tailored especially for Hedin's visit and lecture, is an illustration of the free and flexible attitude characteristic of Oriental studies at Kyoto Imperial University during this period.

Naitō Konan, then a lecturer in Oriental history, is believed to have played a major role in curating the Chinese texts listed in Tables 6.1 and 6.2. Many of these texts are now held by the Library of the Graduate School of Letters at Kyoto University, among which are several editions from Naitō Konan's personal library. While the current collection includes many Chinese texts cataloged prior to 1908, we do not know whether the Chinese texts exhibited at the time were in fact those held by the College of Letters or on loan from personal collections. One such, for which clues have been left outside the text now held by Kyoto University, is the *Kang you cao* listed in Table 6.2. A cycle of poems was composed during the Qing era by Chen Zhongxiang as meditations on natural scenery and landscapes, including those found in Tibet. Although the work has been anthologized in collections of Chen's work such as the *Quyuan chuji wu zhong* and *Yiyin-zhai shichao*, there are very few copies of the individual volume in Japan or elsewhere, and no copy held by Kyoto University. According to Japan's National Database of Chinese Classics (http://kanji.zinbun.kyoto-u.ac.jp/kanseki), the Naitō Bunko collection at Kansai University Library is the only institution in Japan known to have a copy. From the fact that the Naitō Bunko collection at Kansai University grew out of Naitō Konan's personal library, we may presume that the copy of the *Kang you cao* exhibited was probably Naitō Konan's personal copy, and was returned to his collection after the exhibition.

Finally, we introduce a few points concerning "(6) Western Chinese Buddhist Scriptures, including Tibetan Buddhist Scriptures" (Table 6.3) As mentioned, these texts are Buddhist scriptures from the collections of Hongan-ji Temple or from Tō-ji or Ishiyama-dera, both temples belonging to the esoteric Shingon school of Buddhism. For example, the *DaTang Xiyu ji* manuscript presented by Ishiyama-dera and known in Japanese as the *Chōkan shahon Dai Tō saiikiki* (Chōkan era Manuscript of the *Great Tang Records on the Western Regions*), is an important manuscript as a source marked with reading aids (it is also known as the *Chōkan ten bon* or "manuscript with marks and dots"), and includes a postscript dating the completion of the manuscript to 1163 AD, specifically "the sixteenth day of the eighth month of the first year of the Chōkan era," at the closing of the Heian period.[12] The *Song ban DaTang Xiyu ji*, from the collection of Tō-ji Kannon-in Temple, is a manuscript dating to the Song dynasty (960–1269), and of course has world-heritage significance.

Also notable are the five texts presented by Hongan-ji Temple prefaced as "Books from the 龍蔵本 *Longzang ben* (the version of Dragon Canon)", namely the *Foguo ji* (Record of the Buddhistic Kingdoms), *DaTang Xiyu ji* (Great Tang Records on the Western Regions), *Ci'en si Sanzang zhuan* (Biography of the Tripitaka Master of Ci-en Monastery), *Nanhai jigui neifa zhuan* (An Account of Buddhism Sent from the South Seas), and *Xiyu qiufa gaoseng zhuan* (Biographies of Eminent Monks in Search of the Law in the West). The "龍蔵 (Dragon Canon)" is the general name for the edition of the Buddhist Canon of the *Tripitaka* (Ch. *Dazangjing*) printed in China during the Qing Dynasty in the Qianlong era, so-called. It was published by imperial edict for distribution to temples throughout China. Because 龍 (Dragon) was the symbol of the Chinese Emperor, the character of 龍 (Dragon) was used in the name of the imperial edition of the Buddhist Cannon. The circumstances by which the "Dragon Canon" was brought to Hongan-ji Temple have been discussed in detail by Kida Tomoo (2008), who notes that Ōtani Kōzui had requested a printed edition of the canon on an 1899 visit to Beijing. In response to this request, "forty cases of the canon" were conferred as a gift by the Empress Dowager Cixi and given into the keeping of Ryūkoku University in 1904 (then known as Bukkyō University) (Kida 2008: 114; cf. 2017: 74). On another visit to Beijing in 1907 – i.e., the year before Hedin visited Japan – Kōzui had a direct audience with Emperor Guangxu and Empress Dowager Cixi, on which occasion he expressed his gratitude for the gift of the "Dragon Canon" (Kida 2008: 117–118; cf. 2017: 78–79). This "Dragon Canon" was "showcased many times at the Tripitaka Association (*Daizōe*) exhibition hosted by the Association for Kyoto's Buddhist Universities of All Sects," and while the

---

11 Incidentally, two years later, an article entitled "Sven Hedin-shi Chūō Ajia ryokō-dan" (An Account of the Travels of Central Asia by Sven Hedin) was serialized in 1898 under byline of "U. I. 生" over two issues of *Chigaku zasshi* (10–6 and 10–8) However, the identity of whoever was writing under the name of "U. I. 生" remains unknown.

12 For detailed discussions, see e.g., Nakada (1958) or Tsukishima (1963).

display at the inaugural *Daizōe* exhibition in November 1915 has been referred to as "an example in the earliest period" (Kida 2008: 120; cf. 2017: 81), its exhibition at Kyoto Imperial University in November 1908 predated this by seven years. Accordingly, the exhibition might be the first time that the "Dragon Canon" was on public display in Japan. The fact that Kōzui, for the occasion of Hedin's visit, had selected those texts pertaining to the Western Regions from among the books of the Dragon Canon that had been conferred on him directly by the Imperial Household of the Qing Dynasty, and moreover brought them to Kyoto Imperial University to be placed on display regardless of the fact that the university was not a Buddhist institution, further attests to the importance that Kōzui had invested in Hedin's visit to Kyoto.

Hedin's interest in Chinese texts and Oriental studies

Let us now consider the ways in which Hedin made use of a variety of Chinese texts and materials, including the *Shuidao tigang*, in the context of his own research. In this section, we examine Hedin's relationship with Chinese texts in light of the interest shown in Oriental studies in his own studies.

Chinese texts and the composition of *Southern Tibet*

Let us begin by considering how Chinese texts were used in the report of Hedin's third expedition, published as *Southern Tibet* (1917–1922). First, we look at the overall composition of this scientific report.

The publication is extensive, running to nine volumes with additional atlases. A breakdown of the contents of the report is listed below (including English translations for parts published in other European languages). The years in which each volume appeared are included in parentheses ( ). The English translations are, in necessary cases, included in parentheses ( ).

Southern Tibet. Discoveries in Former Times Compared to My Own Researches in 1906–1908
- Vol. 1. Lake Manasarovar and the Sources of the Great Indian Rivers: From the Remotest Antiquity to the End of the Eighteenth Century (1917)
- Vol. 2. Lake Manasarovar and the Sources of the Great Indian Rivers: From the End of the Eighteenth Century to 1913 (1917)
- Vol. 3. Trans-Himalaya (1917)
- Vol. 4. Kara-Korum and Chang-Tang (1922)
- Vol. 5. Petrographie und Geologie, von (Petrography and Geology by) Prof. Dr. Anders Hennig (1916)
- Vol. 6. Part 1. Die meteorologischen Beobachtungen / bearb. von (Meteorological Observations / edited by) Prof. Dr. Nils Ekholm; Part 2. Les observations astronomiques / calculées et rédigées par (Astronomical Observations / calculated and written by) Dr. K. G. Olsson; Part 3. Botany / Prof. Dr. C. H. Ostenfeld; Part 4. Bacillariales aus Innerasien. Gesammelt von Dr. Sven Hedin / von (Bacillariales in Central Asia Collected by Dr. Sven Hedin) / by Friedrich Hustedt (1922)
- Vol. 7. History of Explorations in the Karakorum Mountains (1922)
- Vol. 8. Part 1. The Ts'ungling Mountains / by Sven Hedin and Albert Hermann. Part 2. Die Westländer in der chinesischen Kartographie / von (The Western Regions in Chinese Cartography / by) Albert Hermann. Part 3. Zwei osttürkische Manuskriptkarten / unter Mitwirkung von (Two Eastern Turkish Manuscript Maps / with the participation of) A. von Le Coq; Herausgegeben von (edited by) Albert Hermann. Part 4. Chinesische Umschreibungen von älteren geographischen Namen / zusammengestellt von (Chinese Descriptions of Ancient Geographic Names / compiled by) A. Hermann (1922)
- Vol. 9. Part 1. Journeys in Eastern Pamir; Part 2. Osttürkische Namenliste mit Erklärungsversuch / von (A List of Eastern Turkish Names with an Attempt at Interpretation / by) A. von Le Coq; Part 3. Zur Geologie von Ost-Pamir, auf Grundlage der von Sven Hedin gesammelten Gesteinsproben / von (On the Geology of East Pamir, Based on Rock Samples Collected by Sven Hedin / by) Bror Asklund; Part 4. Eine chinesische Beschreibung von Tibet vermutlich von Julius Klaproth / nach Amiot's Übersetzung bearbeitet. Herausgegeben von Erich Hänisch; Das Goldstromland im chinesisch-tibetischen Grenzgebiete nach dem Großen Kriegswerk vom Jahre 1781 dargestellt von Erich Hänisch (A Chinese Description of Tibet, probably by Julius Klaproth (after Amiot's translation) transcribed and edited by Erich Hänisch; The "Land of the Gold Stream" (Jinchuan) in the Chinese-Tibetan Borderlands, according to the History of the Great War of 1781 / presented by Erich Hänisch); Part 5. General index (1922)

Volumes 1 and 2 consist of exhaustive reviews of the historical and international literature concerning Lake Manasarovar and the major rivers of India. Volumes 3 and 4 are reports of Hedin's field surveys, while Volumes 5 and 6 present appraisals by experts in various fields concerning geological, botanical, and other specimens collected by Hedin during his expedition. Volumes 7 and

8 are bibliographic surveys of Central Asian cartography, toponyms, and natural surroundings, while Volume 9 consists of a collection of articles on Eastern Pamir and a general index of the entire work. Based on this configuration, two things are immediately obvious: first, that Hedin conducted a meticulous and extensive study of the relevant literature, and second, that he obtained cooperation from a variety of fields.

Volume 8 draws the most attention from the point of view of the utilization of Chinese texts. All four parts of the volume draw on the use of Chinese textual materials in some fashion. Part 2, which contains a historical discussion by the Silk Road Scholar Albert Hermann[13] on Chinese cartography as it pertains to the Western Regions, incorporates a vast store of information. After beginning with an explanation of the characteristics and outline of Chinese maps, Hermann cites a wealth of maps and geographical treatise, from ancient times to the Qing Dynasty, as well as maps created by foreign hands, developing a detailed discussion that unfolds over thirteen chapters copiously furnished with figures and tables. He also discusses several noteworthy figures in the history of the cartography of the Western Regions, such as 張騫 Zhang Qian,[14] 裴秀 Pei Xiu,[15] and 賈耽 Jia Dan,[16] and a 1607 edition of "南瞻部洲圖 Nansenbushū-zu"

(Map of Jambudvīpa, the Island of the Terrestrial World, as imagined in the cosmologies of Hinduism, Buddhism, and Jainism).[17] Also, based on "西域圖識 Xiyu tu zhi" (1776), the volume includes a set of twelve maps (redrawn by Hermann) for historical periods from the Western Han (206 BC–8 AD) to the Ming (1368–1644) dynasties with place names transcribed into European text. Similarly, for maps that include extensive toponymic notation, lists of place names are provided separately along with map reference coordinates.

In collaboration with the archaeologist and Turkey specialist August Albert von Le Coq,[18] Volume 8 also includes a list of East Turkish toponyms with an accompanying map. Moreover, Volume 9 includes two articles written by the sinologist Erich Haenisch.[19] Although not written by Hedin himself, these articles by prominent researchers of Chinese and other Asian texts, share the diversity and richness found in the natural sciences research papers collected in *Southern Tibet*.

The value of *Shuidao tigang*: The accuracy of Chinese geographical knowledge

The chapters of *Southern Tibet* discussing the *Shuidao tigang*, as treatments of a Chinese text, have a distinct character in that rather than quoting the works of other researchers, Hedin examines cautiously and in detail

---

13 Albert Hermann (1886–1945) was a German archaeologist and geographer. Author of *Die alte Seidenstraßen zwischen China und Syrien: Beiträge zur alten Geographie Asiens* (The Ancient Silk Roads Between China and Syria: Contributions to the Ancient Geography of Asia) (Berlin: Weidmannsche Buchhandlung, 1910) and *Lou-lan: China, Indien und Rom im Lichte der Ausgrabungen am Lobnor*) (Loulan: China, India and Rome in Light of the Excavations at Lop Nor) (published with a foreword by Sven Hedin, Leipzig, F. A. Brockhaus, 1931). Cf. the respective translations into Japanese of these texts by Yasutake Osamu (Tokyo: Kasumigaseki Shobō, 1944) and Matsuda Hisao (Tokyo: Heibonsha, 1963)

14 A native of Chenggu district east of Hanzhong (now in Shaanxi Province), Zhang Qian (d. 114 BC) lived during the Han dynasty. As an envoy of the emperor Han Wudi, he made overtures to the Yuezhi pastoralists to negotiate an alliance against the Xiongnu. Although he ultimately failed to secure an alliance, Zhang Qian brought the Han Imperial Court information on the situation in the Western Regions, which until then had been largely obscure.

15 A native of Wenxi in Hedong (now in the Shanxi province), Pei Xiu (224–271) was a statesman and geographer in the state of Cao Wei during China's Jin Dynasty. He is known for setting out six principles of cartography in the introduction to his eighteen-volume compilation of maps (the *Yu gong di Yu tu* (Maps of Regions of Tributary to the Great Yu)) and his creation of the *Fangzhang tu* (1 *chun* on map corresponds to 100 *li* on terrestrial sphere) on a scale of (1:1,800,000). This served as the model for cartography in China until the introduction of European map projections.

16 A native of Nanpi in Cang Prefecture (now Cangzhou, Hebei Province), Jia Dan (730–805) was a statesman and geographer during the Tang Dynasty. Although known for his authorship of works such as the *Gujin junguo xiandao Siyi*

shu (Descriptions of Commanderies, Counties, Circuits, and the Four Barbarians from Past to Present) and the *Hainei Hua Yi tu* (Map of both Chinese and Barbarian Peoples within the Four Seas), which juxtaposed contemporary and older toponyms, but these have been lost. The map's original contours can only be imagined from the *Hua yi tu* (Map of China and the Barbarian Countries), a rubbing taken from a stone engraving.

17 In Buddhist cosmology, human beings are considered to inhabit the southernmost of the four island-continents that surround Mount Meru, known as Jambudvīpa, "the land of Jambu trees." The *Nansenbushū-zu* is a map of this putative continent.

18 August Albert von Le Coq (1860–1930) was a German archaeologist and explorer of Central Asia. His account of the Fourth German Turfan Expedition (*Von Land und Leuten in Ostturkistan: Berichte und Abenteuer der vierten Deutschen Turfan-Expedition* (An Account of the Activities and Adventures of the Fourth German Turfan Expedition)) was published in Japanese translation by Hatori Shigeo as *Higashi Torukisutan fūbutsu-shi* (Hakusuisha, 1986). Cf. also his report of the Second and Third German Turfan Expeditions, published in English translation by Anna Barwell as *Buried Treasures of Chinese Turkestan* (London: George Allen & Unwin, 1928).

19 Erich Haenisch (Hänisch) (1880–1966) was a German Mongolist and sinologist. He is known for his studies of the *Mongɣol-un niɣuča tobčiyan* (Ch. *Yuanchao Mishi*, or "Secret History of the Mongols") and the *Erdeniin tobchi* ("The Summary of the Khans' Treasure").

Table 6.4: Principal works cited by Hedin

和漢三才圖會 *Wa-Kan sansai zue* (Illustrated Sino-Japanese Encyclopedia) (1712)	(Klaproth 1826)
大清一統志 *DaQing yitong zhi* (Records of the Unity of the Great Qing) (1744) (Introduction)	(Klaproth 1828) (de Rhins 1889) (Bretschneider 1910)
衛藏圖識 *Wei-Zang tu zhi* (Topographical Description of Tibet) (1792) (Introduction)	(Klaproth 1829, 1830) (Rockhill 1891)
西招圖畧 *Xi zhao tu lue* (Outline of Tibetan Maps) (1847) (Introduction)	(Rockhill 1891)
大清一統輿圖 *DaQing yitong yutu* (The Atlas of the Great Qing Dynasty) (1863)	(de Rhins 1889) (Bretschneider 1910)

the texts translated from Chinese to English by Ogawa exclusively for Hedin himself. Let us take a closer look at the way in which Hedin discussed the *Shuidao tigang*, which he quotes in the second of the four constituent parts of the first volume of *Southern Tibet* (Hedin 1917–1922, Vol. 1).

In Part 2 ("Chinese and Tibetan Geographers" comprising Chapters 6 to 13), Hedin opens the first chapter (on "Chinese Works on the Hydrography of Southwestern Tibet") as follows.

> In the preceding chapters I have tried to show how hopeless a task it is to search in the ancient Indian, Greek, Roman, Arabian and other Mohammedan writers for any valuable and trustworthy information about Tibet. In later chapters we shall see how Europe got acquainted with this country only in very recent times. The only people which has since many centuries possessed really reliable and partly very detailed and correct information of Tibet is the Chinese. [...] At an epoch when Tibet was still unknown to Europe, the Chinese had a rather clear conception of its geography, more especially of its eastern and southern portions, while central and northern Tibet has remained nearly unknown even to them. But being a practical people the Chinese did not care very much for those parts of the country, which were uninhabited and where nothing was to be gained. (Hedin 1917–1922, Vol. 1: 79)

Here we can see Hedin's great respect for the utility of the geographical information in Chinese books and maps relating to Tibet.

In Part 2, while citing various texts and maps, including some from Japan, Hedin is chiefly concerned with the Brahmaputra, Sutlej, and Tsangpo Rivers, as well as Lake Manasarovar. Many of the documents he cites were used as sources for works by European authors, and Hedin had not necessarily read them in the original. The principal works are listed in Table 6.4.

Works cited in parentheses ( ) indicate previous studies that have made use of these materials.[20]

Hedin also mentions other works, such as "大唐西域記 *DaTang Xiyu ji*" (Great Tang Records on the Western Regions) (646) and "西藏圖考 *Xizang tu kao*" (Atlas of Tibet) (1886). The *DaQing yitong zhi* and the *Xizang tu kao* were included among the books exhibited alongside his lecture in 1908.

Hedin's discussion of the description in the *Shuidao tigang* is developed in Chapter 12, entitled "The Shui-tao-ti-kang on the source of the Brahmaputra and the Satlej." The most salient feature of this chapter is Hedin's appraisal of the accuracy of the *Shuidao tigang* in comparison with the maps of other cartographers such as Jean Baptiste Bourguignon d'Anville[21] and Nain Singh Rawat.[22] His quotation of Ferdinand von Richthofen[23] on the point that the Chinese produced extremely accurate descriptions of areas that they saw for themselves is interesting in its suggestion that Hedin's regard for Chinese texts may have been influenced by his former teacher (Hedin 1917–1922, vol. 1: 121).

---

20 Information missing or incomplete in Hedin's bibliography has been supplemented as appropriate.
21 Jean Baptiste Bourguignon d'Anville (1697–1782) was known in his day as Europe's foremost cartographer.
22 Nain Singh Rawat (1830–1895) was engaged as a surveyor by Great Britain to explore the Himalayas, which resulted in his drawing the "Map Showing the Route Survey from Nepal to Lhasa, and Thence Through the Upper Valley of the Brahmaputra, Made by Pundit" (Montgomerie and Pundit 1868).
23 Baron Ferdinand Freiherr von Richthofen (1833–1905) was a German geographer. He conducted surveys in China from 1868 to 1872, summarized in his major treatise, *China: Ergebnisse eigener Reisen und darauf gegründeter Studien* (China: The results of my travels and the studies based thereon) (1877–1912, 5 vols. and atlas). Sven Hedin was one of Richthofen's pupils during the latter's tenure as Professor at the Friedrich Wilhelm University of Berlin (Hedin 1941).

Employing longitudinal and latitudinal coordinates, the *Shuidao tigang* clearly identifies the source of the Brahmaputra as "35°W [from Beijing] and 29°N" and the source of the Sutlej as "35°5'W [from Beijing] and 29°1'N." Considering questions about the accuracy of astronomical surveying techniques at the time, the conversion of latitudinal and longitudinal coordinates is something that must be approached very carefully. Hence, when Greenwich is taken as the reference point for longitude rather than Beijing, the *Shuidao tigang* locates the source of the Brahmaputra slightly southwest of 81°E and 29°N, and the source of the Sutlej slightly northwest of the same point. Neither of these points is far off the location of these sources on current maps, and the proximity of the two sources is also clear. The *Shuidao tigang* also describes in detail the relative positional relationship between the mainstream and the tributaries, the direction of flow path, flexion, length, etc., in a wide range of the water head regions. The translation by Ogawa about these descriptions is fairly long, extending to ten paragraphs.

The details in the *Shuidao tigang* are relevant to the identification of the source of the two rivers, which was one of the major findings of Hedin's third expedition. Again, we note that Hedin did not cite the translations of Chinese texts published in other researchers' literature, but instead he used the material that was translated for him by Ogawa. Ogawa had translated the detailed geographical description of the headwater region, which Hedin was eager to understand. This perhaps well explains Hedin's own excitement that is conveyed by his writings. Please refer to Appendix 1 for detailed discussion of Hedin's Chapter 12.

The evolution of Hedin's scientific reports over his first three expeditions

It is worth considering whether the strong interest in Oriental studies so clearly evident in the report of Hedin's third expedition was already there in the beginning, when he commenced his first Central Asia expedition. We now look to the reports of his previous expeditions for comparison.

Hedin's first Central Asia expedition was conducted between 1894 and 1897, with the publication of a scientific report in 1900 (Hedin 1900). Chapters 1 to 6 of this report present Hedin's own report of the expedition, while the Appendix in Chapter 7, as well as an overview of relative elevations at various points, includes an index of East Turkestan toponyms and nomenclature, an appraisal of algae collected by Hedin in northern Tibet by N. Wille, the results of botanical analysis co-written by W. B. Hemsley and H. H. W. Pearson, an analysis by H. Bäckström of young volcanic ejecta collected in Tibet, and an explanation of attached maps by B. Hassenstein.[24]

The report of the second expedition, between 1899 and 1902, consisted of seven volumes with atlases (Hedin 1904–1907). Hedin's own report constitutes Volumes 1 to 4. Volume 5 includes a meteorological study by N. Ekholm (Part 1) and astronomical observations by K. G. Olsson (Part 2). Volume 6 comprises a zoological study by W. Leche (Part 1), a geological study by H. Bäckström and H. Johansson (Part 2), and an album of Hedin's sketches of various ethnic groups from Western and Central Asia (Part 3). The end of Volume 2, on "Lop-Nor" (1905), features a list of Central Asian toponyms, with commentary by Karl Bernhard Wiklund (1905).[25]

What the first two expeditions have in common is that in both cases Hedin collaborated with experts in various fields of the natural sciences (e.g., astronomy, geology, and botany). Notably, aside from the toponyms, we find almost no analyses from the perspective of the humanities. Accordingly, the most significant difference in the third expedition's report is the important position given to collaborations with scholars in Oriental studies.

Two abiding interests: Toponymy and Chinese geography books describing Central Asia

While Hedin's interest in Oriental studies is apparent in his scientific report, even if we assume that it dated only from the time of his third expedition, it seems worth considering how he came to such an interest. Wahlquist points to two closely interrelated spheres of interest within Hedin's scholarly concerns, namely toponomy as the study of place names and the ancient geography of Central Asia as shown by documents written in Chinese and other Asian languages (Wahlquist 2001: 31).

We find that Hedin's interest in toponyms remains consistent from his earliest explorations. On his first expedition, he carefully surveyed toponyms along his route, collecting local place names and associated vocabulary, and then summarizing this data as a list of "Ostturkestanische Namen (East Turkestan Names)" (Hedin 1900: 350–370). In the second expedition report, he collaborated on the toponymic notation for Central Asian place names with the Finno-Ugric linguist Wiklund

---

24 Bruno Hassenstein (1839–1902) was a German cartographer. As well as drawing many maps for A. Petermann's geographical journal, *Petermanns Geographische Mitteilungen*, published by the firm of Justus Perthes in Gotha, he also produced and compiled maps based on the observations of travelers and explorers like Hedin and an atlas of Japan (Hassenstein 1885).

25 Karl Bernhard Wiklund (1868–1934) was a linguist specializing in Finno-Ugric languages, especially the Sami languages.

(Wiklund 1905). For the third expedition report, he sought commentary on the list of East Turkish place names from August Le Coq, an archaeologist and scholar of Turkey (Le Coq 1922).

Another of Hedin's interests is the literature of Oriental studies, especially the geographical information recorded in classic Chinese texts. While this interest is evident in *Southern Tibet* (Hedin 1917–1922), the report of the third expedition, there are indications that he was aware of the importance of geographical and archaeological information written in Chinese classics from an early stage (Wahlquist 2001: 31–32). Hedin's keen interest in Chinese texts may have been influenced by the China studies of his teacher, Ferdinand von Richthofen.

Section 2 of the first volume of Richthofen's great work on China, entitled "Entwicklung der Kenntnis von China (Development of the Knowledge of China)," spans more than 450 pages. This section consists of Chapter 8, which presents details from "禹貢 *Yu Gong*" (Tribute of Yu) concerning the geography of ancient China, and Chapter 9, which presents a detailed description of the development of geographical knowledge among the Chinese over five historical stages from the ancients to the Ming period, as well as the period when surveys of China began to be carried out by European missionaries and explorers (Richthofen 1877, Bd. 1.). Given that Richthofen's field of expertise was physical geography, particularly geomorphology, the attention to detail shown in this historical discussion based on both Eastern and Western sources is astonishing.

Ogawa Takuji held a high regard for Richthofen's studies of China. Ogawa had pointed out that, as a country, China was unparalleled in terms of its abundance of geographical literature, and that making full use of this heritage would be of great assistance for observations in the field. Discussing Richthofen, Ogawa praised the Prussian scholar's emphasis on Chinese characters and meticulous attention to spelling the place names mentioned in his treatise on *China*, as well as his extensive references to Chinese literature (Ogawa 1902). Richthofen's orthographic consideration for Chinese characters can be seen in the explanation provided concerning "Orthographie der chinesischen und anderen asiatischen Sprachen entnommenen Worte (Orthography of words taken from Chinese and other Asian languages)" in the "Vorerläuterungen (Prefatory Notes)" in the first volume of his great work (Richthofen 1877, Bd. 1: XIX–XXI).

Nevertheless, even as he recognized the importance of Chinese books of geography, Hedin frankly acknowledged his lack of training in deciphering these original sources. Accordingly, he had no choice but to rely on collaborations with sinologists or to cite documents indirectly from the works of other researchers of Central Asia.[26] This is no doubt why Hedin left the examination of various archaeological artifacts and documents collected on his first two expeditions to specialists in Oriental studies, sinology, and the archaeology of Central Asia (Wahlquist 2001: 30). This attitude is also evident in his turning to experts in petrography, botany, and meteorology for data analysis and appraisal of his specimens. Nevertheless, it is also clear that Hedin's ability to bring interdisciplinary research interests into the frame of a single project was an indispensable factor for the realization of the large-scale and comprehensive survey that would later be undertaken by the Northwest Scientific Expedition.

Hedin's exchanges with faculty at the College of Letters during his visit to Kyoto

Accepting the premise that Hedin had long harbored a keen interest in geographical information about Central Asia contained in Chinese texts, the opportunity to interact with faculty members at the College of Letters at Kyoto Imperial University, which had been established as a base for Oriental studies research in Japan, would have been something like a dream come true. It is not hard to imagine that Hedin would have been well pleased at seeing the collection of Chinese texts exhibited in reflection of the spirit of his own expeditions and surveys. This was undoubtedly even more the case for his encounter with Ogawa Takuji, who as a geographer also known as a scholar of classical Chinese texts emphasized the importance of Chinese geographical treatises.

There is ample evidence that Hedin's exchanges with faculty members at the College of Letters were not limited to the official welcome reception or exhibition at the University. Among the Hedin materials in the National Archives (Riksarkivet) in Stockholm is a file of Hedin's correspondence with Japan.[27] The file contains several letters demonstrating relationships with members of the College of Letters. One such is a letter addressed to Hedin from Tomioka Kenzō (then a lecturer in Oriental history) dated December 10, 1908. The letter, handwritten on illustrated stationery, expresses the author's gratitude for an evening spent in conversation with Hedin. The evening before this

---

26 According to Wahlquist, Hedin was fully cognizant of the importance of documents written in Chinese and other Asian languages, as were other Central Asian researchers he counted as peers, such as Marc Aurel Stein, Paul Pelliot, and August Le Coq. Their strengths – which Hedin lacked – were derived from a mastery of materials stemming from their systematic training in Sanskrit, Chinese, and Turkish, respectively (Wahlquist 2001: 61 n. 98).

27 Stockholm, Riksarkivet Marieberg, Sven Hedins arkiv, 417.

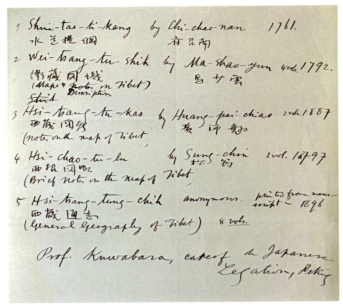

Figure 6.1: A list of five Chinese texts (with English translations)

Source: Stockholm, Riksarkivet Marieberg, Sven Hedins arkiv, 417.

letter was written, i.e., December 9, was shortly before Hedin left Kyoto to begin his return journey to Sweden, after the activities associated with his official welcome reception in Kyoto had mostly concluded.

Also in the file is a memorandum listing five Chinese texts (Figure 6.1). The titles are listed in Chinese characters along with a transcription in Roman letters and appended with a brief English-language description of their contents, along with authors and years of publication. It is notable that *Shuidao tigang* is at the top of this list. This part was translated by Ogawa.

While we do not know when this memo was written, it would not be a stretch to speculate that it may have been at a dinner party where Hedin would have been in the company of Tomioka Kenzō and other members of the College of Letters. This is supported by the fact that Kuwabara Jitsuzō is listed at the end of the memo as "care of the Japanese Legation, Peking." Dispatched by the Ministry of Education to study in China in April 1907, Kuwabara would eventually return to Japan in April 1909 to take up an appointment as Professor of Oriental History at the College of Letters. That he could not have been present at a dinner party held in Kyoto in December 1908 is consistent with the suggestion that Hedin would have to contact him in Beijing. While the memo does not contain any information enabling us to infer its authorship, the English handwriting is certainly not that of Tomioka Kenzō. And while we do know precisely who would have been at this gathering, it seems likely that Ogawa Takuji and Naitō Torajirō were in attendance.

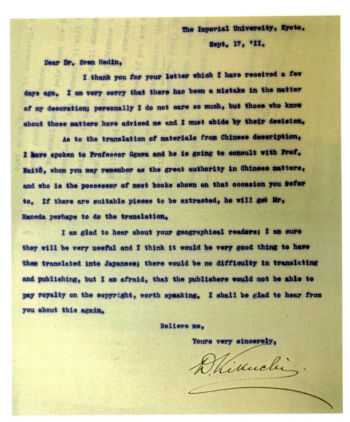

Figure 6.2: A letter to Hedin from Kikuchi Dairoku (Dated September 17, 1911)

Source: Stockholm, Riksarkivet Marieberg, Sven Hedins arkiv, 417.

One passage that could be speculated as a descriptive reference to such a meeting on the evening of December 9, 1908 in the company of faculty members at the College of Letters is found in Chapter 9 in the discussion of the tributaries of the Tsangpo River in the first volume of *Southern Tibet*, where he writes, "So far as I have had an opportunity to control the Chinese statements I have found their drawing of these rivers very incorrect" (Hedin 1917, vol. 1: 96). We cannot completely eliminate the possibility that the "opportunity" Hedin references here occurred on the evening of December 9, alluded to above. Chatting with the members of the faculty of the College of Letters would have been an opportunity to discuss these various Chinese texts and speak frankly about their respective merits and the geographical information contained within, which for Hedin would surely have been a meaningful and significant occasion.

Collateral evidence supporting the speculation that Hedin felt a sense of trust and familiarity toward Ogawa and the other faculty at the College of Letters may be found in a letter sent to Hedin by Kikuchi Dairoku (Figure 6.2).[28] Dated September 17, 1911, Kikuchi's letter

---

28 Stockholm, Riksarkivet Marieberg, Sven Hedins arkiv, 417.

states that he had given instructions to Professors Ogawa and Naitō concerning the translation of the Chinese texts that Hedin had requested, then notes that "if there are suitable pieces to be extracted, he will get Mr. Haneda [Tōru, then a lecturer in Oriental history] perhaps to do the translation." Kikuchi also writes about Naitō as "the great authority in Chinese matters, and (…) the possessor of most books shown on that occasion you refer to" – namely, the books that Hedin had seen during his visit to Kyoto Imperial University. Unfortunately, we have not been able to determine which Chinese texts Hedin had requested translations for, whether they were in fact translated, or how they were utilized in his research and writings. These remain future tasks.

Chapter II-2 of the present volume, pointed out that Hedin's visit to Kyoto in 1908 was an almost perfectly timed opportunity for the College of Letters, which had been established with the objective of situating Oriental studies as one of the pillars of its research activities. Conversely, in appealing to his keen interest in Chinese texts, especially maps and Chinese books of geography, the visit also seems to have been the realization of an eagerly anticipated encounter.

Ogawa's translation of the *Shuidao tigang* was born out of the exchange that took place in Kyoto between Hedin and the College of Letters, one that took on tangible form as an academic outcome through its incorporation into Hedin's work. It is possible that the influence of Hedin's encounters and conversations with Ogawa and Naitō may not have ended there. Namely, they may have provided a stimulus for the conception of the scientific report for Hedin's third expedition, which in its extensive incorporation of materials from Oriental studies and emphasis on elements from the humanities, represented a major departure from the reports of the first two expeditions, whose strengths were in their natural scientific elements. By extension, they may have planted the seed that grew into the plan for the resultant cross-disciplinary academic project many years later in the Northwest Scientific Expedition.

Conclusion

In this chapter, we have focused on Hedin's relationship with Chinese texts, examining Hedin's exchanges with faculty members in the College of Letters at Kyoto Imperial University concerning the *Shuidao tigang*, as well as their background and significance.

In 1908, an exhibition of Chinese texts concerning Tibet and the Western Regions (i.e., Central Asia) was staged in conjunction with a lecture delivered by Hedin at Kyoto Imperial University. One of these texts was the *Shuidao tigang*. A passage of this text was translated into English by Ogawa Takuji and given to Hedin during his stay in Kyoto, a passage that was later quoted on two occasions in Hedin's own writings. The contents translated by Ogawa from the *Shuidao tigang* were descriptions pertaining to the headwaters of the Brahmaputra and Sutlej Rivers. For Hedin, this geographical information was important, being closely related to one of the major achievements of his third Central Asia expedition (1906–1908), namely the discovery of the sources of these two rivers.

The *Shuidao tigang* is a book of geography compiled by Qi Shaonan during the Qianlong era of China's Qing dynasty. As well as being an extremely reliable catalog of the topography of each area with reference to local river systems and based on the latest and most important sources of its day, it was also the first geographical treatise to systematically present a method for describing China's "waterways" (*shuidao*). A notable characteristic of the Chinese texts displayed in the exhibition is that they were classified as "Chinese Geographical Treatises on Central Asia" rather than on "the Western Regions." The use of the comparatively new regional classification of "Central Asia," thought to have been used for the first time in 1844 by naturalist Alexander von Humboldt, and the curation of suitable books of geography in accordance with Hedin's own interests, are two points of reference that suggest the free and versatile academic attitude and reliable scholarship characteristic of Oriental studies at Kyoto Imperial University at this time.

While Hedin was not able to read books in Chinese, he was keenly interested in the accuracy of the information in the Chinese texts, especially books about Central Asian geography. This interest appeared clearly for the first time in the scientific report of his third expedition, in terms of both the structure of the report and its contents. On the 9th of December 1908, a dinner party could be thought to have been held for Hedin by faculty members at the College of Letters who had prepared the exhibition. The party served as a valuable opportunity for Hedin to talk with them about the Chinese texts. Hedin's visit to Kyoto not only coincided with the course of his own approach to Oriental studies, but also was in some ways implicated in the evolution of his expeditionary style from solo surveys to comprehensive and organizationally structured surveys that included both the natural sciences and the humanities. Hedin could understand the Chinese text explaining the headwater areas of Brahmaputra and Sutlej Rivers in the *Shuidao tigang* through Ogawa's English translation. Later, Hedin quoted Ogawa's translation without alteration into his works. This may have been a small but significant milestone for Hedin's own research.

The translation and quotation of the *Shuidao tigang* that came out of the encounter between Ogawa Takuji and Sven Hedin at the beginning of the twentieth century, while relying on maps and documentary sources, represents a collaboration that was carried out with regard to the description of the real world; it is in some ways also a result born from an exchange between Hedin's Central Asia Expeditions and Oriental studies at the College of Letters. This collaboration from a century ago can be regarded as being of great significance in that it can also be understood in the context of the interdisciplinary and collaborative research projects of today. In addition, the excitement and enjoyment that were derived therein from the stirring up of each other's interests are also important elements not to be forgotten.

References

Bretschneider, B. 1910. *Mediæval Researches from Eastern Asiatic Sources Fragments Towards the Knowledge of the Geography and History of Central and Western Asia From the 13th to the 17th Century.* 2 volumes. London: K. Paul, Trench, Trübner.

Chen Ruiping 1995. "Shuidao tigang tiyao (Summary of the 'Guide to the Network of Waterways')," In Tang Xiren, ed. *Zhongguo kexue jishu dianji tonghui. Dixue juan* (General Introduction to Comprehensive Compendium of Materials and Sources on Chinese Science and Technology: Vol. 5 Geography). Zhengzhou: Henan jiaoyu chuban she, 643–645.

de Rhins, J.-L. D. 1889: *L'Asie Centrale, Thibet et Régions limitrophes: Texte et Atlas* (Central Asia, Tibet and neighboring regions: Text and atlases). Paris: E. Lerou.

Fujitani, Takao, translated by. 1888. *Joshi chiri kyōkasho: Chūtō kyōiku* (Alexander Keith Johnston's Textbook for Intermediate Geography Lectures), folio 2, volume 2. Tokyo: Uchida Rōkakuho.

Hassenstein, Bruno 1885. *Atlas von Japan: Sieben Blätter im Massstabe von 1:1,000,000 und eine Übersichtskarte im Massstabe von 1:7,500,000* (Atlas of Japan: Seven sheets in the scale of 1:1,000,000 and an overview map in the scale of 1: 7,500,000). Gotha: J. Perthes.

Hedin, Sven 1900. *Die geographisch-wissenschaftlichen Ergebnisse meiner Reisen in Zentral-Asien 1894–1897* (The Geographic-scientific results of my travels in Central Asia 1894–1897). Ergänzungsband 28 zu *Petermanns Mitteilungen* (Supplement 28 to Petermanns Mitteilungen). Gotha. 399 S. + Karten.

Hedin, Sven 1904–1907. *Scientific Results of a Journey in Central Asia and Tibet 1899–1902.* 6 volumes and atlas including 3 parts. Stockholm: Lithographic Institute of the General Staff of the Swedish Army.

Hedin, Sven 1909–1913. *Trans-Himalaya: Discoveries and Adventures in Tibet*, vol. 1–3. New York: MacMillan. (First edition issued 1909 to 1912).

Hedin, Sven 1917–1922. *Southern Tibet: Discoveries in Former Times Compared with My Own Researches in 1906–1908*, vol. 1–9. Stockholm: Lithographic Institute of the General Staff of the Swedish Army.

Hedin, Sven 1941. "Omohide (Memories of my teacher)." translated by Y. Takayama. In *Richthofen Den* (Biography of Richthofen). Tokyo: Keiō Shobō, 35–102. (Richthofen, F. 1933. *Meister und Schüler. Ferdinand Freiherr von Richthofen an Sven Hedin* (Master and Student. Ferdinand Freiherr von Richthofen to Sven Hedin). (A correspondence.) Mit einer Einleitung und Erläuterungen von Sven Hedin (With Introduction and Explanations by Sven Hedin)... Herausgegeben von Ernst Tiessen, etc. (Ernst Tiessen etc. eds.), (With portraits.) Berlin: Verlag von Dietrich Reimer.)

Heng mu yi, zhu bian (A. W. Hummel, ed.) 1990. *Qingdai Mingren zhuanlüe* (Eminent Chinese of the Ch'ing period (1644–1912)), Xining: Qinghai renmin chubanshe, 106–108. (Original text: A.W. Hummel, ed. 1943–1944. *Eminent Chinese of the Ch'ing Period (1644–1912).* Washington, D.C.: U.S. Government Printing Office. Translated by the Institute of Qing History, Renmin University of China).

Humbolt, Alexander von, 1844 *Central-Asien: Untersuchungen über die Gebirgsketten und die vergleichende Klimatologie* (Central Asia: Studies of mountain chains and comparative climatology). Berlin: Verlag von Carl. J. Klemann.

Kida, Tomoo 2008. "Ryūkoku daigaku shozō no ryūzō ni tsuite (On the Qing Dragon Canon at Ryukoku University)." *Ryukoku Daigaku Lonshū* (The journal of Ryukoku University), 471: 104–129.

Kida, Tomoo 2017. "Ōtani Kōzui's Tripitaka Diplomacy in China and the Qing Dragon Canon at Ryukoku University." In Jiang Wu and Wilkinson, G. eds. *Reinventing the Tripitaka: Transformation of the Buddhist Canon in Modern East Asia*. Lanham, MD: Lexington Books, 67–94.

Kikuchi Kōji 1884, *Bankoku sangyō ibun* (Curious episodes of world sericultures). Fūsui-lō's woodblock, Komatsu Seiichi Printing.

Klaproth, Julius 1826. "Éclaircissement sur une Carte Chinoise et Japonaise de l'Asie et de l'Inde. Mémoires relatifs à l'Asie (Enlightenment on a Chinese and Japanese Map of Asia and India)." *Mémoires Relatifs a l'Asie, Contenant des Recherches Historiques, Géographiques et Philologiques sur les Peuples de l'Orient* (Memoirs relating to Asia containing historical, geographical and philological research on the Peoples of the Orient), Tome II, 411–432.

Klaproth, Julius 1828. "Mémoire sur la Cours de la Grande Rivière du Tubet, Appelèe Iraouaddy dans la Royaume des Birmans (Memory on the course of the great river Tubet, Called Iraouaddy in the Kingdom of Burma)." *Mémoires Relatifs a l'Asie, Contenant des Recherches Historiques, Géographiques et Philologiques sur les Peuples de l'Orient* (Memoirs relating to Asia containing historical, geographical and philological research on the peoples of the Orient), Tome III, 370–417.

Klaproth, Julius 1829, 1830. "Description du Tubet, Traduite du Chinois en Russe par le Père Hyacinthe, et du Russe en Français par M.*** ; Revue sur l'Original Chinois, et Accompagnée de Notes (Description on the Tubet, to Translate from Chinese to Russian by Père Hyacinthe, and from Russian to French by M.***; Review on the Chinese original, and accompanied by note)," *Nouveau Journal Asiatique* (New Asian Journal), Tome 4, 81–158, Tome 6, 161–246, and 321–350.

Le Coq, August von 1922. "Ostürkische Namenliste, mit Erklärungsversuch (Eastern Turkic name list, with explanation attempt)." In Hedin. S., *Southern Tibet: Discoveries in Former times Compared with My Own Researches in 1906–1908*, vol. 9, Part II. Stockholm: Lithographic Institute of the General Staff of the Swedish Army, 87–123.

Matsushima, Gō 1895. *Shin chirigaku: gaikoku no bu* (New geography: Chapters of foreign countries). Tokyo: Shunyō-dō.

Montgomerie, Thomas G. and Pundit 1868. "Report of a Route-survey Made by Pundit, from Nepal to Lhasa, and thence through the Upper Valley of the Brahmaputra to its Source." *The Journal of the Royal Geographical Society of London*, 38: 129–219.

Nakada, Norio 1958. *Kotenbon no kokugogakuteki kenkyū. yakubun hen* (The Japanese linguistic study of glossed texts. vol. translation). Tokyo: Dai-Nippon Yūbenkai Kōdansha (Tōkyō: Bensei-sha, revised edition, 1979).

Nishi, Tokujirō 1886. *Chū-Ajia kiji* (Chronicle of Central Asia). Tokyo: Rikugun Bunko.

Ogawa, Takuji 1896. "Chūō Ajia no sōi ni tsuite (On the stratigraphy of Central Asia)." *Chishitsugaku Zasshi* (The geological magazine), 3 (33): 276–278.

Ogawa, Takuji 1902. "Hokusei zakki (Dai ichi kō) (Notes on Chinese Classic Books of Geography (Part one))." *Chigaku Zasshi* (The Journal of Geography), 14 (8): 562–565.

Richthofen, Ferdinand von 1877–1912. *China: Ergebnisse eigener Reisen und darauf gegründeter Studien* (China: Results of my own trips and studies based on them). Bd. 1–5, Atlas 1–2. Berlin: D. Reimer.

Rockhill, W. Woodville 1891. "Tibet: a Geographical, Ethnographical, and Historical Sketch, Derived from Chinese Sources." *The Journal of the Royal Asiatic Society of the Great Britain and Ireland*, January.

Tanaka, Kazuko 2015. "Kyōto daigaku ga shozō suru Sven Hedin ni kakawaru kaiga shiryō ni tsuite (A preliminary observation of the drawings and paintings related to Sven Hedin stored at Kyoto University: A legacy of his stay in Japan in 1908)." *Jimbun Chiri* (Japanese Journal of Human Geography), 67 (1): 57–70.

Tanaka, Kazuko, and Kizu, Yūko 2011. "Kokuritsu kokyu-hakubutsu-in zō "Shanzi bianyuan tu" oyobi "Shanxi sanguan bianyuan tu" to Kyōto daugaku zō "Shanxi sanguan bianyuan buzhen tu" tono hikaku" (Comparative study on maps along the Great Wall in Shanxi stored in National Palace Museum of Taiwan and in Kyoto University)." *Kyōto Daigaku Bungaku-bu Kenkyū Kiyō* (Memoirs of the Faculty of Letters Kyoto University), 50: 1–29.

Tōkyō chigaku kyōkai hen (Tokyo Geographical Society ed.) 1908. *Hedin gō* (Special Issue on Hedin). *Chigaku Ronsō* (The Geographical Review), No.4.

Tōkyō Chigaku Kyōkai (Tokyo Geographical Society) 1909. "Hedin hakase tairaku kiji (Dr. Hedin in Kyoto)," *Chigaku Zasshi* (The Journal of Geography), 21 (6): 1–12.

Tsukishima, Hiroshi 1963, "Ishiyama-dera bon Daitō Saiiki-ki no wakun no tokusei (On the Characteristic of the Vernacular Readings in Daitō Saiiki-ki Held by Ishiyama-dera Temple)," In Tsukishima, Hiroshi. *Heian jidai no kanbun kundokugo ni tsukiteno kenkyū* (The Study of Diacritical Languages in Heian Era). Tokyo: University of Tokyo Press, Chapter 2–3.

Wahlquist, Håkan 2001. "Saiiki Kouko-gaku no Tanjo to Tenkai (Central Asia archaeology from Sven Hedin to Folke Bergman: Notes on the early history of Swedish contributions to the archaeology of China and China's Western Provinces)." In Tomiya, I. ed. *Ryūsa Shutsudo no Moji-shiryō – Loulan- and Niya-monjo o Chūshin ni* (Written materials excavated from the sands). Kyoto: Kyoto University Press, 3–78.

Wiklund, Karl Bernard 1905. "Transcription of Geographical Names in Central Asia." In Hedin S., *Scientific Results of a Journey in Central Asia 1899–1902*, Vol. 2, Lop-Nor. Stockholm: Lithographic Institute of the General Staff of the Swedish Army, 647–660.

Yamasaki, Naomasa 1908. "Masa ni kitaramu to suru daitanken-ka Sven von Hedin shi (A great explorer Sven von Hedin is now approaching Japan)." *Chigaku Zasshi* (The Journal of Geography), 20 (11): 757–785.

Column 1
Hedin's Suit of Armor

TANAKA Kazuko

I first learned that Sven Hedin had visited Kyoto University when I saw his name in the *Equipment Inventory for the Geography Department in the College of Letters at Kyoto Imperial University* (1908–1936).[1] Figure C.1 shows the relevant entry in the Equipment Inventory, which I had been consulting in search of clues to the name and date of purchase for an old map of China that had lost its identification slip (Tanaka et al. 2010). So, my first impression of Hedin was that his visit had occurred very shortly after the Department of Geography was established in 1907 and the idea that the university gifting him a suit of armor was incomprehensible. It was incomprehensible to me, in the passing moment, because I had misinterpreted the term "suit of armor" (*gusoku*) to mean "greaves" – i.e., gaiters for the lower legs.[2] If the bequest was for supplies necessary for exploration, I thought it would have been better to have donated at least a dozen sets. I had overlooked the listed value of 360 yen. After that, I completely forgot about Hedin.

In 2014, Hedin's presence at the Kyoto University was felt again, when I learned that the sixty reproductions I had found in a cabinet in the Department of Geography might have been reproductions of pictures he had drawn. I immediately recalled the entry in the Equipment Inventory. Hedin really *had* come to Japan in 1908, the same year that the suit of armor was purchased and gifted to him (Tokyo Geographical Society 1909).

Attracted by the charm of these vivid reproductions and the curious mystery of how they came to be, I worked in cooperation with colleagues from related fields to conduct a study of the pictures and Hedin's visit to Japan. Nothing of Hedin's visit to Kyoto Imperial University was mentioned in retrospectives or similar materials published by the Faculty of Letters (Kyoto University Faculty of Letters 1935). It nevertheless became clear that Hedin had been welcomed as an academic guest of Kyoto Imperial University (Sakaguchi 2013), and that a record of the gifts given to him was listed in the *Gaikoku meishi shōtai kankei shorui* (Archive Documents Relating to Invitations to Celebrated Foreign Nationals) (for 1908 to 1912) kept in the University Archives (Figure C.2).

The gifts were delivered to Hedin, who was staying at the Sawabun Ryokan, by Kikuchi Dairoku, the President of the University himself, on December 6. While I have been unable to find any documents to prove that this breastplate and helmet (*katchū*) is the one given to Hedin by the Department of Geography, it seems unlikely that

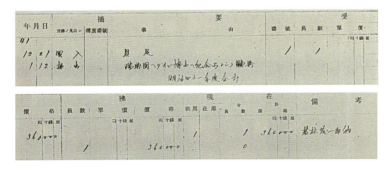

Figure C.1: A record of the purchase and gift of the suit of armor noted in the Equipment Inventory (top: left page; bottom: right page).

Source: *Meiji 41 – Shōwa 11 bihin suitōbo Kyōto teikoku daigaku bunka daigaku chirigaku kenkyūshitsu* (Equipment Inventory for the Geography Department in the College of Letters at Kyoto Imperial University (1908–1936)).

---

1   *Meiji 41–Shōwa 11 bihin suitōbo Kyōto teikoku daigaku bunka daigaku chirigaku kenkyūshitsu*, is kept in the archive of the office of the Faculty of Letters at Kyoto University.

2   The term *gusoku* used here to mean "suit of armor" may be translated more literally as "fully equipped set" and is written using the kanji characters 具 (equipment) and 足 (sufficient). My confusion perhaps stemmed from the fact that the latter character can also mean "leg" or "foot".

Figure C.2: Catalogue of commemorative gifts presented to Hedin.

Source: Kyoto Imperial University (1908–1909)'s *Gaikoku meishi shōtai kankei shorui* (Archive Documents Relating to Invitations to Celebrated Foreign Nationals) (for 1908–1912).

Figure C.3: Suit of Japanese armor given to Hedin at the Museum of Ethnography, Stockholm. Photo by the author.

Figure C.4: A mannequin of Hedin wearing long leather boots. Photo by the author.

he received gifts of multiple sets of armor. The price of the suit of armor purchased by the Department of Geography is listed as 360 yen (Figure C.1). The *Gaikoku meishi shōtai kankei shorui* also features a memorandum regarding the preparations for Hedin's welcome, with a note reading "Matter of the budget for a commemorative gift / 500 yen or less / breastplate and helmet, long sword (contact Dean Inoue at the College of Law…)".[3] While the price of the sword in question is unknown, in monetary terms, the price of the armor was less than the 500 yen budget limit.

Compared with the pair of flower vases presented to Hedin by Tokyo Imperial University, the sword and armor seem rather unsophisticated. However, considering that arrangements were made for Hedin to visit martial arts demonstrations in both Tokyo and Kyoto, it is conceivable that arms and armor would have suited his tastes (Tokyo Geographical Society 1909a, 1909b). The sword and suit of armor were sent to Hedin's home in Stockholm separately from the baggage that Hedin carried on his trip home (Kyoto Imperial University 1908–1912). A photograph in the collection of the Sven Hedin Foundation shows the suit of Japanese armor on display in Hedin's own home. Had the armor caught the explorer's fancy?

Later, the suit of armor that had graced Hedin's home was donated to the Museum of Ethnography (Etnografiska Museet) in Stockholm, where it is currently on display as a specimen of samurai armor (*ō-yoroi*) in an exhibition dedicated to Japan (Figure C.3). Two Japanese long swords are placed next to the suit of armor, but not the one gifted by Kyoto Imperial University.[4] When I visited the Museum of Ethnography to see the suit of armor in person, I felt a tangible sense of the exchanges between Hedin and the Department of Geography, and between Hedin and Kyoto Imperial University, after the passage of more than a century.

Along the way, realizing that the suit of armor gifted to Hedin was not a set of greaves, I began to also wonder what Hedin had worn during his expeditions. Figure C.4 shows long leather boots worn by a mannequin representing Hedin in the "Hedin Corner" of the Museum of Ethnography in Stockholm. Judging from the mannequin's clothing, they appear to be the long boots from the Northwest Scientific Expedition, which began in 1927.[5] Figure C.5 is a photograph of Hedin published in *Trans-Himalaya* (1910, vol. 2; illustration no. 343), an account written for a popular audience describing the Central Asia Expedition he had completed just before coming to Japan. Hedin was dressed in clothing resembling that of the local inhabitants so as not to be an obvious European. In this photo, he appears to be wearing long leather boots on his feet – but neither gaiters nor greaves. It is

---

3 "Dean Inoue" is a reference to Inoue Mitsu (1867–1916), then Professor and Dean at the College of Law.
4 According to Dr. Håkan Wahlquist, Director of the Sven Hedin Foundation.
5 A scientific expedition carried out in Xinjiang and northern China over three phases between 1927 and 1935. Its members included researchers from Sweden, China, and Germany.

obvious that gaiters were not suitable for exploring the mountainous and arid areas of the Himalayas.

The commemorative gift from Kyoto Imperial University was a suit of armor, and Hedin wore long leather boots. "Hedin's suit of armor" proved to be a valuable clue for investigating the circumstances of Hedin's visit to Kyoto, and serves as a testament to the link between Hedin and Kyoto.

References

Hedin, Sven 1910. *Trans-Himalaya: Discoveries and Adventures in Tibet*, vol. 2, New York: MacMillan. (First Edition was issued from 1909 to 1912).

Kyōto Teikoku Daigaku (Kyoto Imperial University) 1908-1909. *Gaikoku meishi shōtai kankei shorui (Ji Meiji 41-nen shi Meiji 42-nen* (Documents Relating to the Invitation and Welcome of Foreign Celebrities for 1908-1909). Materials held in the Kyoto University Archives (ID: 01A19469).

Kyōto Teikoku Daigaku bungaku bu (Faculty of Letters of Kyoto Imperial University) 1935. *Kyōto teikoku daigaku bungaku bu sanjū shūnen shi* (The 30th-year Memorial Book of Faculty of Letters, Kyoto Imperial University). Kyoto: Faculty of Letters, Kyoto Imperial University.

Sakaguchi, Takahiro 2013. Sven Hedin no kōydai hōmon (Sven Hedin's Visit to Kyoto University). *Kyōto Daigaku Bunsho-kan Dayori* (Kyoto University Archives newsletter), 25: 8.

Tanaka, Kazuko, Kizu, Yuko, and Usami, Bunri 2010. "Shan xi zhèn bian yuan bu zhen tu" (kashō) ni kansuru chirigaku, bunkengaku, kaigaron-teki chōsa – yobi-teki kōsatsu (Study on "Defense Map along the Great Wall in Shanxi" from the viewpoints of geography, Chinese philology, and Chinese theory of arts: a preliminary observation). *Kyōto Daugaku Bungaku-bu Kenkyū Kiyō* (Memoirs of the Faculty of Letters Kyoto University), 49: 1–53.

Tōkyō Chigaku Kyōkai (Tokyo Geographical Society) 1909a. Dokutoru Sven Hedin shi kangei hōkoku (Report on the Welcome Given to Dr. Sven Hedin), *Chigaku Zasshi* (The Journal of Geography), 21 (6): a1–a31.

Tōkyō Chigaku Kyōkai (Tokyo Geographical Society) 1909b. Hedin hakase tairaku kiji (Dr. Hedin in Kyoto), *Chigaku Zasshi* (The Journal of Geography), 21 (6): b1–b12.

Figure C.5: Photo of Hedin in ethnic garb published in *Trans-Himalaya*. Source: Hedin, S. 1910. *Trans-Himalaya*, vol. 2 (Illustration no. 343).

Column 2
What Did Hedin See in Osaka? An Unsung Episode of Unringable Bell

Deguchi Yasuo

During his trip to Kyoto, Hedin accepted an invitation from newspaper companies in the neighboring city, Osaka, and visited there on 7 and 8 December 1908. Around midday of the 7th, he arrived at Umeda station, the city's main train station, then went to see Osaka castle and Shitennōji temple, one of the oldest temples in Japan. After that, taking a rickshaw ride, he passed through Osaka's busy downtown areas such as Douton-bori and Shinsai-bashi, attended a dinner party arranged by the companies at a Japanese-style restaurant in central Osaka, and returned to Kyoto the following day (Osaka Asahi Newspaper 1909b: 3, Tokyo Daily Newspaper 1908: 3).

In Osaka Hedin was accompanied by Takuji Ogawa, professor of geography, Kyoto University, Kenyū Hori, a close associate of Abbot Ōtani Kōzui of Nishi-honganji temple and a journalist who had reported Hedin's activities in Kyoto (Osaka Asahi Newspaper 1908c: 3, Osaka Mainichi Newspaper 1908: 2).

According to a news report, Hedin was not very interested in Osaka castle, where he mounted the foundation of the main keep. (The castle's main keep had not been restored when he visited the site.) But he was, according to the report, quite impressed by the cultural assets of Shitennōji temple (Osaka Asahi Newspaper 1908a: 2). He was especially excited by "the world's biggest" bell which the temple had installed a few years earlier (Osaka Asahi Newspaper 1908a: 2). It seems that Shitennōji temple's bell was the highlight of Hedin's trip to Osaka.

The newspaper report described it as follows:

> In Shitennōji, [Hedin] was very fond of the huge bell, admiring it as the greatest bell in the world. [He said that] though being also quite large, the bell of Moscow was smaller than this. Even worse, since being cracked, the Moscow bell could not make good sounds. He badly wished to toll the bell, insisting that he would lavish money on it. But he was very disappointed by [being told that] for some reasons, he couldn't ring the bell. He asked when he could do so, telling that he would come to Japan again just for tolling this bell. (Osaka Asahi Newspaper 1908a: 2)

Let me ring this bell. I splash money on it. If I cannot do it now, tell me when I will be able to do so. I will come all the way back to Japan to ring it… This childish response to being refused the joy of ringing the bell seemed to surprise the reporter. Of course, he was jokingly expressing his disappointment. But there may be something a bit more than that. Perhaps the temple's representatives did not clearly explain why he could not ring the bell, offering only the vague "for some reasons". Hedin's response might reveal a nuance of slight irritation about the temple's unexplained refusal.

There was indeed a reason for the unexplained refusal. The great bell was cast in 1903, five years before Hedin's visit, and was proclaimed to be "the one and only in the world." But it was cast with a crucial structural defect; an uneven horizontal thickness where it should have been uniform (Ichimura 1998: 59). As such, the world's biggest bell was a failure. At its public inauguration ceremony, the gathered crowd learned that it made only mere a metallic sound when struck, rather than the resonant peal of a bell. When Hedin visited, it was already notorious as an unringable bell that should never be tolled again. Since Hedin had already referred to the fault of its nearest rival, the Tsar Bell in the Kremlin, the temple's personnel might have found it difficult to admit that their bell was also defective. Anyway, the highlight of Hedin's brief tour of Osaka was, bluntly, one of the world's biggest failures at the time.

※

Based on his visit to the great bell, Hedin wrote the following record of his travel experience in later years.

> If you wish to see something else which does not exactly belong to the small things of Japan you should visit a temple in Osaka, the chief manufacturing town of Japan. There hangs a bell which is 25 feet high and weighs 220 tons. In a frame beside the bell is suspended a beam, a regular battering-ram, which is set in motion up and down when the bell is sounded. And when the bell emits its heavy, deafening ring it sounds like thunder. (Hedin 1912: 194)

This is a passage from a chapter titled "Japan 1908" of his book, *From Pole to Pole*, published as a travelogue for the young in 1912. It confirms that Shitennōji's great bell was the highlight of his Osaka visit, because the book contains no other reference to the city. Also we can see that he dramatized the sound of the bell which he had not heard. Of course, "making things up" is a questionable practice. But if the temple had frankly admitted that their bell was defective, he would not have needed to fictionalize it. At any rate, thanks to such human errors as the misleading hesitation and the lack of confirmation, the unringable bell could ring pealing sounds in the travelogue.

※

Let us now ask why Shitennōji temple wanted to construct the world's biggest bell. In 1900 the temple decided to mold it, aiming to complete its construction three years later. The temple officially announced that the bell was built to commemorate the 1300th anniversary of the death of its founder, Prince Shōtoku. But the 1300th anniversary year was, in fact, 1922, not 1903. It seems strange to aim to complete it 19 years before the anniversary. At the same time, however, the prospectus for the bell's construction expressly referred to the 5th domestic industrial exposition, which was to be held in an adjacent park in 1903 (Ichimura 1998: 57). These domestic expositions were important national events for Meiji Japan. Since the 1903 exposition was the first ever to be held in Osaka, the locals had high expectations. Hence, the intention was for bell's inauguration ceremony to be held during the exposition, but it was not ready in time due to difficulties in its construction. In short, the bell was intended as a spectacle, taking advantage of one of the largest national events. This spectacular bell was expected to attract a great many visitors. The catchphrase, "the world's greatest bell" was advertising copy to enhance the spectacle and thus draw more visitors. If it had truly been commissioned as a linchpin of the local's faith, it would not need to be the biggest. It needed to be the greatest of all because it was expected to be a spectacle that appealed to visitors.

While Shitennōji temple planned to create a spectacle, to take advantage of an opportunity, the Osaka citizens enthusiastically responded to the temple's call for donations, providing funds and materials for the construction. At the time, Osaka was experiencing a remarkable transformation as a modern city. Its modern port facilities were under construction. In the year of the expedition, the first tram and private bus services in Japan began operations there. Against this backdrop, Osaka had come to be known as "the center of Japan's commerce and industry". Hedin used the phrase in his speech at the banquet on his night in Osaka, flattering his hosts (Osaka Mainichi Newspaper 1908: 2), and cited it again in his travelogue, as quoted.

A newly rising city wants a symbol of its emerging economic power. The symbol also embodies its desire to stand out from its rivals and to develop further. Growing cities often compete to build the world tallest edifices, manifesting their ambitions to be the world's top city. This was also the case for early 20th century Osaka. For its citizens, "the world greatest" bell was a symbol that embodied their pride in the city's economic power and aspirations for further growth.

Osaka Newspapers might have arranged Hedin's visit to Shitennōji temple. They also expected that he would be guided to the world biggest bell there. Hedin was showed the bell, rather than simply seeing it. And what he was showed was a symbol of Osaka's pride and desire.

※

But, as we have seen, the world biggest bell was defective. Its defect resulted from "a primitive failure"; at the time of pouring, a sand mold was misplaced in its cast (Ichimura 1998: 59). A specialist diagnosed that its molders, one of Japan's top foundries, made this simple mistake because they had ventured too far beyond their experiences (Ichimura 1998: 59). He also suggested that the problem stemmed from insufficient casting material due to a shortage of funds (Ichimura 1998: 61). Frankly, the failure might be attributed to *hubris*; a failure to recognize the limitations of their techniques and funds. The unringable bell is a consequence of overreach – trying to do something beyond one's capabilities.

Similar examples of overreach can be seen all across Japan around that time. In 1908 Japan had begun operating the South Manchuria Railway in Northeast China after its military victory over Russia the previous year. It would annex Korea within a few years. The collapse of the empire a few decades later makes clear that its imperialistic expansion was an overreach, because it was triggered by Japan's inability to control the Manchurian branch of its military.

Two years after Hedin's visit to Osaka, Sōseki Natsume, a prominent writer of Meiji Japan, conducted a lecture tour around the Kansai area, including Osaka, criticizing social conditions of the time as "superficial and slippery Westernization" (Natsume 1986:34). Though the molding of the bell is an enlarged reproduction of an Eastern tradition rather than Westernization, the overreach in its construction is of the sort that Sōseki was criticizing. From this perspective, what Hedin saw in Osaka was a manifestation of the chancily overreaching sprits of the time.

※

Another newspaper article names the Shitennōji priest who received Hedin; "Major Prelate Ichikawa" (Osaka Asahi Newspaper 1908b: 3). Probably this Major Prelate, Enjō Ichikawa, was the temple's representative who refused Hedin's request to ring the bell. I have a personal connection to him. Two years after Hedin's visit, a ten year old boy became Ichikawa's first live-in apprentice. This boy is my grandfather, who later succeeded Ichikawa's position in the temple, and for whom Ichikawa was a sort of foster grandfather. Though Ichikawa died before I was born, I also took him as my foster great-grandfather, who was often mentioned in my family as "the old priest".

Later my grandfather, Jōjun Deguchi, majored in Indian Buddhism at Faculty of Letters, Kyoto Imperial University, went to Europe to study, contacted Albert von Le Coq, another explorer of central Asia and a rival of Hedin, at Berlin, bought a parcel of the documents that he had excavated in Turfan, and brought it back to Japan. Those documents are now known as Deguchi collection. In front of the collection unearthed in Central Asia, what conversation did grandfather and Ichikawa have? Did Ichikawa begin to tell an old story of Hedin's visit and bitterly smile, muttering that he was troubled by Hedin's tantrummy demand to ring the unringable bell? No one knows now.

※

Later, the unringable bell cast its lot with the Great Japan Empire, which had continued to bite off more than it could chew. In December 1943, the great bell was delivered to the government to be melted down to produce munitions for the ever deteriorating war situation. Upon delivery, a big ceremony was held for its last ring, and it once again revealed the shrill voice that had been quiet for forty years. This was precisely "the next occasion" which Hedin had enquired about.

Many people of high station such as the governor of Osaka and the division commander attended the ceremony (Ichimura 1998:59). Among them was my mother, a four-year-old girl, who never thought that she would marry into a family who lived next to the campanile. The little girl remembered only that when the unringable bell was rung, the thick dust which had accumulated on it for forty years fell on the gatherers, including her. In comparison to such imperialistic expansions as management of Manchuria railways and the annexation of Korea, the overreach of construction of the world's biggest bell was harmless and peaceful. The farcical last cloud of ashes may be an appropriate upshot of such a smile-provoking overreach.

If the bell had a mind, did she remember at her final moment the day she was visited by a foreign celebrity, Hedin, when she was only five years old and still attracted much public attentions, as one of a few grand occasions in her relatively short and ill-fated life? Of course no one knows.

Appendix 1

"Chapter XII. *The Shui-Tao-Ti-Kang* On the Source of the Brahmaputra and the Satlej." (Hedin 1917, vol. 1, Chapter 12: 114–122)

The Original Text and Editor's notes

Tanaka Kazuko

Regarding annotations to the text

1. Hedin's footnotes on each page of the original text have been changed to endnotes and numbered sequentially (1 to 32).
2. Additional editor's notes are distinguished by parentheses, from (1) to (30).
3. Please refer to Appendix 3 for place names, and Appendix 4 for major water systems and mountains in the Brahmaputra and Sutlej headwater regions.

In the *Shui-tao-ti-kang* or *Outlines of Hydrography*, Book 22nd, complied by Chi Chao Nan in the 26th year of Emperor Chien Lung (1762 A. D.), we find the following description of the source of the Brahmaputra, which was translated for me by Professor Ogawa during my stay at Kyoto[1]. Under the heading: »*Waters of Hsi-tsang*» or Tibet, the author says:

»The *Ya-lu-ts'ang-pu-chiang* is the *Ta-chin-sha-chiang* (= Great Gold Sand River). It is supposed by some geographers to be the *Pa-pu-chuan* of olden times. Some consider it to be the *Hei-shui* (= Black Water) in *Yü-kung*,[1] but it is too far situated. Its sources come out from *Ta-mu-chu-ko-k'a-pa-pu-shan*[2] standing at a distance more than 340 li northwest of *Cho-shu-tê*[3] tribes in the western frontier of *Tsang*. [The north-western part of the mountain is near the source of the Lake *Ma-piu-mu-ta-la*[4, (2)] in the *Lang-ch'ien-k'a-pu-pa-shan*[5]. This mountain (*Ta-mu-chuk-k'a-pa-pu-shan*) is situated 300 li S.E. of *Kang-ti-ssu-shan* (Kailas Mountain). The mountain is very high and great, and its form resembles a horse, whence it is named. The source of the *Ya-lu-tsang-pu-chiang*[6] is 35°W. (of Peking)[(3)] and (the altitude of the north) Pole 29°.][7] There are three sources, all of which flow north-eastwards and unite into one river. The river flows at first turning eastwards, then south-eastwards for more than 200 li. A stream of fore mountains of *Ku-mu-kang* comes from S.W. to meet the river. The river now turning to the north-east for 100 li, receives the *Chiang-chia-su-mu-la-ho* which flows south-eastwards from *Sha-ku-ya-la-ma-shan* on the north-west. [The river *Chiang-chia-su-mu-la* is in the west of *Cho-shu-tê*. Its source comes out from *Sha-ku-ya-la-ma-la-shan* and *Nieh-li-ling* of *Cha-ko-chia-la-shan*. There are four streams, which run eastwards, and unite in one. After the confluence the river flows southwards, and receiving the *Cha-êrh-ho* coming from the west, eastwards into the *Ya-lu-tsang-pu* River.]

The *Ya-lu-tsang-pu* River flows now eastwards for 50 or 60 li, and receives *A-la-chu-ho* coming from the fore mountains of *Sha-la-mu-kang*. The river now runs southwards for 50 li, then turns east by north for more than 100 li, to be met by the *Na-yu-ko-tsang-pu*[8] which flows south-westwards from Lake *Sang-li*[9] receiving several streams before the confluence. [The river *Na-yu-ko-tsang-pu* lies 30 li south-west[(4)] of *Cho-shu-tê*. Its source comes out from Lake *Sang-li* on the north-east, flows westwards for more than 250 li, and receives from the north two streams coming out from *Shang-li-ko-pa-ling* and *Mu-ko-ling*, and from the south three streams originating in *La-chu-ko-shan*, *Tsu-lun-shan* and *Yang-pa-mu-shan*. Passing the west of *Yang-pa-mu-ling* it turns southwards, and after flowing for 80 li, receives from the N.W. two streams coming out from *Ya-la-ling* and *Ta-ko-lung-shan*. Then it flows southwards for more than 60 li before entering the *Ya-lu-tsang-pu* River.]

The river flows south-eastwards more than 200 li, and receives the *Kuo-yung-ho* which comes from *Ang-tsê-ling* on the S.E., and which flows north-eastwards and receives several tributaries before meeting the river. The river flows now south-eastwards for 50 li and then receives a stream coming from the S.W. It now turns south-east, then north-eastwards, for more than 200 li. The course becomes now more south-easterly, and the river receives a stream coming from the fore mountains of *Ni-ya-lung-kang* on the S.W. Further east it receives the *Sa-chu-tsang-pu* which comes with tributaries from N.E. [The river *Sa-chu-tsang-pu* lies more than 200 li S.W. of *Sa-ko* tribes. Its source comes out from the mountains of *Ye-lo-kang-kan*. There are six streams, all of which

Appendix 1

flow southwards for more than 100 li, and unite into the *Chia-pa-lan-ho*. The *Chia-pa-lan-ho* flows more than 50 li, and receives five streams, three from N.W. from *La-chu-ko-tsu-lêng-yang-pa-mu-shan*,[(5)] and two from S.W. from *Ang-sê-ang-lê-sung-shan*. All these streams unite in one, and flow S.E., then turn S.W. The river, after receiving from north-east two streams of *Cha-sa-kung-ko-êrh-shan* and from south-west two streams of *Nieh-mu-shan* and *Liu-tsê-li-yang-ku-shan*, becomes the *Sa-chu-tsang-pu-ho*. It now flows south-westwards for more than 100 li before entering the *Ya-lu-tsang-pu* River.]

Further S.E. for 70 li, the river receives a small stream coming from the north. Further east for 30 li, the *Yung-chu-ho* comes from south to meet the river. Further east for 90 li, the *Shi-êrh-ti-ho* comes from south with its three affluents. Further east for 30 li the *Man-chu-tsang-pu-ho* comes from north to meet the river. [The river *Man-chu-tsang-pu-ho*, otherwise called the *Ma-chu-tsang-pu-pi-la*, lies in the south-west of the *Sa-ko* tribes. Two streams flow for more than 200 li southwards from *Hsieh-êrh-chung-shan* and *Pieh-lung-shan* on the north. After receiving three streams coming from *Kang-chung-cha-ta-ko-shan* on the east, and further one from *La-ko-tsang-cho-li-shan* on the west, the river becomes the *Man-chu-tsang-pu-ho*, and flows south-eastwards for 50 li before entering the *Ya-lu-tsang-pu* River.]

The river flows further eastwards for 60 li, and receives a stream coming from south. Further east for 70 li a stream comes from *A-li-tsung-chêng* on the south to meet it. Further east for 80 li, it turns to the north-east, and meets the *Sa-ko-tsang-pu-ho* which comes from Lake *La-pu* on the north-east, and which at first flows south-westwards but after gathering several streams turns south-eastwards to enter the river. [The river *Sa-ko-tsang-pu*, otherwise called *Sa-êrh-ko-pi-la*, lies on the south-east of *Sa-ko* Province. Its source is Lake *La-pu* on the north-east, and at first flows underground, and appearing on the surface, it has a sinuous course towards south-west for more than 400 li. A stream comes from *Pi-pu-ta-ko-la-ko-shan* on the north, and taking a south-easterly course and receiving a stream from *La-lung-a-êrh-shan* on the north-east, flows southwards to meet the river. Flowing further south-west for 150–160 li, another stream comes from north-west, and further 170 li south-west a stream from *La-pu-kang-chung-shan* on the north-east. Further 100 li south-west, a stream from *Lung-kan-shan* comes from the west to meet the river. The river now flows southwards for 60 li, then turns south-westwards, and receives a small stream from the north; further to south-west it receives another from the west. The river then takes a southerly course, and after receiving two streams from *Kang-lung-shan* and two from *Chao-yu-la-chung-shan* on the north-east, turns to the south-west, and receives further a stream coming from *Chi-pu-lung-shan* on the south-east with another from the east. The river flows further for 80–60 li south-westwards, then south-eastwards. The river is called the *Sa-ko-tsang-pu-ho* from here down to the confluence with the *Ya-lu-tsang-pu* River for 150–160 li. The length of the river is 1,000 li long.» [10 (6)]

Here again, in the description of the rivers of Hsi-tsang or Tibet, the source of the »Yaru-tsangpo-chiang» or Brahmaputra is placed in the »Tamchuk-khapap-shan». We are told that the north-western part of the Tamchok-kabab mountain is near the »Langchien-khapap» mountain, which in this description is called the source of the lake Mapam or Manasarovar. This is also interesting because it does not leave any doubt as to *which* affluent to the lake the Chinese text regards as the source or main feeder of the lake, namely Tage-tsangpo. The statement is important, as the original Chinese author has been at the place. Tamchok-kabab is said to be 300 li S.E. of the Kailas and is very high and great. The latitude is given more than one degree too far south.

When it is said that »there are three sources», one should at first think of Kubi-tsangpo, Chema-yundung and Maryum-chu, but this is not right, for with »there» is meant the astronomically given source of the Ya-lu-tsang-pu-chiang, and then it is said that all three sources flow north-eastwards and unite into one river, which is the Kubi-tsangpo or uppermost Brahmaputra. At first sight this statement seems to be correct[11]. For, indeed, the three principal source branches of the Kubi-tsangpo come out of three mighty glaciers, of which the one farthest west is double, although it gives rise only to one stream, namely the source of the Brahmaputra. But in reality the Chinese text does not at all mean the three sources of the Kubi. It means the Angsi-chu, Chema and Kubi, which we have found joined much too early on the Ta-ch'ing map.[(7)] But the Chema seems to be regarded as the principal source.

The next passage of the Chinese text tells us that the river »at first» turns eastwards and then south-eastwards, of which the first is true for the Kubi-tsangpo, and Chema-yundung the second for the Tsangpo. From the S.W. a tributary meets the Yere-tsangpo and comes from a mountain called Kumu-gangri or something like it. As this tributary must be identical with Kubi-tsangpo, it may be that this river is not included in the three source branches mentioned above. Then Tamchok is obviously placed at the head of Chema-yundung, as appears clearly from the Ta-ch'ing text,[(8)] where Kouben gang tsian is placed at 258 li and Tam tchouk khabab at 340 li west of Djochot. The Shui-tao-ti-kang, which has the same distance, makes the bearing, in Ogawa's translation, N.W. of Cho-shu-tê (Djochot).

The next tributary mentioned comes from the left side and is called Kiang-chia-su-mu-la-ho. It corresponds to Kiankia somla of d'Anville's general map⁽⁹⁾ and Kiankia Somla R. of his detailed map, and Giangghia sum la of de Rhins.⁽¹⁰⁾ Its source comes from a mountain called Sha-ku-ya-la-ma-la-shan, which may be a transcription of Shakya-lama-la or »the pass of the Buddha priest«. The Sha-ku-ya-la-ma-la-shan and Cha-ko-chia-la-shan are identical with de Rhins' Changou Yarak ri and the Chadziar ri. Comparing the Chinese text and d'Anville's map with Ryder's map⁽¹¹⁾ we find again that this river comes from the Transhimalaya and that the Maryum-chu, or rather the minimal brook coming from the pass Maryum-la, is only one of the smallest tributaries to the Chiang-chia-su-mu-la-ho, which itself is only a tributary to the Yere-tsangpo. The fact that it, in its lower parts, is called Maryum-chu, as I was told by the Tibetans, probably depends upon the *tasam*⁽¹²⁾ which follows up the brook to Maryum-la. The Chinese text does not even mention Maryum-chu. So all attempts to proclaim the Maryum-chu as one of the sources of the Brahmaputra has no foundation whatever.

As to the Chema-yundung it is not mentioned in Ogawa's version either.

The following tributaries from the north seem very doubtful, at any rate their derivations. A-la-chu-ho is d'Anville's Artchou R., but the Sha-la-mu-kang cannot be identified. The Na-yu-ko-tsang-pu is d'Anville's Naouc Tsanpou R. and is probably identical with Ryder's Nakchak and Nain Sing's Chu Nago.⁽¹³⁾ It is said to come from the lake Sang-li, d'Anville's Sanc-li, which, perhaps, may be Senit-tso, a lake situated on the southern side of the Transhimalayan water-parting as the Tibetans told me. But the river Na-yu-ku-tsang-pu cannot be S.W. of Cho-shu-tê, if this is the district of Toshut or Hor-toshut as I believe, for then it is N.W. of that district.

The mountains from which the tributaries come are as yet impossible to identify, unless Ya-la-ling is Yor-la, one of the chief passes of the Transhimalaya.

In the description of the many tributaries of Sa-chu-tsang-pu or Tsachu we easily recognise the reality. Most of the water of this river seems to come from Lunpo-gangri and flow to the S.W. The Man-chu-tsang-pu is my Men-chu.

The general description of the course of Sa-ko-tsang-pu is admirable. It is the same river which Nain Sing more than a hundred years later called Charta Sangpo and which I call Chaktak-tsangpo. The Chinese author simply gives it the same name as the province in which it is situated, Sa-ko, the Sarka-jong of Nain Sing, Saka-dzong of Ryder and myself. It is said to come from the lake La-pu on the N.E., and indeed, as I found in 1908, it comes from a lake Lap-chung-tso situated N.N-E. of its junction with the Tsangpo. It is also perfectly right to say that the river first flows south-westwards and, after receiving several tributaries, turns south-eastwards to join the Tsangpo. But when he comes to the explanatory details within brackets, he is difficult to follow. The La-pu-kang-chung-shan is all right, for the whole country round the lake is called Lap-chung, and there may easily be a Lap-chung-gangri. Kang-lung-shan may be my Kan-chung-gangri. The length he gives to the river, 1,000 li, is very much exaggerated, if the distance between the Kailas and the Tamchok-kabab shall be used for comparison and which is given as 300 li. For the distance from the Lap-chung-tso to the mouth of the Chaktak-tsangpo is not even so much as 300 li. But the general description of the river is incomparably better and more correct than the fantastical representation given on d'Anville's map, where the river in a straight line goes to the S.W. the whole way. The Lio L. of d'Anville is meant to be the La-pu lake of Chi Chao Nan. About half way between the lake and the mouth of the river d'Anville has a range of mountains he calls Lop M., an echo from the Lap-chung mountains. He calls the river the Sanki Tsanpou.

We have seen that some of the Chinese writers makes the Chema the principle branch, coming from Tamchok-kabab, others say that Chema is only a tributary joining the Kubi. In all instances, both western and eastern, the Kubi-tsangpo has, however, been almost ignored. The Chinese authorities do not mention its name, although at least in one case, it is called the Yere-tsangpo. Only Kawaguchi seems to have heard its name, Kubi-chu.⁽¹⁴⁾ The Chinese and d'Anville cut the Chema into two parts, of which the upper joins the Kubi, the lower the Maryum-chu. Even on Ryder's map it is difficult to tell which river is meant to be the Kubi.

The source of the Brahmaputra has, in other works, wandered about in the periphery of a semi-circle, the centre of which is at the confluence of the different branches.

I have already once published[12] an extract from the Shui-tao-ti-kang about the Satlej and its relation to the two lakes[13].

»The *Kang-ka-chiang*[14] comes out from *Kang-ti-ssu-shan*[15], on the south-east of which there stands *Lang-chuan-ka-pa-pu-shan*[16], magnificent like an elephant. [The relief is gradually accentuated more and more towards the south-western frontiers, and culminating at Kang-ti-ssu-shan[17]. The mountain has a circumference more than 140 li. On all sides the mountain forms precipitous walls, more than 1,000 feet high above the surrounding mountains, and accumulated snow seems as if hung on cliffs. Hundreds of springs pour down from the top, but flow under the ground on the foot of the mountain. It is situated on the extreme west of the Ts'ang Region, 310 li north-east of *Ta-ko-la-chêng*[18] in

A-li[19], more than 5,590 li south-west of Hsi-ning-fu in Shensi Province. Its longitude is 36°4′W. and its latitude 30°5′N[20]. In olden times the place was unknown, but can be doubtfully referred to as A-nok-ta-shan in the annotation of Shui-ching.[15] In the neighbourhood there are four high mountains, of which the southern is called Lang-chuan-ka-pa-pu-shan lying 250 li south by east of Kang-ti-ssu-shan, and 270 li east of Ta-ko-la-chêng. The natives call it so, because the form of the mountain resembles an elephant. On the east of this mountain there stands *Ta-ma-chu-ko-ka-pa-pu-shan*[21], which is the source of the *Ya-lu-tsang-pu*-River[22]. This mountain runs south-westwards to *Men-na-ko-ni-êrh-shan* and then to *Sa-mu-tai-kang-shan*, and extends to the south of A-li to the country of *E-no-tê-ko*.] Springs come out from the northern foot of the mountain, and accumulate into a lake [35°5′W. and 29°1′N.]. The water flows north-westwards for 70 li and receives a stream coming from the north-east. [The stream lies in the mountains 80 li north-west of Lang-chuan-ka-pa-pu. Two streams flow westwards from the mountain and turn north-westwards after their junction. It now takes a sinuous course for 60 li, turns south-westwards, and joins the main river. This is a source.]

The river flows further to the west-by-north for 40 li, then to the north-east, to be met by the water of Lake *K'ung-shêng*[23] [16] which sinks underneath the ground of the lake basin, but which, after reappearing, and after receiving three northern affluents, runs south-westwards to the river.

[The Lake of *K'ung-shêng-o-mo* has two sources, one coming from the north-east, from *Ta-ko-la-kung-ma-shan*[24], and flowing 150–160 li, the other from the east, from the western foot of *Man-êrh-yo-mu-ling*[25] in the western frontiers of *Cho-shu-tê*. This last-mentioned mountain forms the eastern boundary of A-li and is the chief range going south-eastwards from Kang-ti-ssu. The water (of the Lake Kung-shéng) flows westwards for more than 50 li and forms another lake, 80 li wide and without an outlet. However, more than 10 li farther to the west, there is a third lake with a subterranean source and with a length of 30 li. A stream comes from north to the lake. The river now flows south-westwards for 60 li, and receives a stream coming from the north-east. 40 li farther south-westwards it receives a stream coming from the northern mountains, further south-westwards, the river meets the water from Lang-chuan-ka-pa-pu-shan.]

The water forms Lake *Ma-piu-mu-ta-lai*[26] [17]. [From south to north it is 150 li long, from east to west 80 or 100 li wide, and has a circumference more than 200 li. On the northern side of the lake there are two streams coming from the north. The lake is situated 120 li to the south of Kang-ti-ssu.] The water flows out from the west of the lake into Lake *Lang-ka*[27] in a distance of 60 li. The latter lake receives a stream coming from the N.E. [Lake *Lang-ka* has a narrow rectangular shape, pointed and elongated, the length from south to north being 170 li and the width from east to west 100 li. Its northern pointed corner has the stream coming from north-east. There are three sources on the southern foot at a distance of 70 li from a southern branch of Knag-ti-ssu; they flow southwards, unite into a stream, which takes a south-westerly course for 150–160 li before entering the lake. The lake is same[28] in circumference and area, but different in outline.]

The water (of Lake Lang-ka) flows out from the west, and after running westwards for more than 100 li, it turns to the S.W. It is now called the *Lang-chu-ho*[29], and takes a sinuous course for more than 200 li. Then it receives the *Chu-ka-la-ho* coming from N.E. [The Chu-ka-la-ho comes out from the southern foot of Ts'ang-wên-ling, and first flows southwards, then south-westwards, and passing to the S.E. of *Ku-ko-cha-shi-lu-mu-po-tse-ching*, turns south-westwards and joins the Lang-chu-ho. The length of this stream is more than 200 li.]

This description is, according to Professor Ogawa, published in the 26th year of Chien Lung's reign. When reading it again and again I cannot help getting the impression that it dates from the same documents and sketches which were delivered to the Jesuit Fathers and by them sent to d'Anville. For the description is in perfect harmony with d'Anville's maps in du Halde[18] and even the same names are to be found in both cases and written very much like each other, disregarding the French transcription of the Chinese syllables. And as the Shui-tao-ti-kang is only a compilation its author had to use any reliable material he could get hold of. From wherever it comes, this description is admirable and distinguished by the same careful conformity with the truth and conscientiousness as all other Chinese geographical descriptions[30].

The case is the same so far as the Shui-tao-ti-kang is concerned. A description in a few words of the Kang-ti-ssu (d'Anville has Kentaisse) could not possibly be more graphic and correct. The same mistake about the Ganges as on the Lama map is made here, when the author thinks the Kang-ka-chiang or Ganges is a continuation of the river which »comes out from» the Kailas, and which, on d'Anville's map is called Latchou R., or one of the feeders of Gar-chu, the S.W. branch of the Indus. In a preceding chapter I have tried to explain why the Lamas confounded the Indus and the Satlej with the Ganges, which gives an example of a geographical object they had not seen with their own eyes, and in which they therefore were mistaken.

The most interesting passage is, however, the one about the »high mountain» Langchen-kabab, which, quite correctly, is said to be S.E. of the Kailas and east of

Taklakhar. It resembles an elephant, a quality which is now transferred to a little hill on the bank of the Satlej at Dölchu-gompa, west of Langak-tso. Then follows a description of the uppermost Satlej on its way from the northern foot of Langchen-kabab towards the N.W. When the author says that this river, which is the Tage-tsangpo, is met by a river from Gunchu-tso, he is wrong, for the Tage-tsangpo goes its own way to the Manasarovar and the statement that the water from the Guncho-tso should »sink under the ground» for a certain distance is of course impossible as the Guncho-tso is salt[31]. The Guncho-tso is said to have two source streams, one from the N.E., from the mountain Ta-ko-la-kung-ma, which is also to be found on d'Anville's map, under the name of Tacra Concla; the other comes from the west side of the pass Maryum-la, which agrees with Ryder's map in all particulars. Maryum-la is said to be on the western frontier of Cho-shu-tê, a district on the southern slopes of the Transhimalaya, and certainly identical with the Hor-toshut or Toshut-horpa of which I heard several times in 1908. Of the two lakes said to be situated west of Guncho-tso, only one is marked on d'Anville's map, but both may be quite small and temporary.

It is worth while[19] to notice that the compilor[20] of the Chinese hydrography regards the Mapama-talai simply as a formation of the water from Langchen-kabab or as a part of the hydrographical system, which from several points of view is correct. At the western side »the water», i. e. the water from Langchen-kabab flows into the lake Lanka, or Lanken as d'Anville writes. The distance between the lakes is said to be 60 li, which corresponds to my 5 ½ miles. As a rule the distance are very unreliable. For if it is 60 li between the lakes along the channel, it should be 180 li and not 120 between lake Mapama and the Kailas. And if the lake is 150 and 80 or 100 li across, its circumference must of course be much more than 200 li. At any rate we have here a positive statement regarding the channel, and a perfectly true view of its character of being the continuation of the Satlej from Langchen-kabab.

Finally, »the water»[32], i. e. the water from the uppermost Langchen-kabab or Satlej flows out from the western side of the lake and is now called Lang-chu-ho, the Lanctchou R.[21] of d'Anville. From the Chinese text it seems that this name was not used for the uppermost part of the river-course. This is doubtful. For the name Langchen-kamba is still used for a spring on the Tage-tsangpo. But Tage-tsangpo is at least nowadays the name of the uppermost Satlej.

Finally it is said that Chu-kar (Chu-ka-la) comes from the N.E. and joins the head river. Unless there are two rivers of this name, the statement is wrong, as the Chu-kar of Strachey[22] comes from the south. But even here it is pointed out that the Satlej is the head-river and the Chu-ka-la a tributary.

Hedin's Notes

1. To avoid misunderstandings I give Ogawa's translation literally, as I got it from him.
2. Tamchok-kabab.
3. Choshut.
4. Mapam-tala, Manasarovar.
5. Langchen-kabab-mountains.
6. Yere-tsangpo-river.
7. Professor Ogawa tells me that the passages within brackets [ ] in the original Chinese text are given with smaller characters as annotations or explications to the geographical names mentioned in the text.
8. The Naouc Tsanpou R. on d'Anville's map.[23]
9. The L. Sanc-li on d'Anville's map.[24]
10. According to Rockhill Chi Chao Nan was also one of the principal editors of Ta-ch'ing-i-t'ung-chih;[25] Shui-tao-ti-kang was, according to Rockhill, written in 1776.[26] The resemblance between the two works depends, therefore, on the fact that the author is the same, or that he, in both cases, has used the same material.
11. Compare »Trans-Himalaya», Vol. II, pp. 96 and 101, and the map.
12. Trans-Himalaya, Vol. II, p. 183 et seq.
13. Professor Ogawa of Kyoto has kindly made the translation for me. I have not altered his English.
14. Kang-ka-chiang means the Ganges river.
15. Kang-tise, Kailas.
16. Langchen-kabab-mountains, or the mountains of the source of the Satlej, as Langchen is the Tibetan name for Satlej and ka means mouth, and bab (pa-pu) pouring out; thus the mouth from which the Elephant river is pouring out.
17. The passage within brackets are printed in the original Chinese text with smaller characters as explanatory notes to the geographical names mentioned in the text.[27]
18. Taklakhar.
19. Ngari(-khorsum).
20. In reality its latitude is 31°2½'.
21. Tamchok-kabab or the Source of the horse-river, i. e. Brahmaputra.
22. Yaru-tsangpo or Brahmaputra.[28]
23. Gunchu-tso.
24. Tacra Concla on d'Anville's map.
25. Maryum-la.
26. Mapama-talai, or Manasarovar.
27. Langak-tso or Rakas-tal.
28. i. e. of the same size as Mapama-talai.
29. i. e. the Satlej.
30. Nobody has ever known Chinese cartography better than the late Baron von Richthofen who, speaking of the maps of the Jesuits, says: »Mehr und mehr waren sie mit dem überaus reichen Material der einheimischen Kartographie bekannt geworden; sie mussten sehen, dass dasselbe hinsichtlich der Eintragungen von Flüssen und Ortschaften den Ansprüchen an Gewissenhaftigkeit und Treue in so weit entsprach, als nur wirklich Vorhandenes aufgezeichnet war, dass aber den Chinesen das Geschick in der richtigen Zusammenstellung des Materials abging, da sie nicht fähig waren, astronomische Ortsbestimmungen mit Genauigkeit auszuführen.» (China, I, p. 681)[29] In his classical article on Lop-nor the same great authority has pointed out the fact, that the Chinese topographers never enter any geographical feature upon their maps unless they have themselves actually seen it. Verhandlungen der Ges. f. Erdkunde, Berlin, Vol. V, 1878, pp. 121 et seq.[30] Compare also my book Through Asia, London 1898, I, p. 18 and II, p. 867, as well as my Scientific Results of a

Journey in Central Asia 1899–1902, Vol. II, p. 263 et seq. And everybody who has had an opportunity to travel in parts of Asia which has been surveyed by Chinese explorers will have been struck by their reliability.

31 The Guncho-tso cannot have had fresh water and an underground outlet 150 years ago; the Chinese explorers have made a mistake in this point.

32 In his translation Professor Ogawa has put between brackets: (of lake Lan-ka), which of course is also correct.

Editor's notes

(1) The *Yu gong* [Tribute of Yu] is the name of a chapter in the *Shujing* [Book of Documents]. Its year of creation is unknown. The text divides all of China into nine provinces, and as an ancient geographical treatise listing the mountains, rivers, and products of each region, has enjoyed a lasting impact on subsequent scholarship.

(2) The part of "*piu*" of "*Ma-piu-mu-ta-la* is considered to be a phonetic notation of a Chinese character of "品". Given this interpretation, this notation should not be "*piu*", but "*pin*". This notation is as printed in Hedin's *Southern Tibet* as well as his manuscript for the book (Stockholm, Riksarkivet Marieberg, Sven Hedins arkiv, 204). According to Hedin (please refer to Author's note 1), he used Ogawa's English translation literally. The manuscript by Ogawa himself has not yet been found in Hedin's Archive.

(3) In Ogawa's English translation, longitude is parenthetically annotated with "West (of Peking)" and latitude with "(the altitude of the North)." Incidentally, the longitude of Beijing today is 116° 17′ East, meaning that 35° W of Peking would correspond to 81° 17′ East.

(4) In Ogawa's English translation, this is represented by a single term, *La-chu-ko-tsu-lêng-yang-pa-mu-shan*, but this seems to correspond to the three mountains mentioned above as sources of tributaries feeding the *Na-yu-ko-tsang-pu*, namely *La-chu-ko-shan*, *Tsu-lun-shan*, and *Yang-pa-mu-shan*. In the *Shuidao tigang*, the course of the *Na-yu-ko-tsang-pu* is described as flowing northwest from these mountains, while the course of the *Chia-pa-lan-ho* is described as flowing southeast from the same mountains.

(5) This hyphenation is as printed in Hedin's text. A word of "southwest" is written in his manuscript for the book (Stockholm, Riksarkivet Marieberg, Sven Hedins arkiv, 204).

(6) In the text of *Southern Tibet*, the bracket] indicating the end of the annotation to the Chinese text is missing. It is also missing from Hedin's manuscript (National Archives of Sweden, Sven Hedin: No. 204).

(7) The most likely candidates for the "Ta-ch'ing Map" to which Hedin refers here include the *DaQing yitong yutu* [The Atlas of the Great Qing Dynasty] (copper plate edition of 1760), the *Huangchao Zhongwai yitong yutu* [The Atlas of the Great Qing Dynasty] (1863 edition), and the *Qinding DaQing huidian tu* [Maps Approved by His Majesty for the Book on Institutions and Laws of the Great Qing Empire] (vols. 235 to 237, on Xizang [Tibet]) (1899).

(8) This seems to refer to the text of the *DaQing yitong zhi* [Records of the Unity of the Great Qing]. The *DaQing yitong zhi* was published in three editions, consisting respectively of 356 volumes (completed in 1744), 424 volumes (although the imperial edition completed in 1784 had 424 volumes, this was revised into 500 volumes for circulation), and 560 volumes (completed in 1842). The edition used by Rockhill in the source cited by Hedin was the 500-volume 1784 edition (Rockhill 1891: 3).

(9) "d'Anville's general map" refers to "Carte générale du Thibet ou Bout-tan et des pays de Kashgar et Hami" (d'Anville 1737). This atlas was drawn for the Jesuit J. B. Du Halde's four-volume treatise *Description géographique, historique, chronologique, politique, et physique de l'empire de la Chine et de la Tartarie chinoise* [Geographical, historical, chronological, political, and physical description of the Empire of China and Chinese Tartary] (Du Halde 1735), which was compiled based on reports by missionaries dispatched to China. d'Anville used data from surveys carried out by missionaries under the Kangxi Emperor, resulting in the creation of an extremely precise map. This book and atlas had a major impact on eighteenth-century Europe.

(10) On de Rhins's *Cartes No. 21* and *No. 22*, entitled "Tibet Sud-Occidental," this is shown as "Dxian dzia" rather than "Giangghia sum la" as attributed to de Rhins by Hedin (de Rhins 1889: Cartes No.21, No.22). De Rhins (1846–1894) was a French explorer and cartographer.

(11) Ryder's map is "Tibet: Map showing explorations by Major C. H. D. Ryder, R. E., D. S. O. and Captains H. Wood, R. E. & H. M. Cowie, R. E. of the Tibet Frontier Commission 1904" (Ryder 1905). Ryder's text also contains a description of Saka-dzong (Ryder 1905: 383).

(12) The term *tasam* is also drawn as a "post station" (*yi zhan*) route on Hedin's map. According to Ikeda Takumi (Professor at the Institute for Research in Humanities, Kyoto University), the pronunciation of the Tibetan term *rta zam* corresponds to either *tazam* or *tasam*. Since it translates directly into a compound word consisting of "horse" and "bridge," its translation as "post station" (*yi zhan*) seems appropriate. It refers to a relay point (or village) used for changing horses on a route used for relaying official documents and the like by horseback. On Hedin's map, this route, equipped with its post stations (i.e., traversable by horse) is indicated by a black line and labeled with the word *tasam*. Since these post stations would have been situated at trading points that could be described as "caravanserai," they may be thought of as settlements where supplies could be obtained.

(13) "Nain Singh" produced the "Map showing Route Survey from Nepal to Lhasa and thence through the upper valley of the Brahmaputra, made by Pundit" (Montgomerie and Pundit 1868). Nain Singh Rawat explored the Himalayas and charted a map of the Brahmaputra river basin on behalf of Great Britain in the late nineteenth century.

(14) Kawaguchi Ekai spells this "Kobei-chu" (Kawaguchi 1909: 185), following the transliteration published in his original Japanese account (Kawaguchi 1904, vol. 1: 211). Hedin interprets the river that Kawaguchi calls "Kobei-chu" as being the lower reaches of the Kubi-tsangpo (*Southern Tibet*, vol. 2, 1917: 240–241), citing it as "Kubi-chu" (*Southern Tibet*, vol. 1, 1917: 118–119). Kawaguchi Ekai (1866–1945) was a monk who belonged to the Ōbaku school of Zen Buddhism. He was the first Japanese person to enter Tibet, where he traveled seeking Buddhist scriptures in the Sanskrit and Tibetan languages.

(15) The *Shuijing zhu* [Commentary on the Water Classic] is a treatise on China's waterways, compiled during the Northern Wei Dynasty by Li Daoyuan. Consisting of a total of 40 volumes, it is estimated to have been completed around 515. Focusing primarily on rivers listed in the *Shuijing* [Water Classic] believed to have been compiled in the third century, the *Shuijing zhu* is a rich historical and

geographical work based on contemporary literature and firsthand observations, listing local products, historical sites, and myths and legends associated with the respective watersheds of each river.

(16) Ogawa's English translation reads "the river flows to the west-by-north for 40 *li*, then to the north-east, to be met by the water of Lake *Kung-shêng*." However, this is inconsistent with the text of the *Shuidao tigang* (see Appendix 2), as well as what is depicted in the *DaQing yitong yutu*. Based on three geographical conditions, namely that the course of the river runs northwest, that Lake *Kung-shêng* is situated to the northeast of this river, and that it flows into Lake Manasarovar in the west, it becomes difficult to grasp the positional relationships if we take "then to the north-east" literally. Notably, "then to the north-east" also appears in Hedin's original manuscript (National Archives of Sweden, Sven Hedin: No. 204).

(17) This notation is as printed as in Hedin's *Southern Tibet* as well as his manuscript for the book (Stockholm, Riksarkivet Marieberg, Sven Hedins arkiv, 204). Please refer to the above note (2).

(18) This separated spelling of "worth while" is as printed in Hedin's text as well as in his manuscript for the book (Stockholm, Riksarkivet Marieberg, Sven Hedins arkiv, 204).

(19) The spelling is as printed in Hedin's text. In his manuscript, the spelling likely seems not to be "compilor", but "compiler" (Stockholm, Riksarkivet Marieberg, Sven Hedins arkiv, 204).

(20) "R." is considered to mean "River."

(21) Du Halde's book refers to his four-volume *Description géographique, historique, chronologique, politique, et physique de l'empire de la Chine et de la Tartarie chinoise* (Du Halde 1735).

(22) "Chu-kar" appears in the text of Strachey's article and on its accompanying map ("Map of West Nari, with the adjoining Provinces of the Indian Himalaya; to illustrate Capt. n H. Strachey's Memoir on the Physical Geography of Western Tibet") as "Chukar" (Strachey 1853: 39, and map).

(23) Map 8 (d'Anville 1737).

(24) Map 8 (d'Anville 1737).

(25) Rockhill (1891: 3).

(26) Rockhill (1891: 3).

(27) Passages in brackets [ ] in the English translation by Ogawa Takuji are written in the original Chinese text in smaller characters in a double-line format splitting a single line into two (or else as inserted notes) as annotations to the geographical names mentioned in the text.

(28) Map 8 (d'Anville 1737).

(29) Baron Ferdinand Freiherr von Richthofen (1833–1905) was a German geographer and explorer. He helped establish the modern science of topography, and through his regional studies of China, was the first to propose the idea of the "silk roads" (*Seidenstraßen*). Hedin was one of his students at the Friedrich Wilhelm University of Berlin. Among his principal works is a five-volume study of *China* (Richthofen 1877–1911).

(30) Richthofen's paper on Lop Nur (Richthofen 1878).

[Literature]

Chinese books referred to by Hedin

Hu Linyi ed. (corrected by Yan Shusen). *DaQing yitsu yutu* [The Atlas of the Great Qing Dynasty], 1760. (The following two books were also referred to in translating Hedin's text: *Huangchao Zhongwai yitong yutu* [The Atlas of the Great Qing Dynasty] (31 books and the first volume) (1863), and Tianlong changcheng wenhua yishu gongsi ed. *DaQing yitong yutu* [The Atlas of the Great Qing Dynasty] (2003), (reprinted version of copper plate edition of 1760)]).

Kun Gon et al. eds. *Qinding DaQing huidian tu* [Maps approved by His Majesty for the Book on Institutions and Laws of the Great Qing Empire] (270 books and the first volume) (1899) , (vols. 235 to 237, on Xizang [Tibet]).

DaQing yitong zhi [Records of the Unity of the Great Qing] (500 books and the first volume) (Authorized Version) (1764) (the Reprinted version by stone-lithography was published in 1902).

Western books referred to by Hedin

d'Anville, J.-B. B. 1737. *Nouvel atlas de la Chine, de la Tartarie chinoise et du Thibet*. 42 maps. GDZ Sammlung Sibirica.

de Rhins, D. 1889. *L'Asie centrale*, Thibet et régions limitrophes: texte et atlas. Paris: E. Leroux.

Du Halde, J. B. 1735. *Description géographique, historique, chronologique, politique, et physique de l'Empire de la Chine et de la Tartarie chinoise: enrichie des cartes générales et particulières de ces pays, de la cartes générales & des cartes particulières du Thibet, & de la Corée, & ornée d'un grand nombre de figures & de vignettes gravées en taille-douce.* 4 T., Paris: Chez P. G. Le Mercier.

Kawaguchi, E. 1909. *Three years in Tibet with the original Japanese illustrations*. Benares: Theosophist Pub. Society. (Kawaguchi Ekai, 1904. *Chibetto ryokōki* [The Journey in Tibet] (two volumes). Tokyo: Hakubun dō).

Hedin, Sven 1898. *Through Asia*, vol. 1–2. London: Methuen.

Hedin, Sven 1905. *Scientific Results of a Journey in Central Asia and Tibet 1899-1902*, vol. 1–3. Stockholm: Lithographic Institute of the General Staff of the Swedish Army.

Hedin, Sven 1909-1913. *Trans-Himalaya: discoveries and adventures in Tibet*, vol. 1-3. New York: MacMillan. (First Edition in 1909–1912).

Hedin, Sevn 1917. *Southern Tibet: discoveries in former times compared with my own researches in 1906-1908*. Vol. 1: Lake Manasarovar and the souces of the great Indian rivers. From the remotest antiquity to the end of the eighteenth century; Vol. 2: Lake Manasarovar and the sources of the great Indian rivers. From the end of the eighteenth century to 1913. Stockholm: Lithographic Institute of the Staff of the Swedish Army.

Montgomerie, T. G. and Pundit 1868. "Report of a route-survey made by Pundit, from Nepal to Lhasa, and thence through the upper valley of the Brahmaputra to its source." *The Journal of the Royal Geographical Society of London*, 38, 129–219.

Richthofen, F. F. von. 1877–1911. *China: Ergebnisse eigener Reisen und darauf gegründeter Studien*. 5 Bd. Berlin: D. Reimer.

Richthofen, F. F. von. 1878. Bemerkungen zu den Ergebnissen von Oberstlieutenant Prjewalski's Reise nach dem Lopnoor und Altyn-tagh. *Verhandlungen der Gesellschaft für Erdkunde zu Berlin*, Bd. 5, 121–144.

Rockhill, W. W. 1891. "Tibet: a geographical, ethnographical, and historical sketch, derived from Chinese Sources." *Journal of the Royal Asiatic Society*, 23, 1–133, 185–291.

Ryder, C. H. D. "1905. Exploration and survey with the Tibet Frontier Commission, and from Gyangtse to Simla viâ Gartok." *The Geographical Journal*, 26(4), 369–391.

Strachey, H. 1853. "Physical geography of Western Tibet." *The Journal of the Royal Geographical Society of London*, 23, 1–69.

Appendix 2
水道提綱 卷二十二 (*Shuidao tigang* [Guide to the Network of Waterways], Volume 22nd)
The Original Text and Editor's notes

Kizu Yuko

Regarding annotations to the text

1. Editor's notes are from (1) to (23).

水道提綱 卷二十二
　　　　　　　　　原任禮部侍郎臣齊召南編錄

西藏諸水

雅魯藏布江即大金沙江(1)，疑即古之跋布川(2)。或指為禹貢黑水(3)，則太遠矣。源出藏之西界，卓書特部落西北三百四十餘里之達木楚克哈巴布山(4)。
　　注)(5)山西北與郎千喀普巴山(6)馬品木達拉(7)池源相近。即岡底斯山之東南三百里也。山甚高大，形似馬，故名。雅魯藏布江源，西三十五度，極二十九度。

三源俱東北流而合，折東流而東南二百里，有枯木岡前山(8)水，自西南來會。又東北百餘里，有江加蘇木拉河，自西北沙苦牙拉麻拉山，東南流來會。
　　江加蘇木拉河在卓書特西，源出西北沙苦牙拉麻拉山及查克佳拉山(9)涅立嶺，四水東流合為一。又南流，合西來之查爾河，又東流，入雅魯藏布江。

又東數十里，有阿拉楚河(10)北自沙拉木岡前山(11)來會。折南流五十里，又東稍北百餘里，有那烏克藏布必拉(12)自東北桑里池西南流，合數水來會。
　　河在卓書特西南三十里。源出東北桑里池，西流二百五十餘里，受北來尚里噶巴嶺及木克龍山流出之二水，南來拉主客山、祖倫山、羊巴木山(13)流出之三水，由羊巴木嶺西轉，南流八十里。又受西北來牙拉嶺、達克龍山流出之二水，又南流六十餘里，入雅魯藏布江。

又東南二百餘里，有郭永河自東南昂則嶺，東北流，合數水來會。
　　河在卓書特東南，有四源。一出昂則嶺名龍列河，一出蓋楚岡前山名蓋楚河，一出塞丹山名朱克河，一出拉魯岡前山，名拉出河。俱東北流三百餘里，合為一水，又東北流，入雅魯藏布江。○此水，源流五百里。

又東南五十里，受西南來一水。又東南，折東北流二百餘里，稍東南，有一水西南自你牙隆岡前山(14)來會。又東，有薩楚藏布河自東北合諸水來會。
　　河在薩噶部落西南二百餘里，源出岳洛岡千(15)諸山。有六水，俱南流百餘里，會為加巴蘭河。又流五十餘里，西北有拉主克、祖楞、羊巴木山之三水，西南有昂色、昂勒宗山之二水，俱會為一。又東南，折而西南，與東北查公噶爾他拉山之二水，西南捏木山及六色立羊古山之二水，會為薩楚藏布河。又西南流百餘里，入雅魯藏布江。

又東南七十里，受北來一小水，又東三十里，有甕出河自南來會。
　　河在薩噶部西南二百里。有四源，一出西南查木東他拉泉，如星宿然，東北流二百餘里。一出南稍西之圖克馬爾他拉泉，東北流五十里。一源出正南那木噶山之北，北流七十里來會，又東北流四十里。一源出東南達克拉他泉，泉眼尤多，匯西流六十里來會。三水既合，北流曲曲七十里，與西南源合，又北四十里，入雅魯藏布江。

又東九十里，有式爾的河，自南合三水來會。
　　河在薩噶部西南百數十里。有三源，一出西南沙盤嶺，東北流二百餘里。一源南出舒拉嶺者，東北流，折而北百餘里來會，北流五十里。一源出東南，出岡里窪千山(16)者，北流二百里，折西北而西流百餘里來會，又北流曲曲百餘里，入雅魯藏布江。

又東三十里，有滿楚藏布河，自北來會。
　　亦曰馬楚藏布必拉，在薩噶部西南。北有斜爾充山(17)、撒龍山二水，南流二百餘里，合東來岡充查達克山之三水，又合西來拉克藏卓立山之一水，合為河。又東南流五十里，入雅魯藏布江。

又東六十里，受南來一小水，又東七十里，有河南自阿里宗城來會。
　　河二源。一出西南岡里窪千山之東北麓，東北流。一出南牛拉嶺，北流，合而北，經阿里宗城西，又北，而東北二百里，有一水自東南來會，又北九十里，入雅魯藏布江。

又東八十里，折東北流，有薩噶藏布河(18)自東北拉布池，西南合諸水，折東南流來會。
　　亦曰薩爾格必拉。在薩噶部東南。源自東北拉布池，伏地復出。西南流，曲曲四百餘里，有一水北自必普塔克拉克山(19)，

Reproduction of a page from volume 22nd of the *Shuidao tigang* [Guide to the Network of Waterways] by the Qing period scholar Qi Zhaonan 齊召南 (1776 imprint by Chuanjing shuwu) (in the collection of the Library of Graduate School of Letters, Kyoto University)

東南流，合東北拉攏阿爾山水，而南來會。又西南百數十里，合西北來一水，又西南百七十里，有拉普岡沖山水自東北來會。又西南百里，有隆千山[20]水自西來會。正南流六十里，又西南流，合北來一小水，又西南，合西來一水。又南，有東北岡隆山[21]流出之二水，交烏拉沖山[22]流出之二水，合而西南流，合東南几布隆山一水，又合東一水，而西來會。又西南數十里，折而東南流，曰薩噶藏布河。又百數十里，入雅魯藏布江。○此河，源流長千里。

岡噶江，源出岡底斯山東南，有狼千喀巴布山，高大如象。
地勢自西南徼外漸高，至岡底山而極。周一百四十餘里，四面峯巒陡絕，高出眾山百餘丈，積雪如懸崖，頂上百泉流注，至麓即伏地。在藏地極西。阿里之達克喇城[23]東北三百十里，直陝西西甯府西南五千五百九十餘里。西三十六度四分，極

出地三十度五分。實諸山之祖，前古未知其地，疑即水經注所言阿耨達山也。相近有四大山，其南幹所始，曰狼千喀巴布山，在岡底斯南稍東二百五十里，達克喇城之東二百七十里，土人以山形似象，故名。其東即達木楚克喀巴布山，為雅魯藏布江源所出。而此山蜿蜒西南，為悶那克尼兒山，為薩木泰岡山，亘阿里之南，入厄訥特克國。

山北麓泉出。匯為池。
西三十五度五分，極二十九度一分。

西北流七十里，合東北來一水。
水在狼千喀巴布山東北八十里。山中二水，西流而合，西北曲曲六十里，折西南流九十里，與會，亦一源也。

又西稍北四十里，而東北公生池水伏而復出。合北來三水，西南流來會。
公生鄂模兩源。一東北出達克拉公馬山，西南流百數十里。一東出卓書特西界麻爾岳木嶺西麓，阿里之東界，即岡底斯向東南之榦山也。水西流五十餘里，匯為池，廣八十里而不流。西十餘里有池，湧地而西，長三十里，有一水自北來會，西南流六十里，又合東北來一水，又西南四十里，有一水自北山來會。又西南而狼千喀巴布山水會焉。

為馬品木達賴池。
南北百五十里，東西徑八十里或百里。周二百餘里，池北又有二水自北來會。○池，直岡底斯南百二十里。

自西流出六十里，為郎噶池，受東北來一水。
郎噶池似狹方，四角尖長。南北徑百七十里，東西徑百里。其水北尖。受東北一河，即岡底斯南支峯七十里南麓水，三源南流，合而西南百數十里入池。池周廣與馬品木達賴同。但方圓形異耳。

從西流出百餘里，折向西南，曰狼楚河，曲曲二百餘里。有楚噶拉河，自東北來注之。
楚噶拉河，出藏文嶺南麓，南流折而西南，經古格札什魯木布則城東南。又西南流，入郎楚河。○此水源流二百餘里。

Editors notes[1]

(1) The Tibetan word *tsang-pu* means "river." Notably, although the name *Ta-chin-sha-chiang* 大金沙江 first appears in "明史" (*Ming shi*) [History of Ming] in the seventh Treatise on Geography, concerning "Yunnan," this refers to what is now called the Jinsha River (*Chin-sha-chiang* 金沙江) in the Yangtze's upper basin, and does not correspond with the *Ya-lu-ts'ang-pu*, which is situated inside the borders of Tibet.

(2) The name *Pa-pu-chuan* 跋布川 first appears in "新唐書" (*Xin Tangshu*) [New Book of Tang], in the first volume dealing with Tibet (vol. 1st of 216).

(3) The expression of "禹貢黑水 (*Yu Gong Hei-shui*)" corresponds to the description of "華陽黑水惟梁州……黑水西河惟雍州"

written in "夏書·禹貢 (Xia Shu, Yu Gong)" of "書經" (Shujing). The *Hei-shui* of the *Yu Gong* [Tribute of Yu] refers to a river flowing across the two regions of 梁州 (Liang Zhou) and 雍州 (Yong Zhou). The Yu Gong describes that Liang Zhou covers the area from Huayang to Hei-shui, while Yong Zhou covers the area from Hei-shui to Xi-he. Liang Zhou and Yong Zhou are both among the nine regions listed in the *Yu Gong*, and are thought to indicate an area stretching from the current Sichuan Province to the vicinity of Hanzhong in Shaanxi Province and an area straddling Gansu Province, respectively; it is also acknowledged in a note in the original that "this is too far."

(4) This is the same as the *Ta-mu-chuk-k'a-pa-pu-shan* 達木楚克喀巴布山, which appears later. While the name does not appear in "大清一統志" (*DaQing yitong zhi*) [Geography on the Great Qing], it seems likely that this is the same mountain that appears as 打母朱喀巴珀山 (the same pronunciation using different characters) in the *Weizang tuzhi* [Chorography of Ü-Tsang] (Central and Western Parts of Tibet).

(5) Here and below, the notes all appear as double-line notes in the original text.

(6) This is the same as the *Lang-ch'ian-k'a-pu-pa-shan* 狼千喀巴布山, which appears later. The name appears in the *DaQing yitong zhi* as 狼千喀巴布山 and in the *Weizang tuzhi* as 郎千喀巴珀山.

(7) The name of Lake *Ma-piu-mu-ta-lai* 馬品木達拉 appears in the *DaQing yitong zhi* as 馬品木達賴. As for the notation of "品 *piu*", please refer to Appendix 1, Editor's note (2).

(8) While Ogawa Takuji translates this as the "fore mountains of *Ku-mu-kang*," in this Appendix 2, I regard the character 前, which he translates as "fore," as a phonetic character for the Tibetan word *chen*, a stem adjective meaning "large." In the *Shuidao tigang*, this is also shown using the character 千. The same is true for all mountains mentioned in the text ending in "*chen-shan*" (written 前山 or 千山; e.g., 沙拉木岡前山 / 拉魯岡前山 / 蓋楚岡前山 / 隆千山 / 岡里窪千山).

(9) While the characters 查克佳拉山 are not used in the *DaQing yitong zhi* for *Cha-ko-chia-la-shan*, there is a reference to "*Cha-ko-la-ling* 查克拉嶺, which sits 27 *li* west-and-south of (*P'ang-to-*) *ch'eng* (蓬多) 城, and it seems likely that *Cha-ko-la-ling* refers to *Cha-ko-chia-la-shan*.

(10) In the *DaQing yitong zhi*, this is written as *La-chu-ho* 拉楚河 rather than *A-la-chu-ho* 阿拉楚河 as in the *Shuidao tigang*.

(11) Ogawa Takuji interprets this as the "fore mountains of *Sha-la-mu-kang*." Regarding the interpretation of "fore," please see note (8) above.

(12) *Na-yu-ko-tsang-pu-bira* 那烏克藏布必拉 is written in the *DaQing yitong zhi* as 那烏克藏布河, with the final character meaning "river." The characters 必拉 appearing in the *Shuidao tigang* are phonetic characters for *bira*, the Manchu word for river.

(13) *La-chu-ko-shan* 拉主客山, *Tsu-lun-shan* 祖倫山, and *Yang-pa-mu-shan* 羊巴木山 seem to indicate the same mountains referred to later as *La-chu-ko-tsu-lêng-yang-pa-mu-shan* 拉主克、祖楞、羊巴木山. This may reflect variation in the phonetic transcription from the Tibetan.

(14) Ogawa Takuji interprets this as the "fore mountains of *Niya-lung-kang*." Regarding the interpretation of "fore," please see note (8) above.

(15) Due in part to a lack of clarity in the printing, Ogawa Takuji reads the final character of 岳洛岡干 as the similar-looking character 干, offering the reading *Ye-lo-kang-kan*. However, the correct reading is not *kan* but rather *chen* 千. This is the character that appears in other publications, including the *DaQing yitong zhi*. Regarding the use of the suffix -*chen* on the names of mountains, please see note (8) above.

(16) Not translated by Ogawa. In the *DaQing yitong zhi*, this is written as 岡拉窪千山 rather than 岡里窪千山.

(17) In the *DaQing yitong zhi*, *Hsieh-êrh-chung-shan* 斜爾充山 is also written simultaneously as 斜爾沖山.

(18) In the *DaQing yitong zhi*, the next note mentions 薩爾格必拉 and 薩爾格藏布河 as other names for *Sa-ko-tsang-pu-ho* 薩噶藏布河.

(19) This is listed in the *DaQing yitong zhi* as 必普達克拉克山 rather than 必普塔克拉克山.

(20) Ogawa Takuji reads the character 千 in 隆千山 as the similar-looking 干, offering the reading *Lung-kan-shan*. Given that this mountain is written as 龍前嶺 and 龍前山 in the *DaQing yitong zhi*, again, *chen* 千 is the correct reading. Here, the characters 千 and 前 are phonetic transcriptions of the Tibetan stem adjective -*chen*, meaning "big." Please see the note (8) above.

(21) In the *DaQing yitong zhi*, *Kang-lung-shan* is written as 岡龍前山 instead of 岡隆山.

(22) In the *DaQing yitong zhi*, *Chao-yu-la-chung-shan* 交烏拉沖山 is also written simultaneously as 角烏爾沖山.

(23) In the *DaQing yitong zhi*, *Ta-ko-la-chêng* 達克拉城 is also written as 達克喇城.

Acknowledgement

In preparing the notes here pertaining to the Tibetan and Manchu languages, I obtained guidance from Ikeda Takumi at the Institute for Research in Humanities, Kyoto University.

Appendix 3

List of place names relating to the description of Brahmaputra and Sutlej headwater regions

KIZU Yuko & TANAKA Kazuko

Place name no.	In-Chinese-character-scripted place names in *Shuidao tigang*	Place names in *DaQing yitong zhi* and other books (*DaQing yitong zhi* is not indicated as a source; place names in the other works are presented with (the book title))	In-alphabet-scripted place names in *Southern Tibet*, Vol. 1, Chapter 22 [Author who indicated the place name] (in cases where a place name differs to the original literature, the original name is also indicated)
1	西藏	西藏	Hsi-tsang [Ogawa][a]
			Tibet [Hedin][a]
2	雅魯藏布江	雅魯藏布江／雅魯藏布江（『衛藏圖識』）	Ya-lu-ts'ang-pu-chiang [Ogawa]
			Ya-lu-tsang-pu-chiang [Ogawa; Hedlin]
			Yere-tsangpo-river [Hedin]
			Yaru-tsangpo-chiang [Hedin]
			Ya-lu-tsang-pu-River [Ogawa; Hedin]
			Yaru-tsangpo [Hedin]
			Tsangpo [Hedin]
			Brahmaputra [Hedin]
	大金沙江	大金沙江／大金沙江（『明史』地理志七）	Ta-chin-sha-chiang [Ogawa]
	跋布川	跋布川／跋布川, 跋布川（『新唐書』吐蕃伝上）	Pa-pu-chuan [Ogawa]
3	黒水	黒水（『尚書』「夏書」禹貢』,『山海経』「南山経」雞山・昆侖山）	Hei-shui [Ogawa]
4	達木楚克哈巴布山	—	Ta-mu-chu-ko-k'a-pa-pu-shan [Oagwa]
	達木楚克哈巴布山	—	Ta-mu-chuk-k'a-pa-pu-shan [Ogawa]
	達木楚克喀巴布山	達木楚克喀巴布山／打母朱喀巴珀山（『衛藏圖識』）	Ta-mu-chu-ko-ka-pa-pu-shan [Ogawa]
			Tamchok-kabab [Hedin]
			Tamchok-kabab-shan [Hedin]
			Tamchok [Hedin]
			Tam tchouk khabab [Hedin]
5	卓書特	卓書特	Cho-shu-tê [Ogawa]
			Co-shu-tê [Ogawa]
			Choshut [Hedin]
			Djochot [Hedin]
6	藏		Tsang [Ogawa]
7	馬品木達拉池	—	Lake Ma-piu-mu-ta-la [Ogawa][b]
	馬品木達賴	馬品木達賴池／馬品木達賴（『清史稿』）	Ma-piu-mu-ta-lai [Ogawa][b]
			Mapama-talai [Hedin]
			Mapam-tala [Hedin]
			the lake Mapam [Hedin]
			Manasarovar [Hedin]

Place name no.	In-Chinese-character-scripted place names in *Shuidao tigang*	Place names in *DaQing yitong zhi* and other books (*DaQing yitong zhi* is not indicated as a source; place names in the other works are presented with (the book title))	In-alphabet-scripted place names in *Southern Tibet*, Vol. 1, Chapter 22 [Author who indicated the place name] (in cases where a place name differs to the original literature, the original name is also indicated)
8	郎千喀普巴山	—	Lang-ch'ien-k'a-pu-pa-shan [Ogawa]
	狼千喀巴布山	狼千喀巴布山／郎千喀巴珀山（『衛藏圖識』）	Lang-chuan-ka-pa-pu-shan [Ogawa]
	狼千喀巴布	—	Lang-chuan-ka-pa-pu [Ogawa]
			Langchen-kabab [Hedin]
			Langchen-kabab-mountains [Hedin]
			Langchien-khapap [Hedin]
9	岡底斯山	岡底斯, 岡底斯山／岡底斯, 岡底斯山（『衛藏圖識』）	Kang-ti-ssŭ-shan [Ogawa]
			Kailas Mountain [Ogawa (in his annotation)]
			Kentaisse [d'Anville]c
			Kang-tise [Hedin]
			Kailas [Hedin]
	阿耨達山	阿耨達山, 阿耨達山（『史記』大宛列傳，『洛陽伽藍記』卷五等）	A-nok-ta-shan [Ogawa]
10	枯木岡	枯本岡前山／枯木岡（『清史稿』）	Ku-mu-kang [Ogawa]
			Kum-gangri [Hedin]
11	江加蘇木拉河	江加蘇木拉河	Chiang-chia-su-mu-la-ho [Ogawa]
			Kiang-chia-su-mu-la-ho [Hedin]
			Kiankia somla [d'Anville]
			Kiankia Somla R. [d'Anville]
			Giangghia sum la [de Rhins] / Dxian dzia [de Rhins 1899: Carte No.21]d
12	沙苦牙拉麻拉山	沙苦牙拉麻拉山	Sha-ku-ya-la-ma-shan [Ogawa]
			Changou Yarak ri [de Rhins]
			Shakya-lama-la [Hedin]
13	涅立嶺	涅立嶺	Nieh-li-ling [Ogawa]
14	查克佳拉山	查克拉嶺	Cha-ko-chia-la-shan [Ogawa]
			Chadziar ri [de Rhins]
15	查爾河	查爾河	Cha-êrh-ho [Ogawa]
16	阿拉楚河	阿拉楚河；阿拉楚河（『清史稿』）	A-la-chu-ho [Ogawa]
			Artchou R. [d'Anville]
17	沙拉木岡	沙拉木岡；沙拉木岡（『清史稿』）	Sha-la-mu-kang [Ogawa]
18	桑里池	桑里池	Lake Sang-li [Ogawa]
			Senit-tso [Hedin]
			L. Sanc-li [d'Anville]
19	那烏克藏布必拉	那烏克藏布河／那烏克藏布河（『清史稿』）	Na-yu-ko-tsang-pu [Ogawa]
			Na-yu-ku-tsang-pu [Hedin]
			Naouc Tsanpou R. [d'Anville]
			Nakchak [Ryder]e
			Chu Nago [Nain Shingh]f
20	尚里噶巴嶺	尚里噶巴嶺	Shang-li-ko-pa-ling [Ogawa]

Place name no.	In-Chinese-character-scripted place names in *Shuidao tigang*	Place names in *DaQing yitong zhi* and other books (*DaQing yitong zhi* is not indicated as a source; place names in the other works are presented with (the book title)	In-alphabet-scripted place names in *Southern Tibet*, Vol. 1, Chapter 22 [Author who indicated the place name] (in cases where a place name differs to the original literature, the original name is also indicated)
21	木克龍山	木克龍山	Mu-ko-ling [Ogawa]
22	拉主客山	拉主客山, 拉祖克	La-chu-ko-shan [Ogawa]
23	祖倫山	祖倫山	Tsu-lun-shan [Ogawa]
24	羊巴木山	羊巴木山	Yang-pa-mu-shan [Ogawa]
25	羊巴木嶺	羊巴木嶺	Yang-pa-mu-ling [Ogawa]
26	牙拉嶺	牙拉嶺	Ya-la-ling [Ogawa]
27	達克龍山	達克龍山	Ta-ko-lung-shan [Ogawa]
28	郭永河	郭永河	Kuo-yung-ho [Ogawa]
29	昂則嶺	昂則嶺	Ang-tsê-ling [Ogawa]
30	你牙隆岡山	—	Ni-ya-lung-kang [Ogawa]
31	薩楚藏布河	薩楚藏布河	Sa-chu-tsang-pu [Ogawa]
			Tsachu [Hedin]
32	薩噶	薩噶	Sa-ko [Hedin]
			Saka-dzong [Hedin; Ryder]
			Sarka-jong [Nain Shingh]
33	岳洛岡干	岳洛岡千	Ye-lo-kang-kan [Ogawa]
34	加巴蘭河	加巴蘭河	Chia-pa-lan-ho [Ogawa]
35	拉主克, 祖楞, 羊巴木山	拉祖克, 祖楞, 羊巴木山	La-chu-ko-tsu-lêng-yang-pa-mu-shan [Ogawa]
36	昂色, 昂勒宗山	—	Ang-sê-ang-lê-sung-shan [Ogawa]
37	查薩公噶爾他拉山	查薩公噶爾他拉山	Cha-sa-kung-ko-êrh-shan [Ogawa]
38	捏木山	—	Nieh-mu-shan [Ogawa]
39	六色立羊古山	六色立羊古山	Liu-tsê-li-yang-ku-shan [Ogawa]
40	甕出河	甕出河	Yung-chu-ho [Ogawa]
41	式爾的河	式爾的河	Shi-êrh-ti-ho [Ogawa]
42	滿楚藏布河	滿楚藏布河	Man-chu-tsang-pu-ho [Ogawa]
	馬楚藏布必拉	—	Ma-chu-tsang-pu-pi-la [Ogawa]
			Man-chu-tsang-pu [Ogawa]
			Men-chu [Ogawa]
43	斜爾充山	斜爾充山, 斜爾沖山	Hsieh-êrh-chung-shan [Ogawa]
44	撇龍山	撇龍山	Pieh-lung-shan [Ogawa]
45	岡充查達克山	岡充查達克山	Kang-chung-cha-ta-ko-shan [Ogawa]
46	拉克藏卓立山	拉克藏卓立山	La-ko-tsang-cho-li-shan [Ogawa]
47	阿里宗城	阿里宗城	A-li-tsung-chêng [Ogawa]
48	薩噶藏布河	薩爾格藏布河	Sa-ko-tsang-pu-ho [Ogawa]
	薩爾格必拉	薩爾格必拉	Sa-êrh-ko-pi-la [Ogawa]
			Chaktak-tsangpo [Hedin]
			Charta Sangpo [Nain Shingh]
			Sanki Tsanpou [d'Anville]
49	拉布池	拉布池	La-pu (Lake) [Ogawa]
			Lio L. [d'Anville]

Appendix 3

Place name no.	In-Chinese-character-scripted place names in *Shuidao tigang*	Place names in *DaQing yitong zhi* and other books (*DaQing yitong zhi* is not indicated as a source; place names in the other works are presented with (the book title)	In-alphabet-scripted place names in *Southern Tibet*, Vol. 1, Chapter 22 [Author who indicated the place name] (in cases where a place name differs to the original literature, the original name is also indicated)
50	必普塔克拉克山	必普達克拉克諸山	Pi-pu-ta-ko-la-ko-shan [Ogawa]
51	拉攏阿爾山	—	La-lung-a-êrh-shan [Ogawa]
52	拉普岡冲山	—	La-pu-kang-chung-shan [Ogawa]
53	隆千山	龍前嶺, 龍前山	Lung-kan-shan [Ogawa]
54	岡隆山	岡龍前山	Kang-lung-shan [Ogawa]
			Kan-chung-gangri [Hedin]
55	交烏拉冲山	角烏爾冲山	Chao-yu-la-chung-shan [Ogawa]
56	几布隆山	—	Chi-pu-lung-shan [Ogawa]
57			Tage-tsangpo [Hedin]
58			Satlej [Hedin]
	狼楚河	狼楚河	Lang-chu-ho [Ogawa]
			Lanctchou R. [d'Anville]
59			Kubi-tsangpo [Hedin]
			Kubi [Hedin]
			Kubi-chu [Kawaguchi] / Kobei-chu [Kawaguchi 1909: 185][g]
60			Chema-yundung [Hedin]
			Chema [Hedin]
61			Maryum-chu [Hedin]
62			Angsi-chu [Hedin]
63			Tsangpo [Hedin]
64			Kumu-gangri [Hedin]
65			Kouben gang tsian [Hedin]
66			Maryum-la [Hedin]
	麻爾岳木嶺	麻爾岳木嶺	Man-êrh-yo-mu-ling [Ogawa]
67			Toshut [Hedin]
			Hor-toshut [Hedin]
			Toshut-horpa [Hedin]
68			Yor-la [Hedin]
69			Lunpo-gangri [Hedin]
70			Lap-chung-tso [Hedin]
71			Lop [d'Anville]
			Lap-chung [Hedin]
72			Lap-chung-gangri [Hedin]
73	岡噶江	岡噶江／岡噶江 (『衛藏圖識』)	Kang-ka-chiang [Ogawa]
			Ganges [Hedin]
74	達克喇城	達克喇城, 達克拉城	Ta-ko-la-chêng [Ogawa]
			Taklakhar [Hedin]
75	阿里	阿里	A-li [Ogawa]
			Ngari(-khorsum) [Hedin]
76			Ta-ma-chu-ko-ka-pa-pu-shan [Ogawa]

Place name no.	In-Chinese-character-scripted place names in *Shuidao tigang*	Place names in *DaQing yitong zhi* and other books (*DaQing yitong zhi* is not indicated as a source; place names in the other works are presented with (the book title)	In-alphabet-scripted place names in *Southern Tibet*, Vol. 1, Chapter 22 [Author who indicated the place name] (in cases where a place name differs to the original literature, the original name is also indicated)
77	悶那克尼兒山	悶那克尼兒山	Men-na-ko-ni-êrh-shan [Ogawa]
78	薩木泰岡山	薩木泰岡山, 薩木泰岡諸山	Sa-mu-tai-kang-shan [Ogawa]
79	厄訥特克	厄訥特克, 厄訥特克國	E-no-tê-ko [Ogawa]
80	公生	公生池（『清史稿』）	K'ung-shêng [Ogawa]
			Gunchu-tso [Hedin]
81	公生鄂模	—	K'ung-shêng-o-mo [Ogawa]
82	達克拉公馬山	—	Ta-ko-la-kung-ma-shan [Ogawa]
			Ta-ko-la-kung-ma [Hedin]
			Tacra Concla [d'Anville]
83	郎噶	郎噶池	Lang-ka [Ogawa]
			Langak-tso [Hedin]
			Lanka [Hedin]
			Lanken [d'Anville]
			Rakas-tal [Hedin]
84	楚噶拉河	楚噶拉河（『清史稿』）	Chu-ka-la-ho [Ogawa]
			Chu-kar [Hedin; Strachey] / Chukar [Strachey 1853, and Map][h]
			Chu-ka-la [Hedin]
85	藏文嶺		Ts'ang-wên-ling [Ogawa]
86	古格札什魯木布則城	古格札什魯木布則城	Ku-ko-cha-shi-lu-mu-po-tse-ching [Ogawa]
87			Latchou [d'Anville]
88			Gar-chu [d'Anville]
89			Dölchu-gompa [Hedin]
90			Langchen-kamba [Hedin]

Notes: The Roman alphabet-scripted place names in the final column are cited from the following source materials.

a. All place names attributed to [Hedin] and [Ogawa] are cited from *Southern Tibet*, Vol. 1, Chapter 22.
   Hedin, S. 1917. *Southern Tibet: Discoveries in former times compared with my own researches in 1906–1908.* vol. 1: *Lake Manasarovar and the sources of the great Indian rivers. From the remotest antiquity to the end of the eighteenth century.* Stockholm: Lithographic Institute of the Staff of the Swedish Army.

b. The part of "*piu*" of "*Ma-piu-mu-ta-la*" is considered to be a phonetic notation of a Chinese character of "品". Given this interpretation, this notation should not be "*piu*", but "*pin*". This notation is as printed in Hedin's *Southern Tibet* as well as his manuscript for the book (Stockholm, Riksarkivet Marieberg, Sven Hedins arkiv, 204). According to Hedin (please refer to Author's note 1), he used Ogawa's English translation literally. The manuscript by Ogawa himself has not yet been found in Hedin's Archive.

c. d'Anville, J.-B. B. 1737. *Nouvel atlas de la Chine, de la Tartarie chinoise et du Thibet.* 42 maps. GDZ Sammlung Sibirica with "Carte Generale de Thibet ou Bout-tan et des pays de Kashgar et Hami".

d. de Rhins, D. 1889: *L'Asie centrale, Thibet et régions limitrophes: texte et atlas.* Paris: E. Leroux.
   Although, in *Southern Tibet*, Hedin cited "Giangghia sum la" according to de Rhins, de Rhins had written "Dxian dzia" on his maps of "Thibet Sud-Occidental" [de Rhins 1889: Atlas, Carte No. 21 and Carte No. 22]. Hedin reprinted part of de Rhins' Carte No. 21 [Hedin, Vol. 1: 1917, Pl.VII]. On the reprinted map, the place name of "Dxian dzia" appears as de Rhins presented it.
   Hedin, 1917: Pl. VII. The region of the Manasarovar and the Sources of the great Indian rivers, as represented on the Ta-ch'ing Map. (After Dutreuil de Rhins) In Hedin, S. 1917. *Southern Tibet*, vol. 1.

e. Ryder, C. H. D. 1905: Exploration and survey with the Tibet Frontier Commission, and from Gyangtse to Simla viâ Gartok. *The Geographical Journal*, 26(4), 369–391 with "Tibet: Map showing explorations by Major C.H.D. Ryder, R. E., D. S. O. and Captains H. Wood, R. E. & H. M. Cowie, R. E. of the Tibet Frontier Commission 1904".
   "Nakchak" is presented on the map published in the article, and "Saka-dzong" is described in the main text [p.383].

f. "Map showing Route Survey from Nepal to Lhasa and thence through the upper valley of the Brahmaputra, made by Pundit" In Montgomerie, T. G. and Pundit 1868. Report of a route-survey made by Pundit, from Nepal to Lhasa, and thence through the upper valley of the Brahmaputra to its source. *The Journal of the Royal Geographical Society of London*, 38, 129–219.

Appendix 3

g. Kawaguchi, E. 1909. *Three years in Tibet with the original Japanese illustrations*. Benares: Theosophist Pub. Society. (Kawaguchi, Ekai 1904. *Chibetto ryoko ki*, 2 volumes. Hakubun do.)
   Kawaguchi presented "Kobei-chu" in Roman letters [Kawaguchi, 1909: 185]. In contrast, he wrote "Kōbei chu" in Japanese *katakana* [Kawaguchi 1904, Vol.1: 211]. Hedin understood that the river of Kobei-chu referred to by Kawaguchi should be the most downstream part of Kupi-tsangppo [*Southern Tibet*, Vol. 2, 1917: 240–241]. Based on this interpretation, Hedin credited Kawaguchi with identifying Kubi-chu [*Southern Tibet*, Vol. 1, 1917: 118–119].
h. Strachey, H. 1853. Physical geography of Western Tibet. *The Journal of the Royal Geographical Society of London*, 23, 1–69 with "Map of West Nari, with the adjoining Provinces of the Indian Himalaya; *to illustrate* Capt. n H. Strachey's *Memoir on the Physical Geography of Western Tibet*".
   Although, in *Southern Tibet*, Hedin cited "Chu-kar" according to Strachey, Strachey had written "Chukar" in his article and map [Strachey 1853: 39, and map].

List of place names presented in the Annotations of *Shuidao tigang*
(Ogawa did not translate these annotations into English)

Place name no.	In-Chinese-character-scripted place names in *Shuidao tigang*	Place names in *DaQing yitong zhi*
91	龍列河	龍列河
92	蓋楚岡前山	蓋楚岡前山
93	蓋楚河	蓋楚河
94	塞丹山	塞丹山
95	朱克河	朱克河
96	拉魯岡前山	拉魯岡前山
97	拉出河	拉出河
98	查木	查木
99	他拉泉	他拉泉
100	圖克馬爾他拉泉	圖克馬爾他拉泉
101	那木噶山	那木噶山
102	達克拉他泉	達克拉他泉
103	舒拉嶺	舒拉嶺
104	沙盤嶺	沙盤嶺
105	岡里窪千山	岡拉窪千山
106	牛拉嶺	—

Appendix 4

Map of the water systems and mountains in the headwater areas of the Brahmaputra and Sutlej Rivers

TANAKA Kazuko

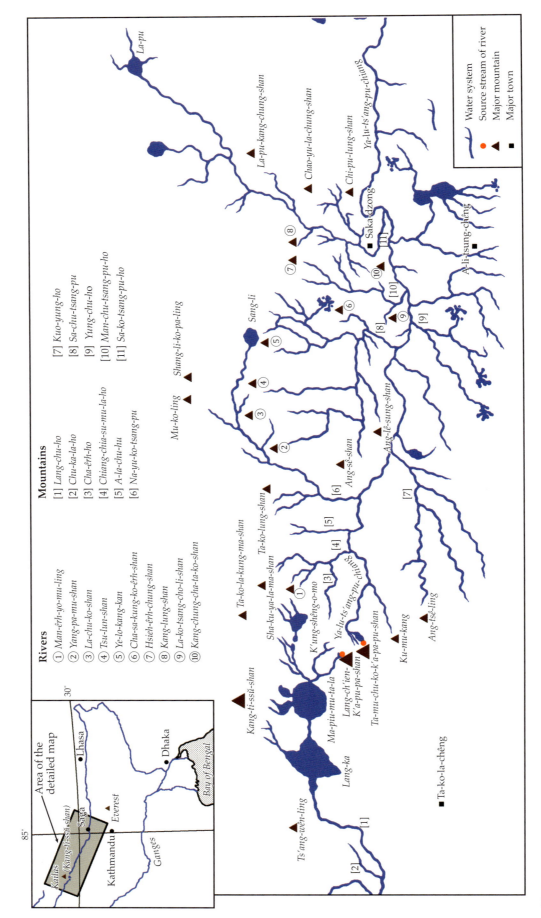

Rivers
① Man-êrh-yo-mu-ling
② Yang-pa-mu-shan
③ La-chu-ko-shan
④ Tsu-lun-shan
⑤ Ye-lo-kang-kan
⑥ Cha-sa-kung-ko-êrh-shan
⑦ Hsieh-êrh-chung-shan
⑧ Kang-lung-shan
⑨ La-ko-tsang-cho-li-shan
⑩ Kang-chung-cha-ta-ko-shan

Mountains
[1] Lang-chu-ho
[2] Chu-ka-la-ho
[3] Cha-êrh-ho
[4] Chiang-chüa-su-mu-la-ho
[5] A-la-chu-hu
[6] Na-yü-ko-tsang-pu
[7] Kuo-yung-ho
[8] Sa-chu-tsang-pu
[9] Yung-chu-ho
[10] Man-chu-tsang-pu-ho
[11] Sa-ko-tsang-pu-ho

Notes:
a. The base maps are partial maps depicting the headwater areas only, which are shown in *Daqing yitong yutu* [Complete Map of the Great Qing Dynasty] (Hu Linyi, ed., and Yan Shusen, corrected, 1760). The following two maps were used to draw this map: *Huangchao zhongwai yitong yutu* [Complete Map of the Dynasty and Surrounding Areas] (31 books and 1st volume, 1863), and 'Reprinted Map after the Copperplate-printed Map in Qin Qianlong 25th year' (Tianlong changcheng wenhua yishu gongsi, ed. 2003. *Daqing yitong yutu* [Complete Map of the Great Qin Dynasty]).
b. Major place names are presented on this map. These are described in *Shuidao tigang* [Guide to the Network of Waterways] and *Southern Tibet*. Please refer to Appendix 3 (List of Place Names).

256

Index

Name Index

Adachi Itarō 2, 12, 36, 42, 44, 50, 56, 72, 74, 76, 100, 104, 107, 116, 121, 128, 171, 173, 176
Asai Chū 173, 175–6, 179–80

Hedin, Sven xi ff., 152–7, 165–6, 171, 173–4, 181, 183, 185, 189–90, 194, 197, 199–214, 217–19, 221, 224–30, 232, 234–5, 237
Hori Ken'yū 152, 154, 157, 168, 175, 179, 237
Humboldt, Alexander von 200–1, 208, 221, 231

Imanishi Kinji 147–8, 180–1, 196–7
Ishibashi Gorō 159–60, 168, 176–7, 179–80
Ishida Kinzō 2, 64, 66, 68, 90, 102, 110, 125–6, 171, 173, 176
Ishikawa Hajime 157, 175–6, 179, 181

Kaizuka Shigeki 2, 223
Kanokogi Takeshirō 8, 173–81
Kawaguchi Ekai 2, 7, 20, 191–2, 245
Kikuchi Dairoku 157–8, 164–5, 175, 230–1, 234

Livingstone, David 184–5, 189, 192–5

Naitō Torajirō (Konan) 8, 147, 157, 159, 162, 164–8, 174, 217, 221, 224, 230–1
Nakao Sasuke 147, 196
Nakazawa Iwata 158, 175–6, 179, 181
Nishibori Eizaburō 147, 180–1
Nishikawa (Nishimura) Junji (Jun) 2, 14, 26, 30, 32, 34, 38, 52, 58, 60, 65, 67, 78, 80, 84, 86–9, 94, 97–8, 106, 108, 112, 122–4, 130, 132, 134, 171, 173–4
Nordenskiöld, Nils Adolf Erik 152, 199, 201, 208, 212

Ogawa Takuji xi, 2, 7–8, 157–60, 164–9, 174–81, 217–18, 221, 223–4, 227–31, 237
Ōtani Kōzui 152–4, 156–7, 164–8, 177, 179, 221, 224, 237

Panchen Lama 9, 12, 14, 16–17, 19–23, 25–6, 28, 30, 33, 35, 37–8, 42, 45, 61, 120, 129–30, 137, 209
Przhevalsky, Nikolay Mikhaylovich 201, 212

Qi Shaonan 162, 219–22, 231

Richthofen, Ferdinand Freiherr von 152, 186–7, 190, 201, 208, 227, 229

Stanley, Henry Morton 189, 192–5
Stein, Marc Aurel 7, 160–1, 186, 229
Suzuki Buntarō 175–6, 179

Tanaka Kaoru 180
Tanaka Zennosuke 28, 40, 46, 92, 171, 176
Tomioka Kenzō 159, 165–6, 168, 229–30
Torii Ryūzō 147, 189, 191
Tsuboi Shōgorō 147

Umesao Tadao 147–50, 196

Yamasaki Naomasa 179, 217, 233
Younghusband, Francis Edward 137, 160–1

Subject Index

Brahmaputra 63, 164, 190, 205–6, 217–18, 227–8, 231

College of Letters, Kyoto Imperial University 147, 152, 157–62, 167–9, 171, 174, 176, 180–1, 217–18, 221, 223–4, 229–32, 234

DaQing yitong zhi 160, 162, 164, 219–22, 227, 249, 256
Department of Geography (College of Letters, Kyoto Imperial University) xi, 1–2, 4, 160, 164, 168, 171–4, 177–9, 181, 234–5
Dragon Canon 163, 223–5

field note 149–50, 202, 206

Grand Cordon of the Order of the Sacred Treasure 153–5

Higashi Hongan-ji Temple 157

Japanese Alpine Club 148, 154
Justus Perthes 207, 212, 214, 228

Kansai Art Academy (Kansai Bijutsu-in) 11, 173–6, 179, 181
Kyoto Higher School of Arts and Technology 173–6, 179, 181
Kyoto Imperial University 2–4, 7–8, 147, 152, 155–8, 160, 164, 166–9, 171, 173–6, 179–81, 196–7, 217, 221, 223–5, 229, 231, 234–6, 239

L'Exposition Universelle de Paris (Paris Exposition) 178–9
Lhasa 2, 4–5, 10–12, 16–17, 20, 29, 35, 47, 50, 54–5, 57, 63–4, 70–1, 75, 78, 85, 91, 106, 111, 119–21, 137, 161, 192, 194, 197, 200, 227
Lop Nur 152, 190

Nishi Hongan-ji Temple 152–7, 164, 167–8, 174, 177, 179

Northwest Scientific Expedition 190, 229, 231, 235

panorama 10, 62–3, 68, 117, 122, 201–2, 204–9

route map 64–8, 81, 97, 99, 101, 103–4, 107, 113, 132, 201–2, 205–8, 212–14

Shigatse 3–4, 6–8, 10, 12–13, 16–17, 19, 23–4, 48–61, 65, 67, 70, 75, 77, 88, 90–5, 99, 105, 113, 116–17, 121, 130, 137, 190, 209
Shimla 137, 172–3
Shitennō-ji Temple xi, 156, 237–8
Shōgoin Institute of Western-style Painting 173, 175
Shuidao tigang 8, 160, 162, 164, 169, 217–22, 225–8, 230–1, 245–56
Silk Road 152, 186, 226, 246
Society of Historical Research 152, 165–9

Southern Tibet 164, 208, 217–18, 225–30
Sutlej 71, 114, 121–2, 131–2, 137, 164, 190, 217–18, 227–8, 231

Taklamakan Desert 186, 190, 210
Tashi Lunpo 25–8, 35, 45, 209
Third Central Asia Expedition 3, 65, 90, 121, 132, 135, 152, 217, 231

Tibetan fever 191
Tokyo Geographical Society 152–8, 160–4, 166, 168–9, 174, 177, 179–81, 188, 217–18, 234–5
Tokyo Imperial University 147, 152–5, 157–8, 160, 165, 167–9, 180–1, 189, 223, 235
Trans-Himalaya xiii, 3–4, 8–9, 14, 17, 25–6, 28, 30, 33, 35, 37–8, 45–6, 50, 53, 55–71, 73, 75, 77–8, 81, 83, 85–9, 91, 93, 95–7, 99, 101, 103–7, 109, 111, 113–15, 117–18, 121–6, 129, 131–2, 135, 152, 164, 172–3, 217–18, 225, 235–6

Wandering Lake 152, 190
Writing Culture 192, 194, 197